CW01176264

PUBLIC SCHOOL LITERATURE, CIVIC EDUCATION AND THE POLITICS OF MALE ADOLESCENCE

Ashgate Studies in Childhood, 1700 to the Present

Series Editor: Claudia Nelson, Texas A&M University, USA

This series recognizes and supports innovative work on the child and on literature for children and adolescents that informs teaching and engages with current and emerging debates in the field. Proposals are welcome for interdisciplinary and comparative studies by humanities scholars working in a variety of fields, including literature; book history, periodicals history, and print culture and the sociology of texts; theater, film, musicology, and performance studies; history, including the history of education; gender studies; art history and visual culture; cultural studies; and religion.

Topics might include, among other possibilities, how concepts and representations of the child have changed in response to adult concerns; postcolonial and transnational perspectives; "domestic imperialism" and the acculturation of the young within and across class and ethnic lines; the commercialization of childhood and children's bodies; views of young people as consumers and/or originators of culture; the child and religious discourse; children's and adolescents' self-representations; and adults' recollections of childhood.

Also in the series

The Nineteenth-Century Child and Consumer Culture
Dennis Denisoff

*Fashioning Childhood in the Eighteenth Century
Age and Identity*
Edited by Anja Müller

*Women and the Shaping of the Nation's Young
Education and Public Doctrine in Britain 1750–1850*
Mary Hilton

The Idea of Nature in Disney Animation
David Whitley

Public School Literature, Civic Education and the Politics of Male Adolescence

JENNY HOLT
Meiji University, Japan

ASHGATE

© Jenny Holt 2008

All rights reserved. No part of this publication may be reproduced, stored in a retrieval system or transmitted in any form or by any means, electronic, mechanical, photocopying, recording or otherwise without the prior permission of the publisher.

Jenny Holt has asserted her moral right under the Copyright, Designs and Patents Act, 1988, to be identified as the author of this work.

Published by
Ashgate Publishing Limited
Wey Court East
Union Road
Farnham
Surrey GU9 7PT
England

Ashgate Publishing Company
Suite 420
101 Cherry Street
Burlington, VT 05401-4405
USA

www.ashgate.com

British Library Cataloguing in Publication Data
Holt, Jenny, 1973–
Public school literature, civic education and the politics of male adolescence. – (Ashgate studies in childhood, 1700 to the present)
   1. Children's literature, English – History and criticism 2. School children in literature
   3. English literature – 19th century – History and criticism 4. English literature – 20th century – History and criticism 5. Boys – Books and reading – Great Britain
   I. Title
   820.9'9282

Library of Congress Cataloging-in-Publication Data
Holt, Jenny, 1973–
  Public school literature, civic education and the politics of male adolescence / by Jenny Holt.
   p. cm. — (Ashgate studies in childhood, 1700 to the present)
  Includes bibliographical references.
  ISBN 978-0-7546-5662-3 (alk. paper)
  1. Children's literature, English—History and criticism. 2. School children in literature. 3. English literature—19th century—History and criticism. 4. English literature—20th century—History and criticism. 5. Boys—Books and reading—Great Britain. 6. Children—Books and reading—England—History—19th century. 7. Children—Books and reading—England—History—20th century. 8. Education—Great Britain—History. 9. Adolescence in literature. 10. Education in literature. I. Title.

PR830.E38H65 2008
820.9'9282—dc22

2008017878

ISBN: 978-0-7546-5662-3

FSC Mixed Sources
Product group from well-managed forests and other controlled sources
www.fsc.org Cert no. SA-COC-1565
© 1996 Forest Stewardship Council

Printed and bound in Great Britain by
MPG Books Ltd, Bodmin, Cornwall.

To my grandparents and all other good and active citizens who never got the education they really deserved.

Contents

Acknowledgements		*viii*
Introduction		1
1	The Crisis of Youth and the Public School Reformation	15
2	An Education for Active Citizenship: *Tom Brown's Schooldays*	59
3	'Beastly Erikin': Nature, God and the Adolescent Boy	83
4	What Exactly Does 'Moderate and Reasonable' Mean? Debates on Discipline in Victorian Public School Literature	113
5	'It's not Brutality ... It's Boy; Only Boy': Public Schools and Adolescence at the Turn of the Century	157
6	The Death of an Ideal	209
Bibliography		*239*
Index		*257*

Acknowledgements

This project was funded in part by a Japanese Ministry of Education grant for young university lecturers.

Thanks are particularly due to Dinah Birch and Francis O'Gorman, who supervised me as a postgraduate, to Claudia Nelson for her advice and to Ann Donahue at Ashgate for her help and assistance. I also owe gratitude to colleagues and students at Niigata and Meiji Universities for their encouragement, especially to Kiyotaka Sato, who helped me to apply for the Ministry of Education grant.

Finally, I must also thank my mother and Yasuhiro, without whose daily support nothing would be possible at all.

Introduction

The term 'adolescence', which comes from the Latin *adolescere*, meaning 'to grow up', has a long history, but it is hard to pin down the precise meaning of the word or the length of the period it refers to. The *Oxford English Dictionary* defines it loosely as 'The process or condition of growing up; [...] the period which extends from childhood to manhood or womanhood [...] ordinarily considered as extending from 14 to 25 in males, and from 12 to 21 in females', though this estimate seems very conservative, particularly in regard to males. By contrast, *Webster* classes adolescence as 'the period of life from puberty to maturity terminating legally at the age of majority' – in other words, lasting nowadays until about eighteen or twenty, depending on the culture to which the individual belongs. The word 'adolescence' appears in the work of Augustine of Hippo ('*adolescentia*')[1] and in medieval medical treatises; it also occurs in English texts from the fifteenth century onwards. Cowper's *Tirocinium* of 1785 uses it specifically to describe school pupils.[2] However, the concept of 'adolescence' as we now recognize it in the West only came into general currency around the time of the epochal two-volume study by the American sociologist Granville Stanley Hall, *Adolescence: Its Psychology and its Relations to Physiology, Anthropology, Sociology, Sex, Crime, Religion and Education*, published in 1904. The precise understanding of the idea has changed, and continues to change, through history, as well as differing between cultures. Nonetheless, most people agree that adolescence is a prelude to mature citizenship, and our assumption must be, therefore, that adolescence is the place where the values of citizenship are learned.

I have here used the public school novel to chart the evolution of ideas of adolescence and citizenship during the nineteenth and early twentieth centuries for several reasons. The public school story occupies an interesting place in the social, cultural and political history of adolescence. Indeed, the genre developed while the sociological concept was evolving, at a time when increasing democracy dictated that adolescents should be given some kind of introduction to their role as future citizens. The first sociological texts specifically concerned with 'adolescence' appeared in the 1900s and the first novel to feature the word 'adolescence' in its title, Harry Jermyn's *The Adolescence of Aubrey* (1913), was a public school story. The question of appropriate civic education for adolescents (usually males) attracted increasing attention alongside this sociological interest. H.O. Arnold-Foster's best-selling *The Citizen Reader* appeared in 1885 and was followed by

---

1 Hanawalt 1992, p. 342.
2 'Schools, unless discipline were doubly strong, / Detain their adolescent charge too long', Cowper 1967, ll. 218–19.

a significant number of texts dealing with civics,[3] culminating at the turn of the century in key discussions of citizenship education such as *The Higher Education of Boys in England* (1909) by Cyril Norwood and Arthur H. Hope. The public school story, which often depicted the educational institution as a miniature world ruled (at least in part) by boyhood statesmen, was also a popular vehicle for the transmission of civic values, but a very problematic one. Writers for boys, usually themselves products of the public school system, used the genre both to relive their own boyhood days and to discuss the experiences that prepared young people for an active role in social and political life at a time of great national change. Part of the glamour of public school stories, which made them so universally successful and marketable, was that they depicted life among the offspring of the elite, many of whom were destined for illustrious public careers. However, many of the readers of the genre were working class, had no contact with the real-life public school system and were considered by the class of men who were writing the works to be ineligible for political responsibility. These readers, it was thought, needed to be educated in ideas of duty and obedience rather than initiative and ingenuity. This was so that, as newly enfranchised citizens, they would value conformity and social stability and adhere to the status quo. Writers thus struggled with the problem of how to tailor their works for the largest possible audience, and how to produce a civic message for the less well off while capitalizing on the national obsession with the boyhood of the elite.

As the phenomenon of adolescence attracted greater discussion, middle- and upper-class boys at public school became the main focus of attention for writers, sociologists and policy-makers eager to investigate and influence this period of life. Christine Griffin argues that the revolution in public school culture which occurred during the nineteenth century, and which was largely attributed to the Rugby school headmaster Thomas Arnold, had, along with 'Muscular Christianity' (for which some of Arnold's students were in part responsible), a decisive effect on approaches to adolescence:

> the 'discovery' of adolescence coincided with the emerging cult of heterosexual masculinity; with the determined avoidance (especially by elite males) of all things 'feminine', and with the construction of 'homosexuality' as a new judicio-legal category which was synonymous with sexual deviance, evil and pathological sickness.[4]

---

3   Examples include: F.W. Farrar's *Social And Present Day Questions* (1891), *The English Citizen* (1893) by C.H. Wyatt (Director for Elementary Education for Manchester), *The Civic Reader* (1893) by J. Harris Stone, *The Model Citizen* (1907) and *A Short History of Citizenship and Introduction to Sociology* (1904) by sociologist H. Osmond Newman, *Civics: As Applied Sociology* (1904) by Patrick Geddes and *British Citizenship: Its Rights and its Duties* (1906) by Frederick Peaker, of the Leeds School Board.

4   Griffin 1988, p. 12.

It was predominantly male, middle-class, public school educated writers, sociologists and educationalists who developed ideas of 'normal' adolescence and who fashioned it in their own (retrospective) image. Some justified this bias by arguing that boarding school was the ideal environment in which to study young people. For example, the *Saturday Review* of 1882 likened the boy at home to a savage in a missionary settlement who seems to conform to civilized standards of behavior but who is, at heart, a barbarian. At school, in contrast, in his natural environment, he inhabits a 'primitive kind of society with barbarous laws of its own'. The writer of this particular article recommends that novelists and schoolteachers therefore take full advantage of the public school as a sociological resource.[5]

Although they were created by and focused on the activities of a small social elite, therefore, public school stories and novels were designed to have a wider impact. In particular, the public school experience of adolescence was held up to working-class children as the optimal way to experience youth. In *What Books to Lend and What to Give* (1887), C.M. Yonge recommended *Tom Brown* for use in state elementary schools because, 'though the sphere is so different from that of the elementary school-boy, his tone may be raised by it'.[6] The fictional upper-class adolescent represented in public school literature was deemed to be an ideal standard that could profitably be placed before working-class schoolchildren for their moral edification. This idea was present right from the birth of state education. In 1867, Robert Lowe MP commented that working-class juveniles should be taught to feel a sense of awe and respect towards their upper-class counterparts. He remarked that 'the higher classes ought to be educated in a very different manner, in order that they may exhibit to the lower classes that higher education to which, if it were shown to them they would bow down and defer'.[7] The Board of Education in its 1910–11 report reiterated C.M. Yonge's advice that *Tom Brown* be included in every elementary school library.[8] Major school stories such as F.W. Farrar's *Eric: Or Little by Little*, Talbot Baines Reed's *The Sixth Form at St Dominic's* and *Tom Brown* were distributed until the 1950s (with occasional reprints since) by state-school oriented publishers such as Schofield and Sims, Nelson, Macmillan and Collins' Clear-Type Press.[9] Circulating libraries also maintained the more conservative school stories. Mudie's 1891 catalogue shows which titles of the past forty years still remained popular. F.W. Farrar's *Eric*, Thomas Hughes's *Tom Brown's Schooldays*, Talbot Baines Reed's *The Fifth Form at St Dominic's* and F. Anstey's *Vice Versa* are listed, which suggests they were still being read. The same

---

5 'Boys' 1882.
6 Yonge 1887, p. 31.
7 McCulloch 1991, p. 17.
8 Yonge, p. 31. See also Musgrave 1985, p. 226.
9 Nelson grew in the 1870s from supplying Board schools with stationery to educational publishing. Macmillan published textbooks and stories (see Bratton 1981, p. 192). Henry Newbolt was appointed Editor in Chief of Nelson's Teaching of English series in 1921, carrying the Public School ethic into State education. See Chitty 1997, p. 254.

books appear in Whiteley's 1909 catalogue, along with H.C. Adams's *Schoolboy Honor* and Kipling's *Stalky*.[10] More politically challenging books are absent.

Girls were also major consumers of boys' school stories. Edward Salmon in 1888 found that one of the principal organs for publishing public school stories, *The Boy's Own Paper*, was popular among girls as well as among 'the sons of working men'.[11] Stanley Hall lamented in 1904 that, in one sociological and literary study, two-thirds of eighteen-year-old girls reported that they favored male role models over those presented in girls' literature.[12] Hall said that reading boys' books gave them too many ideals, which distracted them from their proper role in life, and he insisted that they should be taught using special women's textbooks that would promote a proper degree of resignation and self-denial. He admitted they would find these books oppressive, but asserted that it was in the 'interests of the race'.[13] Girls seem to have had the opposite idea. As Peter Musgrave has observed, large numbers of girls patronized boys' school stories until girls' school stories started appearing more regularly during the 1900s. Moreover, *The Times Literary Supplement* remarked in 1917 that girls were still the principal consumers of boys' magazines.[14] Stories about girls' schools actually predate those about boys' schools, beginning with Sarah Fielding's *The Governess: Or, the Little Female Academy* of 1749,[15] but they only achieved a commercial boom in the late-nineteenth century when they started to imitate boys' school narratives and to avoid the girl-specific or domestic. This topic is, however, a subject for a different study that merits a separate volume of its own. Although the relationship between girls and the school story is important, the emphasis of this work is on the role played by public school literature in the formation of male adolescents as civic subjects in the public sphere.

In this study I have chosen to emphasize in particular how public school stories tackled ideas of appropriate adolescent education in terms of training for citizenship and statesmanship. Public schools were originally designed to create a ruling and administrative elite which would have the 'correct' impact on society in adulthood. Public school stories, however, had a much wider range of social, political and ideological functions. Some writers aimed, for example, to prepare upper-class boys for public school life, to edify those who had no access to public school, to indulge the nostalgia of former public schoolboys, or to campaign for change in the system itself. Others, particularly those writing for magazine publications such as the *Boys' Own Paper*, used the public story to transmit certain ideological values to working-class boys who would have no chance of experiencing public school life at first hand. Many tried to satisfy more than one perceived social need,

---

10 Whiteley 1909, pp. 565–673, Mudie's Library 1891.
11 Salmon 1888, p. 185.
12 Hall 1925, vol. II, p. 385.
13 Ibid., pp. 391–92.
14 Musgrave 1985, p. 231 and *TLS* December 13, 1913.
15 Clark 1996, p. 6.

and the fact that these needs were often conflicting meant that the genre labored under a host of contradictions. The issue that seemed to trouble authors most, however, was the question of whether readers were to be encouraged, as future citizens, to embrace social change, or to accept and promote the status quo. I will return to this question shortly.

Most of the characters in public school stories aimed at upper- and upper-middle-class readers seem, ostensibly at least, to be working with a view to becoming socially and politically influential citizens when they mature. They frequently go on to influential positions in society, usually connected in some way with promoting what the author regards as social justice (as members of parliament, charitable workers, barristers, soldiers, writers and so on). Their school careers direct them towards these occupations but their motive is never profit. Most appear to have private incomes or investments to live on, which enable them to take a disinterested, statesmanlike role in society. When Tom Brown grows up, for instance, we discover that he is going to be involved in education in some way and that he will be 'poor' (or, at least, too poor to afford a personal maid for his wife). Presumably, he will rely on inherited money to support his socially improving work, although Thomas Hughes does not elaborate on this question, seeming to think financial practicalities too unimportant to discuss. The way of life Tom and his ilk look forward to is perhaps described most succinctly in H.G. Wells's *The New Machiavelli* (1911), written at a time when the number of those with sufficient private means to enjoy such a career was diminishing. Wells's novel, of course, is not a public school story (although the protagonist attends public school), but it is peopled almost entirely by the kind of individual depicted by many public school texts. The typical disinterested upper-class citizen, remarks Wells,

> is a flat contradiction to all the ordinary doctrine of motives, a man who has foregone any chances of wealth and profit, foregone any easier paths to distinction, foregone marriage and parentage, in order to serve the community. He does it without any fee or reward except his personal self-satisfaction in doing this work, and he does it without any hope of future joys and punishments.[16]

Because their protagonists are supposed to be disengaged from the profit motive, public school stories often neglect or denigrate science, technology, modern languages, or anything else related to industry or the economy. This literary cold-shouldering of practical subjects reflected attitudes in real schools. Thomas Arnold notoriously said that, rather than his son being preoccupied by science, 'I would gladly have him think that the sun went round the earth, and that the stars were so many spangles set in the bright blue firmament'. According to Arnold, the most important aspect of education was the inculcation of skills necessary to citizenship and statesmanship, and he remarked that 'Surely the one thing needful for a Christian and an Englishman to study is Christian and

---

16 Wells 1978, p. 108.

moral and political philosophy'.[17] This concern for citizenship education is one reason why school stories debate human relations rather than discussing the intellectual development of their characters, and why they focus on the 'extra-curricular' aspects of school life. In demonstrating how conflict can be resolved in a 'miniature world', they act as manuals in citizenship, teaching principles that can later be applied to the outside world. However, only a very small number of writers – for example, Bracebridge Hemyng in his *Butler Burke* stories (1865–1870) – wholeheartedly encourage readers take an active role in changing school or society. More often, they are torn between a reforming and a conserving agenda, especially if the target audience includes working-class youth. In this book, I will discuss a variety of forms of citizenship education described in school stories and explore how various kinds of plot motif are used to promote both active and less active ways of being a citizen.

In a British context, there are several different ideas of what 'citizenship' means. In the 1940s, the sociologist T.H. Marshall attempted to classify the ways in which the citizen could be engaged in society. 'Civil citizenship', he said, defines the citizen as a person who possesses an understanding of individual rights and civil liberties. 'Political citizenship' sees the citizen as having the right to be involved actively in political processes. 'Social citizenship', in contrast, focuses on the responsibilities, duties and obligations an individual has to society and the rights he or she acquires through their observance.[18] The heirs of Tory paternalism on the traditional British political right often emphasize the latter form of citizenship by encouraging an awareness of duties and obligations towards nation or empire and promoting a patriotic sense of imperial or national identity. This kind of citizenship could, feasibly, be classed not as true citizenship but as subjecthood (ultimately as being the subject of the monarch and his or her government), since it emphasizes obedience rather than participation in the legislative decision-making process. This perspective is still reinforced to some extent in Britain by the lack of a written constitution enshrining citizens' rights. In contrast, the liberal tradition tends to see the well-educated citizen as conversant with and defending his or her civil rights and participating actively in the democratic decision-making process (though liberalism in Britain is not synonymous with socialism or left-leaning ideology, as it might be in the United States).

The liberal approach to citizenship is inherited to some extent from the ideas of thinkers such as J.S. Mill, as well as from more conventionally classical liberals, for example, Adam Smith and Richard Whately, who put faith in the ability of ordinary people (as opposed to the elite) to make rational choices – a belief which, taken to an extreme, leads to libertarianism.[19] However, liberals often struggle to balance libertarian values with the social liberalism inherited from Gladstonian paternalism which holds that certain freedoms must be limited (generally under

---

17 Stanley 1882, vol. II, p. 37.
18 Edirisingha 2000, p. 33.
19 Eccleshall 1986, pp. 2–3, 121, 157.

the influence of a social elite) for the general good. Modern British and European liberal democracy, therefore, despite a superficial commitment to classical liberal concepts such as free trade, still errs towards 'institutional liberalism', relying on elite governmental and social structures to curtail the exploitations that arise from unbridled social and economic freedom.[20] This double meaning behind the British understanding of the term 'liberal' has always caused trouble for writers involved in the 'liberal education' movement who, as I will show, demonstrate conflicting attitudes towards the idea of individual autonomy.

To complicate our present understanding of education and liberty further, during the last thirty years the right wing in Britain has also adopted the libertarian rhetoric of choice, chiefly in the fields of business and economics. Nonetheless, it often still adheres to authoritarian principles when making social and educational policy, despite a superficial commitment to, for instance, parents' rights to choose schools. The Thatcher government demonstrated its authoritarian stance when it emphasized the importance of humanities as a force for transmitting traditional citizenship values in the National Curriculum.[21]

When civics first appeared on school curricula following the 1884 Reform Act, it took the conservative track and focused on the duties and obligations of citizens. Books such as Arnold-Forster's *The Citizen Reader* (1885) taught basic facts about the structure of local and national government, but did little to encourage active participation.[22] As Ian Lister remarks, up until the 1944 Education Act, civics in elementary schools 'aimed to create obedient and passive subjects, not active, democratic citizens'. In the public schools, which were designed 'to produce leaders and achieve sufficient civic cohesion for a divided society to hold together', there was 'political education through the hidden curriculum of roles and rituals' but 'little explicit teaching about politics for citizenship'[23] (although, as I will show, the more elite a public school was, the more active the modes of citizenship it fostered). The encouragement of political consciousness in the general population was condemned by some educationalists, for example Cyril Norwood, who wrote in 1943 that 'nothing but harm can result from attempts to interest pupils prematurely in matters which imply the experience of an adult'.[24] Until the 1960s, indeed, civics classes in schools failed to address issues such as human rights or trades union participation. In encouraging, as Ian Lister puts it, 'conformity and deference', classes continued to aim to produce 'subjects' rather than 'citizens'.[25] In recent decades, attempts have been made in some quarters to promote more participatory concepts of citizenship education. The Council of Europe in 1993 advised that young people should be educated to

---

20 Sweeney 2005, p. 249.
21 For a discussion of this issue, see Bhattacharyya 1991, pp. 4–19.
22 Edirisingha 2000, p. 40.
23 Lister 1998, p. 256. See also Kennedy 1992.
24 Norwood Report, 1943, quoted in Edirisingha 2000, p. 41.
25 Lister 1998, p. 258.

understand issues surrounding democratic processes, racial equality, social justice and the protection of the environment.[26] Recently in the UK, the Department for Education and Science defined citizenship education as inculcating an awareness of rights and responsibilities, including the right to air views and to participate in the democratic process. In 2002, the UK became one of the last parliamentary democracies to introduce lessons in democratic, participatory citizenship to its National Curriculum.[27] I hope that this study, which covers a genre in which citizenship is of such central importance, will give some insight into how ideas of adolescent citizenship and citizenship education evolved.

One thing that complicates our understanding of adolescence and its social role is the fact that the relationship between physical and intellectual maturity is difficult to assess objectively. This is demonstrated by the fact that different societies accord 'adult' rights to the individual at different ages. Some scholars have questioned biologically-determinist views of adolescence (and childhood) using arguments already familiar to students of gender, maintaining that adolescence is an event shaped by society as much as by hormones. Barbara Hanawalt, for instance, revisits the claim by the early-twentieth-century anthropologist Arnold van Gennep that '"physical puberty" and "social puberty"' are 'very distinct and not necessarily coinciding.' Societies can lengthen or shorten the passage from childhood to adulthood according to their needs, or put an individual through the rituals of adolescence 'either earlier or later than the onset of puberty'.[28] Some historians 'argu[e] that puberty can be culturally suppressed or at least well camouflaged, even from those experiencing it'.[29] James Kincaid goes so far as to claim that the idea of 'puberty' was invented by the Victorians as a way of defining and delimiting their idea of childhood:

> The creation of puberty seems to have solved a good many problems. It provided a means for preserving childhood innocence, more important childhood difference and childhood emptiness. It showed how the child could be considered a separate species without violating utterly the metaphor of 'development': one simply posited that puberty marked the moment of metamorphosis, where the child was recast as an adult.[30]

Hanawalt argues that adults and juveniles 'struggle' over the delimitation of adolescence, with one group attempting to attain adult privileges (marriage, enfranchisement, financial independence and so on) and the other trying to withhold them.[31] In this study, I do not intend to join the nature/nurture debate but to demonstrate how changing adult priorities conditioned popular views of youth

---

26 Holden 1998, p. 13.
27 Edirisingha 2000, p. 46.
28 Hanawalt 1992, p. 343.
29 Ibid., p. 342.
30 Kincaid 1994, p. 125.
31 Hanawalt 1992, p. 344.

and to show how public school literature sought not only to influence adolescent behavior, but to define adolescence itself.

During the past few decades, scholars have increasingly debated the extent to which literature seeks to shape our expectations of the young. Patricia Meyer Spacks has used literary examples to argue that adults project their concerns about social and cultural issues onto narratives of adolescence, often blaming wider social problems on youth and its supposedly inherent instability. She observes that 'the grand polarities that surface repeatedly in the thought of any given historical period help to determine that period's understanding and evaluation of adolescence'. Eighteenth century thinkers preoccupied by the twin principles of reason and sensibility, for example, produced juvenile narratives that traced the individual's progress from irrational childhood to rational adulthood. In contrast, for the twentieth century, the rebellious, socially isolated adolescent protagonist enabled writers to vent their feelings of alienation in an age of mass production.[32] Adolescence also allows the writer to access an intensified sense of self, since the adolescent 'yield[s] to no one in his or her capacity to concentrate on, and in some ways to attain, self-gratification and self-development'.[33] Similarly, viewing a situation from the perspective of an adolescent who is struggling to establish his or her social position by either internalizing or resisting social norms gives the writer opportunity to reassess the 'value' of society.[34]

Psychologist Christine Griffin also offers insight into the ways in which the sociological and political establishment constructs perceptions of adolescence. Dominant attitudes to adolescence, she explains, are often 'characterized by the tendency to investigate young people as both the source and the victims of a series of "social problems" adopting the victim-blaming thesis in the search for the cause(s) of specific phenomena'. Thus, the innate psychological and emotional instability of the young is often held to be at the root of phenomena such as unemployment, crime and the breakdown of the family, and studies of adolescence therefore focus on mental problems, criminality and sexuality.[35] The political elite is preoccupied by an exaggerated belief that the young are in the midst of various moral or social 'crises' because the condition of youth is deemed to be an 'indicator of the state of the nation itself':

> it is expected to reflect the cycle of booms and troughs in the economy; shifts in cultural values over sexuality, morality and family life; and changes in class elations, concepts of nationhood, and in occupational structures. Young people are assumed to hold the key to the nation's future, and the treatment and management of 'youth' is expected to provide the solution to a nation's 'problems'.[36]

---

32 Spacks 1981, p. 10.
33 Ibid., p. 9.
34 Ibid., p. 15.
35 Griffin 1988, p. 3.
36 Ibid., pp. 6, 9–10.

It is through a negotiation of these (real or imagined) crises that the boundaries of 'normal' and 'deviant' adolescent behavior are set out, prescribed and enforced, and dissenting voices are marginalized. My study responds by suggesting some ways in which members of the nineteenth- and early-twentieth-century establishment tried to demarcate 'normal' and 'deviant' adolescent behavior through public school literature. Of course, society does not have one unitary standard of 'normality'; any single writer's account of adolescence, therefore, will inevitably be an attempt to deal with various, sometimes conflicting, social ideologies that dictate what adolescence is or should be. Recently, Robyn McCallum has contributed to the theoretical debate over adolescence and subjectivity by reading adolescent literature from a post-structuralist perspective, using Bakhtinian ideas of dialogism and heteroglossia to investigate the ways in which writers negotiate the social formation of adolescent identity.[37] I will return briefly to this idea in Chapter 1.

The remaining task of this introduction is to explain what kinds of literary work and what kind of school this book will deal with. The educational historian J.A. Mangan defines the British public school as 'expensive, predominantly boarding, independent of the state, but neither privately owned nor profit making'.[38] The most prestigious public schools were founded in the late medieval and early modern periods, often as charitable institutions, sometimes under Royal Charter. They were originally intended to provide a classical education for promising boys whose families could not afford private tutors, but were gradually monopolized by aristocrats and the wealthy. The Clarendon Commission of 1861 was established to inspect what were believed to be the topmost public schools: Eton, Harrow, Westminster, Rugby, Shrewsbury, Charterhouse and Winchester, along with St Paul's and Merchant Taylors'. Among the older institutions there were also various sectarian or charitable boarding schools such as Stonyhurst College and Christ's Hospital. In the Victorian period a glut of new schools appeared that challenged the prominence of older public schools which, at the beginning of the nineteenth century, had suffered in popularity, partly because of indiscipline and an out-of-date curriculum. New foundations included proprietary or 'joint stock' schools such as University College School (1828), the City of London School (1837), Cheltenham (1841), Marlborough (1843) and the Woodard schools (for example, Lancing and Hurstpierpoint Colleges) founded by Nathaniel Woodard to remedy the barbarism of the middle classes.[39] As Robert Kirkpatrick's list of 'real schools' represented in fiction shows, almost every public school has provided the setting for at least one story or novel, some for more than one.[40] The books I discuss here deal with a range of schools, some fictional, some genuine. Indeed, a number of authors, most notably Talbot Baines Reed, had never attended public school, but applied the public school model to wholly imaginary institutions. What the texts

---

37 McCallum 1999.
38 Mangan 2000, p. 2, quoting V. Ogilvie.
39 Armytage 1965, p. 106.
40 Kirkpatrick 2000, pp. 379–81.

have in common is that they all deal with situations in which boys were taken from their families to be educated away from mainstream society, independently of government control.

This study deals with several kinds of text. First, I have offered re-readings of core texts by Thomas Hughes, F.W. Farrar, F. Anstey, H.A. Vachell, H.O. Sturgis, Rudyard Kipling, Arnold Lunn and Alec Waugh, which have already been covered by the genre's major critics. Rather than reading them for historical veracity, I have considered them alongside contemporary periodical literature on adolescence and youth, religious tracts and juvenile advice manuals, in order to determine what kind of role models and ideologies they presented. Secondly, I have introduced a number of hitherto neglected works, for instance, those by Bracebridge Hemyng, in order to give a more complete perspective on the subject. I have also included some autobiographical works designed to be read both by adults and boys, such as those by George Melly and P.H. Fitzgerald. I would class most of the fictional works considered here as 'serious' public school novels. These works usually involve older boys and are markedly different in tone and content to 'humorous' preparatory school stories about younger boys, such as Frank Richards's *Billy Bunter* or Anthony Buckeridge's *Jennings* stories, which post-date the period considered here.

A number of the more significant works discussed in this book were reviewed in major periodicals and discussed in terms of their value to the educational and literary worlds. They were certainly not dismissed as ephemera. *Blackwood's* mentioned *Tom Brown's Schooldays* in an 1859 review of *Adam Bede* which focused on aspects of literary realism and called it 'a "novel" in the most genuine sense'.[41] The same publication commended *Tom Brown* and George Melly's *School Experiences of a Fag* for their accuracy in describing life at Rugby.[42] F. Anstey's *Vice Versa* was discussed in the *Saturday Review* and the *Spectator* in 1882, J.E. Welldon's *Gerald Eversley's Friendship* featured in the *Saturday Review* of 1895 and Kipling's *Stalky* was reviewed in *The Academy* in 1899. Twentieth-century publications such as H.A. Vachell's *The Hill* (1905), Arnold Lunn's *The Harrovians* (1913), Alec Waugh's *The Loom of Youth* (1917) and Shane Leslie's *The Oppidan* (1922) received attention from the *Times Literary Supplement* as they emerged; the *TLS*'s review of *The Hill* also mentioned H.O. Sturgis's *Tim* with approval.[43] The opinions of the reviewers were often ambivalent, but the very fact that the works were mentioned in major literary organs implies that they were considered to merit attention from the intellectual elite. However, this interest seems eventually to have waned. This study will therefore end with the close of the First World War, because this was where most public school literature ceased to debate the particular concepts of citizenship that had been current since before the Victorian period and began to concentrate on purely personal experience. I

---

41 '*Adam Bede*' 1859, p. 491.
42 'A Visit to Rugby' 1862, p. 559.
43 'The Hill', 28th April 1905, p. 137.

have not subdivided the works into those written for adults and those written for juveniles (as Kirkpatrick has done in his *Encyclopaedia of Boys School Stories*) because, as I will argue, intended audiences were never as rigidly defined as this.

Much work on public school fiction to date, notably Isabel Quigly's *The Heirs of Tom Brown* (1984), has concentrated on historical veracity and compares school records and anecdote with textual events while delivering qualitative judgment. Peter Musgrave's *From Brown to Bunter* (1985) and Jeffrey Richard's *Happiest Days: The Public Schools in English Fiction* (1988) give insights into the reception of and influences on the genre.[44] In describing how various social movements (for instance, that of 'Muscular Christianity') affected the development of public school literature, they offer mainly biographical/psychosexual interpretations.[45] Here, however, I interpret public school literature not as a mirror of real adolescent life (although some works may have reflected it quite accurately), but as documents that reveal the processes by which ideas of the adolescent as a developing citizen changed over the period in question. I follow more contemporary trends in juvenile literary criticism which have suggested that, far from representing the young with accuracy, children's and young adult literature often suppresses their voices, interests and needs in order to create a satisfactory world for adult readers. Jacqueline Rose has remarked on how children's books look backwards to a Rousseauian 'conviction that both sexuality and social inequality were realities that the child somehow be used to circumvent' and how the fictional child 'is rendered innocent of all the contradictions which flaw our interaction in the world'.[46] Karín Lesník-Oberstein adds that, unlike alienated adults, children have no way of reasserting their 'real voices', which leaves them even more open to misrepresentation.[47] However, adolescence is a time when young people, given the chance, begin to comment on the disparity between the way the adult world sees them and the way they see themselves. Obviously, it is harder to idealize an articulate adolescent than to idealize a child. A very small number of critics have observed that some writers infantilize adolescents, arrest the development process or confound adolescence and childhood, in order to silence the dissident adolescent voice. In R. Bator's *Signposts to Criticism of Children's Literature* (1983), J. Abrahamson comments that modern 'Teen novels' often show a 'failure to respect' their audience's emotional resilience and understanding of complex issues, while D.L. Burton argues that adolescent fiction reinforces dependency on parents, and stifles political debate.[48] In Chapter 6, I have therefore included a number of texts by adolescents in my debate, in a small attempt to acknowledge that those who

---

44 Richards 1988. General historical overviews of juvenile literature include Avery 1975 and Darton 1999.
45 See, for example, Carpenter 1985.
46 Rose 1994, pp. 8–9.
47 Lesník-Oberstein 1994, p. 34
48 Abrahamson 1983, p. 320, Burton 1983, pp. 311–17

are often denied a voice do have opinions worth listening to, especially when they themselves are the topic of debate.

The starting point of this work is, therefore, that claims about the 'real' nature of adolescence, boyhood or youth should be examined for their ideological content before they are accepted as fact. I work under the premise that when adults write literature for and about the young, their own needs are at least as prominent in their minds as the needs of their audience. Lest this approach seem reductive or cynical, I acknowledge that much of the literature discussed was enthusiastically received by the young and that, in order for this to have been so, it must have rung true with many of their aspirations and experiences. For teenagers to laugh at (and with) Kipling's Stalky does not necessarily mean they are colluding with a cunning adult plot to subject them. It just means they live within a shared culture of signs and values, some understood by adults, some by adolescents and some neither understood, nor even consciously considered, by either.

Chapter 1

The Crisis of Youth and the Public School Reformation

The school-boy, above all others, is not the simple being the world imagines. In that young bosom are often stirring passions as strong as our own, desires not less violent, a volition not less supreme.[1]

—Benjamin Disraeli, *Coningsby* (1844)

What especial cloud hangs over this one part of our life's current, that the stream here will ever run dark and sullen, while on its earlier and its later course it is either all bright and lively, or the impurity of its waters is lost to the distant view in the breadth and majesty of their volume?[2]

—Thomas Arnold, *Sermons*

At the climax of the 1788 story *The History of a Schoolboy*, the hero, George Manly, comforts a vagrant former slave who has been abused by his violent, insensitive and conformist schoolmates. George, weeping, addresses the man as 'my brother', and expresses the fervent wish that slavery might be abolished.[3] At this point in the story, the anonymous author interjects and compares abused slaves to schoolboys who are beaten by their masters. Juveniles and slaves, he implies, have reason to feel commonality, and both are in need of liberation. The egalitarian *History of a Schoolboy* is thus of essence a protest text and it is interesting that a book of this kind should have been probably the very first male-oriented school story.[4] Robert Kirkpatrick suggests that it was written by Thomas Day and, indeed, the narrative fits well with the ideals of Day and his circle.[5] This group included figures such as Joseph Priestley and Richard Lovell Edgeworth, who were striving to establish a tradition of liberal schooling on nonconformist, egalitarian grounds, with a greater emphasis on practical subjects.[5] Like many other types of juvenile literature, therefore, the school story has roots in the

---

1 Disraeli 1989, p. 48.
2 Findlay 1897, p. 130.
3 *The History of a Schoolboy* 1788, pp. 117, 119–20.
4 Girls' school stories predate this by nearly four decades.
5 See Armytage 1965, ch. 4, for a summary of the 'rationalist' dissenting tradition and its educational aims and objectives.

traditions of nonconformists, whose ideals were reflected in the images of youth and citizenship training which it sought to promote.

For George Manly, a boy of the aspiring middle class, education is all about learning how to become a rational civic subject in a world making its first steps towards democracy. Before the age of fourteen, Manly, a regimental trumpeter's son, is educated by a parson at a small school. The parson gives him guidance on moral matters and cultivates his sensibility. Detecting in George 'an inclination to reason and reflect',[6] the parson tells him that the world is a 'theatre' of morals.[7] By observing this world carefully, he explains, we can learn how to exercise good judgment. By fourteen, Manly has developed enough force of personality to be transferred to a residential grammar school to prepare for university. This school, however, proves a true test of his moral strength; it is nothing but a watered-down version of the degenerate outside world, where the status quo is maintained by the tyranny of the strong over the weak. The pedagogy is crude. The boys write '*Nonsense verses*', with the aim of mastering the grammar of classical languages, which, divorced from literary or historical context, are meaningless to them.[8] The master '*thrash[es]*' any student guilty of academic failure.[9] Discipline is coercive, bullying and conformity are endemic, and the boys have no idea of attempting to organize a civilized community among themselves, preferring instead blindly to follow the strongest members of the group.

The History of a Schoolboy teaches boys that they can assert their independence against the forces of convention and conformity without descending to the levels to which other young people often sink.[10] George is constantly bullied for refusing to bow down to the strongest boys in the school, but he nevertheless decides to imitate Christ and 'pursue the most peaceful and inoffensive mode of behavior towards every body'.[11] Because he is a true hero, George serves other people's interests before his own and sees justice done: 'Heroism', we are told, 'may be displayed in every action of our lives' and involves self-denial rather than force.[12] The book's message is one of enlightened individualism. The current school system, suggests the writer, is one that beats boys into conforming to a pre-determined, established system. Social progress, however, demands that identity be formed in the private, domestic sphere and a new brand of individual with new values is needed to establish principles of social justice in society.

George Manly's story would seem to constitute something of an anomalous beginning for a genre that has often been heavily criticized for promoting

---

6   *History of a Schoolboy* 1788, p. 11.
7   Ibid., p. 18.
8   Ibid., p. 67.
9   Ibid., p. 58.
10 Ibid., p. 108.
11 Ibid., p. 52.
12 Ibid., pp. 29, 24.

(as Kenneth Allsop said of *Tom Brown's Schooldays*), 'cruelty' and 'conformity'.[13] In fact, however, far from displaying a unitary view of youth and its place in society, the public school genre is fraught with a whole array of political contradictions, many of them resulting from conflicting attitudes towards the role of young people as emergent citizens. *The History of a Schoolboy* appeared at the beginning of a revolution in the way the period we now describe as 'adolescence' was perceived.[14] Before the Industrial Revolution, adolescence, more usually termed 'youth', was marked by a variety of social rituals, in particular apprenticeship, which lasted for around seven years, starting between the ages of fourteen and seventeen and lasting until the mid-twenties. A common practice in this period was for young people to be sent away from home, usually to become apprentices or to work in another family's household. John Springhall describes this practice as a 'rite of passage' into 'a transitional stage which was meant to prepare [young people] for adulthood and citizenship'.[15] This process averted the conflict that might otherwise have arisen between older generations in the family and young people who were beginning to assert themselves.[16] English public schools, originally intended to produce an elite mandarin class, had a similar function, giving boys an opportunity to make social contacts and experience a range of socialization rituals. These practices suggest that there was a common acceptance that a period existed between childhood and adulthood which required its own special treatment. However, the extent to which childhood was recognized as an entity in itself is a matter of debate among historians. Thus, whereas Philippe Ariès argued in the 1960s that the early moderns saw young people merely as miniature adults, Linda Pollock has shown more recently how childhood was recognized as a specific stage of life before the eighteenth century.[17] It is arguable, nonetheless, that adolescence drew far more attention from writers from the eighteenth century onwards. The first question this chapter will discuss, therefore, is why writers from the governing classes became interested in documenting the real and fictional lives of the young and, in particular, in discussing the development of civic values among teenaged schoolboys. One of the reasons for this increased attention on the young was the perception that schools were failing to educate their charges to fulfill the moral duties of conscientious citizens. I will, therefore, proceed to detail some of the ways in which public schools inculcated certain ideas of citizenship, pointing out how and why reformers with different political agendas attacked traditional notions of public school education. Finally, I will discuss the

---

13 Hartley 1969, 216. Allsop's article, 'A Coupon for Instant Tradition', was published in *Encounter* (November 1965).

14 For a general analysis on the historical impact of the Industrial Revolution on ideas of adolescence throughout Western Europe, see Gillis 1974, ch. 2.

15 Springhall 1986, p. 17.

16 Ibid., p. 20.

17 See Pollock 1996, ch. 4, for evidence of parents' attitudes to children from the early modern period.

conflicting Enlightenment and Evangelical attitudes towards adolescence which contributed to some bewilderingly contradictory agendas for reforming the way future citizens were brought up.

It seems that adolescence, or youth, carried a symbolic value during the Industrial Revolution stretching far beyond the individual, private concerns of the young. To Benjamin Disraeli, for instance, the narrative of national political reform was intimately bound up with the personal development of the young people involved in it. 'The history of Heroes', explains the Jewish intellectual Sidonia in *Coningsby* (1844), 'is the history of Youth'.[18] He remarks: 'Do not suppose [...] that I hold that youth is genius: all that I say is, that genius, when young, is divine. Why, the greatest captains of ancient and modern times both conquered Italy at five-and-twenty!'[19] Pascal, he continues, wrote 'a great work' at sixteen, and Grotius was in legal practice at seventeen. The intense focus on young people and their relationship to political reform demonstrated by Disraeli and other writers of the *Bildungsroman* tradition was, in one sense, a result of political change and industrialization. Philip Abrams explained in the 1970s how industrialization can, in some cases, create an environment where political activism flourishes among certain groups of young people. An industrialized society 'drives a wedge' between the domestic sphere of childhood and the 'occupational system' (the sphere occupied by working adults), because the 'division of labor' requires formal work to be done outside the home.[20] Adolescence, at least for classes not compelled by poverty to send their children to work in their early teens, thus becomes a distinct stage of life bridging the two spheres, in which young people learn how to make the transition between home and the outside world.[21] Liberal capitalist societies organize adolescence as 'a period of freedom and role-experimentation' set aside for re-appraising identity and behavior. Youth radicalism is often a by-product of this process, since young people often feel that society denies them the power and autonomy they deserve, a feeling which leads them, in response, to construct their sense of self in opposition to the status quo. For instance, in an industrial capitalist system, youths might try to seek ways of expressing themselves which 'reaffirm [...] the world of kin, community, rural innocence and childhood'.[22] As will be seen later, public and private secondary schools, which during the Industrial Revolution were accommodating increasing numbers of young people, were perceived as having the potential to generate a significant level of politicized activity.

Whatever the extent of actual political involvement among the young during any particular period, adolescence is also a useful metaphor for a nation which is experiencing upheaval and uncertainty while moving towards industrialization and political 'maturity' (however that is defined). Countries undergoing this change are

---

18 Disraeli 1989, p. 146.
19 Ibid., p. 145.
20 Abrams 1970, p. 185.
21 Ibid., p. 188.
22 Ibid., p. 186.

sometimes described as being in a state equivalent to adolescence (hence the titles of numerous nineteenth-century European political reform movements, 'Young England', 'Young Germany' and 'Young Italy', among others). John Matthews argues, for example, that in *Coningsby*, 'The Condition-of-England is [...] treated as though it were a single literary character, subject to the same pressures [...] that individuals reveal in their behavior'.[23] It is easy to go from this idea to observe that, for Disraeli and others, the protagonist and his country follow similar paths of development. In *Tom Brown's Schooldays*, Thomas Hughes (1857) remarks that 1850s society is itself exhibiting symptoms of adolescence ('we as a nation [...] are in a transition state'[24]). Hughes echoes Disraeli's remark that the English people during the reform period were, in a political sense, 'literally children', who needed re-educating in 'self-government'.[25] Chapter 2 of this book will show how Hughes presents Tom Brown's small personal narrative alongside the macro-narrative of English social and political history.

It would be interesting to see how often societies with a linear idea of progress use narratives of youth to express their hopes or frustrations during periods of transition. Perhaps modernity itself creates a heightened consciousness of youth, engendered by a feeling that society is aiming towards maturity. Indeed, since secondary educational provision generally expands under industrialization, there may be a strong sense that the education of adolescents in particular helps society to reach this goal. Increasing levels of democracy may also give previously disenfranchised individuals the feeling that they are achieving social maturity. In the British Industrial Revolution, increasing social mobility offered greater political and economic autonomy to many whose forbears had lived in a state of 'childlike' dependency under aristocratic landowners. The process of learning to cope with this autonomy could be compared to adolescence. On a further level still, there is a sense that what a nation becomes in the future – and the level of civility it achieves – depends on how it educates its young (especially its young elite) as citizens. One historian of the public schools claimed that

> If a composite history of all the public schools is ever written it will be, in reality, the history of England, since the British Empire has been in the main built by the founders of the schools and the pupils who [...] had their characters molded in those institutions.[26]

On the other hand, if what happens among the young is a useful predictor of what tomorrow holds, the narrative of youth can also be used to give salutary warnings, as in F.W. Farrar's *Eric: Or, Little By Little* (1858), which I will discuss in Chapter 3. The way writers treat adolescence, as I will show, is often determined by whether they perceive society as in a process of advancement or decay.

---

23 Matthews 1984, p. 184.
24 Hughes 1989, p. 41.
25 Disraeli 1989, pp. 99, 98.
26 Webster 1937, p. 9.

In the years between the appearance of *The History of a Schoolboy* and the publication of probably the most well known public school story, Thomas Hughes's *Tom Brown's Schooldays*, great changes took place in the way literature dealt with young people, particularly with regard to young males. The German Romantics had already developed the *Bildungsroman* genre specifically to deal with ideas of adolescence, partly in response to the emphasis Enlightenment philosophers placed on youth. England responded, somewhat later, with works such as *Great Expectations*, *The Mill on the Floss* and *Jane Eyre*.[27] There were significant gender issues at work here, because Romantic writers and philosophers had made it 'respectable' for male authors to discuss juvenile issues, previously regarded as a 'woman's subject'. According to Cynthia Buffington Davis, until the 1850s,

> chronicles of childhood or autobiographical development were considered too trivial for public consumption, one commentator remarking: 'only to two or three persons in all the world are the reminiscences of a man's early youth interesting; to the parent who nursed him; to the fond wife or child mayhap who afterwards loves him; to himself always and supremely'.[28]

For several reasons, however, it became not only attractive but also necessary for early Victorian men to write about their juvenile experiences. Firstly, social mobility meant that boys could no longer follow the educational paths set by their forefathers. They needed guidance from outside in the form of the boyhood histories of successful men. Secondly, cheap printing was flooding the market with popular literature which boys, to the horror of moralists, were more than happy to read. Thomas Arnold, head of Rugby School from 1827 to 1842, whose role in public school reform will be discussed in more detail below, insisted that reading mass-produced literature, including novels, stimulated a kind of 'vice' in boys which had not existed before. Works of literature of an earlier time, he commented, 'were less exciting, and therefore less attractive', as well as being 'dearer, and therefore less accessible'. They did not come in periodical form, so 'they did not occupy the mind for so long a time, nor keep alive so constant an expectation'.[29] Publications such as 'Pickwick and Nickleby, Bentley's Magazine &c',[30] on the other hand, encouraged 'childishness'. Not only were they bad for the intellect; they also depleted bodily energy and encouraged physical excess and gluttony:

> this weak and delicate appetite [...] presented [with] an abundance of the most stimulating and least nourishing food possible [...] finds its full gratification in the

---

27 See Buckley 1974, for an analysis of how the English *Bildungsroman* built on the original German model pioneered by Goethe.
28 Davis 1981, p. 22.
29 Sermon IV.IV in Findlay 1897, pp. 159–60.
30 Stanley 1882, vol. II, p. 137.

details of an exciting and protracted story, and then lies down as it were gorged, and goes to sleep.[31]

Arnold complained that 'the weakness of mind' produced by novel reading 'is [...] adverse to quiet study and thought, to that reflection which alone is wisdom'.[32] In response, his protégés, including Thomas Hughes, took it upon themselves to add their own matter to the flood of new works being written for the young, in the hope of neutralizing the evils of popular fiction.

By the time *Tom Brown* appeared, the school story seems also to have become a good excuse for men to indulge a retrospective on their own juvenile years under the guise of higher pedagogical motives. Previous authors of school stories had often been female (for example, Maria Edgeworth, Harriet Martineau and Dorothy Kilner, who also wrote about a character called Tom Brown[33]). This female presence seems to have made some men anxious to reclaim the genre for themselves. James Fitzjames Stephen expressed immense relief when he discovered that a male author had finally written a story of school life for 'boys and men', 'an attempt in which', he crowed, 'Miss Edgeworth failed'.[34] One reason so many male authors subsequently chose exclusively masculine expeditions or ships, or indeed, schools, as locations for juvenile stories may have been the desire to distinguish themselves from the world of the nursemaid, governess and Sunday School teacher associated with authors such as Sarah Trimmer and Mrs Sherwood.

The upsurge in interest in specifically public school adolescence was also part of a drive to examine changes in ideas of upper-class male identity, which were evolving all the way through the long nineteenth century. In particular, from the mid-nineteenth century onwards, former public and grammar school boys constantly, obsessively and often repetitively re-lived their own schooldays in the form of hundreds of school histories and biographies, as well as in fiction. Many of these works, such as those by H.C. Adams, A.D. Coleridge, C.F. Johnstone and Eric Parker, are cited in this book. Old Etonians alone published so many memoirs that some felt obliged to apologize for adding to the pile. Lionel Cust wrote in the preface to his *A History of Eton College* in 1899: 'It would seem as if some apology were due for the publication of this book. Eton has been a fruitful, perhaps too fruitful, source of inspiration to writers of all ages in the nineteenth century'.[35] For a man to revisit his schooldays by writing such a history may have helped him to make sense of the social changes that had occurred in his lifetime. He might also have been searching for the key to his own successes or failures, in order to give some idea of the best way to raise the coming generation. Many of these

---

31 Findlay 1897, p. 160.
32 Ibid., p. 161.
33 Dorothy Kilner's *First Going to School: The Story of Tom Brown and His Sisters* was published in 1804. See Kirkpatrick 2000, p. 176.
34 Stephen 1858, p. 172.
35 Cust 1899, p. v.

books (such as those quoted in this work) follow a highly formulaic pattern. There is a brief exposition of the school's history, then a semi-autobiographical account of the author's own experiences, and finally a list of recent modernizations and improvements. There is also usually a hagiography of headmasters and school heroes. The history of the school is usually divided into three stages. In its first stage, during the eighteenth and early nineteenth century, the school is described as a hotbed of anarchy, where physical conditions are hard and educational mediocrity prevails. The author then describes the process of enlightenment which took place during his own adolescence, and then details how the school became the ideal, civilized, organized pedagogical institution of the present time. Again, the emphasis falls on the way in which the author's own adolescence coincides with a great transitional process within the school itself.

There were private reasons, too, which led men to indulge in recollections of their own schooldays and to contemplate the activities of the next generation of boys. From Thomas Gray's 'Ode on a Distant Prospect of Eton College' (1747) onwards, the spectacle of youth at play was recognized as a powerful emotional stimulus to disenchanted adults. The Rugby School headmaster Thomas Arnold, in spite of some hard-line Evangelical attitudes towards the juvenile sin (see below), had his own fantasies of regression:

> I want absolute play, like a boy, and neither riding nor walking will make up for my leaping-pole and gallows, and bathing, when the youths used to go with me, and I felt completely for a time a boy as they were.[36]

He also commented:

> I enjoy [...] the society of youths of seventeen or eighteen, for they are all alive in limbs and spirits at least, if not in mind, while in older persons the body and spirits often become lazy and languid without the mind gaining any vigor to compensate for it.[37]

This emphatically Romantic attitude echoes Wordsworth, a friend of Arnold's during the Rugby years. The urge to regress into one's own childhood featured heavily in Romantic literature because childhood was central to changing notions of individual identity. According to Carolyn Steedman, the development of child- and adolescent-centered narratives in the late eighteenth and early nineteenth centuries was a response to a fundamental change in the idea of 'self'. Citing Foucault's *History of Sexuality*, she comments that 'it is not so much the sense of the self that is a development of the modern world: rather it is the *location* of the self that is new'. The pre-Enlightenment 'self' was defined according to its social context. After the Enlightenment, the 'self' became more private, individual and internal. Steedman remarks that 'child-figures, and more generally the idea of

---

36 Stanley 1882, vol. II, p. 82.
37 Ibid., vol. I, p. 33.

childhood, came to be commonly used to express the depths of historicity within individuals, the historicity that was "linked to them, essentially"'.[38] Some figures, such as Wordsworth and Rousseau, even suggested that the inborn self was actually corrupted and damaged by society. The desire of authors to recover their 'true' selves through narratives of youth is, therefore, something more that needs to be kept in mind when assessing the portrayal of adolescence in literature. The school story was not only a means of educating the young but could also function as a regression fantasy, giving the kind of therapy to world-weary adults that Gray, Wordsworth and Arnold craved. Because childhood and adolescent experiences had become so crucial to sense of identity, public school stories, which are often based on personal recollections, show an especially strong conflict of authorial interests, between satisfying a forward-looking juvenile readership and a nostalgic adult readership. As Peter Musgrave observes, some authors deliberately wrote novels with a 'dual readership in mind'.[39]

Public school stories, therefore, grew out of an incredibly complex mixture of motivations, and often had multiple, contradictory aims. For example, Percy Hetherington Fitzgerald in *Schooldays at Saxonhurst* (which describes a time of strong Irish nationalism at Stoneyhurst), makes amusing political quips while nostalgically recalling youthful transgressions. However, the text also includes cautionary advice for the young and was published as part of a series of boys' books. George Melly's *School Experiences of a Fag*, also semi-autobiographical, provides an explanatory defense of the fagging system for worried parents while simultaneously giving boys advice and celebrating the author's experiences at Rugby. *Tom Brown's Schooldays* works on multiple levels. Primarily, the book seems oriented towards fathers who are reading with their sons. There are, for instance, numerous cultural and literary tags which might stimulate discussion between parent and child. By invoking the 'gentle reader, or simple reader',[40] Hughes aims his story both at the initiated (the 'gentleman', well-educated and mature) and the – as yet – uneducated child. His register is split between a didactic voice ('now, my boys, you whom I want to get for readers') and one which is simultaneously sentimental and sardonic.[41] At times, the narrative begins to resemble a contemporary political or moral tract. At one point, Hughes harangues both 'young England' (adolescents and students who travel over Europe in the summer) and 'rising Parliamentary Lords'.[42] Another time he addresses his audience as 'My dear boys, old and young, you who have belonged, or do belong, to other schools and other houses',[43] attempting to unite his disparate readership by evoking the common experience of school. This attempt to satisfy all levels of reader means

---

38 Steedman 1995, p. 12.
39 Musgrave 1985, p. 85.
40 Hughes 1989, p. 5.
41 Ibid., p. 15
42 Ibid., pp. 6, 43.
43 Ibid., p. 125.

that Hughes's narrative, which sometimes seems dangerously unplanned, vacillates self-consciously. As a narrator, he is unreliable, or at least quixotic. His opinions change freely and he sometimes pompously states a principle merely to knock it down shortly afterwards. For example, after having alternately decried and praised the recent vogue among the young for foreign travel, he writes:

> having succeeded in contradicting myself in my first chapter [...] I shall here shut up for the present and consider my ways; having resolved to '"sar" it out ,' as we say in the Vale, 'holus bolus,' just as it comes, and then you'll probably get the truth out of me.[44]

Hughes invites us to read and experiment with him, and his authorial persona feels his way through the story, struggling to find a self, a voice and firm principles. Indeed, what Hughes has in common with Tom, England and Rugby itself is the fact that they are all struggling and searching for identity, moral certainty and maturity. This idea – that both the institution and the boy inside it are in a process of travelling from darkness to enlightenment – is almost universal among public school oriented writers of this period.

Robyn McCallum's use of Bakhtinian ideas of hereroglossia and dialogism to analyze the formation of subjectivity and authorial voice in adolescent literature is a useful approach in understanding the public school text. The novel, according to Bakhtin, 'is an inherently heteroglottic and intertextual genre which appropriates and represents various primary speech genres as well as other socially stratified languages, both literary and extraliterary, from within a heteroglossia'.[45] If this is true of the novel, how much more so of a genre such as the public school story that recycles its predecessors and that is addressed to a community of readers who are immersed daily in a plethora of texts ranging from novels through Latin primers and school histories to sermons. The presence in these works of multiple, often conflicting social ideologies and multiple-voiced narratives is also entirely consistent with Bakhtin's ideas about the relationship between literature and subject formation. As McCallum explains,

> For Bakhtin, an individual's subjectivity is formed through the selective appropriation and assimilation of the discourses of others, and these discourses position a speaker within a heteroglossia and equip speakers with socio-ideological viewpoints. Subjectivity is the product of an intense struggle for hegemony among various ideological discourses and voices.[46]

This process of 'assimilation' is particularly important to the development of subjectivity in adolescence, when the individual emerges as a social being and launches into dialogue with the competing social claims around him or her. As I

---

44 Ibid., p. 20.
45 McCallum 1999, pp. 25–26.
46 Ibid., p. 10.

have said, the public school story was developing at a time when not just adolescent subjectivity, but all kinds of ideas of subjectivity, were under question. Writers such as Hughes, unsure of their own textual and social authority, find themselves juggling with a number of conflicting ideologies of identity and the role of the citizen, and end up as a result with narratives written seemingly from several different viewpoints. This issue was especially serious for educators desiring to enforce a particular authoritarian stance, such as F.W. Farrar, writing primarily as an Evangelical cleric with a moral agenda, but also as a Darwinist. Farrar struggles painfully – and unsuccessfully – to sustain a monologic voice in his most famous work, *Eric: Or, Little By Little*.[47] Caught up between the competing meta-narratives of evolution and creationism, each of which presents a radically different account of the meaning of human subjectivity and development, Farrar despairs not only of his own authority but even of the authority of God Himself. Through the course of this book, I will examine the conflicting discourses and ideologies that went together to form the sometimes contradictory accounts of adolescence in the works I consider. I do not want to complicate my own narrative by using Bakhtinian terminology, because any discussion of the public school system already requires the introduction of concepts that are alien to many readers and require explanation. However, I do think that it is worth pointing out that, while many of the writers considered here seem very conscious of a need, as educationalists, to create monologic, unified, authoritative texts, they invariably fail to do so.

Central to the narrative of school history promoted by Victorian writers is the idea that, in pre-Victorian times, schoolboys and schools were unremittingly barbaric. This myth was rooted in social and economic anxieties, in a changing sense of what was appropriate adolescent behavior and in a more general sense of panic surrounding the conduct of the young. Historians have identified several reasons, some demographic, as to why the behavior of young people attracted so much comment at this time. John Gillis remarks that life expectancy for professionals and aristocrats increased from 42.4 years in 1729 to 54.9 years by 1830.[48] At the same time child mortality over Western Europe fell, bringing a rise in population and resulting in a slump in professional employment opportunities for young middle- and upper-class males. The nineteenth-century German writer W.H. Riehl spoke of these jobless youths as an 'intellectual proletariat' who were alienated by lack of professional employment and the subsequent delay of marriage prospects and proper citizenship, and presented a potential source of trouble.[49] Barbara Hanawalt, discussing lower-class juveniles, suggests that a socio-economic 'crisis' in youth identity occurred when artisans and farmers stopped using long indenture between 1750 and 1844. The existence of masterless, unanswerable working-class adolescents, many with disposable incomes, 'left modern Western Europe's newly disempowered adults struggling to define and

---

47 See Chapter 3.
48 Gillis 1974, p. 40.
49 Ibid., p. 76.

control what they perceived as an unfortunate transformation in the behavior of youth'.[50] Across all classes, therefore, increased youth leisure time was popularly associated with violence and crime. In England, the public schools served as repositories for surplus rich young men waiting to enter society. To the popular imagination, the Regency public school, full of privileged young men with plenty of spare energy, fostered a type of masculine identity that found expression in social disruption and violence. As Jeffrey Richards comments:

> public schools merely reflected the prevailing values of a dissolute aristocracy, whose world was one of hard drinking, ruinous gambling, horse racing, blood sports and prizefighting. The measure of a man was how much he could drink and how tough he was. It was an ethic that the aristocracy shared with the 'rough' working class.[51]

The biographer of Thomas Arnold, A.P. Stanley, remarked on how pre-Victorian schoolboys had been 'left for a large portion of their time to form an independent society of their own'. This independence made them liable to organize themselves into self-sufficient groups over whom adults had little control[52] and they became rebellious when their autonomy was challenged.

Victorian commentators usually documented the frequent rebellions that plagued pre-Victorian schools as outpourings of barbarous insubordination. However, it is important not to forget that public schoolboys were living in a world unsupervised by governmental agencies, without the benefit of child abuse legislation. Parents were often several days' journey away and boys were left to themselves to survive in, and defend themselves against, a system overwhelmingly devoted to providing maximum profit and ease for schoolmasters. Winchester had rebellions in 1774, 1793 and 1818. The 1793 episode arose from rising indignation against the school Warden who would frequently 'break his word, lay traps for [the boys'] youthful inexperience and their quixotic loyalty to each other, take back a promised amnesty and quell by a trick what by a trick he had incited'.[53] H.C. Adams, the boys' story writer, recorded that students became angry when the whole school was punished for the wrongdoing of one individual. They entered into a respectful written correspondence – in Latin – with the Warden, explaining (correctly) that he had broken the statutes of the school. Gaining no satisfactory response, they then began a siege of the school and entered into a long (and seemingly well-argued) debate with the authorities.[54] The boys raised the 'red cap of liberty' over the Middle Gate, and held fort with 'swords, guns and bludgeons'.[55] In 1818 a quarrel with a Tutor over a breach of confidentiality led to boys seizing

---

50 Hanawalt 1992, p. 347.
51 Richards 1988, p. 9. See also Mangan 1986, pp. 265–87.
52 Stanley 1882, vol. I, p. 97.
53 Firth 1949, p. 90.
54 Adams 1878, p. 151.
55 Ibid., p. 148.

the school buildings, causing the Riot Act to be read and the military to be brought in.[56] At Eton in 1768, boys rebelled against Dr Foster over a meaningless rule that dictated that they had to hide from masters if they saw them in town ('shirking').[57] In 1783, they joined their tutors in a strike against the head, Dr Davies, and handed him a list of grievances.[58] In 1818, they rebelled against Keate when they felt a boy called Marriott had been unjustly expelled.[59]

Adult commentators, however, tended to aim their criticism more at the insubordinate youths than at the institutional flaws which had contributed to their rebellious tendencies. The 1835 *Quarterly Review of Education* (quoted by John Chandos), remarked that 'Boys are sent to school among other purposes, to be instructed in the knowledge of social life, not a social life founded on their own notions, but one which shall be a fit introduction to the social state of manhood'.[60] H.C. Adams maintained that the Winchester boys' 'whole conduct in openly refusing obedience to the authorities was *per se* blamable',[61] even though he pinned primary responsibility for the hostilities on staff who failed to keep promises and lacked an aptitude for the teaching profession. However, he did express admiration and sympathy for the Winchester rebels, as well as implying that things in the school improved after the rebellion and vindicating the boys involved by saying how well they turned out in later life.[62] Adams's comments place him in an uncomfortable no-man's land between the Victorian and pre-Victorian ages. Victorian commentators tended to insist that even if boys were legally and morally in the right, insubordination against masters was in essence wrong. In theory, Adams respected the boys' mastery of the debate on the nature and rights and authority, but he could not condone the independent nature of their actions.

The behavior of public schoolboys, whether justified or not, offended the sensibilities of social reformers among the ascendant middle classes. These reformers, who occupied themselves during the first few decades of the nineteenth century with reform of state, economy, family and public institutions – including schools – were a diverse group who are hard to fit into one single category. However, the Evangelical lobby doubtlessly accounted for a large number of them. As Boyd Hilton has explained, these Evangelicals were the heirs to the Wesleyan revival.[63] They included both dissenters and Anglicans, and their most influential luminaries were members of the Clapham Sect, which included William Wilberforce, Henry Thornton, James Stephen and Hannah More. Their religious convictions centered

---

56 Ibid., pp. 186–87.
57 Benson 1899, pp. 206–7.
58 Ibid., pp. 216–17.
59 Ibid., p. 290.
60 *Quarterly Journal of Education* 10, 1835, p. 103. Quoted in Chandos 1984, p. 172.
61 Adams 1878, p. 151.
62 Ibid., p. 189. Adams lists 'Bishop Mant, Field-marshal Lord Seaton, Lord Chancellor Hatherley, and Sir Alexander Malet'.
63 Hilton 1988, p. 7

on individual conversion and revelation, and on a belief in original sin, life as a moral trial and salvation through faith in Christ's atonement.[64] They also adopted an attitude of what Ian Bradley calls 'moral seriousness', which saw every decision and action taken by an individual to be of decisive importance as regarded his or her chances of salvation.[65] Evangelicals varied in the degree to which they believed that the condition of man on earth could be ameliorated and how social improvements might be achieved, and these differing beliefs lead them to ally themselves to a variety of political factions. Some embraced a reforming agenda, believing that suffering on earth was God's way of telling mankind to change its ways in readiness for the second coming. Believers responded to God's warnings by devising interventionist state policies such as Lord Shaftesbury's Ten Hours Act of 1847. Religiously-motivated reform was associated with enlightened Tory paternalist factions,[66] although it sometimes had elements in common with more radical agendas, such as Robert Owen's New Lanark project. Other Evangelicals, such as Richard Whately, applied religion to social matters in a quite different way, believing that divine providence could operate through free trade and the activity of individual choice in the market. They adhered to classical economic liberalism, while still expressing concern for the moral wellbeing of the nation.[67] At times, Evangelicals vacillated between political ideologies, particularly during the Corn Law and Poor Law debates.[68] Allied with Evangelicals on the specific issue of educational reform were Unitarians, such as Harriet Martineau and Joseph Priestley, who had the same intensely serious attitude to life but a different theology, and their rationalist associates, including Thomas Day, the Edgeworths and other members of the Lunar Society. The leading light of school reform, Thomas Arnold, saw himself as an intermediary between high and low church and between traditionalism and reform, rather than as an Evangelical. Nonetheless, as I will show later, Arnold combined elements of Evangelical thought with other current ideas in his sermons.[69]

Arnold's student and biographer, A.P. Stanley, commenting on the state of the pre-reform public schools, remarked that the

> evil of the absence of systematic attempts to give a more directly Christian character to what constituted the education of the whole English gentry, was becoming more and more a scandal in the eyes of religious men, who at the close of the last century and the

---

64 See ibid., p. 8
65 For a debate on the impact of Evangelical belief on social behavior, see Bradley 1976.
66 Hilton 1988, p. 92.
67 Ibid., p. 53.
68 Ibid., pp. 201–53.
69 For a full analysis of Thomas Arnold's relationship to Evangelicalism, see Newsome 1961.

beginning of this – Wilberforce, for example, and Bowdler – had lifted up their voices against it.[70]

In the literary world, Tobias Smollett, Thomas Day and William Cowper also criticized schools for failing to give a useful education and for not supervising boys adequately in their spare time. In the *Edinburgh Review*, Henry Brougham and Sydney Smith complained about the misappropriation of scholarships earmarked for poor students and exposed the vice and physical abuse which was allowed to happen amongst boys who were not supervised properly.[71] Moreover, the middle classes – those without long-established inherited wealth or power, who were anxious to gain the privileges accorded to the established upper classes – coveted public school education, but wanted it on their own terms.[72]

This body of people found their most notable spokesman in Thomas Arnold, son of the Collector of Customs for Cowes and headmaster of Rugby school, who spent his life trying to unite Evangelicals with the Anglican establishment. Arnold was credited by the Victorians as having reformed the public schools, but debunked in the twentieth century for failing to implement any substantial reforms at Rugby other than introducing Modern History, Modern Languages and Mathematics into a fundamentally very conservative curriculum. Nevertheless, his moral ideologies were widely proliferated through Thomas Hughes and other of his most publicly vocal students, through the Working Men's College and the Co-operative and Trades Union movements, A.P. Stanley's biography and his published sermons and writings.[73] Arnold was passionately involved in political debate, particularly in promoting a 'middle way' between High Church Anglicanism and Evangelicalism in order to consolidate moral and political power in the hands of the middle classes. Stanley remarks that he also ascribed 'a peculiar importance [...] to political questions'.[74] However, since his ability to get his hands on real political power was limited, he worked instead on the children of the powerful, probably gaining a wider influence than he could have achieved in other middle-class professional or bureaucratic roles (a strategy followed, arguably, by many of the educationalists and authors discussed here). He once commented, rather disingenuously, 'I should like to be *aut Caesar aut nullus*, and as it is pretty well settled for me that I shall not be Caesar, I am quite content to live in peace as *nullus*'.[75] The frustrated Caesar undoubtedly emerged in his approach to headmastership. As J.E. Adams observes,

---

70 Stanley 1882, vol. I, p. 85.
71 Chandos 1984, pp. 36–37.
72 Richards 1988, p. 10. Shrosbree 1998 also notes that the middle classes were founding their own schools which, when compared to traditional public schools, showed the older institutions in a poor light (p. 16).
73 See Vance 1985, Newsome 1961 and Adams 1995, ch. 2, for analysis of the Arnoldian influence on education, religion and social activism.
74 Stanley 1882, vol. I, p. 172.
75 Stanley, quoted in Adams 1995, p. 68.

Stanley's biography of Arnold reveals how he ran Rugby 'precisely on the same principles as he would have governed a great empire'.[76] The drive to reform the education received by the ruling elite at public schools gave Arnold an arena for exercising the social and political power he so craved.

The aspects of public school education that most appalled nineteenth-century reformers were the combative model of male citizenship they promoted, the ascetic, often brutal living conditions, the large amount of leisure time which allowed boys to take part in subversive or politicized activities and the tendency of school to alienate young men from domestic values. In the next few pages, I will describe how the 'traditional' model of the emergent male citizen manifested itself in public school education, before explaining why this model upset reformers – including early feminists. As M.V. Wallbank has observed, the old public school system was based on the idea of 'combative learning'.[77] The curriculum consisted of classical languages, classical (and sometimes English) literature, verse-making and rhetoric, along with debating and (occasionally) drama as leisure-time activities. A great deal of time was spent making verse and prose compositions using pre-set classical formulae. The system was designed to groom boys in 'the development of political ambition, political character and political skills'.[78] Although noblemen automatically qualified for such an education, foundations (theoretically) allowed promising local boys to participate and status at school was supposed to be determined not by birth, but through academic ranking.[79]

Success at school was measured according to a boy's performance in the rhetorical, dialectical and 'histrionic' skills deemed essential for public men.[80] Canning advised Gladstone, preparing for a political career at Eton in 1824, to 'Give plenty of time to your verses', since 'Every good copy you do will set in your memory some poetical thought or well-turned form of speech which you will find useful when you speak in public'.[81] As James Brinsley-Richards commented, before the introduction of scholarships and examinations Eton allowed considerable free time for political writing and debating. Many schools – among them Eton, Winchester, Westminster, St Paul's, Merchant Taylors and Stonyhurst – also had a history of formal and informal dramatic performance in Latin and sometimes in English. The Lower Chamber theatre at Eton was internationally acclaimed and, although supposedly illicit, was indulged by the head.[82] According to Lawrence Tanner (writing in the 1930s), dramatic performances at Westminster were 'held to have high educational value from the point of view both of deportment and

---

76 Ibid., p. 70.
77 Wallbank 1973, p. 4.
78 Ibid., p. 3.
79 Ibid., p. 4. In reality, upper-class gerrymandering often meant that scholarships were appropriated by the rich, one reason the 1861–1864 Clarendon Commission was established.
80 Ibid., p. 12.
81 Brinsley-Richards 1883, pp. 411–12.
82 Ibid., p. 100.

elocution'.[83] They were rare survivals from the medieval festivals of the Boy Bishops, Lords of Misrule and 'King of the Beans'; 'licensed bufoonery' which had been mostly repressed with the Protestant Reformation and the Civil War.[84] Drama was also a means by which boys could experiment with and create personae for themselves that would be useful later in public life. Rupert Wilkinson suggests that a theatrical cultivation of manners was essential to those who later went into government. A diplomat, for instance, was, in the words of Walter Bagehot, 'not simply an agent; [but] a spectacle', and ruling-class youths were accordingly 'trained for the theatrical side of life'.[85] Thomas Spateman, author of *The School-Boy's Mask* (1742), a play designed for educational use, reminds his boy actors in his introductory preface that personality is as much a performance as an inborn quality, remarking that 'Life, in fact, / Is just, just such a mask, as here we act'.[86]

However, boyhood rituals of dressing up and performance came under attack from critics of the public school system as encouraging insincerity and a love of the superficial among the ruling orders. This criticism was rooted partly in the Evangelical and Romantic emphasis on the 'inner' self as the root of moral feeling and character. As James Eli Adams has remarked, the early nineteenth-century distrust of theatrical display was articulated by Thomas Carlyle in his attack on 'dandies' in *Sartor Resartus* (1833). The dandy, a 'fundamentally theatrical being',[87] relied on dress, rhetoric, public display and a careful cultivation of a public *persona* to build himself a place in society, rather than, for example, entitling himself to public respect by championing good causes. I will return to this theme later in the chapter when discussing opposition to the public school system in more detail.

The rhetorical culture of the pre-reform public schools encouraged not only poetry and drama, but also a certain amount of political debate. John Keate, headmaster at Eton from 1809 to 1834, encouraged political independence, and remarked to W.E. Gladstone, 'I wish I could hear you [debate] without your being aware of my presence'. This was despite the fact that Keate was widely thought to be a 'graceless, senseless little martinet'.[88] Gladstone, at one point debating society president, edited the 1827 *Eton Miscellany*, where he was permitted to publish 'Ode to the Shade of Watt Tyler', sympathetic to the Cato Street Conspirators. Late in life, he recalled being allowed to boo at Keate during sermons and commented to A.C. Benson, 'I am sorry that booing has died out – it gave us a sense of our national privilege of disagreeing with constituted authority'.[89] Many aspects of the public school curriculum contained elements of combat, and even literature

---

83 Tanner 1934, p. 55.
84 Ibid., pp. 56–60.
85 Wilkinson 1964, p. 23.
86 Spateman 1742, pp. vii, 55.
87 Adams 1995, p. 22.
88 Brinsley-Richards 1883, pp. 401, 423.
89 Benson 1899, p. 499.

became a weapon. As B.G. Smith observes, 'Boys who beat and bruised each other while they competed for prizes in their studies followed a junior version of the model found in Caesar or Cicero – [...] who waged war and politics but who also wrote'.[90] Combat was physical as well as verbal and boys fought with masters as well as each other. One early nineteenth-century Westminster head even encouraged boys to challenge their masters physically.[91] At Eton, Keate mounted a highly theatrical 'campaign' against his pupils, his 'epic' canings accompanied by 'jests and laughter'.[92] Such traditions led Edward Gibbon, who was at Westminster for a short period, to remark that 'the mimic scene of rebellion [...] displayed in their true colors the ministers and patriots of the rising generation'.[93]

The line between legitimate horseplay and illicit rebellion, however, was thin. Gladstone at Eton got away with making openly political statements, but Robert Southey was expelled from Westminster for publishing a magazine in 1792 entitled *The Flagellant* – which included a satirical, articulate and reasonable condemnation of corporal punishment – because it supposedly challenged the national status quo.[94] Southey and his friends set themselves up as a pseudo-order of flagellant monks, whose task it was to 'scourge' with satire the faults of the age. They announced that 'four Westminsters, quitting the noise, the *dissipation* of Dean's Yard, have betaken themselves to this habitation, resolved to pursue their observations aloof from mankind and form into "a band of BROTHERS"'.[95] *The Flagellant* debated a number of social issues, such as the plight of girls hired as companions to old ladies and the problems faced by poor students employed as servitors at Oxford.[96] Southey and his friends also fabricated a letter from an imaginary correspondent at a private school, debating disciplinary relationships between educators and students. The letter alleges that the boy's master, Mr Thwackum, had confiscated a copy of *The Flagellant*, remarking that these were 'Pretty times indeed, if boys are allowed to think for themselves!'[97] Their 'correspondent' wrote:

> these words struck forcibly upon my mind, [...] till at last I concluded that boys *have* a right to think and judge what is proper for themselves; and that the dread, should thy exert the faculties of reason, that all the master's illegal authority would be resisted, was the cause of Mr Thwackum's contumelious usage of your production. I have often heard of the divine right of Kings, and by the bye, as often doubted; but I never yet heard of the divine right of *school-masters*. [...] They endeavor, by discipline, to inculcate the doctrine of passive obedience, enforce it by stripes, and sour the tempers, and break the

---

90 Smith 1993, p. 576.
91 Wallbank 1973, p. 7.
92 Tucker 1892, pp. 181–83.
93 *Memoirs of my Life*, in Wallbank 1973, p. 11.
94 G.F. Russell Barker, 'Westminster School' in Webster 1937, p. 248.
95 Southey 1792, p. 33.
96 Ibid., No. 4, pp. 55–56, 57–69.
97 Ibid., No. 5, p. 75.

spirit of their unfortunate subjects, who in their turn, exercise the same tyranny over their inferiors, till the hall of learning becomes only a seminary for brutality![98]

Such a direct statement was clearly unacceptable. A libertarian atmosphere was obviously only perceived to be beneficial in the education of future statesmen if it did not cause inconvenience, damage profits or injure the individual sensibilities of school staff.

Another idea fundamental to pre-reform schools was asceticism. The fagging system, where everybody below the fifth form performed menial tasks for the sixth, regardless of parentage, supposedly stripped boys of social sensitivity. Harsh living conditions assisted in the process of social and physical desensitization, and boys endured 'privations [...] thought inhuman if inflicted upon a galley slave'.[99] In Eton's Long Chamber lived

> 52 boys, ordered during the evenings and nights only by their evolved ritual, [...] without wash basins and without adequate food, [...] liable to find on waking in winter a layer of snow on their beds which had drifted in [...]. Animals, both of the sporting and edible sort, were sometimes kept in the Chamber.[100]

Letting the boys live in this kind of squalor was a way of keeping housing cheap and profits high, but it also had a pedagogical rationale. Wallbank attributes the lack of supervisory care to 'the traditional Whig affection for the idea of liberty'.[101] The approach was also, however, part of a post-Renaissance idea of male citizenship which existed until the Victorian period. As Linda Dowling has pointed out, writers such as T.B. Macaulay, Joseph Addison and Richard Glover advocated an ideal of citizenship 'drawn from Aristotle and Cicero and Machiavelli'. The ideal citizen was a *zōon politikon* who 'subordinat[ed] his private desires to the public good, and in so doing create[ed] a sphere in which his fellow citizens may in turn realize their own natures as human beings'. The willingness to fight for 'the survival of the polity as a whole, its art and its thought and its ordinary life of field and village', was fundamental to this idea of citizenship.[102] Its antithesis was the *effeminatus*, who dwelt in luxury and thought only of ease, physical appearance and selfish wants.

One of the more startling aspects of this *laissez-faire* system is the amount of unsupervised free time boys had. An article on Eton published in the *Edinburgh Review* in 1830 complained:

---

98 Ibid., pp. 76–77.
99 Coleridge 1896, p. 2.
100 Wallbank 1973, p. 9.
101 Ibid., p. 10.
102 Dowling 1994, p. 7.

In a common week there is one whole holiday, on which no school-business is done, but every boy is required to go twice to chapel; one half holiday, on which there are two school-times and one chapel; and on Saturday there are three school-times and one chapel. On each of the three other days, there are four school-times, three of which last respectively for three-quarters of an hour; the other has no fixed length, but probably averages for each boy about quarter of an hour. The school-times would, therefore, amount to less than eleven hours in a week.[103]

This somewhat empty curriculum seems today like a parlous waste of time, and such freedom certainly gave some boys opportunity to inflict hideous cruelty on each other, to drink to excess and to create a public nuisance, activities already described in sufficient depth by John Chandos and Colin Shrosbree.[104] However, not everybody considered free time to be a bad thing, because it allowed for a variety of creative leisure-time activities such as Southey's foray into publishing. In particular, it gave space for role-play activities in which boys experimented with social roles and different kinds of communal organization. Indeed, the fagging system itself is presented by some school story writers as a kind of social role play. What the schools offered by providing free time was a process of socialization – the development of skills for living in a certain kind of society – rather than academic or practical skills. Even the writer and donnish head of Marlborough, F.W. Farrar, remarked that since the number of boys who could distinguish themselves academically was very few, the real purpose of attending school was not to achieve scholarly distinction but '*to be trained*' which was 'a higher end'.[105] Some Arnoldians also believed that the lessons in human nature learned in a non-regulated environment actually made boys into more perceptive citizens, providing experiences which could not be found in the classroom. Thomas Hughes commented in *Tom Brown's Schooldays* that 'The object of schools is not to ram Latin and Greek into boys, but to make them good English boys, good future citizens; and by far the most important part of that work must be done, or not done *out of school hours*' [emphasis added].[106] The importance of play and leisure time in Hughes's depiction of Arnold's Rugby will be discussed in Chapter 2.

The kind of leisure-time activity schools indulged depended on their ethos. There is autobiographical evidence that schoolboys during the 1830s and 1840s were engaged in political debate and that adults, taking it for granted that boys would be interested in politics, allowed a measure of freedom for them to indulge in political play. *School Days at Saxonhurst* (1867), by the Irish barrister and writer Percy Hetherington Fitzgerald, describes the Jesuit-run Stonyhurst College as a highly politicized community. Stonyhurst was built on a foundation of political

---

103 'Public Schools of England – Eton' 1830, pp. 67–68.
104 For example, in 1825 Ashley-Cooper was killed in a sixty-round Eton fistfight. See Shrosbree 1988, p. 20.
105 Farrar 1876, p. 193.
106 Hughes 1989, p. 63.

and religious controversy. The original school, St Omers, had been established in Normandy in 1568 for the children of Catholic recusants, and its Victorian biographers were proud to boast of the number of former students who subsequently 'shed their blood on the scaffold, or died of their hardships in prison'.[107] Fitzgerald's senior at Stonyhurst by eleven years was Thomas Meagher (1823–1867), leader of the nationalist 'Young Ireland' movement, who died in the year Fitzgerald's book was published, and who was involved in the Irish Uprising (1848) which coincided with Fitzgerald's schooldays.[108] It is possible to speculate that nationalism among Irish students, as well as a tradition of dissent, contributed to a politically charged atmosphere at the school.

Fitzgerald describes Saxonhurst as a former abbey set in 'rough blustering county' (Lancashire).[109] It had 'eagle-capped towers' overlooked by a mountain, Hendle (Pendle) which 'frowned on us solemnly always, from afar off, stern and like a wicked master'.[110] The gothic environment suited the 'survival of the fittest' ethic which governs the school: 'There were a few plums and good things to be struggled for; and, as in the world also, the strongest and most forward got them – the shy and weaker went to the wall'.[111] The ascetic environment, where 'all about one was a gauntness and a prison-like rawness', forced each boy to 'become a man' quickly.[112] However, this harshness also stimulated the boys' political consciousness. Fitzgerald, writing in 1867, makes frequent allusions to the political climate of the 1840s and points out that the boys have a political awareness reaching far beyond their isolated world – something their masters fear.[113] The boys ally themselves to contemporary political factions and their out-of-class activities revolve around role-play scenarios that mimic events in the political world. Their two leaders, Jack and Bob, compared to Disraeli and Gladstone, labor under a 'secret discord' (an allusion to the strife-ridden 'Young England' movement).[114] In their opposition to the harsh conditions at school, the boys rehearse the political arguments of Young England as well as showing an interest in Radicalism and Irish Nationalism. One boy's father has worked with Orator Hunt,[115] which gives him the right to arbitrate in disputes. Another boy, an Irish dandy called T.W. Bridges, later to be 'engaged in ill-fated attempts to enfranchise [Ireland]', has the air 'of a *heros de roman* h[anging] about him' because he is 'always involved in some struggle with authority'.[116]

---

107 Gruggen 1901, p. 18.
108 *Catholic Encyclopaedia.*
109 Fitzgerald 1867, p. 3.
110 Ibid., pp. 4, 70.
111 Ibid., p. 17.
112 Ibid., pp. 13–14, 5.
113 Ibid., p. 165.
114 Ibid., pp. 33–34.
115 Ibid., p. 51.
116 Ibid., pp. 251–52.

One wave of agitation at Saxonhurst concerns the quality of school food, referred to as a 'famine'.[117] A High Tory visitor announces that 'famishing [Irish] creatures' would be glad of such food ('b---g soup'), while the boys maintain that the food is bad because that the masters ('Percivals and Castlereaghs'), having suffered in their own schooldays, wish for their charges to suffer equally.[118] They then separate into two factions, 'Republicans' and 'Loyalists', anti and pro the masters. The Loyalists are compared to 'gentry [...] of an effeminate order' and the Republicans receive advice from Paddy, an Irish smallholder who informs them of their 'constitutional right' to gather in the school grounds and protest.[119] At other times agitation is led by boys from mainland Europe, who have experienced the 'freedom of foreign training'.[120] During one episode, when a theft occurs and the school is held collectively responsible, the boys barricade themselves in the schoolroom 'a la Française',[121] evoking the 1848 Paris barricades and the Revolution. When the Gladstonian, Bob, is blamed for this act of rebellion, he defends himself and stands up eloquently for 'his legal rights'.[122] Politicized rebellion is a rite of passage and individual identity is affirmed through the breaking of bounds. When the boys on principle invade the masters' fruit orchard, the authorities seem to view their transgression as a display of 'pluck and skill' and avoid punishing them unless caught in *'flagrante delicto'*.[123]

That Stonyhurst boys were allowed to get away with these antics seems remarkable, especially in light of J.A. Mangan's findings that, later on, the school 'permitted little freedom to the pupils to control and organize their leisure activities'.[124] Maybe the priests were more bothered by religious than political dissent, though Fitzgerald did not enter into any discussion on tfhe subject. However, in the era of Chartism and in the years following Catholic Emancipation, the experience of struggling for self-representation would have provided a valuable training in citizenship necessary for this community's survival. Saxonhurst's head is ambitious for his students to achieve positions in British society which would formerly have been closed to them, informing the parents of new boys that the school would 'make a Lord Chancellor or a Chief Justice of him'.[125] Thus the system teaches the boys to fight their way into the ruling classes, even though it almost destroys itself in the process (in one episode, boys barricade teachers out of a classroom and almost succeed in 'breaking up the whole establishment'[126]).

---

117 Ibid., p. 158.
118 Ibid., pp. 159, 162.
119 Ibid., pp. 184, 179.
120 Ibid., p. 160.
121 Ibid., p. 146.
122 Ibid., p. 152.
123 Ibid., pp. 214–15.
124 Mangan 2000, p. 66.
125 Fitzgerald 1867, p. 6.
126 Ibid., p. 156.

In their political play, the boys develop skills which later prove fruitful (as in the case of Thomas Meagher and the emancipationist Thomas Wyse). In the end, the image of the male adolescent that emerges from Fitzgerald's text is of a miniature hero acting out the role of a great reformer in a narrative of rebellion played out in the relative safety of a sheltered environment. Here, the boy can develop, refine and test his own personal ideology. Paradoxically, however, at the close of the book, after describing his schooldays with relish, Fitzgerald casts his adult self as a shocked bourgeois who remarks that the boys overplayed their hardships, comparing their revolutionary antics to those of a 'contemptible mob' and accusing them of behaving like ungrateful '"potwolloper" voters'.[127] Like H.C. Adams, he is torn between an adult, Victorian concern for order and obedience and nostalgia for his radical youth.

The kind of leisure-time activities described by Fitzgerald excited sharp criticism from some quarters, especially when they were celebrated in literature. In his review of *Tom Brown*, James Fitzjames Stephen complained that Thomas Hughes gave the impression 'that [Rugby] was an immense playground, in which the boys, having the gift of prophecy, talked like the characters in Mr Kingsley's novels'.[128] Hughes, remarked Stephen, attributed too much importance to boys' trivial activities and cared too little about science. He claimed that, in treating the behavior of young people too seriously and debating it in terms of 'the great fundamental principles of right and wrong', Hughes was sure to 'stimulate a diseased consciousness' among boys.[129] Such a 'diseased sensibility' was evident in 'The rebels against society, from Byron and Shelley downwards; [...] the pale-eyed prophets muttering fearful change in religion, politics, literature [and] art'.[130] These 'rebels' were people who, as adolescents, had failed to realize that juvenile life is essentially trivial. Stephen's idea that free time should be limited and supplanted by organized sport, science and modern language training grew in currency in the latter part of the nineteenth century, particularly under the influence of the 1861 Clarendon Commission. Nonetheless, as will be shown below, play retained a deep socio-political value for authors, largely because it was during free-time activities that the development of the qualities required for successful citizenship could take place.

Public schools came under fire, therefore, for their emphasis on combat as a central part of the educational scheme, for their approach to character as something to be consciously created rather than nurtured from the inner self and for a *laissez-faire* ethos that indulged a dangerous amount of free play and gave rise to rebellion and insubordination. For the middle classes, whose own parents had been brought up at home rather than away at school, the public school system was, in short, inimical to family values. These values, held in particular by Evangelicals but

---

127 Ibid., p. 201.
128 Stephen 1858, p. 189.
129 Ibid., pp. 188–89.
130 Ibid., p. 177.

also shared by other reformers, included respect for parental authority, intense supervision and regulation of the young, and detailed attention to the inner spiritual or moral state of each member of the family – a matter which was not to be left to chance. P.J. Rich has also suggested that the all-male atmosphere of the public schools encouraged boys to reject family attachments and that, to outsiders, this rejection seemed like 'a kind of adultery' against home.[131] That boys denigrated their relationships with mothers and sisters seems to have been of particular concern to reformers, and the next chapters will demonstrate how Thomas Hughes and F.W. Farrar tackled this problem.

Before Hughes's time, however, opposition to the anti-domestic ideology of the public schools came mostly from women writers such as Maria Edgeworth and Harriet Martineau, writing with what might be called a feminist agenda.[132] Moreover, in spite of Fitzjames Stephen's dismissals, these writers had a strong influence on later male writers (for instance, Hughes corresponded with Edgeworth as a child[133]). Both Edgeworth and Martineau use public school stories to explore the tensions which existed between adolescent masculinity and the female sphere; tensions which were present in Edgeworth's own home (Francis Beaufort Edgeworth, a model for some of his sister's characters, was reluctant to admit his kinship to his sister while at Charterhouse[134]). Beverly Clark calls the kind of textual production Edgeworth and Martineau undertook, in which a woman writes about an exclusively male experience or vice versa, 'crossgendering',[135] and suggests that it has subversive possibilities. Not being of the public school tradition, such women were able to initiate challenges to its traditions and its configuration of masculinity in a way which men, at that time, possibly could not. Indeed, a good number of early school stories were by women, since writing for young people was considered to be 'an extension of their traditional nurturing and maternal teaching'.[136] Once women had started to undermine traditions, it seems that men were happy to take up and proliferate their ideas, something which no doubt contributed to the feminization of boy characters which Claudia Nelson has observed occurring in mid-nineteenth century juvenile literature.[137] These ideas also started to find their way into educational policy. Thomas Arnold, in spite of his own public school education, seems also to have subscribed to some extent to the idea that schools needed to be domesticated, since he valued his wife's role in forming a 'family' atmosphere at Rugby. He remarked when he began as headmaster that: 'it has been a great delight to me to think that M[ary] will feel doubly and naturally bound to so many of [the boys], that she will have

---

131 Rich 1991, p. 113.
132 For claims regarding Edgeworth's feminism, see Butler 1972 and Bilger 1998.
133 Armytage 1952, p. 11.
134 Smith 1940, p. 101.
135 Clark 1996, p. 2.
136 Ibid., p. 7.
137 Nelson 1991. This debate is covered in Chapter 3.

little trouble in learning to love them'.[138] This emphasis on domesticity inevitably had an impact, for good or ill, on changing ideas of adolescence. The effect of the feminist attack on traditional notions of citizenship education was that, while attempting to counter the anti-domesticity, writers ended up contesting the established idea of adolescence as essentially experimental, combative, political, theatrical and rhetorical.

Edgeworth and Martineau both produced boys' school stories that challenged public school conventions. Edgeworth wrote two school stories about adolescents – *The Barring Out* and a play, *Eton Montem* (both of 1796), published in *The Parent's Assistant*. *The Barring Out* is about a small private boarding school belonging to the rational but authoritarian Dr Middleton and its main ideological message is that the traditional political, combative, rebellious antics of adolescence have no place in rational education. Dr Middleton's is a peaceful school, because it discourages the establishment of '*favorites* and *parties*'.[139] However, that is only the case until a newcomer, the exceptionally bright Archer, arrives. Archer comes from a public school and brings with him its combative ethic, setting himself up in competition to Dr Middleton's star pupil, the conscientious and obedient De Grey. The power-hungry Archer, courting popularity with his derring-do, then raises a rebellion against the headmaster. The cause of this rebellion is a dispute over a playhouse run by the boys. Initially, De Grey is the Stage Manager, but Archer uses his prodigious wealth and self-confidence to persuade the boys to depose De Grey in his favor. He improves the playhouse and intends to put on *School for Scandal*, but the head suddenly, and without explanation, orders him to close it down. Archer objects and plans a revolt which involves a '*barring out*', a common event in school stories in which the boys barricade themselves into a classroom as a form of protest and hold a kind of siege until either the authorities capitulate or until they are starved or physically forced out.[140] This barring out, like the one at Saxonhurst, has strong French Revolutionary overtones. Archer cries 'victory and liberty! – Bar him out, till he repeals his tyrannical law', telling his followers not to be 'slaves'.[141] Adults, he implies, have no right to demand compliance from young people without providing good reasons for their demands.

However, Archer, after being drenched by the gardener, starved because of his own incompetence and disappointed by the low intelligence and ineptitude of his supporters, 'spen[ds] the night as a man, that had the cares of government upon his shoulders'.[142] When Archer's supporters mutiny, De Grey, as ambassador from the head, sneaks in and generously counsels him on the value of friendship and the importance of reason.[143] De Grey explains that it is not reasonable to question the

---

138 Stanley 1882, vol. I, p. 53.
139 Edgeworth 1800, p. 2.
140 Ibid., p. 27.
141 Ibid., p. 36.
142 Ibid., p. 62.
143 Ibid., p. 99.

Doctor's commands, and Archer surrenders. The reason for the theatre's closure is revealed later by the head. Some gypsies, one of whom had a 'putrid fever', had camped there overnight, possibly contaminating the building. The fact that the head did not disclose this information earlier is significant. It seems that he withheld it for no other reason other than that it is his prerogative not to enter into arguments with the boys. As he says, boys should automatically obey adults in authority whether they are given a good reason to or not, because adults, with their greater wealth of experience, are always right. Young people who question adult judgment are irrational and deviant. Moreover, as Edgeworth demonstrates, rebellion and a desire for self-government reveal a suspicious side to a boy's character. Archer's political power comes from his knowing 'too well how to govern fools, to attempt to reason with them'.[144] His supporters, who elect him democratically, are 'not very remarkable for their mental qualifications'. They are boys who 'by their bodily activity, and by the peculiar advantages annexed to their way of life, rendered themselves of the highest consequence'.[145] Edgeworth repudiates the idea that adolescence is a time for competition, political play, dissent against authority and the development of leadership skills, and teaches her readers that political power and authority are adult burdens that young people should shun. To have responsibility for others, particularly to deal with problems of factionalism, is a nuisance. It is better to concentrate instead on building personal, intimate, emotional bonds with individual friends. Thus, in her (bigoted) portrayal of Archer's relationship to the gypsies, who advise him on how to conduct a barring out, Edgeworth casts the political, combative adolescent as dangerous, potentially unhealthy and best avoided by society. As society cleanses itself of the gypsies and their sickness, it must cleanse itself of dissent among the young. The theatre, as a symbolic locus for the display and egotism beloved of the political classes, provides a platform for the dissenting boy to contaminate society. The theatre only gets restored to the boys once it has been symbolically cleansed and, more importantly, once Archer's desire to attack the status quo has been subdued.

Edgeworth's public school play, which continues (paradoxically) the anti-theatrical theme, is *Eton Montem*. This play concerns Eton's Whit Tuesday celebrations, in which crowds of dignitaries flocked to Eton to be accosted by boys in fancy dress demanding money (perhaps with a measure of intimidation: A.D. Coleridge remarks that the guise of Macheath the Highwayman was one 'particularly well chosen'[146]). The money (or 'salt') thus procured was used to send the captain of the school (originally a charity boy) to Cambridge. Montem, essentially a Carnivalesque festival of misrule, resembled the 'Feast of Fools', a connection observed by John Nichols in an article in the 1814 *Gentleman's Magazine* entitled 'The Boy Bishop. – Eton Montem. – Salt-bearers'.[147] The

---

144 Ibid., p. 40.
145 Ibid., p. 21.
146 Coleridge 1896, p. 262.
147 Nichols 1814, pp. 537–39.

practice was abolished in 1847 as a 'dangerous temptation' that ignored the 'spirit of the advancing age'.[148] Edgeworth, who was also skeptical about Montem, used the theme to suit her own ideological ends. Traditionally, she tells us, the eldest boy at Eton would become school captain and receive the Montem 'salt'. In the year the story takes place, the two eldest boys in the school share a birthday, so it is decided that the other boys will vote democratically on who should be captain. However, one of the boys – the hero, Talbot – announces that he will refuse to dress up in Montem clothes or to canvass for votes. Instead, he stands on a ticket of moral righteousness, preaching on the virtues of working for one's living, avoiding debt and fighting for equality between rich and poor. His rival, Wheeler, uses wealth and show to impress supporters and initially commands most respect. However, when Talbot reveals that Wheeler has sold him a lame horse, the tide turns and Talbot wins the captaincy. Talbot dislikes both fancy dress and rhetoric. He advocates 'plain speaking' and counsels a fellow pupil: 'Be yourself, my lord – See with your own eyes, and hear with your own ears'.[149] The two boys have radically different ways of presenting themselves to the public. Wheeler constructs his public persona through artifice, drama, rhetoric and display; Talbot promotes himself as a representative of a distinct body of personal moral virtues. Indeed, Edgeworth suggests that virtuous men lack the rhetorical qualities to succeed in the Georgian political sphere. Talbot is 'chosen for his honorable conduct, not for his electioneering skill', and 'Coriolanus himself was not a worse electioner'.[150] Edgeworth here repudiates not only outward display, but also the ethic of competition, especially when this competition involves rhetoric and debate – the mainstays of public school culture. The boys' choice between Talbot and Wheeler is made on the strength of one simple moral issue. There is no discussion of the candidates' wider social or political outlook, and no consideration of academic ability. Talbot's homely morality, learned from his mother, is more important than any skills learned at school. In order to drive this point home, Edgeworth introduces mothers and sisters into the normally masculine environment of school and portrays Talbot's meek female relatives in stark contrast to the frivolous mothers of the rich and fashionable dandies. Edgeworth's fundamental message is that it is home, not school, which makes a boy into a good citizen.

An insight into why writers such as Edgeworth might have opposed the combative tradition of elite male education is given by Walter Ong, who describes the shift in English education from a Latin-based curriculum to the vernacular. Classical education – in particular the study of Latin – was, Ong argues, a rite of passage which affirmed a particular idea of masculinity by teaching boys to dispute aggressively – not empirically, but through sheer force of argument.[151] However, the advent of increased schooling for girls encouraged educationalists

---

148 Coleridge 1896, pp. 55, 263. Coleridge also clearly disapproved of Montem.
149 Edgeworth 1800, pp. 135, 164.
150 Ibid., p. 223.
151 Ong 1967, p. 251.

to focus more than before on practical, rather than rhetorical skills. Similarly, the feminization of the curriculum made combat and disputation less ideologically acceptable. Moreover, radicals such as Joseph Priestley, William Cobbett and Thomas Paine had promoted vernacular scholarship in order to make knowledge accessible to those without a classical education who sought to improve their station in life.[152] The 'polemic state of mind', with its 'formulaic modes of thought and expression' and its 'exploitation of dispute to clarify issues', became unfashionable.[153] In debate, the use of evidence began to accrue more importance than the use of persuasive rhetoric. At the same time, in the literary field the advent of Romanticism had encouraged a greater emphasis on 'private epiphan[y]', which favored supposedly spontaneous and personal styles of discourse, rather than formulaic composition.[154] Those who subscribed to Romantic notions of spontaneity attacked the public school practice of composing Latin verses. T.B. Macaulay called verse making 'an exotic, [...] far-fetched, costly, sickly imitation of that which elsewhere might be found in healthful and spontaneous perfection'.[155] Ultimately, changes in the way young people were taught to express themselves reflected changes in ideas of how personal identity is formed. Because Romantics (and also Evangelicals) placed emphasis on the inner, essential self, rather than a self that was consciously constructed through rhetorical performance, adolescence itself became a process of searching for that inner self, rather than a theatrical process of building one. In particular, those who repudiated rhetorical training as a good foundation for life in the public sphere argued that identity was best established in the private, domestic realm.

Harriet Martineau's domestication of the boy is even more radical than Edgeworth's. Whereas Edgeworth still allows her boy hero a role in the public sphere, Martineau reclaims him for the private. Martineau's public school story, *The Crofton Boys* (first published in *The Playfellow* of 1841), is a tale of home values triumphing over school. The hero is Hugh Proctor who, at the beginning of the book, is educated at home with his family in London. Hugh spends all day reading *Robinson Crusoe* and dreaming of going abroad, which makes him lag behind his academically diligent sisters. Martineau praises the sisters' acceptance of their limited sphere and remarks that Hugh felt 'ashamed to see how his sisters got on, from the mere pleasure of learning, and without any idea of ever living anywhere but in London'.[156] Hugh's firm and coldly rational mother preaches self-discipline and teaches Hugh that there is no gain without suffering. She is the dominant influence in the home compared to the father, who is nothing more than a bungling playmate. Hugh, always looking outwards beyond the domestic arena, asks to go away to school early. His mother pours cold water on his dreams by

---

152 See Smith 1984, for an analysis of debates on language and class.
153 Ong 1967, pp. 239, 241.
154 Ibid., p. 253.
155 In Salt 1911, p. 81.
156 Martineau 1856, p. 8.

warning him that he 'will find it painful and difficult to learn' after his 'idle habits at home'.[157] At school he continues to fantasize about foreign escapades, despite being punished for academic backwardness and Martineau, while describing the scrapes he gets into, continuously emphasizes the superiority of home over school. In one chapter, entitled 'What is only to be had at home', Hugh's more domesticated brother complains about how 'it is not the way of boys to talk about feelings' or 'their sisters or their mothers'.[158] Injustice is endemic at school, he insists, because 'parents know [...] all that is in their children's minds' whereas 'A schoolmaster can judge only by what he sees'.[159]

Hugh is finally brought to heel when he falls while climbing an orchard wall in the snow and has his leg crushed by a coping stone. This breaching-of-boundaries episode, which might have won acclaim in the world of Saxonhurst, puts an end to Hugh's outward-looking ambitions. The leg is amputated and his mother and sisters set themselves up at school to help him through the trauma. His new disability constricts his outlook and he reflects that he will 'never be a soldier or a sailor – [...] never go round the world'.[160] His mother tells him that the only way to get over the shock is to exercise a kind of masochistic self-discipline. She remarks that 'There is a great pleasure in the exercise of the body [...] but this is nothing to the pleasure there is in exercising one's soul in bearing pain' and advises him, 'smile to yourself and say you will be content at home'.[161] She confiscates his travel books and gives him menial tasks to do, such as papering a room to pay off a friend's debts. Martineau literally smashes up her hero in order to breach the exclusivity of the male domain and to reclaim him for the domestic. Because Hugh goes to school very young (at the age of eight) and gets injured shortly afterwards, his mother has chance to step in before he undergoes any of the adolescent rites of passage that contribute to boys' sense of identity at school. At the end of the book, he is allowed to become a civil servant in India. Notwithstanding the exotic location, it seems little consolation that he has relinquished adventure, exploration and heroism for the banality of spreading the British domestic status quo across the world from behind a desk.

The emphasis of reformers on domesticity, spontaneity and private feeling as an antidote to combative masculinity was shared by Thomas Arnold, who was one of the first public schoolmasters to modify the public school curriculum with the goal of inculcating these values. To Arnold, education meant more than mastering rhetorical formulae. He read vernacular literature with his boys on a Sunday and puzzled over how to persuade his pupils to answer his questions spontaneously rather than 'cramming' themselves with prepared answers before class, as they

---

157 Ibid., p. 29.
158 Ibid., p. 96.
159 Ibid., p. 97.
160 Ibid., p. 114.
161 Ibid., p. 116.

would have done with classics.[162] Believing that education was 'dynamical, not [...] mechanical',[163] and that teacher and pupil should seek enlightenment together, he saw himself as a channel through which knowledge could be deduced. A.P. Stanley recollected that

> he never gave information, except as a kind of reward for an answer, and often withheld it altogether, or checked himself in the very act of uttering it, from a sense that those whom he was addressing had not sufficient interest or sympathy to entitle them to receive it.[164]

Again, the emphasis on 'sympathy' and bonding between teacher and student as part of the educational process is symptomatic of the shift from classical notions of disputational, rhetorical education to the emotional values of Romanticism. In tailoring his sermons specifically for a child and adolescent audience, Arnold would first choose his Biblical text (for instance: 'A man's foes shall be they of his own household', or 'Be ye not unwise, but understanding what the will of the Lord is'[165]), and would then relate the text to boys' experiences at school or home, using 'the language [...] of common life,' and 'cases of common life [...] ennobled and strengthened by those principles and feelings which are to be found only in the Gospel'.[166]

In his approach to preaching, Arnold's most obvious debt was to the 'Preface to the *Lyrical Ballads*', combined with an emphasis on religious 'feeling' borrowed from Evangelicalism. Arnold's pedagogical aim, however, was not only to create emotionally-literate young citizens, but also to inculcate some of the rationalism promoted by Unitarians, who he considered to be full members of the Christian and intellectual community.[167] Some of his ideas reflect Joseph Priestley's 1765 *Essay on Education*, which laid out plans for a new form of civic education for 'all those stations in which a man's conduct will considerably affect the liberty and the property of his countrymen, and the riches, the strength, and the security of his country'.[168] Priestley recommended a curriculum based on 'civil history' and 'civil policy' (to include 'the theory of laws, government, manufactures, commerce, naval force &c').[169] This history was not to consist merely of dates, battles or Royal genealogies, but was intended to focus on topics as diverse as 'alienation of land property', criminal law, dress and 'conveniences in houses'.[170]

---

162 Stanley 1882, vol. I, p. 61.
163 Ibid., vol. II, p. 22.
164 Ibid., vol. I, p. 123.
165 Matt. x. 36 and Eph. v. 17. See Arnold 1833.
166 Stanley 1882, vol. I, p. 47.
167 Ibid., vol. II, pp. 27, 46, 70–72.
168 Priestley 1992, p. 9.
169 Ibid., p. 10.
170 Ibid., pp. 80–81.

The curriculum was to herald a new kind of citizenship, a revision of the Greek and Roman model in which 'the practice of thinking, reading, conversing, and writing about the interest of our country [will] answer the same purpose with the moderns, as fighting for it did among the ancients'.[171] Arnold aimed towards this ideal of civic education in his history scholarship, editing Thucydides by focusing on making 'a living picture of things present, fitted not so much for the curiosity of the scholar, as for the instruction of the statesman and the citizen'.[172] He hoped to combine and balance this pragmatic approach with a respect for traditional classical scholarship in a new educational style, acceptable to both the rational citizen and the academic Divine, which incorporated 'everything that is manly, sensible, and free, and everything that is pure and self-denying, and humble, and heavenly'.[173]

Of course, Arnold's belief that boys should study and compose in the vernacular, his respect for mothers and concerns about the overly macho environment of public schools also owe a great deal to John Locke.[174] In particular, his belief in eliciting ideas from boys rather than focusing on rote-learning echoes what Alex Neill refers to as Locke's 'notion of epistemic individualism or autonomy'.[175] In this scheme, education

> is the process of producing the dispositions and habits in a child that will enable him to think for himself, to reason and act according to the dictates of reason. The role of the teacher is not to impart knowledge, but to provide an atmosphere in which the child's understanding can develop without being indoctrinated by 'the common received opinions'.[176]

It would be an idealization of Arnold to say that he adhered to this principle rigorously or that he set boys free to make sense of the world for themselves. He was too morally dogmatic for that. In addition, while Locke was giving the child the tools to fill his *tabula rasa* with knowledge and experience, Arnold's religiosity and Romanticism would have been leading him rather to draw out his students' pre-existing, 'essential' inner personalities. However, it is fair to say that, in contrast with his peers, Arnold at least attempted to introduce a more liberal approach to education to the public school setting.

Less positively, Arnold also followed Lockean principles in ways that might be hard for many modern-day educators to stomach. His emphasis on training boys to be gentlemen before teaching them to be scholars recalls Locke's hierarchy

---

171 Ibid., p. 33.
172 Stanley 1882, vol. I, p. 169.
173 Ibid., p. 243.
174 For Locke's comments on the vernacular, see *Some Thoughts Concerning Education*, in Locke 1768, p. 109, and on his objections to public schools, see p. 33.
175 Neill 1991, p. 256.
176 Ibid., p. 259.

of values which placed 'virtue' before 'learning' ('Learning must be had, but in the second place, as subservient only to greater qualities'[177]). Locke, in spite of being 'The Father of Liberalism', was no democrat and his conception of education for citizenship remained socially divisive in the hands of Arnold and the other educationalists who followed him. As I will show in Chapter 3, F.W. Farrar incorporated Arnold's version of Lockeanism into his scheme for 'liberal education' which was, in some ways, very anti-democratic. Arnold's son Matthew let the same sense of class consciousness infect his Romanticism and liberalism when he advocated cultivating working-class children's moral sensibilities and emotional attachment to culture by teaching them English literature. While insisting on this education for the working classes, he maintained that Etonians should continue their traditional scholarship in order to inculcate 'a sort of republican fellowship, the practice of a plain life in common, the habit of self-help'.[178] In other words, working-class children were to receive moral and cultural education primarily through a vernacular approach that centered on their feelings, while public schoolboys were to be given more scope for studying political ideas.

Returning to the more general theme of adolescent society, it is fair to say, in summary, that the rituals that had previously defined adolescent male identity in the public schools were eroding, causing a rash of new ideologies to fall upon the adolescent boy. There is, however, one aspect of the argument about adolescent education that has not yet been considered here. Although the authors discussed so far in this chapter wrote from a range of radically different perspectives, they all share the view that adolescence, at least for the upper classes, is a time for cultivating systematic, rational thought, developing an understanding of citizenship and gaining an awareness of abstract social and political principles. But the very question of whether adolescents had sufficient rational ability to benefit from such an education was strongly contested and I will spend the remainder of this chapter considering debates over what kind of social and moral thought adolescents were deemed capable of.

According to Rolf Muuss, the idea that adolescence brings about the ability to reason goes back as far as Aristotle, who said that while children are under the sway of base animal appetites, adolescents have the ability to learn to make rational behavioral choices. The barrier to rational thinking is the fact that it is 'only if the youth voluntarily and deliberately chooses' that he will 'develop the right kind of habits and thus, in the long run, build the right kind of character'.[179] Between Aristotle and the Enlightenment, Scholastic Christianity made little impact on the understanding of adolescent rationality, because 'The difference between a child and an adult was [...] only a quantitative one, not a qualitative one'. A child's

---

177 Locke 1768, pp. 83, 93.
178 Hollingworth 1974, p. 320. See also Matthew Arnold's 'A French Eton' (Arnold 1962) on state control of middle and working-class education. For Locke on the teaching of the art of disputation in schools see Locke 1768, p. 116.
179 Muuss 1996, p. 5.

intellect was a miniature version of the adult's rather than significantly different. Scholastics ignored physical change as a contributory factor in adolescent behavior, because they thought that the process of child development merely expanded faculties that existed in the individual from birth; nothing 'new' developed during adolescence. From the seventeenth century onwards, however, Humanists began to understand childhood and adolescence as discrete stages demanding specific educational approaches. Comenius, Rousseau, Pestalozzi, Froebel and British writers such as Maria Edgeworth identified the stages at which the child's mental faculties were geared to differing objectives. For younger children, whose mental world was oriented towards physical sensation and habituation, education was best conducted through play and practical activities. Adolescence, often thought to consist of two stages, built on foundations established in childhood, but individual thinkers ascribed to it differing degrees of rationality. Rousseau, for example, divided the developmental stages of Émile into infancy, childhood, pre-adolescence (twelve to fifteen) and adolescence. At twelve, heuristic science lessons begin; Émile must work out problems himself and not rely on his tutor for answers. He also reads books for the first time.[180] When he reaches fifteen, history is introduced to his curriculum, so that he can acquire an understanding of human behavior from a spectator's viewpoint, studying civic and social values through the lives of great men.[181] Moral judgment becomes possible at adolescence, because this is the time when reason begins to override animal impulse. Finally, from eighteen to twenty-four, Émile travels with his tutor in order to train his 'will'.[182] 'Will' was the ability to make informed, independent choices – something which John Locke explained as being fundamental to democratic citizenship.[183]

Maria Edgeworth, carrying Rousseauian pedagogy (not uncritically) into English education, also distinguished between 'children' and 'young people':

> Children, before they reason [...] have no power to break their own habits; but when young people begin to reflect, and deliberate, their principles are of much more importance than their habits, because [they...] in many cases govern their future habits.[184]

'Reason' is a key concept here. Adolescents must learn to deal with rational, abstract principles and, like George Manly, develop the skills to hold their own convictions against the crowd. This confidence in the power of reason, free choice and anti-determinism appealed in particular to the emergent middle classes, who were busy during the late eighteenth and early nineteenth centuries asserting themselves against hereditary wealth and power. They used their pervading

---

180 See Rousseau 1993, books 2 and 3 *passim*.
181 Ibid., book 4 *passim*.
182 Ibid., book 6 *passim*.
183 Muuss 1996, p. 10.
184 Edgeworth 1801, vol. I, p. 344.

influence over juvenile literature in order to impress these qualities on the young. Indeed, the rational and democratizing message of some early school literature has aspects in common with self-help manuals for young people of the middle-classes. For example, William Cobbett's *Advice to Young Men* (1829) shows how prudence, self-control and self-denial are essential to maintaining independence of thought and action. Behavior that leads to financial loss and economic dependency (gambling, relying on stocks and shares for income and being a slave to fashion) restricts intellectual freedom. For a young man to be unable to make independent practical and moral choices is tantamount to 'slavery'.[185] Nothing is more tragic, says Cobbett, than when a genius is forced to suppress his ideas because somebody else is supporting him.[186] Victorian school writers also warned against reliance on others. For example, in the conclusion to *Tom Brown at Oxford*, Tom rejects the wealth, fashion, financially irresponsible friends and a socially prestigious career put before him at Oxford to preserve the integrity of his Christian Socialist values.

The question of how to exercise rational choice featured prominently in the growing body of juvenile literature which, during this period, typically placed great emphasis on how an individual character's freely-made choices (no matter how trivial) impact on his future prospects.[187] Samuel Pickering observes that the school story in particular had much in common with allegorical works such as *The Pilgrim's Progress*:

> School stories put great stress upon the individual's determining his own future [...] the student like [Bunyan's] Christian had to acquire not only the ability to withstand temptation or pressure but the knowledge that he had a duty to himself that outweighed secular calls.[188]

An interesting early example of rational allegory in juvenile literature is a morality play written for school performance, *The Schoolboy's Mask* (1742), by Thomas Spateman. This play follows the careers of a group of men – 'Lord Tinsel', 'Guzzle', 'Rakish', 'Rival', 'Wild-Rogue', 'Lord Grand-Clerck', 'Bookish' and 'Goodwill' – through school and university into adult life. For Spateman, education is a preparation for independent, democratic citizenship and the richest field of study is politics.[189] The self-made scholars Bookish and Goodwill, together with the munificent Lord Grand-Clerck, spend their time counseling wealthy libertines not to squander educational opportunities and a moral spokesman called 'Time' appears periodically to remind them of their mortality.

---

185 Cobbett 1829, pp. 12–24, 29.
186 Ibid., p. 72.
187 See Avery 1975, p. 21 on the evangelical roots of children's literature.
188 Pickering 1993, pp. 32–33.
189 Spateman 1742, p. 23.

Spateman's world is meritocratic and noblemen and commoners, educated together, receive their just deserts according to their behavior. When they become adults, the characters cannot escape the choices they have made as boys. Those who have not sought rational enlightenment as adolescents remain in a childish state of unreason. Those who use either inherited wealth or their intelligence for the greater human good rise to powerful roles in society.[190] Those who over-consume become dependent on others (one becomes a curate). This 'rational' education is, however, decidedly anti-domestic. Going to school takes the characters away from the home environment and places them on an even footing with other boys. It also separates them from mothers, who might impede their growth. A spoilt boy, Jack Fondler, reports to his mother that his schoolmaster 'with his Blows / Oft fetches Crimson Currents from my Nose'. She, rebelling against 'these Men', withdraws him from school. Jack's father attempts to reason with her (manfully restraining his impulse to use 'force').[191] He complains that Jack's 'wrong Will' (his lack of discipline and his irrational 'Passions') will make him an inadequate citizen, and asks 'What Duty, when a Man, will he fulfil? / Son, Husband, Father, Master, Friend, unfit'.[192] The mother tries to educate Jack herself, by using rewards to coax him. He becomes unmanageable, abuses his parents, sleeps with the maid at the age of fifteen, has an illegitimate child, marries a rich scold for her money and dies 'so vile a Fellow, that his Life was a Misfortune, and his Death a Blessing'.[193] Thus, the spoiled adolescent who is not removed from the family and forced to undergo the ascetic discipline of school destroys his own home from within and creates social chaos. Democracy and social stability depend on the correct education of the 'Will', self-discipline and the deferral of immediate gratification. On the other hand, if a boy's education is correct, a satisfactory result is assured. Spateman never wavers from the ideology that rational behavior should guarantee an influential job in politics, academia or the church, and concedes nothing to either environmental or biological determinism. In Chapter 4, I will return to the theme of rational discipline and offer a theoretical contextualization of these trends in disciplinary ideology.

This belief – that adolescence was the time when reason blossomed – was by no means universally held, however, during the late-eighteenth and early-nineteenth centuries. Certain sectors of the adult population worried about the impressionability of the young and their powerlessness to resist temptation and moral contamination, particularly at school. Feeling that adolescence was crucial in determining whether an individual would be saved or damned, some called for more intense supervision of the young. Cowper, in his 'Tirocinium' (1784), opined that it was important to 'cast the minds of youth / Betimes into a mould of heav'nly truth', because it was too risky to let them seek their way alone, and 'ignorantly

---

190 Ibid., p. 32.
191 Ibid., p. 4.
192 Ibid., p. 5.
193 Ibid., p. 36.

wand'ring', to 'miss the skies'.[194] Calls for school reform coincided with campaigns to improve conditions for juveniles in prison and some commentators (particularly Evangelicals) developed a tendency to use the same language to discuss the two issues. One metaphor shared by both sets of reformers was that of contamination and disease. For example, the central issue for prison reformers was the moral 'contamination' of juvenile prisoners by adults. John Wesley called the Marshalsea prison 'a nursery of all manner of wickedness', but also used exactly the same phrase in warning parents against the public schools.[195] John Howard called jails 'nurseries of crime',[196] while in his sermons, Thomas Arnold quoted John Bowdler's comment that schools were 'the very seats and nurseries of vice'. For many boys, he said, school was a 'poisoned bowl' which undid the proper moral principles learned at home.[197] Another time, Arnold remarked that a fatal epidemic at Rugby was 'nothing when compared to the existence of any moral evil in the school: far less distressing and far less harassing'.[198]

Even rationalists such as Edgeworth, Cobbett and the author of *The Schoolboy's Mask* all remarked that, since young people learned partly by imitation, they were in danger of having their morals contaminated by bad influences, particularly at school. To Spateman, overly-impressionable boys were 'polluted Swine'.[199] One reason for this focus on juvenile vice and contamination was that, during the early nineteenth century, criminologists shared in the new vogue for studying youth, and were producing reports on the relationship between youth and crime. As Heather Shore remarks, an upsurge in concern about working-class juvenile crime, caused by factors such as changing patterns of apprenticeship, urbanization and post-war unemployment, led to the first specific analyses of juvenile crime, such as the 1816 *Report of the Committee for Investigating the Causes of the Alarming Increase of Juvenile Delinquency in the Metropolis*.[200] All classes of adolescent came under suspicion, since it was believed that youth itself, rather than the environment of the individual delinquent, was the causal factor in crime. I will discuss adolescence as a 'criminal' period further in Chapter 4.

Two biographical texts from the early nineteenth century, both concerning Christ's Hospital, show the manner in which boys could be treated as a source of criminality and contamination. Charles Lamb's 'Christ's Hospital Five and

---

194 Cowper 1913, pp. 105–8.

195 See Journal no. 9 in Wesley 1991, p. 444, and Sermon 94 (1772) in Wesley 1986, p. 343.

196 May 1973, pp. 7–29. See also Shore 1999, p. 30, on the use of 'medical language' and ideas of 'contagion' in discourses on prison reform and juvenile delinquency.

197 Sermon XII, Vol. II in Findlay 1897, pp. 128–29. Arnold was quoting Bowdler's *Remains*, vol. II, p. 153. Chandos 1984 (p. 263) remarks that Bowdler was quoting Fielding.

198 Stanley 1882, vol. II, p. 227.

199 Spateman, p. 18.

200 Shore 1999, p. 6.

Thirty Years Ago' (1820) covers the period from 1782 to 1789.[201] Lamb compares discipline at school – particularly the 'monitor' system, in which older boys supervise younger ones – to that in both prison and mental institutions. Residential schooling confined the boys, controlled them and shielded society from them. The regime of peer surveillance is evocative of a panoptical prison; Lamb says that a boy who collected waste food for starving relatives was spied on by other boys who pursued him until they had 'secured their victim'.[202] Another boy, who ran away from school, was put in 'fetters' and placed in solitary confinement in the 'little, square, Bedlam cells, where a boy could just lie at his length upon straw and blanket [...] with a peep of light [...] from a prison-orifice at top'. The presence of the cells and prison-style discipline in school seems to have been calculated to have a salutary effect on students. Lamb records the impact on his mental health of witnessing the boy chained thus: 'I was a hypochondriac lad: and the sight of a boy in fetters, upon the day of my first putting on the blue clothes, was not exactly fitted to assuage the natural terrors of initiation'. He also adds in a footnote that cases of 'lunacy' and 'attempted suicide' put a stop to the fetters and cells. Lamb makes explicit the link between the use of a jail-like regime at school and juvenile prison reform, remarking bitterly that 'The fancy of dungeons for children was a sprout of Howard's brain; for which [...] I could willingly spit upon his statue'. The sense of vulnerability instilled by the spectacle of prison discipline, together with the uniform, undermines identity, engendering a psychological fear that ensures that the boys conform to the status quo. Once they have become accustomed to seeing their companions dressed alike, a boy without a uniform attracts collective revulsion. The fettered boy, who later disguises himself to escape, is described as having been 'arrayed in uncouth and most appalling attire' and is paraded before the boys as an example of deviance.[203]

E. Ward's description of early-nineteenth century Christ's Hospital, *Boys and their Rulers* (1853) also explores the issue of schoolboys and pathological contamination. This narrative is peppered with constant references to medicine, so much that the school itself seems more like a medical facility than an educational institution (indeed, the playground was connected with Bartholomew's Hospital 'in case of accidents'[204]). The book explains that at Christ's Hospital, boys were segregated into eighteen 'wards' supervised by 'nurses'.[205] The first (rather unusual) thing that happened when new boys arrived was a 'medical examination'. Sickly boys were rejected lest 'disastrous consequences [...] ensue'.[206] Early on, there

---

201 Lamb 1987, p. 14.
202 Ibid., p. 18. For a Foucauldian reading of school discipline, see Chapter 4.
203 Ibid., p. 19.
204 Ward 1853, p. 34.
205 Ibid., p. 30.
206 Ibid., p. 28. Apparently death rates had been disastrously high when the school was founded in the sixteenth century and still amounted to 10 per year in the eighteenth. See Blunden 1953, pp. 8 and 34.

is an entire chapter discussing the sick bay, which seems to have been so overused it almost became a subdivision of the school. Here, Ward developed his first friendship, during an outbreak of fever. Even the friendship, however, has an air of the pathological about it, because it was while Ward has suffering from the fever, which made his imagination 'vivid', that he became acquainted, then obsessed, with the other boy. On Ward's returning to school, the friend, dying in the infirmary, 'engrossed' his 'every thought'.[207] In the next episode, Ward describes how he and other boys were at one point segregated en masse in an attempt to eliminate ringworm ('condemned to be "scalped" [... though] not to be decapitated').[208] The segregated boys vandalized their ward with a battering ram, as if defiantly asserting their own health (Ward remarks: 'it is surprising what school-boys will endure without suffering any ill-effect'). To classify them as 'sick' was a 'misnomer' because 'we were only outwardly touched in the heads, not mentally'.[209] In a later chapter Ward recalls that the ringworm carriers were eventually 'sentenced' to be 'transported' to the school's Hertford annex.[210] In Hertford, a hotbed of political dissent, they were inspired to hold anarchic mock-elections and, again, they caused mayhem. Whatever conditions were really like at Christ's Hospital, Ward clearly seems to have felt that the authorities saw medical control as a way of disciplining the boys and the sick-room as a kind of prison – an approach that appears to have been counterproductive. The salient point that emerges from Ward's narrative is that the control of the supposedly 'diseased' adolescent body was seen by authorities as in some way the key to controlling behavior.

Commentators on youth issues often asserted that some kind of correlation existed between amoral behavior and the growth of the adolescent body, a connection they found physically repellent. Thomas Arnold's sermons, given at Rugby School, give clues as to why. In one sermon, Arnold discusses what he terms 'the intermediate state between childhood and manhood'.[211] A child, says Arnold, possesses 'humility' and 'teachableness'. In the child's mind there is 'nothing which can be called prejudice: he will not as yet refuse to listen, as thinking that he knows better than his adviser'. However, his 'moral sense [...] is exceedingly weak, and would yield readily to the first temptation', so 'the selfish instinct, connected apparently with all animal life' predominates. Adults are less teachable, but less selfishly thoughtless. The problem is that in the worst cases, between childhood and adulthood 'whilst in the one point of teachableness, the change runs on too fast, in the other three, of wisdom, of unselfishness, and of thoughtfulness, it proceeds much too slowly'.[212] The answer is to push young people into adulthood as quickly as possible: 'it is a sin in every one not to try to

---

207 Ward 1853, p. 35.
208 Ibid., p. 36.
209 Ibid., pp. 37–38.
210 Ibid., p. 113.
211 Sermon II.IV in Findlay 1897, p. 147.
212 Ibid., p. 146.

hasten it: because, to retain the imperfections of childhood when you can get rid of them, is in itself to forfeit the innocence of childhood'.[213]

Arnold's understanding of child development anticipated an idea known as 'recapitulation' which received a Darwinian re-interpretation during the nineteenth century. According to the recapitulation theory, while growing up children and young people experience all levels of evolutionary mental development, starting life as the most basic of primitive men and becoming *Homo Sapiens* only at adulthood. The idea had originated with Augustine, was elaborated in the early nineteenth century by Augustus Comte[214] and was followed through by Herbert Spencer and G. Stanley Hall. To Arnold, this theory meant that juveniles were closer to animals, a fact he found monstrous. He observed that in some boys the body grew faster than the intellect and that the mind was unable to control physical impulses ('for with the growth of our bodies evil will grow in us unavoidably'[215]). Juveniles, therefore, needed to be closely controlled and monitored and could not be allowed autonomy. He told his students:

> your bodies, at your time of life, so far outgrow your minds; – that your spirits and bodily strength are so vigorous and active, while your understandings are, in comparison, so feeble. This makes you unapt and unwilling to think; and he who does not think, must surely do one of two things, – he must submit himself entirely to be guided by the advice and direction of others, like young children, or else he must certainly go wrong.[216]

It was not just pathologically naughty juveniles but also healthy ones who repulsed Arnold. He disdained wealthy boys in whom 'one sees nothing but plenty, health and youth',[217] a distaste which is reiterated by many public school writers who portray adolescents as gluttonous, over-sized or over-athletic.

Arnold was not repulsed by children, who, in his eyes, were just as full of animal vice as adolescents, but smaller and easier to control (an observation also made by Augustine in his *Confessions*[218]). His vehement reiteration of the Augustinian horror of adolescence seems at variance with his Lockeanism, his Wordsworthianism and his aversion to Evangelical extremism; but the dangerous instability of adolescence was one of the points on which rationalist social and economic commentators tended to agree with Evangelicals.[219] The popular revulsion that adolescents seem to have attracted may have been caused at least partly by demographic change and an ensuing Malthusian panic. The autonomy and financial independence which the

---

213 Ibid., p. 149.
214 Cunningham 1991, p. 100.
215 Findlay 1897, p. 224.
216 Ibid., pp. 130–31.
217 McCrum 1989, p. 36. Billy Bunter is the comic typification of the monstrous boy.
218 Ezell 1991, p. 240. F.W. Farrar put the Edenic nature of children into his own peculiar form of evolutionary theory. See Chapter 3 below.
219 For examples see Hilton 1988, pp. 65–67.

Industrial Revolution had brought to some young people resulted in a decrease in the age of marriage. The increased fertility this brought, combined with a falling death rate, caused the population to swell from 5.5 million in the first half of the century to 9 million in 1801.[220] Thomas Malthus blamed the population explosion on unfettered adolescent sexuality and warned that 'if we were all to marry at the age of puberty' the subsequent increase in population would bring famine, social disorder and despotism.[221] This Malthusian panic helps to explain Arnold's disgust towards healthy adolescents and his preoccupation with adolescent sin, since the biggest threat to the social fabric had become not disease, but health, fertility and consumption. Linda Berry remarks that

> Malthus makes a historically unique connection between the healthy body and social disease. Because persons in health must eat, and cannot be persuaded to cease procreating, a greater number of healthy bodies means more reproduction – and less food.[222]

Those people who were capable of reproducing but who were not working and contributing to the economy, such as the young or the unemployed, presented the biggest threat to civilization. Malthusian ideas went to the heart of state policy in the agricultural depression of the 1820s and 1830s, at the height of Arnold's career. The 1834 New Poor Law placed unemployed adults in workhouses, where they could eat but not reproduce. According to Berry, it was impoverished children, who could not breed, rather than hungry adults who got most attention from opponents of the New Poor Law.[223] A strict moral division thus appeared between breeders and non-breeders. If these issues seem distant from the public schools, it should be remembered that dependent schoolboys were also consuming and not working and that a considerable number were capable of reproducing. Although Arnold and his contemporaries rarely if ever mention explicitly that their older students were capable of fathering children, their fear of demographic apocalypse must have been aroused by the proximity of large bodies full of energy which were not being invested in useful physical labor.[224]

It may not have been totally coincidental that Malthusianism appeared simultaneously with a heightened awareness of the moral significance of the body. James Kincaid remarks that

---

[220] Trevelyan 1948, pp. 341 and 470. See also Hinde 2003, p. 185.

[221] Malthus 1803, book IV, ch. V, pp. 518–19.

[222] Berry 1999, p. 8. Here Berry is citing the work of Catherine Gallagher in 'The Body versus the Social Body in the Works of Thomas Malthus and Henry Mayhew', *Representations*, 14 (1986), pp. 83–106.

[223] Ibid., p. 36.

[224] Chandos 1984 remarks that Coventry prostitutes used to visit Rugby (p. 285), though he does not specify when.

The modern 'body' is an invention at least as startling as the modern 'child'; there was a time, says A.F.M. Willich (1799), [...] when most people, on a rough-and-ready, day-to-day basis, really were not aware that they had a body: 'Formerly, people were not accustomed to think of the physical state of their body, until it began to be afflicted with pain or debility'.[225]

According to Kincaid, before the development of modern ideas of childhood the concept of 'innocence' had little to do with awareness of sexual matters or lack thereof. This pre-Victorian attitude to innocence and sexuality might explain why, as Chandos remarks, there was little interest in sex as a 'sin' at public schools until the Victorian period.[226] Kincaid argues that children knew about sex as a fact, but that this knowledge was not thought to be corrupting in itself. The idea that children were 'innocent' because they did not have sexual feelings developed with an increased public consciousness of sexual morality and the more sexual morality was dwelt upon, the more children seemed to be morally superior beings. Indeed, it seems that, among all classes, the first three decades of the nineteenth century brought about a greater consciousness of morality. Michael Mason has used autobiographical material by the London political activist Francis Place to suggest that pre-marital and casual sexual activities (the only ones most adolescents could participate in) became publicly less acceptable at this time, as society saw 'a massive shift towards greater moral respectability'.[227] According to Mason, Place attributed this change to factors such as 'the New Police, hygienic clothing, increased prosperity, innovations in schooling' and to political and intellectual movements that came in the wake of the French Revolution, which left serious men with no time for dissipation. Continence also appealed to the aspirational, self-determining democratic imagination. Mason says that 'for Place, and for other working-class radicals, there was [...] a conceptual affinity, between an optimistic commitment to raising the status of ordinary people and the drive towards orderliness, restraint and decency'.[228] This taste for orderliness and self-control doubtless also existed among the aspiring middle classes and among upper-class individuals who subscribed to middle-class values.

For some upper-class individuals, establishing physical self-discipline was a step in the direction of creating social order. In Thomas Hughes's *Tom Brown at Oxford* (1861), Tom goes through a period of dissipation with his aristocratic friends which is an impediment to his development as a social and philanthropic activist when he develops a flirtation with a barmaid. The episode gives Hughes an opportunity to deliver a lecture against 'sowing wild oats'. The best thing for wild oats, he says, is to 'put them carefully into the hottest part of the fire, and get them burnt to dust', because 'If you sow them, no matter in what ground, up they will

---

225 Kincaid 1994, p. 104.
226 Chandos 1984, p. 285.
227 Mason 1994, p. 29.
228 Ibid., pp. 32, 34.

come, with long tough roots like couch-grass, and luxuriant stalks and leaves'. The reason a man ought to exert such self-control is that 'What a man – be he young, old, or middle aged – sows, *that*, and nothing else, shall he reap'.[229] The metaphor of 'luxuriant' weeds – unwanted offspring growing to monstrous proportions and occupying soil meant for legitimate produce – is deeply Malthusian. Hughes urges that young men concentrate their energies on 'higher ends'. He also insists that they pay more attention to women's feelings. The main reason that Hardy, Tom's progressive and supremely moral friend, objects to the barmaid affair is that one should not engage the feelings of a girl one is not prepared to marry. In short, spontaneous, irresponsible sexual impulse is the enemy of progress, control and order. Adolescents and young adults such as Tom, who are in full-time education and upon whom progress depends, are particularly vulnerable to straying since they are not in a position to regulate their sexuality through marriage.

Hughes allows Tom Brown to learn from experience, which means letting him to get very close to sin. Other commentators were less happy to leave boys alone to weather the dangers of temptation and permanent reprobation. Michael McCrum suggests that Thomas Arnold's obsession with boyhood sin made him push Arthur Hugh Clough (head of Arnold's House) and other favorite students towards adulthood and maturity too quickly, causing early 'burn out'.[230] Some writers dealt with adolescence in a different way, recommending that childhood innocence be artificially prolonged. A pre-*Tom Brown* public school story which promotes the prolongation of childhood is *The Cherry Stones*, written in 1842 by William Adams and published posthumously, in 1851, by his brother Henry, who was later a writer for the *Boys' Own Paper*. Addressed to those at the 'time of life which it is in general peculiarly difficult to reach by such means',[231] this story is specifically 'for youth'. The protagonist, Harry Mertoun, aged thirteen and on the brink of adolescence and public school life, attends a preparatory school. Innocently playing cricket one day, he accidentally discovers how to broach the wall between the playground and the headmaster's garden and has a night's foray to steal cherries (a scenario that echoes Augustine's story of the stolen pears from his own adolescence in Book II of the *Confessions*[232]). During the following days, Harry is tortured by his conscience and also by the seemingly supernatural reappearance of the cherry stones (placed in strategic positions in the school by a rival). A little while later, he is presented with a school prize but, convinced he does not now deserve it, he confesses his crime. The headmaster deems the pangs of conscience he has suffered, plus a lecture on the evils of rivalry, to be sufficient punishment.

The beginning of adolescence here is a fall, mirroring the Fall in Eden (Harry literally falls off the garden wall at one point and hurts his foot). Harry blunders

---

229 Hughes 1897, p. 53.
230 McCrum 1989, p. 106.
231 Adams 1851, p. viii.
232 Augustine 1995, p. 53.

upon adolescence haplessly, a victim of his own curiosity and misplaced initiative. His schoolmates celebrate his violation of school boundaries in the same way as the Saxonhurst boys did, because it fits their 'heroic' concept of what a boy should be. But the act awakens in Harry both pride and 'angry and rebellious feelings',[233] strengthening his ties to the boy community and alienating him from adults. It also changes the moral outlook of the other boys, 'produc[ing] a complete revolution in the sentiments of the little world of Charlton School'.[234] One of the things which drives Harry on to do his evil deed is his overactive imagination, which is fuelled by what he reads. He had 'a strong love of the romantic and adventurous':

> Tales of wild and perilous exploits would at all times arrest and rivet his attention, often to the neglect of serious duties: and he was apt to lose all recollection of the folly and criminality of some of his heroes, in his admiration of their unbounded and desperate courage.[235]

Reading heroic narratives over-stimulates the imagination, which is bad, because imagination has 'so much [...] to do with our worst misfortunes'.[236] Harry's heroes resemble characters from the popular 'Newgate Chronicle' narratives and early 'Penny Bloods' such as Jack Sheppard and Dick Turpin.[237] This attack by Adams on the young, self-actualizing heroes of popular fiction was not the first, nor was it the last. In *Practical Education* (1801), Maria Edgeworth had commented on the lack of wholesome juvenile literature and had complained about the dubious heroes 'Gil Blas, Tom Jones, Lovelace [and] Count Fathom'. Although their 'wit, humor and the ingenuity of their contrivances' were entertaining, their careers implicitly taught that 'deceit and dishonesty are associated with superior abilities'.[238]

Adams might have explored through Harry new and more 'wholesome' ways for boys to be heroic, as did the author of *The History of a Schoolboy*. Instead, he rejects adolescence altogether. Harry is inspired to be a better boy by his little brother Walter, who is 'thoroughly honest, [and] simple-hearted'; an obedient, naïve, passive Arnoldian child.[239] In contemplating him, Harry realizes that he has lost his innocence and determines to get it back. In order to return to the Eden of childhood, he opens himself up completely to the headmaster (having hidden from him, as Adam had hidden from God, after stealing the fruit). His regression is now complete. Adolescence, implies Adams, is exciting but dangerous and it is better to seek the safety and comfort of adult protection and passive obedience than to try to think or act for oneself. Although it is entitled 'A Tale for Youth', Adams's

---

233 Adams 1851, p. 10.
234 Ibid., p. 9.
235 Ibid., pp. 18–19.
236 Ibid., p. 10.
237 See Springhall 1998 for a discussion of 'Penny Bloods'.
238 Edgeworth 1801, vol. I, p. 336.
239 Adams 1851, p. 48.

simplistic Biblical allegory erases adolescence as a meaningful social entity by evading issues about the role of young people in society or their physical and emotional development. Adolescence only exists here in its denial.

Between the Industrial Revolution and the mid-Victorian period, therefore, the time of life we now call adolescence attracted more attention than it had ever done before, because adolescent education meant so much, symbolically and practically, to a rapidly industrializing culture. In particular, juvenile development gained a new value as a metaphor for wider social progress and political reform. There were also more negative voices to be heard, particularly from those who had a growing consciousness of sexual morality and who warned that the young were a source of social instability. A broad array of interest groups, from Young Englanders to feminist radicals, found an outlet in the public school story for their political and social ideologies and what they wrote had ramifications far beyond the world of schoolboys themselves. Under the weight of these manifold influences, the public school novel emerged as what could be described as a heteroglossic patchwork of voices and influences that portrayed adolescent subjectivity in some very contradictory ways. Outside the literary sphere, meanwhile, changes in the structure of British society also meant that the cultural construction of adolescence – particularly public school adolescence – had to change. Up until this period, only a small elite had been able to experience the kind of adolescence which involved attending public school and going through the various combative and linguistic rituals which were deemed to fit a man for statesmanship. As British political life became more inclusive, and as the public-school population began to number more and more boys from middle-class backgrounds, there was pressure for different methods of socialization to be introduced to the public school regime. The next chapter will show exactly how one author, Thomas Hughes, conceived of a new model of education for citizenship and statesmanship that would suit the purposes of this changing society.

Chapter 2

An Education for Active Citizenship:
Tom Brown's Schooldays

The idea that adolescence is the time when a child begins to change into a politically literate citizen can be found in very different types of Victorian literature. Disraeli's *Coningsby* and Hughes's *Tom Brown* books, for example, seem worlds apart in tone and focus. Nonetheless, both are set in the context of the political movements of the 1830s and 1840s and there are parallels between the two. These parallels become particularly clear when the sequel to *Tom Brown's Schooldays*, *Tom Brown at Oxford* (1861), is taken into account. Like Coningsby, Tom abandons his forefathers' traditional Toryism to search for a new approach to English social problems and eventually finds a vocation as a reformer. Both Tom and Coningsby attend public school and have intense, almost romantic, friendships with boys from a more liberal background (Millbank in *Coningsby* and George Arthur in *Tom Brown*). Tom and Coningsby both come from landed families (although Tom's father is a squire not an aristocrat) and Arthur and Millbank are from industrial towns. Coningsby saves Millbank from drowning and Tom defends Arthur from bullying. In return, Arthur and Millbank help Tom and Coningsby to establish new attitudes towards social problems. At times, Hughes even repeats Disraeli's comments on adolescence and education. For example, Disraeli, describing the friendship between Coningsby and Millbank, says that 'the influence of the individual is nowhere so sensible as at school'.[1] Hughes, echoing him, remarks that, 'In no place in the world has individual character more weight than at a public school'.[2]

Tom Brown has been criticized for being conservative, violent and anti-intellectual and its ideological messages have been called into question by writers ranging from James Fitzjames Stephen to Richard Usborne and Kenneth Allsop.[3] Lately, Ian Watson has shown how the book reinforces colonialist ideology and defends the hegemony of the landed classes.[4] In this chapter I will offer a different perspective by showing how Hughes's works explore changing ideas of adolescent political growth and citizenship. First, I will give an account of the stages of political growth that Tom experiences through the narrative, explaining how his

---

1   Disraeli 1989, p. 71.
2   Hughes 1989, p. 167.
3   See Usborne 1956 and Allsop 1965.
4   Watson 1981, pp. 116–29.

individual growth fits in with the changing political climate of the nation. Then I will remark on the increasing importance of 'fatherliness' to Hughes's conception of individual male citizenship and describe how he addressed many of the complaints against the excesses of 'Regency masculinity' that I documented in Chapter 1. After this, I will show how, in the course of writing *Tom Brown's Schooldays*, *Tom Brown at Oxford* and a manual on Christian citizenship, *The Manliness of Christ* (1879), Hughes continuously revised his ideas on competition, combat and heroism. Finally, I will demonstrate how Hughes's idealized image of a reformed Rugby school, run by a protective *deus ex machina*-type father figure, acts as a safe training ground in which boys use play and leisure-time activities to learn how to cope with the challenges the real world presents. I will also describe how this ideal education was radically different from the baptism-by-fire of traditional public school education and how, in outlining his ideal, Hughes presents play as the most appropriate kind of work for nascent adolescent citizens.

Hughes, as remarked on in the previous chapter, makes close parallels between the evolution of Tom as a citizen and the social evolution of Britain. Nonetheless, unlike *Coningsby*, or even *The History of a Schoolboy*, *Tom Brown's Schooldays* avoids open political comment. At Coningsby's Eton there is 'a reigning inclination for political discussion' and the pupils are 'agitated' by the question of reform.[5] There is nothing so transparent in *Tom Brown*. Hughes's idealistic depiction of village life in Tom's Berkshire birthplace fails to mention contemporary events that would have been impossible for real-life villagers in that area to ignore, such as the 1834 Tolpuddle Martyrs incident (the year Hughes went to Rugby) and the 1830 'Swing' Riots. As Ian Watson points out, Berkshire 'was a major county of disturbance [where] 162 cases were heard, one rioter was hanged, and 123 were jailed or transported'.[6] Nonetheless, in his early chapters, Hughes's only political reference is to events of the 1790s. A family retainer tells Tom that during the French Revolutionary wars rioters threatened local magistrates and that Tom's grandfather '[rode] in with a big stick in his hand, and held the Petty Sessions by himself'.[7] Watson observes that it would have been unlikely that hard-pressed villagers would pamper the grandson of such a magistrate in the way Hughes describes,[8] and claims that the narrative deliberately erases political history in order to promote paternalism in the face of unrest both at home and in the Empire.

However, it would be unfair to write Hughes off as completely stifling political debate, especially since the sequel to the *Schooldays*, *Tom Brown at Oxford*, engages extensively with the narrative of English labor history. In fact, there are pedagogical reasons why Hughes saves his political commentary for the later work. By temporarily ignoring contemporary events in the earlier parts of *Tom Brown*,

---

5   Disraeli 1989, p. 132.
6   Watson 1981, p. 120.
7   Hughes 1989, p. 27. See also Sanders's footnote on the French Revolutionary wars, p. 389.
8   Watson 1981, p. 120.

Hughes is able to pace Tom's intellectual and social development according to Rousseauian principles. In *Émile* Rousseau commented that 'A child's political knowledge should be clear and restricted; he should know nothing of government in general, beyond what concerns the rights of property'.[9] Thus Tom, and through him the child reader, approach politics gradually, by stages, beginning with issues of individual identity and property and moving on later to more abstract concerns and 'real-world' debates. There is also a wider political rationale to this discursive strategy. Hughes's narrative is designed in such a way that, in political terms, both the protagonist and the society he inhabits mature together. This reinforces the sense that the whole country is in a 'transitional state'. As a child, Tom Brown lives in a childish environment with childlike villagers who hang on their paternalistic Squire's every word. The villagers do not start to mature politically until Tom goes to Oxford, at which point both they and he become Chartists, making a tidy allegory and a convenient (although historically inaccurate) parallel between ideas of individual and community development.

Jeffrey Richards has already made a formal analysis of Tom's development that goes some way to explaining Hughes's understanding of adolescence. Tom, arriving at Rugby School at the age of about eleven,[10] experiences a rite of passage which Richards terms 'socialization into the institution'. During this process he is stripped of his existing identity and rebels against the status quo.[11] Eventually he is tamed and spends the rest of his education learning to accept the school's internal code. Once he has done this, he is finally ready to be absorbed into the nation's social elite.[12] I will elaborate on this model by showing how Tom's political development is divided into discrete stages, in which he struggles not only with issues of personal development but also with changing social ideas of individual identity.

In childhood and early adolescence Tom is in an almost permanent state of revolution, fighting to establish identity and autonomy. His first struggle, which begins when he leaves infancy, aged four, is a 'war of independence' against his mother and nurse.[13] Likened to a Miltonic devil, Tom mounts his insurrection 'from early morning till dewy eve'.[14] In this first step towards the 'fallen' period between infancy and maturity, he battles to define himself as a male subject in his own right, distinct from his mother. The family retainers conspire to free Tom from 'petticoat government', rescuing him from the attentions of his mother's maid.[15] Each of these retainers wears a symbol of the Squire's paternal lineage (Noah

---

9   Rousseau 1993, p. 182.
10   Hughes arrived at Rugby at eleven: see Mack 1941, p. 15. However, Arnold disliked accepting under-twelves (Stanley 1982, vol. II, p. 133).
11   Richards 1988, p. 29.
12   Ibid., p. 30.
13   Hughes 1989, p. 23.
14   Ibid., vid. *Paradise Lost*, ll. 742–43.
15   Ibid., p. 52.

with an inherited wig and Benjy in a hand-me-down jacket, both inherited from dead Browns), and it is their role to teach Tom his place in the feudal hierarchy. The old men encourage deliberately disobedient and disruptive behavior – for instance, stealing curds or gatecrashing the village school –a kind of rebellion that Hughes depicts as fundamental to creating a sense of masculine identity.[16] However, although Tom enjoys rebelling against his mother, his forefathers make him anxious. He views Noah's wig 'with considerable respect, not to say fear'[17] and feels relieved when Noah dies and the wig is buried with him. This lurking anxiety towards the Brown family ideology emerges in full when Tom rejects his father's Toryism at the end of *Tom Brown at Oxford*.

Chapter 1 presents the Browns as a family with a corporate identity, who see themselves as members of a group rather than as individuals. Hughes remarks that '[w]ith them there is nothing like the Browns, to the third and fourth generation'. They even all look the same ('square-headed and snake-necked, broad in shoulder, deep in the chest').[18] That Tom should develop a clan mentality at this point is consistent with Arnold's idea that the individual recapitulates the evolution of the race through childhood and adolescence. Thus while infancy resembles a primeval matriarchy, childhood is a time of tribalism. *Tom Brown*, however, is a story about the severing of continuity and the broadening of perspectives, and as Tom develops, his outlook accordingly begins to extend beyond the Browns and the Vale. Hughes is half inclined to celebrate the Brown philosophy, advocating the preservation of traditional social structures and complaining that stable class and generational relationships collapse when 'sons and daughters have their hearts in London Club-life, or so-called Society, instead of English home duties'.[19] He admonishes those who are fixated on European culture, 'Going round Ireland with a return ticket, in a fortnight; dropping your copies of Tennyson on the tops of Swiss mountains; or pulling down the Danube in Oxford rowing-boats'.[20] Nonetheless, Hughes's perspective gradually begins to widen, despite his 'Brown-worshipp[ing]'.[21] Although he scolds 'Young England' ('why don't you know more of your own birthplaces?'), he remarks approvingly that 'we are a vagabond nation now'.[22] Tom, constantly looking outside the home (admiring, for example, the nomadic barge-people), seems to challenge the static order. The Browns themselves, moreover, are broadening their horizons with the expansion of Empire, having left 'their mark in American forests and Australian uplands'.[23] Continuity and a fixed sense of location, therefore, no longer provide identity.

---

16 Ibid., pp. 22–27.
17 Ibid., p. 25.
18 Ibid., p. 3.
19 Ibid., p. 41.
20 Ibid., p. 6.
21 Ibid., p. 2.
22 Ibid., pp. 6, 19.
23 Ibid., p. 2.

Tom's individual transition into adolescence and out of the family sphere brings up, on a miniature scale, the same questions as do major changes in the national body politic in the face of wider global consciousness.

Entering private school, Tom is deprived of the privileges his father's position has so far given him and must find a new identity. From now on, everywhere he goes he finds the social order in a process of change or decay, and he is surrounded by role models that he can either imitate or reject. His job in late childhood and early adolescence is to establish an identity independent of his father. Having done so, he can spend his time as a senior schoolboy and as a university student carving out a role building a new kind of society in which an individual's prospects are determined by ability, rather than parental status. When Tom first arrives at Rugby, the school is going through the same changes as wider British society and lacks a decisive sense of social and political direction. A crisis descends when the Head of Tom's house, 'Pater' Brooke, the Paternalistic guardian of the microcosmic School House community, leaves and takes with him the conservative moral authority that has held anarchy at bay. As in the feudal world, the Rugby status quo has thus far been maintained by physical force and tradition, in which justice (or lack thereof) has depended on the individual character of the school's boy-leaders, chosen on the strength of their athletic skill. As in the real world, however, when one order collapses, a moral vacuum appears. Flashman, Tom's adversary, enters this moral vacuum. Like the architects of the Corn Laws, Flashman wields power by manipulating the school's internal economy ('by dint of his command of money, the constant supply of good things which he kept up, and his adroit toadyism').[24] Tom's second battle is, therefore, an anti-capitalist, anti-bourgeois challenge to Flashman's regime. Hughes comments that 'brave gallant boys', such as Tom, 'hate easy-chairs, and have no balances or bankers'.[25]

This conflict is illustrated with the following story. In the school's internal economy, poorer students are obliged to borrow from the rich, and Tom intervenes to assist an older boy, Diggs, who has no control over his money and has indebted himself. Tom steps in to redeem the belongings that have been requisitioned to pay off Diggs's debts. This primitive attempt at social welfare eventually benefits the entire community, because the grateful Diggs provides essential backup to Tom and his friend Harry East in their war against Flashman. It is at this point that the previous reference to Tom's grandfather becomes relevant. In 1795, Berkshire magistrates, one of whom is supposedly Tom's grandfather, had established the Speenhamland System of poor relief, designed to supplement the incomes of the poor to prevent starvation.[26] The system was, of course, condemned by Malthus as encouraging the poor to reproduce. Tom's act of charity echoes this policy. Diggs is a big boy and a return to solvency would surely allow him to join the other boys in supplementing their basic provisions with purchases from local

---

24 Hughes 1989, p. 178.
25 Ibid., p. 195.
26 See Marshall 1985, p. 13.

shops.[27] From a Malthusian perspective, charity should only exacerbate Diggs's problems, since he grows so rapidly that his parents cannot afford to clothe him adequately.[28] However, Hughes's logic runs counter to that of Malthus, because Diggs's strong, outsize body is useful to Tom. Hughes seems to imply that social welfare initiatives and economic intervention are worth their cost because of the benefits to social reformers (that is, the middle classes) of getting the collective might of the laboring poor onto their side in the battle against vested interests.

Tom's next 'War of Independence' (Chapter 8) occurs at the first stage in his adolescent growth, a stage that enables him to negotiate basic questions about the nature of the self. This campaign is essentially about the right of the individual to control his own money and to be rewarded for his labor. In this episode, the younger boys protest about the abuse of the 'fagging' system, where the sixth form is entitled to demand menial services such a shoe cleaning or toast-making from 'fags' (boys below the fifth form). When Rugby goes through its crisis, the fifth form, who are not entitled to these services, get into the habit of expecting them nonetheless. Tom rebels against the abuses of the system, albeit not against the system itself. Under a proper fagging system, Hughes explains, younger boys get a good return for their labor; the sixth formers are supposed to protect them from bullying and help them with academic work. Ideally, this patronage eases a boy's passage up the school into a position where he can himself claim service from his juniors in return for protecting them. Any labor a boy performs is therefore an investment in his future and in the future of the school (a system oddly like an idealized version of Japanese corporate culture). Under Flashman's rule, however, social power is bought with money and the fags have neither a fair return nor a stake in the system. Flashman makes them work for him and pays the older boys not to oppose him. According to D.W. Allen, in protesting against Flashman's regime Tom is defending 'the equality of all boys in certain fundamental rights of self-possession and self-determination'.[29] Allen interprets Tom's behavior according to Locke's precept that the body is individual private property and that each person deserves a fair return for any labor that body does. Here again, therefore, Hughes presents an indirectly expressed political subtext. When Hughes puts the word 'strike' into Tom's mouth to describe his rebellion,[30] he draws a parallel between the self-conscious adolescent and the increasingly class-conscious industrial workforce ('strike' was a comparatively new usage in Tom's time, still italicized as a neologism in 1810[31]). Boys and laborers fight not

---

27 See Hughes 1989, pp. 114–18, for a description of the boys supplementing their food after a match. Hughes does not discuss the boys' nutrition specifically but it does seem that larger boys stole younger boys' food (p. 231).
28 Ibid., p. 174.
29 Allen 1994, p. 124.
30 Hughes 1989, p. 170.
31 Knowles 1952, p. 2.

only for fair working conditions but also for recognition of their rights, as citizens, to have a stake in the government of their communities.

Although Hughes identifies Tom with no specific partisan group, he draws parallels during the campaign against Flashman to a number of contemporary political movements. In his rebellious stage, Tom is compared to 'poor gallant blundering men like Kossuth, Garibaldi, [and] Mazzini'[32] (Mazzini's 'Young Europe' movement was established in 1834, the year Hughes entered Rugby). Hughes also quotes J.R. Lowell's *Stanzas on Freedom* (1843), drawing the reader's attention to issues surrounding slavery (abolished in the British Empire in 1833).[33] The story of Flashman's monopoly over supply and demand and his abuse of the fags also makes an oblique reference to the abuses of child labor that prompted the 1833 Factory Acts. Similarly, when Tom and East build 'barricade[s]' against their fifth-form oppressors, Hughes points our attention towards a form of resistance that had symbolic meaning throughout mainland Europe (not least in the persistent unrest in Paris in the early 1830s[34]). By making so many disparate political references, Hughes takes Tom's rebellion out of any specific national or class context. Tom is just one atom in a giant movement campaigning for universal rights. He is as yet too young to get involved in any real-world political cause. Instead, he experiments with general ideas of social right, property and freedom in a 'safe' environment. It is only when we reach *Tom Brown at Oxford* that we learn how he had actually absorbed political ideas, such as the 'wild and violent beliefs and notions' of Chartism, in his later Rugby years.[35]

Tom and East achieve a sense of self-determination by suffering repression and rebelling against it. However, after laying down the basic principles of justice in the school, the boys continue to rebel 'for no earthly pleasure except that of doing what they are told not to do'. Revolution has become a habit and the way in which they find a sense of identity. Their supreme act of defiant egotism is to inscribe their names in capital letters on the minute hand of the school clock.[36] As yet, there is no social contract or understanding between younger boys and older boys, or between boys and masters, and it is taken for granted that masters and boys have separate, opposing interests. Tom has become the combative, revolutionary adolescent of the traditional public school and at this stage would probably be at home in Fitzgerald's Saxonhurst or Keate's Eton. For Hughes, however, this is an immature concept of adolescent citizenship; it is a stage that it is necessary to go through in early adolescence but which must be overcome by something more suited to present social and political conditions.

---

32 Hughes 1989, p. 195.
33 This gave freedom to slaves, unlike the 1807 Act which only curtailed the slave trade. See Davis 1984, pp. 192–205.
34 Hughes 1989, p. 171. Also see Magraw 1992, p. 53.
35 Hughes 1897, p. 435.
36 Hughes 1989, p. 208.

The second stage of Tom's adolescence begins at the age of fourteen, when Arnold puts him in charge of the delicate George Arthur. Arnold creates stability for Tom, in his search for an identity, by introducing him to new ideas of masculinity, particularly of fatherhood, with which he counteracts the destructive side of Tom's revolutionary instincts. Tom learns fathering skills during adolescence and later, at Oxford, learns to teach which, to Hughes, is an extension of fatherhood. Indeed, a central theme to *Tom Brown* is that of old versus new ideas of fathering. Tom's own father, Squire Brown, has a very hands-off approach and refuses, for example, to interfere in Tom's relationships with the village boys (to the astonishment of his neighbors whose children 'never went to the village without the governess or a footman'[37]). His idea is that Tom should mix freely with all classes and learn that 'a man is to be valued wholly and solely for that which he is in himself [...] apart from clothes, rank, fortune and all externals whatever'.[38] In a sense, the Squire's *laissez-faire* approach instills some of the principles of classical citizenship, such as a contempt for luxury, social nicety and privilege. Tom, a 'combative urchin',[39] is, like a Regency schoolboy, allowed to initiate conflicts with members of the village community and is only prevented when complaints are made. This combativeness is central to the role of the Browns in wider society. The identity and authority of the Brown dynasty is founded on their willingness to fight when their community needs them: 'wherever hard knocks of any kind [...] are going, there the Brown who is nearest must shove in his carcass'.[40] This fighting spirit is also fundamental to Squire Brown as a squire and as a father: as Hughes comments, he 'dealt out justice and mercy in a rough way and begat sons and daughters'.[41]

During his school and university days, however, Tom moves away from his father. They finally reach a political contretemps in an argument about whether a landlord has a right to evict a man whose mother, a 'weekly tenant', has died.[42] The tenant's son was a childhood friend of Tom's and the friendship, ironically, was a result of Squire Brown's liberal attitude to social mixing. The episode alienates Tom from his father, but it is arguable that Tom's open display of sympathy for the working-class cause actually reduces the threat of violence breaking out in the village. In a paradoxical and unexpected way, therefore, Squire Brown's *laissez-faire* approach to parenting actually helps a fairer social order to emerge naturally from the old hierarchy, without the need for revolution. Hughes makes it clear, however, that this is not the parenting style needed for the future.

In struggling with these ideas of continuity and change, particularly in father–son relationships, *Tom Brown* sometimes echoes the continental *Bildungsroman* tradition. As Jerome Buckley has explained, in the *Bildungsroman*, the first

---

37 Ibid., p. 61.
38 Ibid., p. 52.
39 Ibid., p. 22.
40 Ibid., p. 3.
41 Ibid., p. 16.
42 Hughes 1897, pp. 372–73.

important event in a rural protagonist's life is loss of, or alienation from, his father, which causes him to 'search for a substitute parent or creed'.[43] At Rugby Tom experiences a *Bildungsroman*-style distancing from his father even though there is little open strife between them until his Oxford years. With Tom's birthright status in the squirearchy losing social currency, he embarks on a romantic quest to 'find himself'. In narrating this quest Hughes shows how changing ideas of identity politics relate to changing social politics. At the start of his Rugby career, Tom, pursuing a revolutionary agenda, slips readily into the persona of the adversarial public schoolboy as seen at Fitzgerald's Saxonhurst, the Eton of Keate and the Winchester described by H.C. Adams. In Book 2, however, he begins to see himself in terms of his more intimate, personal relationships; identity is now a private matter, defined not in relation to other classes or political groups but through personal relationships with teachers, friends, friends' mothers and ultimately in an individual spiritual relationship with the divine.

The new father figure Tom finds is Arnold, a hero worthy of 'Thomas Carlyle himself'.[44] Tom's worship of Arnold finally directs him to the ultimate father figure, God. When Arnold dies, Hughes comments that 'all young and brave souls who must win their way through hero-worship, to the worship of Him who is the King and Lord of heroes'.[45] Religious consciousness, like political understanding, is built in stages, starting with the worship of the concrete (school tradition and school sports heroes) and culminating in the worship of an abstract God. Perhaps with this aim in mind (or perhaps merely through a desire for influence), the historical Arnold deliberately fostered a cult status for himself among his students. A.P. Stanley confessed to having worshipped Arnold and 'felt a love and reverence for him', remarking, 'I well remember that I used to think I would gladly lay down my life'.[46] He explains how Arnold created almost romantic sentiments among students, holding them at arm's length until they proceeded to university, when he finally requited their devotion to him:

> it was now that the intercourse which at school had been so broken, and as it were stolen by snatches, was at last enjoyed between them to its full extent. It was sometimes in the few parting words [...] that they became for the first time conscious of his real care and love for them.[47]

Arnold created a culture where his students, as grown men, continued to rely on his judgment. Even when privately studying the Bible, remarked Stanley, they

---

43 Buckley 1974, p. 19.
44 Hughes 1989, p. 367.
45 Ibid., p. 376.
46 Stanley 1882, vol. I, p. 159.
47 Ibid., p. 160.

would find themselves following 'line[s] of thought that came originally from him, as from a great parent mind'.[48]

The Arnold of *Tom Brown* is first and foremost a father. The first time Tom meets him at close quarters is not in the classroom but in his family quarters.[49] As a father figure, Arnold embodies a combination of qualities Hughes refers to as 'manliness', a new concept of male citizenship that Arnold instills in Tom by placing him in charge of the puny George Arthur. As G.R. Worth has explained, 'manliness' was a quality which 'could conceivably be applied to right-living girls and women as well as to right-living boys and men', which went 'beyond mere bodily strength or athletic prowess'.[50] Arnoldian manliness is a synthesis of paternal and maternal qualities that Tom learns by caring for George Arthur.[51] The episode that introduces Arthur is deeply significant. Now aged fourteen, Tom and East are back from the holidays. We see them rooting around in new boys' trunks, busy poking fun at some nightcaps they have found, 'beautifully made and marked, the work of loving fingers in some distant country home [of a] kind mother and sisters who sewed that delicate stitching with aching hearts'.[52] By mocking the caps, they affirm their sense of masculine identity through a rejection of domestic sentiment. However, the matron chases East away and tells Tom about his new role. Initially, Tom hates Arnold's idea. Arthur is effeminate and Tom worries that he 'would be afraid of wet feet, and always getting laughed at, and called [...] some derogatory feminine nickname'.[53] Immediately after being introduced, however, Tom and Arthur are taken to visit Mrs Arnold in her drawing room. In a move which seems to owe more to Edgeworth and Martineau than the public school tradition, Hughes creates a mystique around Arnold's family life by refusing to describe what happened there, impressing on his readers the idea that home is not a thing to be mocked.[54]

Having established the combative, 'masculine', independent side of his identity in early adolescence, therefore, the next stage is for Tom to develop his social, 'feminine' side, which will equip him for a position at the top of the school.[55]

---

48 Ibid., pp. 159–60.
49 Hughes 1989, p. 155.
50 Worth 1984, p. 310.
51 Harrington 1977 (p. 76) mentions the same changes coming over Kingsley's characters.
52 Hughes 1989, p. 216.
53 Ibid., p. 218.
54 Ibid., p. 219.
55 A number of scholars, including Donald Hall, James Eli Adams and Maureen Martin, have focused on Rugby as a homosocial (sometimes misogynistic) community. As Martin points out, Eve Kosofsky Sedgwick has observed that the homosocial/homosexual continuum was 'less "radically disrupted"' in public schools than in other all-male communities (Martin 2002, p. 483). However, while it is valid to represent the public schools as encouraging networking and male bonding, the idea that they were the female-free hothouses of prurient popular imagination is very questionable. Mrs Arnold is a strong

Tom imitates Arnold's father-like behavior by stage-managing and orchestrating Arthur's life. East berates him for 'cackl[ing] after [Arthur] like a hen with one chick' and scornfully calls him 'dry-nurse',[56] but Tom's job is to make domesticated behavior socially acceptable both to his school contemporaries and to readers. One way in which he copes with the uncertainty of his new identity is to create a scapegoat for his fear of effeminacy. At one point East derides Arthur, remarking, 'That sort of boy's no use here [...] he'll only spoil. [...] Go and get a nice large band-box made, and put him in with plenty of cotton-wool, and a pap-bottle, labeled "With care – this side up", and send him back to mamma'.[57] Tom responds by seeking out and thrashing 'one of the miserable little pretty white-handed curly headed boys, petted and pampered by some of the big fellows, who [...] did all they could to spoil them for everything in this world and the next'.[58] Part of his fight to redefine 'acceptable' male behavior involves finding a new type of unacceptable male character (figured in the 'pretty boy') against whom the 'real' man can define himself.

Transforming the ideal adolescent from fighting misogynist into empathic, nascent father figure is a difficult maneuver to negotiate and comes at a cost to the freedom of expressing other kinds of masculine identity. Hughes makes his own designs for adolescence more socially acceptable by drawing attention to and stereotyping the homosexual boy, stigmatizing him as a representative of 'deviance' and inviting his readers to focus their hatred on him. It is arguable that before this stereotype was created, homosexuality attracted little moral concern in schools. A.P. Stanley's professed surprise on finding in *Tom Brown* that homosexuality had existed at Rugby may or may not have been feigned but, according to Chandos, there is very little documented evidence of it at schools in the early nineteenth century.[59] This lack of documentary evidence does not suggest that homosexuality was nonexistent – rather that the boys' private relationships were a matter that did not worry adults sufficiently to warrant investigation or comment. It is more than mere coincidence, however, that homosexuality began to attract the attention

---

figure in *Tom Brown* and, as I remarked in Chapter 1, it was Arnold's intention that she mother the boys. In later public school stories, women and girls appear in less platonic capacities. As I remark below, the heroes of Bracebridge Hemyng develop romantic associations with girls and women met through school, as does Welldon's Gerald Eversley. In Eden Phillpott's supposedly semi-autobiographical *The Human Boy*, the students' attention is focused on the headmaster's daughter. Moreover, Stalky & Co. are not averse to flirting with and kissing local girls (Kipling 1987, pp. 264–66). Chandos 1984 (pp. 285–87) contains evidence that boys had access to girls, whatever the authorities might have thought. With many traditional public schools situated in or near towns (fewer in isolated locations than was the case with schools founded later on), it must have been difficult to prevent such association – hence Thomas Arnold's sense of Malthusian panic.

56 Ibid., p. 231.
57 Ibid., p. 232.
58 Ibid., p. 233.
59 Chandos 1984, p. 301.

of moralists at the same time as writers such as Hughes were trying to re-shape the character of adolescent masculinity. Fearing being labeled as an 'inauthentic' or 'effeminate' man himself, Hughes was suggesting that sexual, rather than any other kind of behavior, was the new primary criterion for measuring deviance, a stance also taken by F.W. Farrar.

It is possible that these writers chose this approach because sexual morality, as I said in chapter one, had received a new social emphasis during their youth. Hughes classes types of sexual orientation as either legitimate or illegitimate, a division which may not have been widely recognized in Britain in Tom Brown's time but which developed rapidly during the Victorian period. Chandos, who observes this phenomenon happening in real-life schools, explains the developing aversion to homosexuality by arguing that homophobia grew at the end of the nineteenth century along with the idea that sexual orientation was fixed and immutable. He suggests that before the time of J.A. Symonds there was no clear delineation of homosexual identity and that homosexuality was just one of a range of ways of expressing intimacy that a man might take part in at various stages in his life.[60] The conclusion is that homosexuality was not stigmatized in schools before Symonds's time because it was thought to be a temporary rather than an immutable orientation. Rictor Norton, on the other hand, has argued that self-consciously queer subcultures have always existed for individuals who are 'essentially' homosexual. For example,

> many eighteenth-century gay men not only identified themselves as gay men, but also as members of a gay community, which is a gay cultural identity rather than just a gay sexual identity. They lacked political awareness, but they possessed every other feature of the modern gay identity.[61]

The problem for these subcultures has been that throughout history, in times of moral panic, 'natural born queers [are] turned into perverts'.[62] When this happens, members of queer communities are deprived of the right to forge their own identities in self-defined groups, and other identities and classifications are imposed upon them from outside by, for example, the medical establishment or moral commentators.

As I argued in Chapter 1, public school reform occurred in an atmosphere both of moral panic and of a crisis in male identity politics. *Tom Brown* replicates this panic on a miniature scale, and the panic results in the rooting out and stigmatization of homosexual boys. The fear expressed by Harry East that the other boys might nickname Arthur 'Molly' gives a subtle indication that the boys are aware of the existence of queer subcultures.[63] As Norton has explained, 'molly' culture was one

---

60 Chandos 1984, p. 303.
61 Norton 2006, pp. 16–17.
62 Norton 1997, p. 64.
63 Hughes 1989, p. 218.

of the ways in which queer identity was expressed in the eighteenth century in theatrical cross-dressing rituals focused on taverns or coffee houses called 'Molly Houses' which catered for the homosexual community. In 1726, on one of the rare occasions on which English anti-homosexuality laws were implemented,[64] a molly house belonging to a woman known as Mother Clap, was raided and the proprietor and clients prosecuted, resulting in the hanging of three men. The investigation was initiated when rumors spread by a client got out of hand and came to the notice of the police, after which the Societies for the Reformation of Manners became involved as *agents provocateurs*.[65]

The relevance of this story for *Tom Brown* is that, like the schoolboy homosexual, the mollies were inconspicuous until they were disturbed by self-appointed moral reformers. Tom, like the Society for the Reformation of Manners, deliberately calls attention to queer boys in the school by digging one out and beating him publicly, an act Hughes justifies by claiming that a brush with their subculture might contaminate a boy for life ('spoiling' him for 'this world and the next'). *Tom Brown* therefore provides evidence that the later Victorian moral hysteria about schoolboy homosexuality was inseparable from the ideological push to redefine the nature of adolescent citizenship and education. Whether Hughes merely took advantage of a developing vogue for classifying sexuality in terms of 'normal' and 'deviant', or whether the classification process itself was partly spurred on by a more widespread desire to reform male behavior is debatable. Whatever the case, the homosexual boy was a scapegoat who attracted censure away from Hughes's domestic boy. This move, as I will show in Chapter 5, left later generations of queer boys confused and without a tried and tested way of expressing their identity, forced to define themselves according to categories imposed by the establishment rather than through membership of self-defined groups of similar-minded individuals. Thus one boy's freedom to create an identity outside the rigidly structured class and gender systems of the past inevitably resulted in other boys losing this right.[66]

---

64 On the infrequency of prosecutions see Norton 1997, p. 139.

65 See Norton 2006, ch. 3, *passim*.

66 Martin (2002) suggests that Tom and Arthur are engaged in a homosexual relationship in which Arthur plays the role of the Angel in the House and that, through this relationship, Tom learns to transform the love he has felt for his mother into the appropriate husbandly love he will feel for an idealized female Angel when he grows up and joins the adult, heterosexual world. However, this theory is problematized by the fact that, at Oxford, Tom has no idea of how to conduct 'acceptable' relationships with girls and selfishly engages the affections of the barmaid Patty without any thought to propriety or his love-object's feelings, thinking only of his own physical satisfaction. He appears not to have any experience of balancing the *eros* and *agape* elements of love in a stable relationship. I would argue that, rather than the Angel in the House, Arthur resembles the sickly, spiritual child-boy I discuss in Chapter 3, a popular figure in children's literature who combines the moral understanding of a man with the 'innocence' of the child. Tom plays father figure to him, which would explain the 'loving' gestures that Martin detects.

Once Tom has made his relationship with Arthur 'safe' and established his right to redefine masculine identity, the two boys together explore ideas of social organization and social contract in an attempt to replace the old disputational, adversarial system, built on the principle of verbal and physical combat, with one based on empathy and consensus-seeking skills. They tackle these issues during their leisure time, through their seemingly trivial debates and squabbles. At one point, they argue over the use of crib-books (books full of prefabricated Latin phrases which boys could choose and piece together when composing Latin poems). Boys were supposed to create their own Latin poems as an exercise in learning grammar and rhetoric, but using a crib or 'vulgus' was a traditional way of avoiding the chore of being original. In essence, however, this argument is not about the crib-book at all, but about the value of tradition versus originality and individual conscience. It is played out in the language of the High Church/Low Church controversy. Harry East plays the role of conservative High Churchman, while George Arthur presents the 'heretical' idea that each boy should create his own, original verses. East draws a theological parallel by commenting:

> Not use old copy books! Why, you might as well say we ought to pull down Westminster Abbey, and put up a go-to-meeting-shop with churchwarden windows; or never read Shakespere [sic], but only Sheridan Knowles.[67]

What really matters here is neither the Tractarian nor the vulgus debate, but the way in which the argument is conducted. Like Arnold in the real theological debate, Tom adopts a *via media* between the two positions (not using cribs unless all legitimate methods have been tried and have failed). The debate teaches him how to mediate between opposing ideologies and how to reach a compromise which is satisfactory to the individual conscience and sensitive to the school's culture.

For Tom, therefore, leisure-time pursuits no longer revolve around learning how to beat an opponent. The new objective of Tom's play is to develop negotiation and reconciliation skills. Thus, when Tom fights 'Slogger' Williams for having bullied Arthur (a fight terminated by the Doctor), he is glad he has not won; 'he liked it better as it was, and felt very friendly towards the Slogger'.[68] They fight not for domination but to release pent-up aggression ('blood letting'). Even though Hughes comments before the fight that 'Every one who is worth his salt has his enemies, who must be beaten', this beating is not like the one with which Tom and his friends destroy Flashman.[69] Rather, it is a 'moral' beating, following which the victor converts the vanquished to his own way of thinking.

The issue of whether combat and competition were healthy, and whether they were an acceptable part of education and adolescent male identity, seems to have troubled Hughes for most of his career. The combat question was one of the two

---

67 Hughes 1989, p. 327.
68 Ibid., p. 299.
69 Ibid., p. 280.

great 'masculinities' problems (the other being fatherhood), which dominated his books. Fighting men were necessary for upholding the imperial and national status quo and, therefore, an ability to engage in combat had to feature in any definition of the ideal citizen. After all, *Tom Brown* was written in the year of the Indian Mutiny (something of a wake-up call for imperialists), and Harry East goes off to India as a soldier when he leaves Rugby. The problem was how to focus combative energies onto activities that were ideologically acceptable to the domesticated, Evangelical middle classes. In *Tom Brown's Schooldays*, Hughes insists that retaining an element of combativeness in male citizenship is essential to the maintenance of civil society. Fighting is 'the real, highest, honestest business of every son of man', promoting social justice and purging 'spiritual wickedness in high places'.[70] However, some of Hughes's critics, following the anti-combative trend in educational thought I mentioned in Chapter 1, were hostile to any type of pugilism, and Hughes's attempts to soften the fighting ethic in *Tom Brown's Schooldays* did not mollify them. The review of *Tom Brown* in *Tait's Edinburgh Magazine* accused Hughes of overvaluing physical strength, somewhat unfairly placing him in the same category as a father who had fulminated in the *Times* when the Eton–Westminster boat race had been suspended due to one boy's catching cold and dying.[71] This father had said that it was good to weed the sickly out and that sport should not stop just because 'some one's pet lamb has turned sick and been cut off'. *Tait* angrily pointed out that the duty of the good Christian was 'to care for everybody, ESPECIALLY [...] *the weak and sickly*'.[72] The ethic of physical hardening and combat, it said, was an affront to Christianity, law and 'justice' (gendered as 'she'). *Tait* accused Muscular Christians of promoting 'a return to Lynch law' and of advocating the kind of natural selection which upsets the 'harmony of the world'.[73] James Fitzjames Stephen's review of *Tom Brown* was equally critical of Tom's pugilism and held it up as evidence of Hughes's 'Muscular Christianity'.

The phrase 'Muscular Christianity' was used pejoratively here although, as Henry Harrington has pointed out, it was a term that was applied to a number of different philosophies of masculinity, all produced by men who were insecure about their identities.[74] For Hughes, Muscular Christianity had positive connotations and a short digression into his idea of the active Christian citizen will shed light on his attitude to adolescence and its social role. From Hughes's point of view, Muscular Christianity is best understood as an attempt to find a middle way between male combativeness and Evangelical Christian piety. The problem was that combative, Regency-style men had physical prowess but neglected social duties, while dedicated Christians were too passive, lacked physical courage and were therefore socially impotent. Hughes remarked in *The Manliness of Christ* that

---

70 Ibid., p. 282.
71 Muscular Christianity', p. 100.
72 Ibid., p. 100.
73 Ibid., p. 102.
74 Harrington 1984, p. 26.

groups such as the YMCA had failed to attract more active young men because they 'taught, not that they were to live in the world and subdue it to their Master, but were to withdraw from it as much as possible'.[75] Active men, put off by the effeminacy of Christians, went to ruin because they had no satisfactory religious outlet. Hughes, therefore, set out to inject the combativeness and physical vigor of traditional masculinity into Christian social reform, in order to create active Christian citizens.

By the time Hughes wrote *Tom Brown at Oxford* he had taken on board the calls to change his ideas on combat, and was more explicit about his definition of Muscular Christianity. In a chapter entitled 'Muscular Christianity', he commented:

> I know that [Tom], and other youngsters of his kidney, will have fits of fighting, or desiring to fight with their poorer brethren, just as children have the measles. But the shorter the fit, the better the patient [...]. [I]nstead of treating the fit as a disease, "musclemen" professors are wont to represent it as a state of health, and let their disciples run about in middle age with the measles on them as strong as ever.[76]

Hughes here represents the fighting adolescent body not as natural or healthy but as a kind of monstrosity, echoing Arnold's squeamishness about big, uncontrollable boys. The Muscular Christian's body is 'given to him to be trained and brought into subjection, and then used for the protection of the weak, the advancement of all righteous causes, and the subduing of the earth'. However, the fighting man, or 'muscleman', a 'servant' of 'brutal passions' has 'no belief whatever as to the purposes for which his body has been given him', other than for 'belaboring men and captivating women for his benefit or pleasure'.[77] What saves Tom from becoming a muscleman is the St Ambrose Eight. Being a member of this team saves Tom from the unhealthy, self-indulgent lifestyle he temporarily drifts into when he first arrives at university. In fact, the kind of competition promoted in *Tom Brown at Oxford* differs from the *Schooldays*. Instead of celebrating man-to-man fighting or the disorganized version of football played at Rugby, in which individual merit and effort were highly prized, Hughes now advises the young man to sublimate his ego to a common, abstract cause. As Tom's new role model at Oxford, a sailor's son named Hardy, tells him: 'Service! [...] that's what makes every young red-coat respectable'.[78]

Self-interest is alien to Hughes's concept of 'manliness', whether displayed by the soldier, the administrator or the businessman. At Oxford Tom develops an interest in economics that leads him to Bentham, Malthus and Adam Smith

---

75 Hughes 1879, pp. 2–3.
76 Hughes 1897, p. 100.
77 Ibid.
78 Ibid., p. 60.

(grudgingly recommended by his tutor who 'deprecated the waste of time'[79]). He is disgusted by the economists but delighted by Thomas Carlyle; indeed, *Tom Brown at Oxford* is in many ways a rewriting of Carlyle's *Past and Present*. By echoing Carlyle's condemnation of *laissez-faire* and competition while upholding the idea of the hero fighting against abstract moral evil, Hughes manages to retain the ideal of the fighting man without descending to the level of the combative musclemen. Again, there were political reasons for Hughes to condemn competition but not fighting *per se*. Economic competition, the realm of the vulgar *nouveaux riches*, was perceived to be causing havoc in the empire. The Indian Rebellion of 1857 was popularly blamed on *laissez-faire* activities of the East India Company, which was abolished in 1858 for stirring up indigenous resentment.[80] The British needed to find a new justification for remaining in India, and found it in a mission to convert the populace to Christianity and western cultural values. As J.A. Mangan remarks, 'The idea of a messianic mission had become detached from the multiplicity of motives which had brought them to India and had been elevated to the level of an exclusive rationale'.[81] Soldiers and administrators were no longer there to beat the locals into political and economic submission, but to battle with their benighted belief systems. These men needed to be proactive but not competitive, egotistical or aggressive. Hughes contemplated the paradox of the peaceful warrior through the course of his career, and eventually came up with a very peculiar kind of role model for young male citizens – the self-effacing, yet combative, Christ.

The Manliness of Christ (1879) takes the idea of active but disinterested and self-sacrificing citizenship to its extreme. Hughes's Christ is a highly political figure and a reforming outsider ('a stranger from a despised province').[82] In fighting for justice, He retains the combativeness essential to the active male citizen, but, importantly, sacrifices Himself in doing so. However, Christ's identity rests on a very specific idea of 'courage'. Hughes explains that mere courage belongs to the animal kingdom, but that true manly courage requires 'self-sacrifice for the welfare of another' (as displayed by the rescuers at the Pont-y-Pridd mining disaster).[83] In fact, Christ's sacrifice was even more perfect. His final, perfect sacrifice brought him 'humiliation', and loss of dignity. His 'triumph' was, paradoxically, his personal failure, 'to be humbled and slain.'[84] Indeed, Hughes's Christ is practically egoless. He is such a private man that when the Baptist sees Him and proclaims 'This is He! Behold the Lamb of God!' He flees 'into the wilderness'.[85] He doubts His own divinity and seeks John the Baptist in the hope that *he* is the Messiah.[86]

---

79 Ibid., p. 393.
80 See Lawson 1993, pp. 144–68, for an assessment of the rebellion.
81 Mangan 1986, p. 124.
82 Hughes 1879, p. 13.
83 Ibid., pp. 21–23.
84 Ibid., pp. 130, 133.
85 Ibid., pp. 76–77.
86 Ibid., p. 75.

Hughes even diminishes Christ's physical presence, remarking on 'His frail human body' and His deliberate self-starvation.[87] Hughes ends by explaining that the aim of the public schools is to make men like his egoless Christ – 'at once inspiring and pathetic [...] standing apart as they do from, and yet so intimately connected with, the great outside world', but protected from the 'world's slow stain'.[88]

Again, Hughes is pointing to a new idea of civic identity and subjectivity. If the citizen is brought up in seclusion, away from worldly influences, his moral courage may be nurtured without an aggressive, politically ambitious ego developing alongside. In *Tom Brown*, Hughes suggests a scheme by which boys might be educated in the seemingly contradictory qualities that make up the Muscular Christian, in which the school becomes an isolated unit apart from the 'real' world. He shows how a boy might be educated in various political, combative and social ideas without being contaminated by the 'slow stain' of worldliness. The school separates and protects the boy from society and Hughes's training for citizenship means being educated out of the surrounding community, rather than within it. This means that 'Independence' for Tom does not mean what it means for other adolescent protagonists of the period. J.H. Buckley, outlining the typical English *Bildungsroman*, remarks that a key event in many narratives occurs when the protagonist quits 'the repressive atmosphere of home (and also of relative innocence), to make his way independently in the city (in [...] English novels, usually London)'.[89] However, Tom does not venture independently into the outside world and he catches only a brief view of London as he passes through on his way to Rugby (it 'excited him so that he couldn't talk even'[90]). Moreover, Hughes's Rugby, unlike Gladstone's *laissez-faire* Eton, is not a school of hard knocks, despite Hughes's protestations to the contrary. Hughes remarks that bad schools can be places 'where a young boy will get more evil than he would if he were turned out to make his way in London streets'[91] and that at Rugby 'much like the big world, punishments [fell] on wrong shoulders, and matters [went] generally in a queer, cross-grained way'.[92] Paradoxically, though, he also comments that there is 'a special Providence over schoolboys as well as sailors'.[93] This 'Providence' is actually the human hand of the omniscient Doctor Arnold, whose eye is 'everywhere'.[94] As the 'Young Master' explains at the novel's close: 'not one of you boys will ever know the anxiety you have given him, or the care with which he has watched over every step in your school lives'.[95]

---

87 Ibid., pp. 76, 79.
88 Ibid., p. 157.
89 Buckley 1974, p. 17.
90 Hughes 1989, p. 70.
91 Ibid., p. 168.
92 Ibid., p. 101.
93 Ibid., p. 159.
94 Ibid., p. 199.
95 Ibid., p. 365.

Hughes's fictional Arnold creates an environment where boys undergo developmental experiences without any serious physical or moral risk. If Diggs had not saved Tom from being 'roasted' by Flashman, somebody else would have done. Although the boys felt they were alone in their fight against Flashman, Hughes remarks that 'the Doctor [...] had long had his eye on [him]'.[96] Similarly, during Tom's fight with Slogger Williams, Dr Arnold, *deus ex machina*-fashion, watches from a turret and descends to intervene before any real harm is done.[97] He scolds a prefect for allowing the fight to happen, but it is worth remarking that he does not intervene in the affair until Tom has been allowed to make his point. Rugby protects boys from themselves and each other in various ways. They are allowed to borrow, lend, barter and gamble, but all these activities are monitored by a school employee, who keeps accounts. Even their egos are protected. When they try to race with the Rugby stagecoach, the driver slows down because he would 'sooner pull in a bit if he see'd 'em gettin' beat'.[98] In this protectiveness Arnold follows, consciously or not, the teachings of Rousseau, who recommended in *Émile* that teachers should stage-manage their pupils' lives, giving them the impression that they are making decisions for themselves but protecting them against the consequences. 'The disciple', explains Rousseau, 'must do nothing, not even evil, without the knowledge and consent of his master'.[99] However, the fact that privileged boys are protected against their own mistakes lies uneasily with Hughes's social conscience. Rugby boys are immune to legal processes, which erodes their sense of social responsibility. A praepostor (prefect), Holmes, reminds Tom and East that 'There's nothing so mischievous as these school distinctions, which jumble up right and wrong, and justify things in us for which poor boys would be sent to prison'.[100] Boys who break the law are put before the Doctor rather than before a magistrate. When Tom torments a gamekeeper, the Doctor invokes not the laws of trespass, but the school rules, which seem more potent.[101] Although the boys are learning about ideas of freedom and individuality, therefore, they are more immature than their working-class counterparts in terms of understanding the consequences of their actions. It is hard, implies Hughes, to teach young people the principles of responsibility, while providing them with a suitable level of protection from moral contamination.

Despite these problems, a properly managed school, to Hughes, is an arena where juveniles can learn how to tackle real-life situations in comparative safety. Literature and play were also, of course, means by which children could learn about the world without suffering the bad effects brought on by actual experience. As Samuel Pickering has argued, the use of imaginative 'play' in *Tom Brown*

---

96 Ibid., p. 194
97 Ibid., p. 297.
98 Ibid., p. 87.
99 Rousseau 1993, p. 358.
100 Hughes 1989, p. 279.
101 Ibid., p. 207.

(specifically sport) parallels the use of imaginative literature in various examples of the English *Bildungsroman*:

> Jane Eyre [...] spent much time at the Reeds' house poring over imaginative literature. Books like the *Arabian Nights* [...] appealed to her imagination and in the process so expanded it that they became dragon-slayers [...] As Jane's reading enabled her to recognize John Reed as Caligula [...] so Tom's [...] experiences in games like football helped him overcome Flashman.[102]

On a literary level, *Tom Brown* is itself a kind of training-manual for adolescent life. Maria Edgeworth had advocated fifty years before in *Practical Education* that books could be used as a substitute for the society of real children to avoid the threat of moral contamination.[103] She also recommended that public school stories be used to prepare boys to survive in the school environment and to teach them how to retain their moral principles.[104] Thomas Hughes, writing *Tom Brown's Schooldays* for his son, had the same motive. Hughes's schoolboy reader, therefore, enters the 'real world' at two removes, firstly learning about school life vicariously through a book and then learning about the outside world through school activities which involve enacting situations at school that harmlessly mirror much graver scenarios played out in the wider world. Tom himself approaches the world through a dialogic engagement with literature. During his childhood and schooldays, he absorbs a large number of oral, vernacular, classical and European stories, starting by hearing tales of the Browns from Benjy[105] and graduating in early adolescence to reading Marryat, Dickens, Scott and *Don Quixote*. Finally, as he deepens his relationship with Arthur in his later teens, he encounters Homer, Aristophanes and the Bible, which he learns to appreciate both as literature and as social and political discourse. Hughes remarks at one point on how 'Arthur began talking about Joseph [...] just as he might have talked about Lord Grey and the Reform Bill'.[106] Hughes also makes reference during the narrative to a huge number of literary texts ranging from Asser's *Life of King Alfred* through popular ballads, Milton, Shakespeare, *The Swiss Family Robinson* and Charles Kingsley to Herodotus and Virgil. He presents Tom's own narrative as just one strain in a panoply of British and European narratives which contribute to the character he forms for himself as he tests out the roles of revolutionary, father-figure, and statesman. A good deal of Tom's sense of self is created through his reading and Hughes's narrative in turn will help other boys to find their own sense of identity, while opening up new literary avenues to them.

---

102 Pickering, 1993, p. 41.
103 Edgeworth 1801, vol. II, p. 93.
104 Ibid., p. 96.
105 Hughes 1989, p. 26.
106 Ibid., p. 242.

Tom's role-play activities – acted out in this seemingly 'safe' environment of school in response to his reading – are central to his education. The historical Thomas Arnold recognized the connection between formal education and leisure time and encouraged social development by placing pupils in role-playing situations, most notably in the monitor or 'fagging' system, where older pupils took 'statesman'-like positions and held authority over younger boys. Arnold commented famously that school represented a 'little world': an environment where boys could practice adult roles.[107] What emerges in *Tom Brown*, particularly in Tom's imaginatively-fired revolutionary activities, is a kind of ultra-serious 'play' that teaches the values of citizenship. In understanding Hughes's attitude to leisure and play, historical factors need to be taken into account. According to David Cohen, until the time of Rousseau, play was something which children did but which nobody thought worth writing about.[108] Locke thought that the only reason children 'abandon themselves wholly to silly play' was 'because they had found their curiosity balked and their enquiries neglected'.[109] To Rousseau, play offered, in contrast, beneficial exercise, an education in sensibility and a means of making learning more palatable and effective. Enjoyment also made it an end in itself. Nonetheless, Rousseau's idea of play differs dramatically from our own, and works of juvenile literature by authors inspired by him (for example, Day or Edgeworth) give little time to imaginative, role-playing or character-developing activities.

Progressive educationalists faced a huge problem in justifying creative leisure time activity to an industrial society that lay such an emphasis on work. Cohen argues that Rousseau 'failed to convince Victorian capitalists' into wholeheartedly adopting his ideas of play. He remarks that 'as Victorian industry developed it was necessary for it to create a division of work (the normal activity) versus leisure or free time (the abnormal activity).[110] As work became formalized, so did play. Children, freed from factories, were officially granted leisure time. As Cohen remarks:

> If they used some of that freedom to play, then play had to have some purpose. This is perhaps most obvious when one considers the growth of leisure activities in Victorian England. If people had free time, they were meant to use it to improve themselves.[111]

If play for children had to be justified by its utility, the argument that adolescents should also play (other than through sporting activities) was, and still is, an even more difficult issue. Cohen remarks that, to the present day, research on play 'peters out round when children are eleven or twelve' and he asks 'do teenagers

---

107 Robison 1983, 325.
108 Cohen 1987, p. 22.
109 Letter 829, ibid., p. 22.
110 Ibid., pp. 25–26.
111 Ibid., pp. 26–27.

never play?'[112] Specifically for Hughes, the business of justifying leisure time as an arena for imaginatively developing adolescent character is important. As I remarked in Chapter 1, there were some commentators who were attacking the public school practice of giving boys plentiful leisure time. On top of this, the increasing unfashionability of imaginary and theatrical character-development activities for schoolboys must have led, as I suggest in the next chapter, to a feeling that creative, personality-building outlets were decreasing. In acting out the roles of revolutionary, statesman and father, Tom is undeniably 'playing' at *being somebody* in an imaginative way, although obviously not in as clearly identified an imaginative context as that used by later writers such as E. Nesbit or Arthur Ransome. Hughes is obviously, however, uneasy about Tom's leisure time and freedom, because it is the word 'work' rather than the word 'play' that most dominates this text.

'Work' is something of a buzzword in *Tom Brown's Schooldays*. When he is sick, George Arthur has a dream that presents a mystified idea of work and heroism similar to that described by Carlyle in *Past and Present*. In the dream, he sees a river, on one side of which the dead are working and on the other side of which the living are working:

> They worked at some great work [...] and each worked in a different way, but all at the same work. And I saw there my father, and the men in the old town whom I knew when I was a child; [...]. And I longed to see what the work was, and could not; [...Then] I saw myriads on this side, and they too worked, and I knew that it was the same work [...] And as I looked I saw my mother and my sisters, and I saw the Doctor, and you, Tom, and hundreds more whom I knew; and at last I saw myself too.[113]

The most important thing about this definition of work is its breadth; it is not limited to what is economically productive. In this conceptualization of work, Hughes echoes Thomas Carlyle's *Past and Present* (1843). Carlyle, as Herbert Sussman and David Rosen have pointed out, struggled to assert the importance of literary and intellectual pursuits previously associated with the leisured classes, arguing they were as socially valuable as the activities of industrialists.[114] His famous description of a multitude of ideal citizens working against 'Necessity, [...] Barrenness, Scarcity, [...] Puddles, Bogs, tangled Forests [and] the hallucinations of [their] poor fellow men'[115] is clearly echoed in Arthur's dream. Hughes's mystification of work broadens the definition to include activities at school that could also be deemed, from a Utilitarian standpoint, to be the unproductive privilege of the leisured elite. His defense of extra-curricular activities was timely, since the Education Department at Whitehall and the Science and Art Department

---

112 Ibid., p. 11.
113 Hughes 1989, p. 319.
114 See in particular Sussman 1995.
115 Carlyle 1843, p. 256.

at South Kensington had been established with a view to increasing the general efficiency of British education in the year before *Tom Brown* was published.[116]

By categorizing Tom's leisure-time activities at Rugby as 'work', Hughes justifies giving adolescents the kind of leisure time they needed to develop civic character through role-play. Arnold's monitor system itself blurred the boundaries between work, leisure and education. The basic idea of the monitor system was partly derived from the Lancasterian system, an educational technique founded on the idea of the factory and the principle that the 'division of labor' could be used in the schoolroom.[117] In this system, the teacher gave personal instruction to older pupils, who then passed it on to the rest, enabling large numbers to be taught by comparatively few professional teachers. Fagging brought Lancasterianism into boys' extra-curricular activities. In what had previously been unstructured leisure time, younger boys were doing manual tasks, while older boys, who enjoyed more contact with Arnold himself, were taking managerial roles. In Hughes's fictionalization of Arnold's system, therefore, the line between work and play is thin, even more so because the roles of boys in school are, to a certain extent, negotiable and are explored through play and experimentation.

The other important thing about Tom's work and play is that it teaches him not to seek profit from his activities. Hughes seems to be arguing that although the boys are not learning to produce anything, at least they are learning how to contribute to society without taking from it. The issue of self-interest is an aspect of Hughes's writing that is taken up by many subsequent writers, whose characters are almost never destined to become a financial success. Whenever writers allude to their protagonists' future careers, these careers tend to be in the promotion of social justice, as philanthropists, high-minded politicians and barristers, soldiers and so on, but without significant pecuniary reward. When Tom first arrives at Rugby, his attention is centered on material and physical pleasures, food and money. By the end of the novel, however, his values have changed. The Young Master tells him that 'working to get your living' is not as important as scholarship or less materially profitable enterprises.[118] When he leaves Oxford, Tom is sufficiently lacking in material prospects to be viewed as a bad marriage match, because he has decided to devote himself to philanthropy and education.[119]

Hughes grooms the upper-class adolescent to stand outside the economic and industrial machine. Tom is a member of a Coleridgean 'clerisy', destined to teach and aestheticize the nation, fighting what Hughes deems the most pernicious effects of industrial capitalism, utilitarianism and *laissez-faire* economics.[120] He is a statesman who is no longer concerned with performing rhetorical gymnastics in

---

116 Armytage 1865, p. 119.
117 Ibid., p. 90.
118 Hughes 1989, p. 363.
119 Hughes himself supported the Amalgamated Society of Engineers and a proposed the founding of a cooperative ironworks (Mack 1941, p. 66).
120 Armytage 1865, p. 96.

the Houses of Parliament while subduing the earth and the peasants in his country estate, but who sacrifices material interests in the active pursuit of social justice. *Tom Brown* therefore presents a complicated idea of what the emergent citizen should be. Adolescent life is a metaphor for social change in both the *Tom Brown* books and, through Tom's search for identity during the growing-up process, Hughes debates what kind of behavior is appropriate for male civic subjects in a changing society. He was deeply conscious of the fact that society needed a new formulation of elite adolescence which was more acceptable to people who had been brought up outside the aggressively masculine, combative environment of the public school. He therefore attempted to integrate the ideas of reformers with more traditional perspectives on male adolescence and, in particular, he fought against the public schools' traditional anti-domestic ethos by promoting fatherhood as the basis of good citizenship. In making citizenship more 'fatherly', he produced a new idea of the stages an adolescent passed through on his way to maturity, in which traditional, combative masculinity was merely one early step. He also promoted an ideal of education in which adolescents were given much more protection than in traditional public schools. However, Hughes also defended aspects of public school tradition that were under attack from those who were concerned with maximizing national economic efficiency. In particular, he demonstrated how it was beneficial for adolescents to have unsupervised free time.

Hughes's overwhelmingly optimistic vision for education, in which boy and nation develop together, relies heavily on his belief in the possibility of individual and social progress. In *Tom Brown*, the ultimate goal of progress, social justice, is in sight. Not everyone, however, was so sure that such progress was possible, in particular the next author to be discussed, F.W. Farrar, whose conflicting Christian and Darwinist beliefs led him to create a completely different picture of adolescent life.

Chapter 3

'Beastly Erikin':
Nature, God and the Adolescent Boy

Eric: Or, Little By Little (1858) by F.W. Farrar (1831–1903) is usually written off as artistically and pedagogically worthless, a position summarized by Hugh Kingsmill's remark that it was 'the sort of story Dr Arnold would have written if he'd taken to drink'.[1] Farrar's other fictional works for young readers, such as *St Winifred's: Or, the World of School* (1862) and *Julian Home: A Tale of College Life* (1859), rarely attract any critical attention whatsoever. However, even though the twentieth century seems to have appreciated Farrar only in his capacity to be lampooned, this does not reduce his social and pedagogical significance, or negate the fact that many earlier readers found his writing compelling. As editor of *Essays on a Liberal Education* (1867), a response to the Taunton Commission's report on endowed grammar schools, Farrar worked alongside leading thinkers in the movement for liberal education such as Henry Sidgwick and Edward Bowen.[2] At the same time, his fictional work proved highly marketable. When *Eric* was first published, reviews were, as Eric Anstruther points out, on the whole positive, with the exception of *The Saturday Review* which objected to its 'lacrimosity'.[3] When the book's fifth edition appeared *The Quarterly Review* and *Blackwood's* criticized its lack of realism and excessive tragedy,[4] but this did not stop it from going through more than thirty reprintings between 1858 and 1902. My own copy of *Eric* has 'Pat. From Ethel. Xmas 1928' scrawled in childish pencil on the flyleaf, which shows that children were still giving it to each other seventy years after its first publication. During the nineteenth century, Farrar was, seemingly, appreciated by teenagers from widely differing backgrounds. One recent graduate from Shrewsbury wrote to Farrar that 'it was through reading "Eric" that I first learned to hate sin, and ever since that time, about four years ago, I have tried to

---

1 Richards 1988, p. 70.
2 Curtis and Boultwood 1966, pp. 440–45, gives a usefully contextualized summary of this work. A staple at teacher training colleges during the 1950s and 1960s, Curtis and Boultwood's work still provides a very lucid account of Victorian educational issues, providing information on thinkers, like Farrar, who have since all but disappeared from mainstream educational debate.
3 6 November 1858, cited in Anstruther 2002, pp. 54–55.
4 Anstruther 2002, p. 57.

live a pure, brave, and true life at school'.[5] Farrar's biography also reproduces a letter from the curate of Hunslet (at that time a deprived area of Leeds), who remarked that 'both among the very poor of London, and among the better sort of working folk here, boys have always been enthusiastic in praise of "Eric" and "St Winifred's"'. In no way was this letter an attempt at flattery or false praise. The curate admitted that the enthusiasm for *Eric* had 'surprised' him, since he had worried that 'the clothing of the stories would make them somewhat difficult for the less educated' (a tactful way of saying he thought the Evangelical rhetoric would be alienating).[6] The biography cites a number of similar letters.

Young people must, then, have found something attractive in Farrar's books and, despite an emphasis on overwhelmingly passive forms of adolescent citizenship (which I will discuss later), there are aspects of his work that may have made it more liberating to non-public-school boys than *Tom Brown's Schooldays* was. Farrar's books are far less class-conscious than Hughes's. He does not assume that his readers are either male or public school educated and, although the protagonists' parents are middle class, they are not from the gentry. While *Eric* contains its share of unpleasant working-class characters (mainly sailors and publicans), it lacks the 'school versus town' ethos of *Tom Brown* that brands non-public school boys as 'cads'. It also features less privileged boys, such as Eric's friend, Russell. Maybe this lack of patrician bias made Farrar's work appealing, and perhaps empowering, not only to children but also to less well-off parents, teachers and Sunday school teachers who might have bought it as a gift or as a prize.

Eric is also highly melodramatic, which may have been one source of its popularity among readers brought up on penny gaffs and penny dreadfuls, but a factor which lost it favor among the critical elite. The *Quarterly Review* condemned Farrar's lack of positive news for educationalists and complained the narrative was too full of 'exaggerations',[7] particularly as regarded the boys' religious attitudes. However, as P.G. Scott and R.J. Kirkpatrick have shown,[8] the seemingly most far-fetched episodes in Farrar's work were based on real events at King William's College (Isle of Man), where Farrar had been a pupil, at Harrow, where he taught, and at Marlborough, where he was Head. For instance, like Eric's brother Vernon, one of Farrar's schoolmates was killed while bird's nesting on the cliffs.[9] Moreover, Farrar's depiction of schoolboy religious fervor does not necessarily denote a lack of understanding of the way boys spoke or behaved. According to Cynthia Buffington Davis, even boys as robust as Thomas Hughes and his brother used the same kind of language in their letters as Farrar's characters use in *Eric*: 'inquir[ing] about each other's growth in virtue in the same unselfconscious way

---

5   Farrar 1904, p. 80.
6   Ibid., pp. 79–80.
7   Musgrave 1985, p. 77.
8   Kirkpatrick 2000, pp. 118–20.
9   Scott 1971, p. 167.

they ask[ed] about progress in Greek or football'.[10] It is possible, therefore, that Farrar was popular simply because he did not belittle the emotional highs and lows of adolescence. As an obituary said, 'He wrote of the deeper emotions of boy life and touched its inner chord in a way which [...] no writer has ever equaled'.[11]

Later, I will demonstrate how Farrar's Evangelical rhetoric is actually a fig leaf that disguises profound philosophical and scientific doubts not only about adolescence, but about the very nature of education and social progress. Beneath its prim façade, *Eric* reveals a problematic and pessimistic concept of youth that had almost apocalyptic implications for subsequent writers on adolescence and which had grave consequences for the whole idea of civic education. In this sense, Farrar was much more influential on later writers than Hughes was. Thus, the warnings presented in *Eric* are echoed not only by his admirers, but also in the works of his detractors (for example, Rudyard Kipling), as well as in more chilling twentieth-century depictions of juvenile behavior such as William Golding's *Lord of the Flies* or Anthony Burgess's *A Clockwork Orange*, which describe youth at odds with civilized values and social order. This legacy might have shocked Farrar had he known of it, since his second school story, *St Winifred's*, suggests constructive answers to many of the problems posed in *Eric* and foreshadows the 'progressive' work of some of the early-twentieth-century authors discussed in the final chapter of this book.

In order to present as wide a perspective on Farrar's view of adolescence as possible, I will here first discuss *Eric* and then move on to *St Winifred's*, with reference to three of Farrar's other books, *Essays on a Liberal Education*, which he edited in 1867, *Social and Present Day Questions* (1891) and *The Young Man Master of Himself* (1896), an advice book based on lectures given to Marlborough boys between 1871 and 1876. I will first suggest why Farrar betrays his credentials as a liberal educationalist in *Eric* and why he presents a negative image of adolescence. I will then show how *St Winifred's* attempts to deal with the paradoxes Farrar finds in the idea of adolescence and demonstrate how he promotes the teaching of emotional literacy in order to encourage a much more passive mode of citizenship than that advocated by Thomas Hughes.

Eric: Or, Little by Little is the story of a naïve, innocent teenager who battles against the temptations of school only to be overcome by his own weakness and by the temptations put before him by older boys. At the end of the book, entangled in a mesh of misunderstanding and deception, and with the whole school mistakenly convinced that he is a thief, he runs away to sea where he suffers such terrible abuse that he dies when he finally manages to get home. *Eric* is a narrative torn between Wordsworthian Romanticism, Evangelicalism and evolutionary realism. The idea of nature and God as forces that govern individual development, personality and society, is a prominent theme for Farrar, but one with no overall coherence, since his conception of nature embraces the mutually incompatible ideas of

---

10 Davis 1981, p. 165.
11 Farrar 1904, p. 81.

Romanticism and Darwinism and his understanding of God, also partly Romantic, is tainted by an almost Calvinistic Evangelicalism. Before he starts school, Eric is a Wordsworthian child. His early upbringing, neither Evangelical nor sectarian, is based on the idea that children left to themselves in a countryside environment develop an innate sense of morality and piety. Eric's guardian, Aunt Trevor, rejects all 'theories of education', and relies on 'wholesome neglect'.[12] 'Nature', comments Farrar, the 'wisest, gentlest, holiest of teachers – was with [Eric] in his childhood'.[13] However, in sending Eric to the local Latin School where there is a 'mixture [...] of all classes', the family goes considerably further than the Browns in eradicating class sensitivities. Eric learns 'practically to despise the accidental and nominal differences which separate man from man'.[14] Farrar, much more so than Hughes, advocates a politically liberal, democratic infant education. Like Hughes, however, he worries about the egotism fostered by such an upbringing. Eric, before he goes to school, is an 'imperious', 'fearless and self-dependent' child, rapidly outgrowing the capacity of his female relatives to guide him.[15]

Eric's school environment is also Romantic, but owes more to Gothic horror than to the pastoral. Farrar, making plentiful use of pathetic fallacy, describes the environment in terms of the sublime:

> On either side of the bay was a bold headland [...] stretching out in a series of broken crags [...]. To the right lay the town, with its gray old castle, and the mountain stream running through it into the sea; to the left, high above the beach, rose the crumbling fragment of a picturesque fort, behind which towered the lofty buildings of Roslyn School.[16]

When Eric goes to Roslyn, his Wordsworthian childhood gives way to an adolescence ruled by brutal Darwinist principles. Farrar describes the bullying that pervades the school as 'a pseudo-instinctive cruelty, a sort of "wild trick of the ancestral savage"'.[17] The average adolescent boy is no Wordsworthian visionary but, like Arnold's ignoble savage, recapitulates an earlier stage of human development. He does not consciously develop a moral character and social role, like Tom Brown, but passively follows his biological destiny. Adolescence, implies Farrar, is the place where a man's evolutionary battle begins. It is also, bluntly, the place where those who are not fit to become adults die. Evolution works in a perverse way in *Eric*, since the physically strong 'villains' outlast the more intellectual and spiritual heroes. Bullying is part of a struggle in which boys are 'tested and weighed', the means by which the school community 'settle[s] the

---

12 Farrar 1899, p. 7. This is a reprint of the original 1858 edition. The edition in its 1902 manifestation has been re-issued with a study of Farrar's life and work by Ian Anstruther.
13 Ibid., p. 6.
14 Ibid., p. 8.
15 Ibid., p. 6.
16 Ibid., p. 10.
17 Ibid., p. 14.

category under which the boy is to be classed'. Farrar, as the good Evangelical narrator, tries to argue that well-brought-up children have an advantage in the struggle to achieve adulthood and claims that the small but significant details of a boy's 'character and training' determine a boy's success in this 'trying ordeal' and decide what kind of a man he will become.[18] However, the plot of *Eric* undermines the narrator's promises. Those who, like Eric, his brother Vernon and their friend Russell, have been brought up with a keen moral and aesthetic sensibility, are the first to die. Only two consistently 'good' boys survive in *Eric*, the emotionally uncomplicated Owen (who 'took everything without tears and without passion') and Montagu, a reliable and 'jolly little fellow', who is neither academically nor socially outstanding.[19] These boys study hard but lack the kind of intellect Eric and Russell possess.

Prefiguring not only the school stories of H.O. Sturgis and James Welldon but also adult works such as Hardy's *Jude the Obscure*, Farrar presents a pessimistic view of evolutionary change, suggesting that individuals who possess a low degree of intelligence and sensitivity have an evolutionary advantage. In spite of the narrator's Evangelical protestations, the religious torment that characterizes Eric's moral development is of less long-term benefit to the individual than conforming to the general crowd would be. The characters who spend their schooldays drinking, smoking and 'taking up' with other boys become successful citizens; indeed, their future careers differ little from those of Thomas Hughes's disinterested manly Christians. Upton and Wildney, both of whom are responsible for corrupting Eric, become soldiers and Graham, who forces Eric to cheat in class, becomes a barrister. Even the bully Brigson becomes a corrupt, but not necessarily wicked, policeman. None are physically stained, as Farrar earlier warns they will be, by indulging in youthful vice; indeed, 'there are not two finer or manlier officers in the whole service' than Upton and Wildney.[20] Notwithstanding, the narrator presses on, constantly reminding the reader of the ugliness of sin and the beauty of a tortured conscience.

Thus the text of Eric is torn between an Evangelical narrator desperate to promote an ascetic Christian morality to the young and the narrative itself, which gives exactly the opposite message. This paradoxical structure embodies Farrar's dilemma as an Evangelical divine whose intellectual interests led him to engage with contemporary scientific advances. Farrar was a close associate of Darwin and T.H. Huxley and was proposed as an FRS by Darwin for 'applying the evolutionary principle to comparative philology'.[21] Although he had some doubts about evolution, Farrar was no creationist and even taught classical grammar using his Darwinian

---

18 Ibid.
19 Ibid., p. 15.
20 Ibid., p. 130.
21 Scott 1971, p. 164. Farrar not only preached the sermon at Darwin's funeral, but requested that he be interred in Westminster Abbey, something which Darwin's friend T.H. Huxley dared not do. See Farrar 1904, p. 109.

philology.[22] He also, arguably, applied evolutionary ideas to pedagogy, a position which compromised his stance on liberal education and which made *Eric* much more pessimistic about the possibilities for adolescence than *Tom Brown*. Tom Brown's career is one of consistent, linear growth. Even his bad deeds and rebellions are learning experiences which help him to progress. Hughes frames adolescent development within a liberal political narrative, emphasizing self-determination, self-representation and self-improvement, where boys are free to make mistakes and learn from them and where the individual has power to change himself. In *Eric*, which embeds adolescence within a narrative of evolutionary change, development is beyond individual control and mistakes are evidence of character flaws which either deepen and destroy the individual, or which naturally disappear with maturity. Tom's evolution is almost Lamarckian; he adapts to changes in his environment as they occur and solves the problems these changes create. Eric cannot significantly change his own psychological make-up, until, at the end of the book, he regresses into his original state of childlike spirituality. There is a further irony to this in that, despite Farrar's liberal Christian assertion that good works are the key to salvation, nature appears to be as indifferent to individual effort as the Calvinist God.

The boys in Farrar's text, like the author himself, are constantly seeking to understand both nature and God. Their interest in natural history, like Farrar's interest in Darwinism, gives them an arena for discussing these topics. Indeed, natural history was a subject promoted by *Essays on a Liberal Education* and it is a *leitmotif* in *Eric* as much as politics is in *Tom Brown*. Farrar was not the only boys' writer to take this approach. In the same year as *Eric* appeared, R.M. Ballantyne used natural history for pedagogical ends when he published *The Coral Island*, in which three shipwrecked boys demonstrate how, even in the absence of adults, boys can uphold 'civilized' moral values and promote the British Imperial status quo. When they find themselves stranded on an uninhabited island, Ballantyne's boys establish a cooperative, family-like social structure, according to the values they have learned as children. Independent life there gives them the leisure to acquaint themselves with God through Nature and to fulfill the worthy civic role of spreading the values they see reflected in Nature to the 'savage' tribes on neighboring islands, just as Rugby gave boys free space to acquaint themselves with political ideas and to develop as active citizens. Ballantyne's boys are particularly observant of evidence of God as creator that can be seen in the island's wildlife, especially among the seashore creatures they keep in a tank. The narrator, Ralph Rover, comments: 'My heart was filled with more delight than I can express at the sight of so many glorious objects, and my thoughts turned suddenly to the contemplation of the Creator of them all'.[23] Ballantyne follows the example set by Philip Gosse in works such as *The Aquarium* (1854), by showing how nature study can reveal proof of the benign creating hand of God.[24] At the time Ballantyne and

---

22 Farrar 1904, pp. 108, 97.
23 Ballantyne 1993, p. 20.
24 For more on Gosse see Smith 2001, pp. 251–62.

Farrar were writing, natural history was important because it was considered to be a legitimate, morally-sound leisure-time pursuit for middle-class males and a good alternative to the rakish activities Hughes cautioned against in *Tom Brown*. Francis O'Gorman has remarked on how, in *Glaucus: Or, the Wonders of the Shore* (1855), Charles Kingsley promotes natural history as an activity which not only requires a suitable amount of strenuous, masculine labor, but which contributes to the general good through scientific discovery and which 'presents nature as teaching human beings about God's creative power, as revealing God's bounty and invention'.[25] Ballantyne's narrative builds on Gosse and Kingsley's pedagogy of natural history when he shows how scientific observation not only teaches boys about God, but also confirms the moral superiority of British male citizens over the rest of life on earth.

In theory, Farrar's boys, as well-brought up Christians left largely to their own devices on an island teeming with marine wildlife, should have plentiful leisure time to absorb the lessons of God in nature. Being so isolated, Roslyn is also the kind of community where, according to commentators on the public schools, boyhood should reveal itself at its most 'natural', and no doubt were this Ballantyne's narrative the school would bring out the boys' natural proclivities as imperial organizers.[26] Nature study has a different role to play in *Eric*. Because Roslyn has little organized sport, Eric and his friends spend their free time on the shore, which is also the place where Eric bonds with his younger brother and parents in the short time they spend as a family in England. These seaside capers initially promise Ballantyne-like possibilities for the boys. However, in this text, the seashore is of interest only to children; it leaves the adolescent unsatisfied. Eric's transition to adolescence is signaled in an episode where, preoccupied with cricket and with his 'spirit of false independence awake and growing', he refuses to take an interest in some sea anemones his brother has collected.[27] Instead, his more innocent friend, Russell (an idealized moralist), is left to talk to the younger boy about the creatures.[28] From now on, not content to dabble on the shore, Eric seeks stronger stimulation and excitement in the island's more dangerous wild places. In pursuing his taste for such places, however, Eric finds a much grimmer side to God and nature than the one revealed by Ballantyne. In the middle of the narrative, Eric, Russell and Montagu climb 'The Stack', a sublime rocky outcrop: 'one of the extremities of Ellan bay [...] a huge mass of isolated schist'.[29] Initially, this seems like a harmless ramble – a welcome break organized by Russell and Montagu to get Eric away from the nefarious company of an older boy, Upton. On this outing, Russell, like Ballantyne, Gosse and Kingsley, searches for God in the

---

25 O'Gorman 2000, p. 154.
26 I referred in the introduction to the Victorian belief that the public schools were the best places to observe boyhood behaviour at its most authentic.
27 Farrar 1899, p. 27.
28 Ibid., p. 26.
29 Ibid., p. 54

landscape, while watching the sun set. He recalls that a master, Mr Rose, had once compared such a sunset to the 'thought of death, judgement, and eternity, all in one!' The boys pause to ponder on the theological significance of this statement, but are so transported that they fail to notice that the tide has come in and stranded them. When they attempt to jump across to the mainland, Russell, not as agile as Eric and Montague, slips and falls in the sea. Eric, 'a strong and expert swimmer',[30] rescues him, but Russell has serious injuries to his leg and head and later dies.

Eric, Russell and Montague here seek, and fail to find, the kind of positive religious epiphany enjoyed by their predecessors on the Coral Island and which Romantic tradition had promoted as the privilege of youth. Jerome Buckley has explained how, in Romantic texts, 'flashes of sudden insight' (like Wordsworthian 'spots of time') signal a moment in a young person's life 'when the soul, "lost" to immediate selfish concern, catches a brief intimation of some ultimate pattern'.[31] However, although Eric and his friends stand surrounded by sublime nature, waiting for spiritual enlightenment, all they come up with are the half-digested ideas of death and judgment they have absorbed from a well-meaning but largely impotent Evangelical teacher. Indeed, Russell's death eventually brings about a negative epiphany for Eric. After the trauma, he has nightmares of apocalyptic revelation:

> He was wandering down a path, at the end of which Russell stood with beckoning hand inviting him earnestly to join him there; [...] and he hastened to meet him, when suddenly the boy-figure disappeared, and in its place he saw the stern brow, and gleaming garments, and drawn flaming sword of the Avenger. And then he was in a great wood alone, and wandering, when the well-known voice called his name, and entreated him to turn from that evil place; and he longed to turn, – but, whenever he tried, ghostly hands seemed to wave him back again, and irresistible cords to drag him into the dark forest.

Although the narrator claims that 'like all affliction' this vision 'purified and sanctified' Eric, the apocalyptic revelation still offers no further insight in the boys' quest for spiritual knowledge.[32] Indeed, the whole nightmare nature ramble serves not to uncover God's benign handiwork, but to reveal a deeper chaos. Both in this work and *St Winifred's*, nature harbors malignant spirits which, like those in Byron's *Manfred*, spurn the boys' Promethean quest for knowledge and power. Farrar denies Ballantyne's claim that adolescents have a privileged relationship with either God or nature. A questioning imagination and a spirit of adventure, which Ballantyne rewards as 'plucky' and developmentally important, are nothing more than a dangerous failure to concentrate on the prosaic business of staying alive.

Indeed, the adolescent impulse to explore boundaries and go to extremes is punished more than once in this narrative and Farrar advises boys to stay safe

---

30 Ibid., p. 56.
31 Buckley 1974, p. 4.
32 Farrar 1899, p. 64.

by attempting to preserve the innocent conservatism of childhood. 'Extreme' nature study is also fatal to Eric's brother, Vernon, who graduates (like Eric) from playing in rock pools to climbing unexplored cliff-faces, after going through a series of mishaps and moral failings at school. Vernon goes climbing 'beyond bounds', to collect eggs. His friend urges him to come off the dangerous cliffs, but he declares 'I feel as cool as possible. We mustn't give up'.[33] When Vernon falls and is smashed on the rocks below, Farrar presents a perversely aesthetic, lyrical description of his body as passive, beautiful and childlike. The anthropomorphized waves, innocently unknowing, seem to welcome his dead body:

> [The tide] crept up to the place where Vernon lay; and the little ripples fell over him wonderingly, with the low murmur of their musical laughter, and blurred and dimmed the vivid splashes and crimson streaks upon the white stone on which his head had fallen, and washed away some of the purple bells and green sprigs of heather round which his fingers were closed in the grasp of death, and played softly with his fair hair as it rose, and fell, and floated on their undulations like a leaf of golden-colored weed, until they themselves were faintly discolored by his blood.[34]

In both of Vernon's and Russell's accidents, the risk-taking, stimulation-seeking adolescent is bodily smashed up and, in the process, infantilized. Russell, dying slowly and suffering from brain damage, regains his childish innocence ('the blow on the head would certainly affect the brain and the intellect if he lived'). When this happens, he achieves a preternatural spirituality and, during this gradual mental decay, he discourses on Christian morality and makes the other boys 'promise to avoid all evil, and read the Bible, and pray to God'.[35] Indeed, his spiritual authority increases as he regresses and, in spite of his age (fifteen), his voice becomes 'childlike'.[36] Nature here seems to be beating the adolescent into an infantile submission, rather than offering him power and knowledge.

It is hard to deduce a consistent pedagogical or theological principle from these deaths. God has forsaken even the most serious-minded of adolescents, only deigning to appear to them when they are so physically and mentally damaged that they become as feeble as children. Farrar's religious conception of juvenile development is perversely illogical. In childhood, God and nature operate together as benign forces. In adolescence, however, nature begins to assert itself within the adolescent as savagery and the loving God becomes vengeful. Despite Farrar's assurance that God will comfort boys in distress, He fails conspicuously to aid the boys in times of crisis and when He does appear, in dreams, He merely threatens and torments. Indeed, He is rather like Roslyn's headmaster, Dr Rowlands, a male authority figure who does not want close relationships with adolescent boys but

---

33 Ibid., p. 108.
34 Ibid., p. 109.
35 Ibid., p. 63.
36 Ibid., pp. 66, 63.

who blunders into their games at infelicitous moments and wreaks punishment on those who least deserve it. This is not the God Eric's mother is thinking about when she counsels the orphaned Russell to look to 'the Father of the fatherless'.[37] God appears to the adolescent not in the image of the paternal Thomas Arnold, but as Eton's psychopathically sadistic John Keate.

Eric, of course, fails to make it into adulthood and ends up dying in a childlike state of dependency at his aunt's house, where the story began. Some previous narratives of adolescence, such as those of Martineau and William Adams, had, as I have shown, also responded to the problems of growing up by infantilizing their characters. Martineau and Adams's schoolboys, like Eric, fall both spiritually and physically, sustaining injuries and, during their recovery, stepping back away from adolescence. Like *The Crofton Boys* and *The Cherry Stones*, therefore, *Eric* is ultimately a non-heroic anti-adventure story, in which the most desirable outcome for the protagonist is to return to the lost Eden of childhood. In his sermons as Head at Marlborough, Farrar advised his students to seek this kind of Eden, which he described thus:

> Each of us at birth is placed in a garden of Eden; for each of us there grows in that garden a Tree of Life, and a Tree of the Knowledge of good and evil; it is possible for each of us even to the last to walk that garden with peaceful feet unterrified by the flaming sword. We cannot indeed do this – since we are very frail – by being absolutely sinless, as are the angels in heaven, but we can do it by living, through God's grace, free from willful, free from presumptuous, free from habitual, free from deadly sins.[38]

The problem in *Eric* is that for a questing, active boy to achieve this Eden, he must be so physically damaged that he will eventually die.

Farrar's book, of course, was not unique in depicting sick or dying teenage boys lapsing into childlike dependency and turning into religious *idiot savants*. According to Nelson, *Eric* is part of a tract genre that uses youth death as a disciplinary warning to wrongdoers.[39] There are a number of such texts from this time, a good example of which is *The Dying School Boy: By his Tutor* (1863). In this purportedly true story, written by a headmaster, a public schoolboy of about fifteen or sixteen succumbs to an illness with no 'organic cause' following his 'corrupt[ion]' by 'older boys'.[40] The headmaster, as God's agent,[41] steps in when the doctor proves useless and prepares the boy to die. He reads scripture to him daily,

---

37 Ibid., p. 21.
38 Farrar 1876, pp. 285–6.
39 Nelson 1991, p. 59.
40 Anon., *The Dying School Boy: By his Tutor* (1863), p. 8. Similar texts include A.L.O.E. (C.M. Tucker), *The Young Pilgrim* (1858), John Ingle, *The Decease of a School-Fellow* (1858), Ashton Oxenden, *Emily Nigh* (1860), Mary Trench, *Little Richard* (1861) and Richard Faulkner, *The Grave of Emma Vale at Havering Bower* (1859).
41 *The Dying School Boy* 1863, p. 33.

takes confessions and encourages him to contemplate his end.[42] The boy is taken to live with the headmaster's family and gives moral counsel to the headmaster's son, whom he had earlier corrupted. As his condition worsens, his intellect begins to decay and he becomes 'A newborn babe in Christ', and an 'infant believer [in] the lineaments of the Savior's Lordly Character'.[43] Approaching death, he begins to speak in a 'succession of scripture texts'.[44] The headmaster's role is to encourage this gradual infantilization.

Farrar, by adopting this theme, denies his characters a meaningful adolescence and, in doing so, denies adolescence a meaningful place in society. However, this is not only the fault of nature and God, but also a result of structural failures in the school's organization and curriculum. At Roslyn, youth does not exist to inject new life into the existing social order. There is no mechanism set up in the school by which boys can experiment with roles or social ideas and no arena for them to fight for social justice. Even when Eric finally runs away from school and becomes a cabin-boy on a ship with a thoroughly wicked crew, he makes no attempt to assert himself or his beliefs; he has neither the vocabulary nor the understanding of social justice to muster the wherewithal to defend his position. In this, he contrasts sharply with Ballantyne's Ralph Rover, who sees shipboard life as a fine opportunity for proselytism. On board the *Stormy Petrel*, when Eric is abused, he does nothing to help himself and stands 'unresisting' while a sailor ties him up to beat him senseless.[45] When he has recovered enough strength to emerge on deck a week later, he feels not a Tom Brown-like urge to fight for justice, but a 'childlike gratitude, that God suffered him to breathe once more the pure air of heaven, and sit under the canopy of its gold-pervaded blue'.[46] In contrast, Ralph Rover, when abused by 'Bloody Bill', throws the ship's gunpowder overboard and confronts the pirate in an honest man-to-man chat. The boys' responses to abuse on board ship reflect their different approaches to solving problems. Ralph confronts problems by embarking on programs of active moral reform. Eric simply stops doing whatever sin he has been committing, without reaching any more advanced a social or moral position than the one he arrived at school with and without making any positive impact on those around him. It is hard to see how adolescents such as this, barely civilized themselves and impotent in the face of superior force, could ever fit into a scheme of imperialist Muscular Christian citizenship such as that projected by Ballantyne or Hughes.

The helpless adolescence depicted in *Eric* contrasts strongly with the ideas of liberal education Farrar promoted as a pedagogue. In 1867, he edited a volume entitled *Essays on a Liberal Education*, which built on Lockean tradition, discussed the work of Kant, Montaigne and Rousseau and argued for the necessity

---

42 Ibid., pp. 12, 19–20.
43 Ibid., pp. 26, 29.
44 Ibid., p. 40.
45 Farrar 1899, p. 121.
46 Ibid., p. 122.

of teaching the economic theories of Adam Smith. The volume suggested that pupils study 'things not words'[47] and that the curriculum should be 'useful'. It also said that, although adolescence was a 'period of darkness',[48] boys, with their hatred of rote learning, would be able to introduce radically original ideas into the academic forum through 'new' subjects, such as science. W. Johnson's essay on the 'Education of the Reasoning Faculties' promoted vernacular literature as a 'mental [...] homeopath[y]' that purges the volatile emotions of the reader.[49] It also encourages the teaching of drama to this end. Elsewhere, Farrar said that the best place for boys to be was outside the discipline of the classroom, free to observe 'the workings of nature' and to 'search for an understanding of nature's laws as the most rewarding occupation of their leisure hours'.[50] Farrar's 'liberal education' was not, of course, 'liberal' in the classical sense or libertarian in a modern sense. He shows little of the 'egalitarian' confidence demonstrated by classical liberals such as Richard Whately and Adam Smith, who taught that all human beings were fundamentally capable of making independent social and economic decisions when unrestrained by official interference;[51] the 'essentially positive view of human nature'[52] descended from classical liberalism that underlines liberal democratic ideas in modern-day Europe seem to have been alien to him. Farrar's ideas were founded on a paternalist ideology, which sets less store on individual choice and values obedience; like Hughes, Farrar had little time for *laissez-faire* in any sense of the word. The 'liberty' of Farrar's liberalism was more about making vulnerable individuals free to make better decisions regarding their own lives by liberating them from constraints such as poverty or workplace abuse than about having faith in human reasoning ability *per se*. Farrar was essentially anti-democratic, believing that the masses should follow the advice of their betters rather than forming political or economic ideas of their own, and he applied the same logic to boys. His liberal education, therefore, has a strongly authoritarian undercurrent. Nonetheless, Farrar showed a belief in certain kinds of progress (particularly scientific progress), an awareness that the curriculum must alter to suit changing social needs and an appreciation of exploration and independent study as beneficial to educational development.

On reading *Eric*, therefore, anybody with a knowledge of Farrar's stated educational philosophy is liable to be confused at the very least. In the following paragraphs I will suggest why Farrar's liberalism fails so seriously in this work,

---

47 Farrar 1868, p. 60. This remark was written in the essay 'On the History of Classical Education' by the Oxford scholar Charles Stuart Parker.

48 Ibid., p. 106.

49 Probably William Johnson (later Johnson Cory), Assistant Master at Eton and Uranian poet. Ibid., p. 337. The Uranians celebrated love between men and explored different possibilities for male identity.

50 Davis 1981, p. 157.

51 For an interesting discussion of this idea see Levy 2001, pp. 45–46.

52 Sweeney 2005, p. 247.

in order to understand more clearly why ideas of adolescent liberal education sometimes met with resistance. I have already said that Farrar was trying to negotiate between two incompatible metanarratives of human development – creationism and evolutionary Darwinism – as well as trying to balance Romantic and Evangelical ideas of childhood innocence and sin. Another reason Farrar failed to live up to his liberal principles in *Eric* may have stemmed, like Arnold's ambivalence towards his pupils, from an unease with the idea of the adolescent body rather than from any coherent religious or educational philosophy. Physical descriptions of boys in *Eric* fall into two categories. His occasional references to Eric and Vernon's blonde hair are used to evoke childlikeness and innocence. Bad behavior, meanwhile, is associated with contamination and disease. Farrar luridly describes 'the gradual coarseness which seemed to be spreading, like a gray lichen, over the countenance' of Eric's friend Wildney during a drinking bout.[53] Similarly, Eric's teacher, Mr Rose, refers to the bully Brigson as an 'ulcer to this school'.[54] Shortly before running away, Eric dreams of Brigson and the pub landlord Billy, 'their bodies grown to gigantic proportions, and their faces fierce with demonical wickedness'.[55] Literally, the more area a boy's body occupies, the more potential it has for corruption. School, a collected mass of adolescent bodies, multiplies the threat of infection. Those who isolate themselves in small groups, like Eric's friends Russell, Owen and Montagu, have stronger resistance against contamination.

At night, the boys indulge in 'Kibroth-Hattaavah',[56] a Biblical coinage of Farrar's meaning literally 'grave of lust', which seems to comprise of telling rude stories but which inevitably, according to Farrar, leads to worse. In Numbers 11, the travelling Israelites rest at 'Kibroth-Hattaavah'. Some are overcome by lust and then, bored with manna, ask Moses for meat. God gives them quails and those who eat are instantly stricken with plague.[57] The incident at Kibroth-Hattavah, however, is not just about physical lust, but about the insatiability of desire and the burden of a dependent population in a barren wasteland, consuming food and multiplying but not working for its living. Moses asks of God: 'Have I conceived all this people? [...] that thou shouldest say unto me, Carry them in thy bosom, as a nursing father beareth the sucking child, unto the land which thou swarest unto their fathers?' (Num. ii.12). Just as Moses worries about the unsustainability of the Israelites' desires, Farrar panics about the consuming, non-productive adolescent population. Perhaps Farrar was reacting partly to the Malthusian panic about excessive consumption and the wastefulness of non-laboring bodies that I referred to in Chapter 1.

---

53 Farrar 1899, pp. 99–100.
54 Ibid., p. 86.
55 Ibid., p. 114.
56 Ibid., p. 37.
57 *Jobe's Dictionary of Mythology, Folklore and Symbols* (1961).

Adolescence, with its insatiability, is contrasted by Farrar to 'childlikeness', a quality deeply significant to Victorian Evangelicals and often discussed in relation to Paul's instruction in 1 Corinthians xiv.20: 'Brethren, be not children in understanding: how being in malice be ye children, but in understanding be men'. John Caird, Professor of Divinity at Glasgow, described 'childlikeness' as a condition where there is no desire for powerful emotional, aesthetic or physical stimulus. Children have a 'capacity of finding delight in simple pleasures, and extracting materials of unbounded happiness, in absolute independence of any stimulus of excited passion, from the commonest senses and objects and the simple routine of daily life'.[58] W.T. Rosevear in *Christian Manliness and Sympathy* (1872) defines childlikeness as the ability to combine intellect with innocent, childlike desires. Paul enjoins us, he says, to retain our critical faculties, yet to remain 'innocent in heart'.[59] Man has degenerated 'from a state of innocence' and we can 'evolve' again by recovering our innocence. Farrar similarly counsels his Marlborough boys to exchange adult 'leper-flesh' for 'child-flesh'.[60] To revert completely to childhood, however, is no answer. John Caird comments that the child's superficial innocence is actually ignorance, which fails to provide protection against influences that come from outside 'the guarded security of home'.[61] Boys must experience enough independence to understand worldly danger. Thus, when Eric tells the one able teacher at Roslyn, Mr Rose, that he is concerned about his innocent brother, Vernon, coming to school, Rose replies:

> The innocence of mere ignorance is a poor thing; it *cannot*, under any circumstances, be permanent, nor is it at all valuable as a foundation of character. The true preparation for life, the true basis of a manly character, is not to have been ignorant of evil, but to have known it and avoided it.[62]

The paradox of adolescence is, therefore, the same as the paradox of the Fall. Indeed, Farrar quotes Genesis iii.5 ('You shall be as gods [knowing good and evil]') at the head of the chapter that describes Eric's temptations in the dormitories.[63]

Yet another reason Farrar's liberalism fails is that he cannot share Hughes's confidence in fatherhood as a social panacea. I would suggest that this lack of confidence stems partly from a disappointment with authority figures *per se* which in itself derives from the confusion wrought by the evolution/creation debate. From God downwards, Farrar's boys are abandoned by father figures. Maybe with Hughes's Arnold in mind, Farrar comments that Roslyn's Headmaster ('the

---

58 Caird 1871, p. 8.
59 Rosevear 1872, p. 3.
60 Farrar 1876, p. 83.
61 Caird 1871, p. 13.
62 Farrar 1899, p. 68.
63 Ibid., p. 34.

Doctor') was, in the eyes of the boys, 'a regular *Deus ex machina*'.[64] However, the boys are mistaken. The Doctor is absent at key points in their careers and only appears after the most damaging events have happened. He limits his work to schoolroom activities and bouts of repressive discipline and sees no relationship between his job, his family life and the world outside. Entry to his own private space is 'peremptorily forbidden' (although an accommodating wife appears near the end of the book), and, unlike Farrar himself who, under F.D. Maurice's influence, spent time caring for the urban poor,[65] he has no paternalistic contact with the local community.

Eric's world is also devoid of biological fathers, apart from a brief period when Eric's parents visit from India, where they, like Farrar's parents, are missionaries. During this visit, early in the book, Eric's father acts as a kind of *deus ex machina*, 'an unobserved spectator' who steps in to save Eric from his earliest adversary, Barker.[66] Like God, however, he too disappears when Eric's adolescence begins. The ambivalence towards fathers that Farrar demonstrates in this text may have been, in part, a result of personal experience. Farrar's father, who sent his son away to England aged three, was, according to P.G. Scott, 'a rather prickly and unlikable cleric'.[67] The missionary parents who left boys at King William's College were harshly criticized by Farrar's junior, James M. Wilson, who attended the school from 1848–1853. Wilson also commented that the school's interest in Evangelical missionary charities seemed to outweigh its concern for its own charges and implied that parents and school cared more about Christianizing the Empire than about saving the souls of their own boys.[68] The central spiritual figure of the father seems to have been paradoxically absent. Another contemporary, E.S. Beesley, commented that although Farrar was sent to the school for an Evangelical education, 'none of the masters had any religious influence' as far as he knew.[69] In addition to this, Farrar's biography, written by his son, Reginald, remarks that while he worshipped his mother, he was 'never [...] on really intimate terms' with his father.[70] This deep appreciation of motherhood may have been heightened while he was writing *Eric* by the fact that his mother, who died in 1860, was seriously ill.[71]

It is also possible that, even while Hughes was exalting the father as the guardian of civilized male citizenship, there was a more general questioning of

---

64 Ibid., p. 16.
65 Ibid., p. 17, Scott 1971, p. 164.
66 Farrar 1899, pp. 17–18.
67 Anstruther 2002, p. 1, Scott 1971, p. 180.
68 See James Wilson, *Autobiography*. Extracts from this work and other works relating to King William's College are collected at http://www.isle-of-man.com/manxnotebook/fulltext/wi1931.htm.
69 Farrar 1904. p. 17.
70 Ibid., p. 5.
71 Anstruther 2002, p. 57.

the value of fatherhood; indeed, this might have been precisely why Hughes put so much emphasis on it. Some commentators – among them Claudia Nelson, Davidoff and Hall and Peter Keating – have suggested that the mid-nineteenth century was, in some respects, a time of crisis for fatherhood. Nelson remarks that during the pre-Victorian era, especially with the 'evangelical revival that stressed the importance of child-rearing while still celebrating the primacy of the male', the father occupied a position of irrefutable authority. With industrialization, however, fathers, spending less time in the home, were increasingly unable to play the role of God to their children.[72] Legislation such as the 1839 Custody of Children Act and the Matrimonial Causes Act of 1857 was eroding the Biblically-ordained power that fathers held over wives and children, partly as a consequence of high-profile cases such as that of Caroline Norton, publicized by the comparatively new mass media.[73] Similarly, with the Factory Acts, the state began to perceive parents as potential exploiters and began to intervene between fathers and children. According to Nelson, a 'lack of a strong symbolization' of fathers consequently arose, particularly in the media.[74] Many novels published within a decade of *Eric*, such as *Villette* (1853), *Hard Times* (1854) and *The Mill on the Floss* (1860), also show young people let down by weak or inadequate fathers.

A disgust towards the biological business of being male probably also contributed to Farrar's feelings about fatherhood. As Nelson has explained, mid-century Evangelicals considered that male sexual desire embodied some of the worst aspects of human nature, such as egotism, selfishness and a wish to live for the present, which led to an ambivalence towards traditional masculinity. Nelson explains how in *Tom Brown* 'The worship of God, the scorning of worldly position and the reverencing of parents and women are part and parcel of each other and of adult manliness'.[75] I demonstrated in Chapter 3 how Hughes also feminized fatherhood to give it more moral authority. In *Eric*, Farrar takes this to an extreme and rejects fathers altogether, portraying them as blustering incompetents who claim moral authority but who blithely abdicate responsibility the moment it becomes a chore. In particular, Farrar's self-indulgent men abandon boys at the point of adolescence when fatherhood ceases to be fun and starts to get tough – when boys inconveniently begin to challenge the adult male's hitherto unquestioned social dominance.

Much later in his career, in his advice book *The Young Man Master of Himself* (1896), Farrar placed the well-ordered adolescent boy in an atmosphere dominated by the mother, rather than the father. The first chapter, 'The Young Man in the Home', depicts the domestic sphere as the proper place for young men. Farrar describes how the self-disciplined youth emerges from school and, instead of

---

72 Nelson 1991, p. 3. Interestingly Cohoon (2006) reports that American boys' texts show no such ambivalence about fatherhood (p. 65).
73 Keating 1989, pp. 231, 153.
74 Nelson 1995, p. 36.
75 Nelson 1989, p. 539.

going on to enjoy male camaraderie at university or in the army, returns home to pursue his career. He becomes a kind of Christ figure in the home, submitting his interests to those of his family; like the family of Solomon's virtuous woman, 'his brothers and sisters rise up and call him blessed!'[76] Moreover, the good young man refrains from entering the public sphere or getting involved with the outside world; Farrar quotes Confucius's dictum that 'If the home duties be well performed [...] there is no need to go afar to offer sacrifice'.[77] Although youths fight against confinement and trivial chores like birds in cages, 'their cage may be to them a universe, which shall give large scope for their best and highest faculties'.[78] Even when he goes out to work, the youth is not allowed to seek personal gain. Young employees, remarks Farrar, should show '*a certain disinterested devotion to* [their] *employer's service*'.[79] British youths, he says, contrast unfavorably to their German counterparts, who speak four languages and work overtime without payment.[80] Later, Farrar explains how youths should invest spare time in church work instead of wasting energy in romantic love (he tells of a boy who died of having too much '*envenomed pleasure*'[81]). He also describes how the abolitionist Thomas Clarkson, the preacher William Carey and the Earl of Shaftesbury invested their youthful energy for mankind.[82] Young men, he explains, should defer gratification and think only of the future and of others. The young man's primary duty is towards the family and all obligations are rooted in domestic obligations. Farrar's advice contrasts with the depiction of adolescence in *Tom Brown*, where it is necessary for the boy to go through a rebellious phase, gradually rejecting what his family stands for so that he can renegotiate and rebuild his identity on his own terms and to develop his own political outlook. Without boarding school, this would not be possible. For Farrar, however, school is a necessary but unfortunate period where the adolescent learns to withstand the seedier temptations life has on offer. Once he has done this, he can return to the family, resume his previous existence and reconfirm the values he was brought up with.

In creating a narrative that constantly harks back to childhood and childhood values, Farrar demonstrates a similar attitude to youth to that observed by Franco Moretti in English responses to the European *Bildungsroman* tradition. In the continental *Bildungsroman*, the protagonist, frequently rejecting the values of his parents, seeks a new social and political consciousness.[83] He or she also often develops an appreciation of the aesthetic and a capacity to gain satisfaction from

---

76 Farrar 1896, pp. 16–17.
77 Ibid., p. 17.
78 Ibid., p. 24.
79 Ibid., p. 38.
80 Ibid., p. 42.
81 Ibid., pp. 74–75.
82 Ibid., pp. 77, 79, 81.
83 See Ginsburg 1992, p. 175.

art and literature, or to appreciate beauty in natural or man-made things. The English protagonist often does the opposite:

> The young hero's [...] exploits are the very opposite of what we call 'experiences'. They are mere digressions, also in a narrative sense, and they will never shed a different light on, nor force [him] from, the straight and narrow path of asexual love, of *childhood* love. [...] In the English novel the most significant experiences are not those that alter but those which *confirm* the choices made by childhood 'innocence'. Rather than novels of 'initiation' one feels they should be called novels of 'preservation'.[84]

Rather than questioning the status quo, English protagonists uphold 'legal continuity'. The plot of the English *Bildungsroman* is 'a merely "negative" force' and characters 'only agree to take part in it to avert the total disappearance of the violated order'.[85] *Tom Brown*, with its pan-European political perspective, follows a more continental model; its adolescent characters are outward looking and socially oriented. *Eric*, on the other hand, gives a conservative, introverted portrayal of adolescence where the emphasis is on individual conscience, private relationships and the preservation of childhood innocence. School only exists to show the boy what evil is.

However, Farrar was living in a society where going away to school was the norm among the social elite and in *St Winifred's: Or the World of School* he gives a more constructive idea of how adolescent education could be improved. In a way, as I will show, this text also explores the value of what might be called 'motherly' education, this time in the form of vernacular literature. The protagonist of *St Winifred's*, Walter Evson, is another Rousseauian 'natural' boy. Surrounded in childhood by benign Wordsworthian nature in a Lake-District type setting ('low hills [...] gentle slopes [...] the huge green shoulder of a mountain'[86]), Walter and his siblings are the sole concern of his gentleman father who, unlike Eric's father, is dedicated to child rearing. Mr Evson sees in fatherhood an opportunity to 'beg[in] life again', by 'fully sympathis[ing]' with his children.[87] Like Rousseau with Émile, he avoids forcing 'book knowledge' or 'conscious labor' upon his children until they reach the age of twelve or thirteen.[88] Farrar refers to Walter's transition from home to school as an 'old, old story'.[89] St Winifred's, where willful passion catches up with Walter, is situated, like Roslyn, in a harsh and sublime landscape between the sea and menacing mountains and to reach it, pupils 'must drive through [...] dark groves'.[90] This time, however, Farrar criticizes Walter's Romantic childhood

---

84 Ibid., p. 176.
85 Ibid., p. 177.
86 Farrar 1910, p. 9.
87 Ibid., p. 14.
88 Ibid., p. 10.
89 Ibid., p. 9.
90 Ibid., p. 13.

education. Like Eric, despite a careful upbringing, Walter has 'evil tendencies' which should have been 'nipped in the bud' and he is unable to control his emotions.[91] These faults, which the Rousseauian system does not address, are exacerbated by his encounter with the classical curriculum at school. Paton, the classics master, whose discipline is 'iron and inflexible', becomes Walter's foremost adversary. He sets the academic level of his classes with a 'measure [like] that of Procrustes,' which means that 'the cleverest boys could not stretch themselves beyond it, [and] the dullest were mechanically pulled into its dimensions'.[92] He cannot judge character and because of this must rely on corporal punishment, rather than on an understanding of his students, to enforce obedience. Most importantly, however, his classes consist merely of linguistic 'routine work' and do not facilitate creativity.[93] Walter, alienated by his 'mechanical' tasks and discouraged by continual failure, devotes himself to hedonism: 'to enjoy himself; to declare himself on the side of pleasure and self-indulgence'.[94] Absence of pleasure in schoolwork leads the boy, at this 'perilous age', to seek stimulus elsewhere, in destructive acts.[95]

Walter not only struggles with linguistic scholarship but also lacks the resources with which to handle school life. Other boys use literature to cope with everyday difficulties and this, for Farrar, is the key to good discipline and to the successful negotiation of maturity. Walter's classmate Henderson, a prolific reader, quotes Shakespeare and Milton freely, using parody to explain and deal with relationships with both masters and pupils and to diffuse awkward situations. He also writes a drama, the 'Sociable Grosbeaks', celebrating his friendships.[96] During quarrels, he makes 'quick tempered' literary responses and another boy comments that he is like a 'lightening-kite', deflecting harm away from others.[97] Elsewhere, the boys use literature to help them cope with emotionally challenging situations. Later in the story, the boys read *Paradise Lost*, which they use as an allegory when discussing the temptation of Walter's younger brother, Charlie, by corrupt older boys. Initially, however, Walter's lack of reading denies him the comfort of literature and leads him to misconstrue others' ideas. When Walter can endure no more Greek, Henderson tries to comfort him, quoting *Hamlet* asking

> Whether 'twere nobler for the mind to suffer
> The slings and arrows of outrageous fortune,
> Or to take arms against a sea of troubles,
> And by opposing end them![98]

---

91 Ibid., p. 57.
92 Ibid., p. 35.
93 Ibid., p. 42.
94 Ibid., p. 43.
95 Ibid., p. 44.
96 Ibid., p. 137.
97 Ibid., p. 236.
98 Ibid., p. 45.

Walter, unaware of the quotation's context, subsequently resolves to take vengeance on Paton, rather than examining the consequences of such an action.

Although Farrar loathed cheap fiction, he held aesthetics and, above all, vernacular literature (which was forbidden at King William's College), central to his idea of adolescent education. Reginald Farrar remarked that at King William's, 'Scott, Fenimore Cooper, and Captain Marryat [...] circulated almost by stealth'. They were 'eagerly devoured, and [...] the boys used to lie awake at night hotly discussing' their favorite characters in these novels. The only education that benefited Farrar at school was 'the practice of setting passages of English poetry to be learnt by heart'.[99] Literature was also a substitute for other social contact. As Reginald Farrar commented:

> The young cynic of to-day derides the boys of *Eric* and *St Winifred's*, who are represented as eagerly discussing out of school the characters of Homeric heroes; but the fact remains that the more intelligent boys of that epoch, being precluded from such lofty themes as cricket averages [...] *did* find interest in discussing the 'shop' of their school classics, regarded as human literature.[100]

A former pupil, George Russell, commented that Farrar filled his classroom in a most un-Evangelical way with casts of statues and 'Fra Angelico's blue Madonnas and rose-colored angels on golden backgrounds as models of color'.[101] In tune with contemporary thinkers such as John Ruskin, and anticipating Matthew Arnold by two decades, Farrar suggested that aesthetics was essential to creating a civil society and showed through *St Winifred's* how adolescence was the place where aesthetic feeling should be taught.

In *Eric* too, Farrar portrays boys as having an innate need for literature and drama. Under Upton's influence, Eric and his dormitory hold forbidden 'theatricals' when they are supposed to be asleep,[102] performing *Bombastes Furioso* and a parody of *Macbeth*. During a carnivalistic and comic rendition of Duncan's murder (where a boy named Duncan plays Macbeth, which 'tickled the audience immensely'), the Headmaster blunders in and injures himself by stumbling into a crude warning system the boys have created.[103] Consequently, Eric is caned. Because Roslyn suppresses the one creative activity the boys pursue, they have no controlled space in which to negotiate issues of power, conflict and identity (all of which might have been considered were *Macbeth* on the curriculum). Perhaps this is one reason why there is so much more overt violence in *Eric* than in *Tom Brown*, including violence against adults (Eric throws a cane at his favorite teacher, Mr Rose). If boys have no means to create, implies Farrar, they destroy.

---

99 Farrar 1904, p. 13.
100 Ibid., p. 14.
101 Ibid., p. 85.
102 Farrar 1899, p. 39.
103 Ibid., pp. 40, 41.

Although Farrar recognized the value of drama and literature, however, he wrote negatively about play in a sermon on the text 'The streets of the city shall be full of boys and girls playing' (Zechariah xiii:5):

> There is a constant danger of extravagant and foolish misjudgments, which utterly lose sight of the relative values and importance of things ... while you play with all heartiness, do not forget that games, however useful or delightful, are not of first rate, not even third, fourth, or fifth – scarcely even of tenth-rate importance ...[104]

Farrar questions the Romantic idea that play is always an expression of freedom and creativity and shows in *Eric* how play becomes destructive if not properly institutionalized. When Barker the bully 'frames' Eric for a school crime (pinning a rude message about a master on a notice board), the boys, at the Head's behest, hold a kangaroo court.[105] Barker is proved a liar and condemned to 'run the gauntlet of the school'. This involves everyone tying handkerchiefs into knots to make scourges and 'ma[king] a double line down each side of the corridor'[106] which Barker has to run between (somewhat resembling Rabelaisian 'gauntlet weddings',[107] where slanderers were beaten). Again, free play seems to be inextricably bound up with violence. Nonetheless, some kind of outlet for boys' creativity is necessary. In *St Winifred's*, therefore, rather than promoting free play as Hughes had done, Farrar describes how literature might be incorporated into a more structured curriculum.

The 'model' teacher at St Winifred's is Mr Percival, who integrates literature with leisure and encourages vernacular creative writing. Percival's regime revises the competitive values of the classical curriculum. He does not repudiate competition completely, but strips it of its egotism. Under Percival, achievement does not confer extra status or rewards upon the individual, but benefits the group:

> There was a bright and cheerful emulation among [the boys], and they took especial pains with their exercises, which Mr Percival varied in every possible way, so as to call out the imagination and the fancy, to exercise both the reason and the understanding, and to test the powers of attention and research. [...] If in one fortnight *four* separate exercises were [sent to the headmaster as examples of especially fine work], the form obtained [...] the remission of an hour's work.[108]

Constructive competition is, at heart, cooperation and helps the group to survive. Competition between individuals, however, is dangerous. For example, when Walter's friend Kenrick desperately needs a scholarship and has an 'open feud'

---

104 Scott 1971, p. 171.
105 Farrar 1899, pp. 49–50.
106 Ibid., p. 51.
107 Bakhtin 1965, p. 200.
108 Farrar 1910, p. 187.

with his classmates, 'stimulated by a fiery ambition, a mad desire to excel',[109] he eventually suffers a breakdown. Literature, on the other hand, teaches the boys to channel their energies and emotions productively and cooperatively. When faced with the death of a friend, Walter responds by composing poetry,[110] a much more successful approach than Eric's short-lived fits of religious mania. It is worth remarking at this point that Farrar, with his emphasis on aesthetics, fails to address the issues of practical and scientific education that preoccupied other liberal educationalists. Nor does he say how boys might be trained to pass the ever-increasing burden of examinations Victorian society was evolving for entry to careers like the civil service. Indeed, he suggests that adolescents are unsuited to systematic thought; the fault with the traditional classics teacher at St Winifred's is that he is 'devoted to a system' and Walter's problem is that 'He could have easily mastered the facts which the rules were intended to impress, but the empirical process suggested for arriving at the facts he could not remember'.[111] To Farrar, adolescent education is about producing people who behave, feel and express themselves in a certain way, rather than being about teaching facts or skills.

Self-expression is not the only constructive disciplinary method employed at St Winifred's. Boys and masters there are 'on warmer and friendlier terms with each other than perhaps at any other school – certainly on warmer terms than if they never met except in the still and punishment-pervaded atmosphere of the classrooms'.[112] Traditionally, relationships between masters and boys in schools had been predicated on confrontation and physical violence, expressed through rebellion and corporal punishment. '[P]opular papers' and 'magazines', complained Farrar, profess 'that courtesy to, and love for, a master, is impossible or hypocritical'.[113] Farrar recommended that masters and boys spend their leisure time together; indeed, intimacy with masters teaches the boys to regard each other as they would family members. Thus Walter takes an interest (a 'boyish protectorate'[114]) in a younger boy, Eden. This relationship is safer than those at Roslyn, perhaps because the boys' need for emotional stimulus is met through literature. Eden becomes like a 'brother' to Walter and asks 'Will you call me Arthur, as they do at home?'[115] Later on, a boy who protects Walter's brother from bullying shows 'an almost womanly tenderness' towards him.[116] From advocating the vernacular as the proper subject of study for boys, therefore, Farrar goes on to advocate a whole new range of values to be incorporated into school, such as domesticisation, anti-competitiveness and equality among age groups.

---

109 Ibid., p. 271.
110 Ibid., pp. 152–53.
111 Ibid., pp. 38, 36.
112 Ibid., p. 89.
113 Ibid., pp. 87–88.
114 Ibid., p. 187.
115 Ibid., pp. 94, 97.
116 Ibid., p. 268.

Like most school story heroes, Walter goes through a rebellious phase, provoked by unsympathetic discipline and the tedium of classics. As an act of revenge, he burns Paton's manuscript commentary on the Hebrew text of the Four Greater Prophets, thinking he is destroying nothing more than a heap of old essays.[117] Unlike the rebellion in *Eric*, however, this rebellion has a positive function for the school community, because it causes the teacher to re-assess his pedagogical methods. Paton suffers 'greater pain [...] than the breaking of a limb, or falling ill of a severe sickness' from the loss and as a result is (miraculously) transformed. He becomes sympathetic and emotionally articulate and forgives Walter, admitting 'I, too, have learnt a lesson'.[118] What is more, his 'REPAIRED' manuscript is better than the first,[119] improved by his increased emotional literacy. Farrar here describes a reverse of the pedagogical relationship. Adults, he implies, have as much to learn from adolescents as the adolescents have to learn from them (something that never happened in *Tom Brown*, where Arnold was too perfect to question). Violent or rebellious outbreaks among boys signal that a problem in teaching methods exists and should be taken as an opportunity to review the curriculum.

Farrar's re-appraisal of master–boy relationships was timely and topical. In 1860, Matthew Higgins, under the pen-name 'Paterfamilias', alleged in the *Cornhill Magazine* that Eton masters were exploiting boys financially. The consternation arising from this accusation resulted in the 1861–1864 Clarendon Commission enquiry into the public schools, which investigated their curricula, disciplinary codes and finances. Paterfamilias considered that the 'masculine' ethics of the marketplace were inappropriate to the educational sphere. Although Eton masters were supposed to behave like parents (*'in loco parentis'*), he complained, they ran the school as a business, working not through a sense of disinterested vocation but from 'vested interest'.[120] The extravagant lifestyles they supported, moreover, encouraged among boys a taste for 'expense and self-indulgence'.[121] A teacher, explained Paterfamilias, must be truly disinterested. Paterfamilias described the ideal teacher in terms usually reserved by Victorians for roles occupied by women, as embracing a life of simplicity and self-denial.[122] He also suggested tackling the high pupil–teacher ratio (48:1), which maximized profit but prevented personal, sympathetic relations developing between masters and boys and made the proper supervision of leisure time impossible.[123] At Eton, he complained, boys only saw the Head to be flogged.[124] He also implied that friction at school was not caused by the inherent rebelliousness of boys, but by the masters' mercenary attitude

---

117 Ibid., p. 60.
118 Ibid., p. 69.
119 Ibid., p. 73.
120 Paterfamilias (M.J. Higgins) 1865, pp. 70, 61.
121 Ibid., p. 22.
122 Ibid., pp. 22–23.
123 Ibid., pp. 53, 25.
124 Ibid., p. 71.

to their work. Adolescence was now to be protected from the marketplace by teachers who rejected economic gain.

Paterfamilias's idea of disinterested education was shared by G.E.L. Cotton, Head of Marlborough, where Farrar had his first teaching post. Reginald Farrar describes how Cotton reformed Marlborough, which had been a failing school where half-starved boys had broken out in rebellion. Cotton encouraged 'self-denial' among the staff, who 'treated the boys as so many younger brothers'.[125] When he took over, the staff even forwent wages for a year, investing the money in order to use the accrued interest for the benefit of the boys. Cotton also told the boys that 'they should confide in him' if they had any objection to the way he was running the school.[126] Canon Henry Bell, a former pupil, made a connection between this new, intimate, non-violent brand of adolescent education and Farrar's interest in vernacular literature when he remarked that

> Farrar [...] brought the boys who were in his Form a new idea of life, and the conviction that we were made for something better and higher than to be caned and cuffed. Till Farrar came we did our verses out of a book, [...] Farrar pitched the book into the fire, and gave us some poetry instead. [...] Our first copy was, 'Oh, call my brother back to me,' which was followed up by 'Cophetua', 'Yea Mariners of England', and many another.[127]

Adolescents were no longer to be toughened by violence but sensitized by the mother tongue.

In stressing literature, emotional bonds and sensibility, however, Farrar seems to have ignored the development of political consciousness that Hughes found so important. Farrar's emphasis on emotion foreshadows the liberal paternalism that Karín Lesník-Oberstein has investigated in the work of Matthew Arnold, Henry Newbolt and F.R. Leavis and which played a big role in the evolution of juvenile literature. These thinkers, Lesník-Oberstein says, proposed that literature should 'foster humanitarian or liberal attitudes and feelings in people, or the capacities for [...] love, compassion, tolerance, and truthfulness'. The literature they inspired, therefore, concentrated on 'evoking emotional reactions to an almost unique extent'.[128] Thus Farrar aims to create a feeling citizen rather than a political citizen. In terms of political ideas, St Winifred's boys learn to follow something like the Anglican idea of the *via media*. This was a social ideology which David Alderson has described as being an attempt to find a middle way between the Puritan 'ascetic virtue' promoted by Evangelicals and the 'Hobbesian rakishness which tended to

---

125 Farrar 1904, p. 54.
126 Ibid., p. 55.
127 Ibid., p. 57. As Shrosbree (1988) remarks, public schools were reluctant to favour the vernacular because it was associated with liberalism and democracy, in contrast to Classics, which represented hierarchy and order (p. 56).
128 Lesník-Oberstein 1994, p. 24.

be associated with the Restoration Aristocracy'.[129] Commentators who advocated this 'middle way', such as Thomas Arnold and Carlyle, subscribed to a Burkean concept of civility that was hostile to radical political change and that held that bonds between classes evolved organically and could not be replaced wholesale by newly invented systems of social order.[130] This ideology, which shows a different side of Arnold and Carlyle's philosophies to the one that Hughes advocated, seems inimical to the idea that adolescents should experiment with 'new' political and social ideas.

Civic subjecthood, to Farrar, should only exist within the incontestable status quo. As his chapter 'The Ideal Citizen' in *Social and Present-Day Questions* explains, male citizenship is founded on religion and has nothing to do with politics, economics or heredity. Christ is the ideal citizen, the Bible the 'statesman's manual'.[131] The citizen has no concept of self-interest and 'live[s] for mankind, not for a class: still less for individual men; least of all for himself only'.[132] He does not get involved in political movements, even to support others. Farrar discourages political debate ('the clash of controversy') and advocates that his readers search for consensus, exercising 'modesty, sympathy, fairness of judgement, humility, candor'.[133] Political principles are self-evident truths, sanctioned by the Bible and a meritocratic elite, who inform the 'collective mediocrity' that 'for all their anathemas [...] they must accept the truth which they have hated'.[134] Farrar also denies that civic identity can be found in the membership of political groups formed by people with a common interest. This attitude he shares with the broad-church Christian Socialists who, as Donald Hall has shown, taught through their weekly publication *Politics for the People* that 'manhood' and 'duty [to] a class-determined construction of the Godhead' were more important than class allegiance.[135] *Politics for the People* depicted the class-conscious, disobedient poor as a 'monster body', which threatened to destroy the delicate body politic,[136] a vision echoed by Farrar in his depiction of the monstrous multitude of unruly adolescent boys at Roslyn. There is no sense in Farrar's work that boys should see themselves as members of a group with distinct interests, in contrast to Hughes's boys, who had a strong sense of belonging to the school itself, the School House and their form. St Winifred's allows no opportunity for feelings of corporate identity to develop (for instance, through sport) and although houses exist, there is no jingoistic sense of house membership. Walter is focused on personal, not social issues. While rehabilitating after his crime, he withdraws for a crucial period from the rest of school society,

---

129 Alderson 1998, p. 16.
130 See ibid., p. 35.
131 Farrar 1891, p. 216.
132 Ibid., p. 225.
133 Ibid., p. 218.
134 Ibid., p. 223.
135 Hall 1994, p. 52.
136 Farrar 1891, p. 223.

supported by one friend, Power, who stands 'aloof from the herd of boys' and who is 'beautiful and fascinating even in his exclusiveness'.[137] The greatest opportunity for character development comes when the individual is rejected by others. Walter looks back on his period of isolation as 'a time of unmitigated blessing' which 'taught him lessons of manliness, of endurance, of humility'.[138] The solutions to Walter's problems are personal, not political, and he turns his attention inwards.

As I said in the introduction, modern educationalists still debate whether adolescents respond better to personalist approaches to subjects such as literature, history and citizenship, or to a more political approach. Philip Abrams quotes the scholar of Human Development, Kenneth Keniston, as having observed that

> Every responsible study or survey shows apathy and privatism far more dominant than dissent ... the vast majority of students remain largely uncritical of the wider society, fundamentally conformist [...] and basically adjusted to the prevailing collegiate, national and international order.[139]

However, it is arguable that authors from Farrar's period onwards sought deliberately to cultivate apathy among the young to avert political unrest and change. Joseph Bristow has remarked on how the 1867 extension of the franchise led to working-class boys being 'identified as a political danger to the nation'. Newly literate working-class boys, he explains, had to be trained 'not only to read the right things' (as opposed to reading inflammatory penny fiction), but also 'to meet the demands of becoming a responsible citizen.[140] In 1862 Farrar, popular among the working classes and perhaps anticipating greater democratic reform, cautiously primes his readers to conform to the status quo.

In *St Winifred's*, Farrar supports his politically quietist ideology with a new concept of God, nature and discipline which were closely bound to ideas of mental health and emotional literacy. He begins to represent bad behavior as the result of entirely treatable psychological instability rather than as the flexing of emergent political muscle. When Walter burns Paton's manuscript, he is sent straight to the sick room, implying that his outbreak was a pathological act. Walter's literary training, which is a kind of therapy, teaches him not only the art of self-enquiry but also stimulates his interest in the mental health of others, although he does not understand this in scientific terms ('He did not know the very name of psychology, but he did know the unhinging, desolating power of an overmastering spirit of fear'[141]). He recognizes Eden's incipient mental breakdown and contemplates his friend Kenrick's growing depression and mental 'degeneracy' after his mother's

---

137 Farrar 1910, p. 76.
138 Ibid., p. 75.
139 K. Keniston quoted in Abrams 1970, p. 177.
140 Bristow 1991, p. 19.
141 Farrar 1910, p. 101.

death.[142] In adolescence mental stability is precarious, but this is also the time when the ability to investigate psychological matters develops. By discussing mental health so often, Farrar's own text becomes a kind of manual of emotions that teaches boys how to diagnose signs of mental illness.

After suggesting remedies to the problems with adolescent education he had identified in *Eric*, all that remained for Farrar in *St Winifred's* was to try to make sense of the confused depiction of Nature that he had created. Two kinds of nature emerge in *St Winifred's*, the 'Edenic' and the 'savage'. As in *Eric*, the first dominates childhood while the second takes over in adolescence. When Walter goes home for the holidays, he is able to enjoy 'odors snatched from a primal Eden, from a golden age when justice still lived upon the earth, and crime was yet unknown'. Farrar pauses at this point to wonder 'whether the squalid Andaman or the hideous Fuegian ever feel them',[143] a comment that throws light on his idea of nature and adolescence. The Andaman islanders were of great interest to anthropologists at this time. The islands had been absorbed into the Empire in 1858 and the islanders, little touched by the outside world, were thought to be relics of primitive man.[144] Farrar here suggests that ideas of evolution can coexist with ideas of Eden and the Fall. Involved in the debate between polygenist and monogenist interpretations of human evolution,[145] he appears to have constructed a belief that humans degenerated, at some time, from the Edenic into a savage state, a fall which, as he suggests in *Eric*, is revisited during adolescence.[146] This idea allows him to retain both his Wordsworthian view of childhood and his Darwinian concept of adolescence. Family life is a portal to Eden, providing respite for the adolescent who is struggling against his own post-lapsarian savagery and against the corrupt, competitive aspects of nature. Adolescence is about using one's emotional literacy to keep hold of one's access to Eden while fighting to overcome the savage side of nature which fallen humanity must grow up and face.

Making nature an agent of punishment and discipline also enables Farrar to demonstrate that the moral principles he advocates are not negotiable, something which again underlines his conception of citizenship as passive rather than active. Justice, he implies, is natural; it is not made by adults but by abstract forces which must be obeyed at all costs. Law is a non-negotiable entity; adolescents cannot challenge adults over legal matters because those matters are decided on by God and nature. This approach even enables Farrar to hide his own authorial voice. *St Winifred's* has very little authorial 'preaching'; Farrar transmits most of

---

142 Ibid., pp. 101, 184.

143 Ibid., p. 227.

144 Goodheart 2000, pp. 13–44.

145 Farrar 1904, p. 108. Polygenists suggested that so-called 'inferior' peoples had evolved separately from 'civilized' races. See Cunningham 1991, pp. 123–24.

146 Evolutionists interested in childhood recapitulation, according to Hugh Cunningham, exploited the image of the 'savage' in rather disdainful discussions of slum children, with no reference to the 'Eden' Farrar describes. See ibid., pp. 97–132.

his moral messages through episodes in which natural justice takes its course, a technique which enables him to dispense with the clumsy Evangelical narrative style that marred *Eric* for so many readers. The teachers in the text, Mr Percival in particular, also prefer to let the workings of natural justice check the boys' behavior; for example, Percival leaves the erring Kenrick to 'the bitter teachings of experience'.[147] Although the boys theoretically have a choice to obey or disobey the 'naturally' ordained laws passed down to them from their teachers, however, exercising this choice will inevitably bring them to grief. Farrar comments: 'it cannot be denied that in the first bloom and novelty of sin, in the free exercise of insolent liberty, there is a sense of pleasure for many hearts; it is the honey on the rim of the poison-cup, the bloom on the Dead Sea apple, the mirage on the scorching waste'.[148] Farrar does not, therefore, invite adolescents to use their independent rational faculties, but urges them to self-censor ideas which deviate from the 'natural' status quo. In *St Winifred's*, therefore, Farrar produces a narrative which embraces liberal education in terms of creativity, but although his narrative is superficially non-authoritarian, it denies adolescents intellectual freedom. This text seems to be one of the many which Lesník-Oberstein has described as seemingly liberal children's narratives that conceal their authority beneath references to God, nature or 'common sense'.[149] In Chapter 5 I will show how social Darwinists used science in a similar way to disguise authoritarianism as liberalism.

In *Eric*, therefore, Farrar opened up a number of questions regarding the possibility of educating adolescents which he tries to answer in *St Winifred's*. Social and evolutionary conditions make male adolescents ineducable in *Eric*. Farrar attempts to fuse evangelicalism and evolution – irreconcilable ways of interpreting human development – to make a coherent narrative and, as a result, ends up with no coherent educational message for his readers. Unable to find an authoritative way of dealing with issues of adolescence, Farrar depicts a chaotic world without an adequate God or leader and expresses deep doubts about male authority and role of parents. Indeed, these doubts may be a general feature of the school story genre, which lends itself in particular to the analysis of loss of parental love and authority. All stories about boarding schools involve the loss of parents in some way, sometimes in death (for example, Arthur's father in *Tom Brown*) and sometimes through a crisis in mutual understanding (for example, when the young person becomes politically, socially or religiously alienated from the family). Most depict the gradual rebuilding of relationships, either with real parents or with substitutes. When average life expectancy was around forty years of age,[150] it must have been inevitable that losing one or both parents was an unwelcome rite of passage for a large number of adolescents. Even those whose parents survived must have gone through the normal adolescent realization, staple of the *Bildungsroman* genre,

---

147 Farrar 1910, p. 220.
148 Ibid., p. 220.
149 Lesník-Oberstein 1994, pp. 61–63.
150 Hinde 2003, p. 195.

that parents are not perfect oracles on every matter. At St Winifred's, however, boys deprived by lack of family involvement strengthen their understanding of the world through vernacular literature and studying their own mother tongue helps them to understand psychological mechanisms. The vernacular promotes cooperation, emotional literacy and understanding and enables the boys to build a quasi-familial support structure to overcome the feelings of parentlessness (and Godlessness) which so troubled *Eric*. This solution, however, is overwhelmingly inward looking. Unlike Hughes, Farrar does not conceive of adolescence in terms of preparation for a public career, possibly because his intended audience includes boys of a lower social class, whom he was unwilling to politicize. Citizenship to him is a process of creating social consensus rather than fighting for rights and change. The adolescent emerges as a passive citizen, focused on emotion rather than on rational political thought, albeit a figure who is now disciplined less by violence than by moral coercion. In the next chapter, I will discuss how Farrar's successors developed the idea of non-violent discipline and how they addressed the question of whether adolescents had enough reason to justify them having any kind of civic role at all.

Chapter 4

What Exactly Does 'Moderate and Reasonable' Mean? Debates on Discipline in Victorian Public School Literature

Discipline is a perennial concern on the educational agenda. Those who are harrowed by reports of playground and classroom violence are sometimes tempted to imagine a time in the past, usually vaguely Victorian, when attentive children sat in neat rows reciting times-tables in unison. The Victorians, however, seem to have viewed the behavior of the younger members of their society as anything but idyllic and devoted huge amounts of time and space to debating how to solve disciplinary problems. In this chapter, I will discuss the way in which the idea of youth figured in the debate on discipline in the periodical press and in public school stories during the second half of the nineteenth century. I will show not only how the genre promoted new ideas of progressive discipline among the upper classes, but also how it was used, in some cases, to promote a broader idea of social discipline and political quietism among the lower classes. A key event for juvenile discipline at this time was the infamous *R v. Hopley* case of 1860, which involved a schoolteacher who had killed a boy while caning him. The Hopley case not only sparked a significant response from educationalists anxious to discuss the idea of 'reasonable' discipline, but also established the legal concept of 'moderate and reasonable' chastisement for minors which stands to the present day. Here, I will concentrate mainly on works that appeared in the decade before and the two decades following the Hopley case and I will discuss the climate of debate surrounding the judgment. The immediate aftermath of *Hopley* saw a minor outpouring of fiction that opposed corporal punishment and attempted to offer suggestions as to how alternative methods might work. I have focused on these because the revulsion towards corporal punishment that followed on the Hopley case seems to have opened up an opportunity for thinking about adolescence and discipline in new ways. This reforming zeal, however, seems to have died down somewhat by the end of the century, and I have provided some examples (for instance, C.J. Mansford's *Bully, Fag and Hero* of 1896) in a discussion of how a backlash against progressive ideas occurred.

    An understanding of discipline in the Victorian period is essential to discovering how the period viewed adolescence itself. As I have explained, adolescence was, to many commentators, a time when a capacity to reason and a proper appreciation of rights and responsibilities developed. In fact, the concept of 'reason' was at the heart of debates about discipline and punishment. Commentators discussed not only the most 'reasonable' and educational forms of discipline and punishment, but also tried to ascertain what exactly might be expected from young people in terms of rational understanding and moral awareness. Unsurprisingly, public schools were the focus of much of the legal and ethical debate on corporal punishment, at least as regards young people outside the criminal justice system. Commentators presumably emphasized school discipline because most of them had attended a public school and because discipline there was easier to scrutinize than the discipline of day-school students, much of which doubtless took place in the privacy of the home.

Before approaching the topic of adolescent discipline as it appears in literary works, it is necessary to present a brief overview of changing attitudes to discipline during the nineteenth century, then to outline how public schools were responding to trends in educational discipline. From a brief glance at the numerous reports and pieces of legislation produced by the Victorians, it becomes obvious that the state was making a massive effort to bring young people of all classes under systematized control. Consequently, the hitherto private realm of the family became, according to Laura Berry, 'increasingly subject to such diverse and evolving authority as the educational and legal systems, the medical establishment, and the apparatus of social welfare'.[1] As Kathleen Alaimo observes, working-class youth also began to have 'less work, more regular schooling, less informal socialization, more regulation of time'.[2] Government agencies such as the Committee of Privy Council on Education (formed in 1839 to control grants to voluntary schools) and the Education Department at Whitehall (founded 1856) were established.[3] The Newcastle Commission (1858–1861) investigated the schooling of the poor, the Royal Commission on Children's Employment (1861) examined workplace conditions, and the Taunton Commission (1864–1867) reported on standards in 'endowed schools' (secondary schools excluding public schools).[4] William Forster's 1870 Education Act established state-controlled, state-funded school boards.[5] Richer children did not escape scrutiny, either. The post-Arnoldian public schools were investigated not only through fiction, biography and history but also

---

1 Berry 1999, p. 2. Notwithstanding the efforts of the middle-classes, the private realm was a difficult one to penetrate, as Behlmer points out (see below). Government commissions and regulatory bills could be rendered utterly toothless, since enforcement often failed to follow on from inquiries. For example, the 1862 Children's Employment Commission found that legislation banning the use of child chimneysweeps was overwhelmingly ignored. See *First Report of the Commissioners* (1863), pp. lxxxiii–xciii.
2 Alaimo 1991, p. 592.
3 Armytage 1965, pp. 113 and 119.
4 Ibid., pp. 137, 126.
5 Ibid., p. 155.

through the Clarendon Commission (1861–1864), which detailed every aspect of life there meticulously.

From the mid-century onwards, the various stages of childhood and youth also began to be more sharply defined in law, particularly as regards employment and compulsory education. James Kincaid remarks that

> schools [...] did little to mark out childhood prior to the late eighteenth century. Very small children and older adolescents [...] were mixed together indiscriminately and were regarded as a uniform group. [...] By the nineteenth century, schools began separating their charges into 'forms' or 'classes,' thus suggesting a new interest in these people and a determination to understand and control them analytically, by separation.[6]

The London School Board established the norm of educating seven- to ten-year-olds in junior schools and the over-tens at senior schools.[7] According to Anna Davin, the institution of compulsory schooling under the 1870 Education Act 'consolidated the distinctness of childhood' which had been developing during the nineteenth century.[8] Between 1864 and 1867, most industries were regulated by the factory acts and in 1880 it became compulsory to send all children to school until the age of ten. Gradually, moreover, the maximum age at which a child was deemed needful of legal protection was increased. From 1874, children could only be employed from the age of ten upwards. In 1891 the limit became eleven and in 1901, twelve. The Prevention of Cruelty Act of 1889 defined childhood as extending up until the age of fourteen for boys and sixteen for girls. The 1908 Children Act defined children as those under under fourteen and classed fourteen- to sixteen-year-olds as 'young people'.[9] The full entitlements of citizenship, however, did not come until the age of twenty-one and Davin remarks that many young people were in limbo, employed and enjoying a degree of respect in the family as wage earners, but without adult freedoms.[10]

Attitudes also changed in regard to juveniles and criminal responsibility. Heather Shore remarks that while a thirteen-year-old was held responsible and executed for murder in 1831, two eight-year-olds who killed a two-year-old fourteen years later were considered to be 'mere babies themselves who could not have known the crime they committed'.[11] Society was becoming more compassionate, but it was also becoming more paranoid. The 1840s and 1850s saw a surge in publications on juvenile crime and a general moral panic about its increase. For example, in *Juvenile Depravity* (1849), one of the earliest books on juvenile delinquency, the Rev. Henry Worsley (1820–1893) declared that, despite accounting for only 9.9 per

---

6 Kincaid 1994, p. 68.
7 Armytage 1965, p. 146.
8 Davin 1999, p. 16.
9 Ibid., p. 28.
10 Ibid., p. 25.
11 Shore 1999, p. 69.

cent of the population, fifteen- to twenty-year-olds were responsible for 25 per cent of all crime.[12] Worsley was worried that spreading criminality was sapping national 'manly strength' and as a remedy suggested increased state intervention in schooling for all classes.[13] As Shore has commented, such concern did not necessarily reflect any real increase in crime rates among the young but was sparked by a growing interest in childhood and by concomitant issues such as prison reform.[14]

Commentators thus began to regard young people as a separate moral and legal category to adults and as having their own distinct (mostly inferior) understanding of morality. All classes of male juvenile, it seems, were considered to be constitutionally disposed to criminal activity. As a consequence, many popular school stories – for example, Farrar's *Eric* and *St Winifred's* or Talbot Baines Reed's *The Fifth Form at St Dominic's* (1887) – featured crime (usually theft), punishment and rehabilitation as central narrative episodes. It is also worth remarking that in dealing with crime as an age-related phenomenon rather than a product of environment, writers seem frequently to have ignored other causes such as poverty, abuse or adult exploitation. Samuel Phillips Day (1833–1916) remarked in *The Athenaeum* in 1859 that 'no condition of life is exempt' from the scourge of youth crime – 'even [...] the clergy'.[15] Criminality, he warned, was spreading from the bottom of society upwards. Outside the home, in theatres and dancing saloons, middle-class boys, improperly supervised by neglectful parents, were mixing promiscuously with their inferiors.[16] After absorbing the evil influence of the masses, they returned home to contaminate the middle classes with their vice. *Chambers's Journal* proclaimed in 'Against Boys' (1863) that young males were 'dreadful animal[s]' who belonged to 'the dangerous classes'.[17] Etonians, it claimed, were fundamentally no different from street urchins and had 'one shoe in a Whitechapel lane'. Indeed, adolescent boys, as a social category, seemed like a race apart, as 'haughty and reserved as North American Indians'. As a consequence, schools were places that existed beyond the bounds of 'civilization', in which scandalous behavior was treated merely as a 'matter of course'.[18] The imputation of innate, inevitable and irremediable criminality was, of course, strengthened by recapitulation theories, which said that young people partook of the same moral immaturity as was supposedly exhibited by so-called 'primitive' peoples.[19] S.P. Day's solution to the all-pervading juvenile crime problem was a state-supervised

---

12 Worsley 1849, p. 9.
13 Ibid., pp. 1, 200–203.
14 Shore 1999, pp. 20–21. Shore suggests that 'changes in penal and policing practices' were responsible for the apparent increase in crime.
15 Day 1858, p. 121.
16 Ibid., pp. 157–86.
17 'Against Boys' 1863, p. 145.
18 Ibid., pp. 146–47.
19 Cunningham 1991, pp. 123–32 gives a good survey of the recapitulation/juvenile delinquency debate.

'comprehensive system of national education as might embrace all grades of the community, irrespective of their social rank or their theological predilections'.[20] He also recommended the suppression of 'poisonous' street literature.[21] Few others, however, recommended this level of social engineering.

Although lacking in sophistication, these analyses were at least an attempt to investigate the sources of social disorder rather than merely to call for punishments to be meted out to antisocial sectors of society. As such, they can be read as having a place in what Reginia Gagnier terms a 'vulgar Foucauldian' model of the history of discipline.[22] According to the Foucauldian model, the eighteenth and nineteenth centuries saw a dramatic change in the way social order was maintained. Gone was the practice of maintaining power through the public humiliation, beating, mutilation and execution of those who failed to conform to the rules of their rigidly stratified societies.[23] Instead, order was to be imposed through the education of the young, the re-education of transgressors and the scientific treatment of the insane. This new-style education would take place in an integrated system of institutions that used systematized methods to manipulate the individual subject's sense of self and identity, coercing him or her to conform to the status quo.[24] Not only the criminal justice system, but all kinds of disciplinary institution – 'the army, the school and the hospital' – were harnessed to produce a nation of 'docile', pliable subjects.[25] However, there was no way to undertake this vast social engineering project without a full understanding of those who needed to be disciplined, and in order to gain this understanding, detailed studies into the causes of disobedience and anti-social behavior were undertaken. An army of right-thinking, systematically trained bureaucrats, administrators and army officers was recruited to oversee the effort. The newer Victorian public schools – designed, in part, to create a bureaucratic class to unify the nation, consolidate power among the elite and expand the empire – would seem to have been ideal candidates for participation in the disciplinary scheme. Not only could boys at school be trained according to the latest disciplinary principles, they could also be trained to proliferate these principles throughout the nation and empire.

Foucauldian theory, of course, also proposes that social discipline changed not only on the institutional level, but also in the range of punishments an individual wrongdoer might receive. Practical, everyday methods of dealing with transgressors began, very gradually, to embrace 'newer' kinds of punishment appropriate to 'rational', post-Enlightenment societies. As Foucault famously remarked, '[p]unishment had gradually ceased to be a spectacle. And whatever

---

20 Day 1858, p. 346.
21 Ibid., p. 175.
22 Gagnier (1991) argues that 'what boys learned was discipline not knowledge, surveillance not learning' (p. 178).
23 Foucault 1991, p. 8.
24 Ibid., ch. 2, *passim*.
25 Ibid., p. 136.

theatrical elements it still retained were now downgraded'.[26] For progressives, disciplinary systems came less to center on physical coercion and more to aspire to the 'higher aim' of reforming the very thought patterns of the wrongdoer.[27] As I will show later, British educators struggled to find alternatives to the flogging system that had hitherto been practically their only sanction against bad behavior, idleness and academic failure.

Many Victorian trends in educational reform tidily reflect those outlined in *Discipline and Punish*, as I will demonstrate later in this chapter. However, as Lauren Goodlad has pointed out, *Discipline and Punish* with its focus on panopticism ('a totalizing paradigm in which human subjectivity is reduced to the effect of an inescapable mode of domination') fails to account for more specifically British ideas of 'governance' and character building.[28] In Britain, unlike mainland Europe, the 'centralized state was smaller, less intrusive, and more reliant on local and voluntary supports'. Paternalism and a suspicion against mechanical means of ordering the populace were considered to be

> the hallmark of an exceptional liberal heritage including the myth of pre-Norman Anglo-Saxon liberty, the civic republican tradition, Puritan dissent, Lockean individualism, laissez-faire political economy, and, in the nineteenth century, aspects of the romantic movement.

This Lockean perspective led to a distaste towards 'the noxious state interference' purportedly 'endured by Continental and Oriental peoples',[29] and this distrust of the state had an influence on policy making. While government reports and associated pieces of legislation poured forth abundantly, they did not, on the whole, result in an increase in bureaucratic control of public life on the scale seen on the continent. Goodlad comments, for example, on the failure of Edwin Chadwick to implement a systematized public health policy through the 1848 Public Health Act.[30] Similarly, while a grandiose report such as that of the Clarendon Commission into life at the public schools was an impressive piece of state-sponsored research, it resulted, through the 1868 Public Schools Act, not in the government imposing centralized control but in the delegation of school management to independent governing bodies.[31] George Villiers Earl of Clarendon may have been inspired by European educational systems[32] but, far from implementing a continental-style, comprehensive *lyceé* system, the commission actually made private education

---

26 Ibid., p. 9.
27 Ibid., p. 11.
28 Goodlad 2003, p. 2.
29 Ibid., p. 3. Of course, a stubborn conservatism also had a lot to do with resistance to structural reform, particularly in public school governance.
30 Ibid., pp. 86–87.
31 Shrosbree 1988, p. 180.
32 Ibid., p. 61.

more exclusive by abolishing the right of poorer local boys to subsidized education at the schools. This freed the schools from local accountability and brought them a status as being apart from mainstream education. As Colin Shrosbree remarks, 'the public schools' supporters [...] discouraged the government from implementing many of the Report's recommendations'.[33] In their view, rationalizing the system would simply have been un-British: 'The irrationality of public school organization [...] was defended on the grounds that irrationality was an English characteristic and therefore to be admired'.[34] Indeed, there seems to have been a cross-class resistance to state involvement in family affairs, because the family was regarded as an inviolable, private institution. This concern for privacy meant, for instance, that activities aimed at preventing child abuse were generally undertaken not by the state but by charities run by the socially-concerned middle classes, as George Behlmer's work on the NSPCC has shown.[35] The private family realm also extended into independent education, where the teacher, standing in for the parent as a figure of authority, could also be deemed immune from the state. A teacher could even excuse wanton cruelty by claiming that it was legitimate discipline sanctioned by a parent, as was demonstrated in the *R v. Hopley* manslaughter case.[36]

Notwithstanding this ambivalence towards the state, most public schools did engage to some extent in modernization schemes that ostensibly seem rather 'Benthamite' – in building, dress code, teaching methods and so on. However, the writings of those engaged in public school reform frequently urged for more intimate, individualistic, schemes of character formation. These strategies were similar to the ideas of 'pastorship' that Goodlad has highlighted in her analysis of Foucault's works on governmentality, ideas that 'reformulate the paradox of disciplinary individualism by introducing human agency, and, in theory, de-emphasizing the state'.[37] In the national context, 'pastorship' was a process by which influential, charismatic, paternalistic mentors from the upper classes developed close interpersonal relationships with sectors of society they deemed to be psychologically and morally immature (typically, the working classes or the young), in order to help them cultivate a sense of 'character'. Coleridge envisioned this mentorship being carried out by the 'clerisy' – an elite class of culturally educated men who could 'humanize' the populace through education – and this philosophy was promoted by commentators such as Ruskin and Matthew Arnold.[38] Goodlad's discussion of pastorship centers mainly on middle-class attempts to change working-class behavior. However, the ideas are just as applicable to a school context, partly because they resemble so closely the Arnoldian ideas of fatherhood and pastoral care outlined in Chapters 1 and 2.

---

33 Ibid., p. 178.
34 Ibid., p. 8.
35 See Behlmer 1982.
36 See below.
37 Goodlad 2003, p. 18.
38 Ibid. For a good summary of the clerisy idea, see Allen 1969, p. 65.

Many schools, however, seem to have been more willing to reform their physical environments than to engage in a full-scale reappraisal of the disciplinary relationships between boys and masters. Some administrations embraced a peculiar mixture of the modern and the traditional. A snapshot of a school during its transition from pre- to post-Enlightenment standards can be seen in Benjamin Bradney Bockett's autobiographical account of early nineteenth-century Reading School, *Our School: Or, Scraps and Scrapes in Schoolboy Life* (1857). At Reading, the school, the local prison and a museum of punishment were in close proximity. Bockett describes the 'humane architecture' of the buildings, at least some of which had new additions made in the late eighteenth century by social progressives. The headmaster, Richard Valpy (at Reading from 1781 to 1830), a member of the Royal Humane Society, financed the building of a new schoolroom with his own money and encouraged boys to perform dramas in English, Latin and Greek in aid of charity.[39] He forbade pugilism because it caused black eyes and 'bloody noses', which he regarded as a 'stigma', and had the boys practice life-saving techniques in the river.[40] In this seemingly 'humanitarian' institution, however, there were throwbacks to a more violent era. Valpy was a notorious flogger. The boys were uncomfortably close to the jail during public executions (a 'stage of horrors') and seeing justice '"done" upon the body of the unhappy culprit' gave Bockett (an opponent of capital punishment) nightmares.[41] Bockett also mentions that a boy died doing agricultural labor at school.[42] Flogging here firmly remains as a 'ceremon[y] in which power is manifested' for more general edification,[43] the Head seeing no contradiction between his disciplinary policy and his humanitarianism.

In terms of physical environment, indeed, most public schools show evidence of having undergone a re-organization around the middle of the century: an increase in adult supervision, a tightening of the curriculum to limit free time and the modification of buildings both for hygienic and disciplinary purposes. School life began to be organized in a style that to some extent resembles that described by Foucault, where daily life is conducted 'according to a codification that partitions as closely as possible time, space, [and] movement [...] mak[ing] possible the meticulous control of the operations of the body'.[44] A typical example of architectural reform is the manner in which the celebrated but infamous Long Chamber at Eton was partitioned in 1845 into smaller rooms more easily supervised by masters.[45]

---

39 See http://www.readingschool.reading.sch.uk/school/schoolhistory/index.php, Oldfellow 1857, p. 33 and Armytage 1865, p. 86.
40 Oldfellow 1857, pp. 35, 36–37.
41 Ibid., p. 87.
42 Ibid., p. 89.
43 Foucault 1991, p. 46.
44 Ibid., p. 137.
45 Coleridge 1896, p. 8. Since the schools had frequently outgrown their original buildings, most reforms probably had as much to do with practicality as with ideological panopticism.

Some reformers believed keeping boys subject to the scrutiny of masters would stop 'immorality'. Thus Maurice Charles Hime, master of Foyle College, Londonderry, recommended much later in the century that schools provided panoptical open dormitories with a master's room at the end, to enable 'magisterial supervision'.[46] However, documentary evidence demonstrates that mechanistic attempts to produce 'docile' bodies were often mistrusted as undemocratic, 'un-British' and intrusive (indeed, Hime clearly anticipates this accusation, since he takes the trouble to explain that 'Open, honest, above-board supervision' by teachers 'is not espionage' any more than is supervision by the police or lunatic asylum attendants[47]). Some commentators inveighed against the idea of teachers spying on boys. H.C. Adams complained in 1878 that the regimented new quarters at Winchester allowed boys no privacy.[48] The sense of confinement felt by Kipling at the United Services College between 1878 and 1882 under a highly supervisory regime is documented in *Stalky & Co*. When the boys try to find a private space in some furze bushes to read and smoke, they are pursued by their housemaster, Prout, who is eager to force them into communal sports. Good boys, in Prout's book, 'attended House-matches and could be accounted for at any moment'. Prout is the kind of pedagogue who seeks for a deeper knowledge of 'the boy' in order to find a rational way to control him and who is not prepared to allow any degree of privacy, for fear of losing command. Kipling satirizes his theorizing and suggests that his concern for the boys' morals comes from his own unclean imagination (he remarks that 'Mr Prout's imagination leaned to the darker side of life').[49] Kipling's school was typical of schools founded by the Victorians, which offered less freedom of thought and movement than older establishments, as S.P.B. Mais remarked when comparing Rossall (founded 1844) with Sherborne.[50] However, building renovations were sometimes supported by more benign intentions. Edward Thring at Uppingham (1853–1887) had cubicles built specifically to protect boys' privacy.[51]

One way to increase the influence of masters over the boys' everyday lives was for them to take over the management of leisure-time activities that had previously been initiated by boys. Team games, previously the concern of boys alone, were gradually incorporated into the curriculum and organized to fill the time boys had previously had to themselves, giving masters the opportunity to keep an eye on their charges to a greater extent than before.[52] The institutionalization of school sport

---

46 Hime 1899, p. 17. Claudia Nelson suggested to me that Foyle College may have implemented a panoptical regime because it was either influenced by, or was competing with, local Catholic schools, which were likely to be implementing more 'continental'-style disciplinary policies.
47 Ibid., p. 21.
48 Adams 1878, pp. 235–37.
49 Kipling 1987, p. 37.
50 Mais 1937, p. 66.
51 Mangan 2000, p. 45.
52 See Chandler 1991, pp. 171–204.

is popularly credited to George Cotton, Head of Marlborough (1851–1858), who took up his post shortly after a rebellion that began when starved and overcrowded boys turned a fireworks display into a riot.[53] The boys were also in the habit of marauding around the local area poaching and Cotton thought that organized games would burn surplus energy.[54] J.A. Mangan has called the 'Circular to Parents' that explained Cotton's innovations an 'epitaph to unsupervised leisure'.[55] Newer schools and ex-grammar schools – for example, Marlborough and Uppingham (under the pro-sport Edward Thring from 1853 to 1887) – had never developed the tradition of free leisure time that boys enjoyed at Rugby or Eton. Mangan has explained how, at these schools, muscular Christian rhetoric was grafted onto a competitive sports ethos to inculcate discipline, a sense of community and the ability to succeed in the marketplace.[56]

Both Mangan and P.J. Rich have also discussed in great depth how school authorities invented and used symbolic codes, inscribed on newly-introduced uniforms, badges, imperial crests and other paraphernalia, to create a sense of common identity between boys that would reinforce their sense of belonging to a 'cultural hegemony' when they went out to govern the empire.[57] Rich argues that the glamour these symbolic rituals imparted to school life was useful in educating future generations of native elites in upper-class British values.[58] As I remarked before, public schools had always encouraged a certain amount of theatricality and ritual. Victorian schoolmasters capitalized on this appetite for display by inventing activities designed to affirm the national and imperial status quo. However, while newer schools invented pseudo-'traditions' and rituals to create a sense of corporate identity to give them legitimacy, older schools erased long-standing traditions initiated by boys and replaced them by more sanitized versions invented by masters. According to Arthur Duke Coleridge (1830–1913), Eton banned its traditional songs (written by boys) in the 1840s, due to their 'viciousness'.[59] Eric Parker describes how they were replaced in the 1880s with new songs written by masters.[60] Montem was also replaced by the more sedate Fourth of July celebrations.[61] A new apparatus of cultural symbolism was externally imposed on boys, the meaning of which was stringently controlled by adults in order to ensure the maximum possible conformity to the status quo.

There was a desire not only to control boys' bodies and actions but also to control what was in their heads by regulating and standardizing their studies. Gladstone

---

53 Mangan 2000, p. 23, Gathorne-Hardy 1977, pp. 103–5.
54 Money 1997, p. 66.
55 Mangan 2000, p. 23.
56 Ibid., *passim.*
57 See Rich 1993, pp. 16–17.
58 See ibid., ch. 2.
59 Coleridge 1896, p. 37.
60 Parker 1914, p. 255.
61 Johnstone 1870, p. 69.

commented to A.C. Benson that, when he was at Eton, 'a boy might if he chose learn something, or might if he chose learn nothing, but that one thing he could not do, and that was to learn anything inaccurately'.[62] This seems to have changed by the time Charles Frederick Johnstone remarked, in 1870, that Eton boys were no longer 'trusted' to organize their own time.[63] Public bodies demanded to know what boys were learning, among them the Clarendon Commission (1861–1864), which opened the big schools to public scrutiny (prompting *Fraser* to announce that education was 'no longer a secret'[64]). The Commission recommended stricter examination, closer regulation of boys' private time, the supervision of games to prevent idleness and greater state control.[65] It also warned that public schools were not equipping boys to perform at their best in the national examinations that had been proliferating since mid-century, such as those for the army and Oxbridge, since they concentrated on rote-learning Classics rather than on more modern subjects.[66] The Clarendon Commission, however, was not backed up to any great extent in terms of new legislation to deal with the schools and it was competition from newer schools, rather than any concerted effort on behalf of the state, that drove them to reform their curricula.

The reforms described above supposedly 'rationalized' the organization of learning and discipline in schools. However, the actual discipline of individual miscreants – particularly in smaller private schools – often involved somewhat less rational, pre-Enlightenment methods, with publicly inflicted physical punishment still central to school culture into the twentieth century. George Behlmer comments that 'By 1880 the flogging of scholars at both public and school board schools had diminished appreciably, though some masters would continue to wield the birch rod with brutal abandon' and that 'Increasingly, even "mild" scholastic punishment evoked public anger'.[67] Nonetheless, there was a general unwillingness to abandon the legal right to flog, even though the vicious mass floggings of individuals such as John Keate were a thing of the past. As Bishop Welldon, former Headmaster of Harrow, commented in *Recollections and Reflections* (1915), 'Schoolboys, from Horace to Augustine, from Augustine to Luther, from Luther to the victims of Busby and Keate' had always been 'treated as the natural objects of cruelty'.[68]

Attitudes towards the discipline of schoolchildren were out of step with wider developments in British penal law. By the time the humanitarian Henry Salt (1851–1939) wrote *The Flogging Craze: A Statement Against Corporal Punishment* in 1916, most forms of judicial and military corporal punishment had been abolished.

---

62 Benson 1899, p. 505.
63 Johnstone 1870, p. 37.
64 'Public School Education' 1868, p. 301.
65 'Public Schools. – Report of the Commission' 1864, p. 657. See also T. Markby 1867 and 'Public Schools' 1865.
66 Armytage 1965, p. 127.
67 Behlmer 1982, p. 45.
68 Salt 1916, p. 35. Salt had taught and studied at Eton.

Corporal punishment was abolished for women in 1820, restricted to offences 'against the person of the Queen' in 1861 and prohibited for soldiers (except in military prisons) by 1881.[69] It was not until 1987 that it was abolished in British state schools and 1999 in private schools.[70] The fact that flogging remained legal, though, does not mean that the practice went unchallenged. Corporal punishment, and the question of whether it had a place in education, lay at the heart of arguments about the moral capabilities of the young and, as I will show below, the 1860s was a time of particular interest in the subject which saw the rise of a concerted movement to find alternatives. I will discuss below these debates as they appear in fictional and biographical accounts of school discipline, but first I will outline some of the issues that concerned Victorian commentators on corporal punishment, in particular the debate surrounding the *R v. Hopley* trial which, arguably, sparked this upsurge in interest.

So far, historians have discussed corporal punishment mainly in terms of the history of sexuality. John Chandos, Ian Gibson and others have already discussed this side of the corporal punishment debate in great detail. Certainly, some opponents of corporal punishment cited indecency as a reason for its abolition. For example, an early attack on flogging in 1830 by the former Etonian and future Home Secretary George Cornewall Lewis (1806–1863), alleged that beating in school was 'indecor[ous]'.[71] Nonetheless, few mid-Victorian anti-flogging writers, even the most vehement, mention sexual abuse as a reason for terminating the practice. The Rugby chronicler George Melly, at school around the time of Arnold's death, remarked in 1854 that 'such cant was unknown in my school days',[72] which implies that Cornewall Lewis's protests did not achieve as much public attention as they might have done. In this chapter, therefore, I wish to discuss less-often examined aspects of the Victorian debate on corporal punishment that shed more light on attitudes to adolescence.

As I mentioned before, we should be wary here of relying too much on Foucauldian concepts of disciplinary reform and of reading these ideas into the works of Victorian commentators. Anti-floggers were primarily interested not in replacing flogging with more 'modern' systems of social control, but in the impact of flogging on civil liberties and on the paternalistic bonds between teacher and pupil already discussed in previous chapters. When exploring alternatives to the flogging system, educationalists were more likely to use the Lockean language of social contract than to recommend the kinds of coercive domination that feature so highly in analyses of pan-European educational reform. There were several basic

---

69 Ibid., pp. 16–17.
70 King 1987, p. 51. Corporal punishment was banned as violating Article Three of the 1950 European Convention on Human Rights (against torture and inhuman or degrading treatment) and Article Two of the 1952 Convention, supporting the right of all children to education.
71 *Edinburgh Review* no. 101, pp. 65–80, quoted in Chandos, p. 229.
72 Melly 1854, pp. 107–8.

arguments at play in the corporal punishment debate. On the most fundamental level, many opponents to corporal punishment complained that it was simply a poor way of solving disciplinary problems. The Victorians were here pre-empted by Robert Southey who, as a schoolboy, wrote in *The Flagellant* that

> CORPORAL PUNISHMENT appears to be a method equally disgraceful and ineffectual. It requires but a very little fortitude to disregard all the castigation a master can bestow; and if I may use my own observation, as by any means decisive, the greatest dunces are generally the most able to endure their chastisement.[73]

More often commentators took a far more political line, suggesting that corporal punishment was an affront to democratic values and free citizenship. I will now discuss this strand of the argument, starting with a discussion of a key event that sparked unprecedented interest in the subject from the year 1860.

In many people's eyes, teachers, *in loco parentis*, had a natural right to beat their pupils. This right was established in a test case, *R v. Hopley* (1860), which is cited to the present day in legal and governmental debates across the globe. The Hopley case was bizarre, shocking and baffling to the journalistic and educational world. The defendant, Thomas Hopley, ran a private school in Eastbourne and had a modest reputation as a humanitarian, writer of scientific papers, liberal educationalist and campaigner for reduced working hours for the poor. On the evening of 21 April, Hopley beat a pupil, Reginald Cancellor, who had hydrocephalus, for two hours, with a thick stick and a skipping rope.[74] It is unclear how old Cancellor was, but Hiroaki Terasaki, who has written the only full-scale monograph on the case, suggests thirteen or fourteen.[75] After the beating, Hopley carried the child upstairs to bed. Whether Reginald was dead or alive at this point is uncertain, but Hopley claimed he was alive. Hopley then cleaned his staircase, which was covered in blood. When he finally discovered, in the morning, that the boy was dead, Hopley wrapped the body up and sent it to the child's father, claiming that Reginald had had a heart attack.[76]

The beating had taken place because Reginald was unable to do some arithmetic and the court heard how Hopley had beaten his limbs to 'pulp'. The defense argued that Reginald was 'obstinate' and 'slow', that his father had given Hopley written permission to beat him and that the master was a gentleman. With these considerations, the charge was reduced from murder to manslaughter and Hopley received four years' imprisonment.[77] Chief Justice Cockburn then commented that,

---

73 Southey 1792, pp. 77–78.
74 Terasaki 2001, p. 12.
75 Ibid., p. 16.
76 Ibid., p. 13.
77 *The Times* (July 24, 1860), p. 11.

> By the law of England, a parent or a schoolmaster [...] may, for the purpose of correcting what is evil in the child, inflict moderate and reasonable corporal punishment – always with this condition: that it is reasonable and moderate.[78]

This case established the idea of 'reasonable chastisement' in common law. Cockburn determined that corporal punishment could not be deemed acceptable if it

> be administrated for the gratification of passion or of rage, or if it be immoderate and excessive in its nature or degree, or if it be protracted beyond the child's powers of endurance, or with an instrument unfitted for the purpose and calculated to produce danger to the life or limb.

He cautioned that 'if evil consequences to life and limb ensue, then the person inflicting it is answerable to the law, and if death ensues it will be manslaughter'.[79] However, there was no discussion in court about whether physical punishment was an appropriate response to Reginald's problems. All involved seem to have taken it for granted that it was appropriate to beat a boy with a learning disability because he was 'slow'.

The Hopley case was all the more surprising in view of the defendant's record of publishing educational tracts. Indeed, he continued to publish while in prison, issuing 'Facts bearing on the Death of Reginald Cancellor: With a Supplement and a Sequel' during the first year of his sentence.[80] Hopley claimed that Reginald, who had arrived at his school overweight, had benefited from its special exercise regime and he emphasized the boy's 'strong inclination to obstinacy',[81] as he had done in the trial. The use of the word 'obstinacy' was particularly relevant here, because it echoed John Locke's statement in *Some Thoughts Concerning Education* that only 'obstinacy and rebellion' in children were sufficient reasons for administering corporal punishment.[82] Hopley thus depicted himself as an educationalist in the liberal tradition, whose actions were justifiable under Lockean precepts. He even went as far as to claim that he was an opponent of corporal punishment – so much of an opponent, indeed, that he lacked a cane (which is why he used a stick to beat Reginald).[83] The jury, press and educational establishment seem to have swallowed this post-hoc rationalization. *The Brighton Observer* dubbed the case 'The Eastbourne Tragedy', but in the eyes of commentators the tragedy seems to have lain not in the fact that a disabled child had been brutally killed, but that a seemingly good man had committed a terrible act. With a few exceptions, there was no clamour for the abolition of corporal punishment in schools. According to

---

78 King 1987, p. 10.
79 *R. v. Hopley*, 2 F&F 202, 175 ER 1024, Assizes, July 23, 1860.
80 Terasaki 2001, p. 143.
81 Ibid., pp. 156, 158.
82 Locke 1768, p. 41.
83 Terasaki 2001, pp. 166–67.

Terasaki, most educational journals responded to the case by reaffirming the need for corporal punishment, although the *Educational Times* did remark that teachers should be careful to distinguish obstinacy from inability.[84]

The opposition to corporal punishment sparked by *Hopley* seems to have been a specifically literary phenomenon rather than a case taken up by the media in general. The cases of cruelty that did attract media attention – such as those at Harrow (1853) and Winchester (1872) – mostly involved boys beating other boys.[85] For example, when a prefect broke four 4′-long ash saplings on a Winchester boy's back, his father notified *The Times* and the case went to the school governors.[86] The *Saturday Review* observed that the incident was evidence of the headmaster's ineptitude. It remarked that his defence of his prefect was 'vague and confused' and that he showed little knowledge of his boys, having stated that the prefect was a 'good and gentle boy'. However, although the *Review* said the matter should have gone to court, it nonetheless maintained that a moderate beating was a 'salutary discipline'.[87] Not only the media but also the Clarendon Commission failed to find fault with punishment regimes, except at Winchester, where it advised against kicking and the use of implements not intended for punishment (for example, rackets).[88] It never questioned the propriety of adults beating juveniles. Indeed, during a failed attempt to implement a Bill limiting the corporal punishment of minors in 1863, birching was recommended as a way of preventing the use of harsher methods.[89] Both media and government accepted the view that, provided it was not too harsh, corporal punishment *per se* was a 'natural' part of education.[90] Although John Chandos has suggested that there was a conspiracy of silence among ex-public schoolboys 'inhibited by prudery',[91] it is also possible that most people, including those who had no specialist interest in education, took it for granted that corporal punishment was legitimate because children, as minors, were the property of parents, who were entitled to do what they pleased in the privacy of the home. After all, a mitigating factor in the *R v. Hopley* trial was that the father had given permission for the boy to be beaten.

In the decade following the Hopley case, however, an unprecedented number of texts appeared which questioned the propriety of corporal punishment. Indeed, it is difficult to find a work published after *R v. Hopley* that treats corporal

---

84 Ibid., p. 119.
85 For in-depth discussion see Gibson 1978, pp. 71–72.
86 'Judicious Kicking' 1872, p. 660.
87 Ibid., p. 661.
88 Clarendon Commission 1864, vol. 2, pp. 163–74. According to Shrosbree 1988 (p. 23), Lord Clarendon himself was opposed to flogging.
89 Shrosbree 1988, p. 23.
90 An exception was at Shrewsbury in 1874, where the Head caused a scandal by beating a boy for having beer in his room (ibid., p. 20). The boy was a day boy (p. 124), so perhaps his parents felt they had handed less responsibility for disciplining him over to the Head.
91 Chandos 1984, p. 230.

punishment with such blasé indifference as the pre-Hopley *Tom Brown*. The incongruity of a professed liberal educationalist using the Lockean language of reason to excuse murder seems to have spurred writers to go further than Locke and to question the fundamental acceptability of any form of physical punishment. A considerable number of public school stories, especially those by Evangelicals, opposed corporal punishment and suggested alternative modes of discipline: some writers even show evidence of having made a U-turn on the issue of flogging. Thus, in the pre-Hopley *Eric*, Farrar, in Lockean vein, makes little argument against his protagonist being beaten by a rational and humanitarian teacher for 'proud and dogged obstinacy'.[92] However, in *St Winifred's*, he makes plenty of use of the words 'obstinate' and 'obstinacy' in his opposition to corporal punishment, adopting, with irony, Hopley's explicit use of the same terms. Thus, Walter Evson's enemy, Mr Paton, fails to realize that the boy lacks training, believing that he is 'at once able and obstinate, capable of doing excellently, and willfully refusing to do so'.[93] His repeated beatings have the effect of engendering the very 'Lockean' obstinacy to which he first, mistakenly, attributes the boy's failure. Farrar's solution to disciplinary problems has already been addressed. I will discuss other anti-flogging texts soon, but first I will introduce the main points of contention in the corporal punishment debate, particularly those concerning the growth of young people as democratically literate citizens.

Those who defended the corporal punishment of children stressed its divine, natural ordination. The populist, conservative *Family Herald* in 1849, for example, argues that children are physical rather than moral beings, needing the 'basest government'. Pain is nature's discipline: a 'burnt child dreads the fire'. Children know that parents who disregard this law are 'out of step' with the 'Divine'. The writer explains that children naturally demonstrate 'primary instincts' (selfishness), which are controllable only by fear. A fearful child, 'feeble and governable', becomes 'beautiful and interesting'. In a regime of 'physical training', a child should receive regular doses of pain and be denied physical pleasures (for example, 'treacle'). Pain is essential for developing the 'reasoning faculties'; withholding pain is 'sentimental' and 'perverts' these faculties.[94] Furthermore, adults must be careful not to reason verbally with children. Arguing with children degrades parents, especially if mothers begin to cry. The household, warns the magazine, 'must not be kept in uproar, waiting for the logical conclusion between you and a refracting boy'. Children who have been 'reasoned [into] compliance' think they have done their parents a favor. School discipline, like discipline at home, should be physical, not verbal. At school, 'serious and ceremonial' public displays of punishment resembling the 'pillor[y]' and the 'scaffold' should be used to teach boys to feel fear, self-distaste, 'sensitivi[ty] to pain' and 'shame'.[95] The *Family Herald* never

---

92 Farrar 1899, p. 80.
93 Farrar 1910, p. 42.
94 'Pain. – Corporal Punishment &c' 1879, p. 460.
95 Ibid., p. 461.

actually mentions how children are to be taught to make rational moral choices and, since the writer believes that children always pervert reasoned arguments for their own ends, it is hard to imagine how they might be educated to make independent decisions. 'Discipline' here is crude – nothing more than teaching the child what sorts of misdeed result in punishment.

On the other hand, more sophisticated responses to the question of discipline tackled the idea that moral development proceeds by stages, something that foreshadowed the ideas of Jean Piaget, Erik Erikson, Lawrence Kohlberg and Carol Gilligan. In 'On the Discipline of Public Schools' (1835), a reply to an article in the *Journal of Education* that had attacked flogging at Winchester, Thomas Arnold outlined the difference between punishment for children and for adolescents. Although Arnold believed in physical punishment as a last resort, he stated that, among public schoolboys over the age of fifteen, 'there could nowhere be found a set of young men amongst whom punishment of any kind was less frequent, or by whom it was less required'.[96] The reason that adolescents require the rod less is that they have a more developed sense of morality than children. While children decide how to behave by considering nothing more than whether they will be punished for a specific action, adolescents strive to achieve the regard of those around them.

Arnold anticipates Kohlberg's identification of distinct 'levels' of moral reasoning that an individual passes through during his or her development. In the first, the 'preconventional', the child focuses on punishments and rewards; in the second, the 'conventional', he or she seeks to conform to societal norms in order to win social approval; and in the third, the 'postconventional', he or she develops a concept of social contract and an ability to handle the idea of universal ethical principles.[97] Arnold's child resembles the child in Kohlberg's earliest stages, who 'Obey[s] rules to avoid punishment' and 'Conform[s] to obtain rewards'. Arnold's adolescent, on the other hand, has entered Kohlberg's second level, where to 'Conform to avoid disapproval and dislike by others' and 'to avoid censure by legitimate authorities and resultant guilt' take priority.[98] For Arnold, corporal punishment serves to heighten boys' sense of the difference between immature and mature behavior, because it publicly proclaims the antisocial attitude of an offending individual, and draws a sense of collective censure. The fact that it is degrading and childish makes it into a deterrent and boys will strive to behave rationally in order to avoid it:

> whilst corporal punishment was retained on principle as fitly answering to, and marking the naturally inferior state of, boyhood, morally and intellectually, [...] we should cherish and encourage to the utmost all attempts made by the several boys as individuals to escape from the natural punishment of their age by rising above its naturally low tone

---

96 Findlay 1897, p. 225.
97 Kohlberg 1981, pp. 17–19.
98 Ibid., p. 19.

of principle [...] every approach to the steadiness of principle shown in manhood should be considered as giving a claim to the respectability of manhood – that we should be delighted to forget the inferiority of their age, as they labored to lessen their moral and intellectual inferiority.[99]

In fact, Arnold remarks that any boy over fifteen who requires corporal punishment should be thrown out of school because he will be 'intellectually incapable of deriving benefit from the system of the place, or morally indisposed to do so'.[100] In this approach, Arnold again echoes Locke, who stipulated that the 'apprehension of shame and disgrace' should be a tutor's principal weapon against bad behavior in all cases except those involving 'obstinacy and rebellion'.[101] Thomas Hughes shows Arnold's philosophy in action in *Tom Brown*, where Tom is flogged only twice, both times for what might be called 'obstinacy'; once for the criminal offence of poaching, and once for visiting a fair 'for no earthly pleasure except that of doing what [he was] told not to do'.[102]

Arnold's ideas of moral development were further elaborated in George Melly's *School Experiences of a Fag* (1854), an autobiographical work written to defend the disciplinary scheme at Rugby ('Harby') against one of the periodic media attacks on fagging and flogging amongst boys in public schools.[103] This text shows how flogging could be incorporated into a 'modernized' disciplinary system, and how the rhetoric of Lockean English liberty could be used to rebut claims that disciplinary reform in schools was going down the path to panoptical continental methods of control. Melly (1830–1894), a ship-owner and the MP for Stoke-on-Trent, entered Rugby in 1840, two years before Arnold's death.[104] His parents chose Rugby, he explains, because of its disciplinary policies. Melly's previous (private) school had lacked adequate supervision and was a realm of moral chaos in which the strongest boys ruled the others by fear and where boys did things in private 'too gross and revolting to be even hinted at'. When he arrived, he was 'inaugurated into [his] room with rites worthy of a Vehmgericht in their solemnity, and of freemasonry in their secrecy'.[105] The boys abused each other 'in perfect silence' and invented forms of bullying which did not mark the body and were invisible to adults, but which left 'traces' in later life.[106] What concerns Melly most about this abuse, however, is not the bullying itself, but the secrecy. 'Open', visible bullying, he tells us, is not so bad, because it damages the bully's reputation more than it hurts the victim. The basis for better and kinder discipline, explains

---

99 Findlay 1897, p. 227.
100 Ibid., p. 228.
101 Locke 1768, p. 24, 41.
102 Hughes 1989, p. 208.
103 Melly 1854, p. iii.
104 Ibid., p. 100.
105 Ibid., pp. 23–36.
106 Ibid., pp. 38–39.

Melly, is for teachers and parents to supervise boys more closely. He also urges the boys among his readers who might be in similar situations to open themselves to adult scrutiny and make 'confidants of their parents', rather than keeping their school activities secret through 'false honor' and a fear of contaminating home.[107]

Discipline was maintained at Rugby, in contrast, through Arnold's 'monitorial' system, a network of intensive supervision by sixth form pupils reporting directly to the staff, with corporal punishment as an ultimate deterrent. Arnold's system (consciously or not) echoed a 'rational' educational scheme proposed by Jeremy Bentham in his discourse on secondary education, *Chrestomathia* ('Useful Learning' 1815–1817). *Chrestomathia* described how Joseph Lancaster's division of labor principle had been applied to secondary education at Edinburgh High School and recommended a monitorial system as the best way to prevent rebellion and avoid the need for corporal punishment.[108] This system, also known as the 'fagging' system in a public school context, has already been described in Chapter 2 of this volume. However, Melly goes to great pains to differentiate Thomas Arnold's disciplinary policies from the supposedly undemocratic panoptical schemes of continental Europe. Melly explains that not only did Rugby boys have a monitorial system, they also had their own laws, taxes, periodical press and a debating club to discuss contemporary issues. The Headmaster, in using this system, was a 'true liberal', because having boy-monitors rather than staff supervise the school avoided teachers undertaking repressive 'espionage'.[109] Perhaps Melly was here contrasting Rugby to the Catholic systems in mainland Europe which supposedly employed 'espionage' to enforce conformity and obedience to the status quo, such as that described in Charlotte Brontë's *Villette* of the previous year (1853).

Melly seems to be implying here that in a democratic state, adolescents should receive an education that nurtures autonomy while protecting them from the extremes of abuse which *laissez-faire* systems allowed. To Melly, the defining feature of the public school is 'self-government', which gives boys a sense of civic responsibility that will fit them to live in a democratic state. 'The British constitution', he explains, 'is founded on the principle of self-government, and the great value of a public school is its close resemblance to the outer world around it'.[110] Thus, discipline does not end in obedience; the aim of discipline is to produce morally literate subjects who can make independent ethical decisions. Melly's description of the system as a constitutional democracy implies that he considers boys to be capable of making social contracts. In terms of theories of psychological development, this means that he is placing a great deal of confidence in the reasoning abilities of the adolescent. Kohlberg defines social-contract-forming behavior as part of the second 'highest' stage of moral consciousness, a stage in which individuals conceive of morality 'in terms of general individual rights and

---

107 Ibid., pp. 85–86.
108 Bentham 1983, Armytage 1965, pp. 94–95.
109 Melly 1854, pp. 302, 308.
110 Ibid., p. 231.

in terms of standards that have been critically examined and agreed on by the whole society'.[111] Melly implies that most public schoolboys can reach this stage and that British education is peculiar in facilitating this kind of development.

Melly also describes how boys with a less developed understanding of morality were disciplined through a mixture of very basic corporal punishment and a more sophisticated system of social censure. There were two types of corporal punishment at 'Harby': 'lickings' by the monitors (in public) and, for very serious offences, floggings by the Head, which involved letters being sent home and which brought about enormous shame and social ostracism. If the Head had to flog a boy, the sentence would be carried out in private, observed by two of the boy's peers to ensure fair play.[112] To Melly, the corporal punishment of boys by monitors demonstrated sound democratic logic:

> What is more right and fitting than that a boy should, on being detected in bullying and teasing a boy smaller than himself, be publicly bullied and thrashed by a bigger boy than he, before the rest of his schoolfellows? What is more constitutional than that the house should punish those who render its members uncomfortable; that the society should chastise those who commit offences against itself?[113]

The fundamental assumption is that the schoolboy community is capable of making quite complex judicial decisions and overseeing punishment to make sure it is done justly. Melly dismisses other forms of punishment (for example, writing lines) as 'irrational', since they waste time better spent on schoolwork.[114]

To Melly, therefore, it was important that discipline existed in a 'democratic' framework where the adolescent was judged and punished by his peers. This experience of consensus government prepared boys to exercise their future civic and legal responsibilities in a gradually democratizing world. Writers who were committed opponents of flogging also focused on issues of citizenship, identity, liberty and democracy, often expressing a firm belief in the adolescent ability to understand ideas of social contract and abstract morality. Commentators suggested that, on the route to maturity, both individuals and society as a whole evolve moral systems based less on punishment and conformity and more on abstract moral reasoning. The educationalist A.R. Craig commented in 1844 that physical violence belonged to 'inferior tribes', who lived by 'sensation' and 'instinct' rather than 'ethical purity'.[115] In a developed country, he explained, corporal punishment only happens in times of war, when the army maintains strict coercive discipline and where the individual is a mere 'fragment of a machine'.[116] A school that

---

111 Kohlberg 1981, p. 18.
112 Melly 1884, p. 107–8.
113 Ibid., pp. 213–14.
114 Ibid., p. 214.
115 Craig 1844, p. 2.
116 Ibid., p. 4.

maintains flogging in a peaceful country is therefore an anomaly. At the end of the century, Henry Salt elaborated on this argument when he said that corporal punishment undermined identity and autonomy. He said schoolboys were like 'tattooed savages', who submitted to mindless rituals and were 'stamped by school-boy tradition'.[117] When such boys became men, they were incapable of making informed choices about the education of the next generation because they themselves had been trained to respond to pain rather than to think rationally about the motives for their actions.

In short, therefore, the most prevalent argument against flogging was that it failed to develop the young person's sense of honor and reason and was counterproductive to producing democratic citizens capable of understanding the concept of the social contract. Herbert Spencer remarked that

> the culture of our public schools, by accustoming boys to a despotic form of government and an intercourse regulated by brute force, tends to fit them for a lower state of society than that which exists. And chiefly recruited as our legislature is from among those who are brought up at such schools, this barbarizing influence becomes a hindrance to national progress.[118]

Henry Salt added that corporal punishment is a 'disgrace and a punishment for slaves' – a kind of 'slavery of the mind',[119] reserved for those who cannot understand reasoned argument. If children, women, servants, soldiers or criminals are whipped, they will remain at a 'low stage of civilization' and will never learn how to make rational, autonomous decisions, or to evolve moral sensibility and 'perfect honor'.[120] To support his argument, Salt quoted Herman Melville's remark that flogging was 'feudal' and 'repugnant' to 'democratic institutions'.[121]

Opponents of corporal punishment warned that floggers treated young people like criminals and that this attitude in itself encouraged poor behavior. They denounced the idea that a school should be run on the lines of disciplinary institutions (namely prisons or madhouses) as an educational anathema. Youth, they explained, was not a moral disorder and should not be dealt with as such. In the *Westminster Review* of 1899, T.M. Hopkins argued that 'A school is not a reformatory or house of correction' and that 'boys of bad character should be treated in separate establishments'. By permitting corporal punishment, the legal system 'catalogue[s]' boys with 'the worst of criminals'.[122] Herbert Spencer warned that 'With family governments as with political ones, a harsh despotism

---

117 Salt 1916, p. 33.
118 Spencer 1966, p. 111.
119 Salt 1916, pp. 39, 11.
120 Ibid., pp. 53–54.
121 Ibid., p. 12.
122 Hopkins 1899, p. 462.

itself generates a great part of the crimes it has to repress'.[123] Pro-floggers, on the other hand, subscribed to a more Hobbesian view of society, arguing that all civil discipline is, in essence, repressive. When the Department of Education proposed in 1883 that only headteachers should administer corporal punishment in state schools, *Macmillan's* commented that 'Corporal punishment in school is analogous to martial law in society. Law-breakers know that if the policeman fails, the soldier is in reserve. At the root of all law is martial law'.[124] Since there is no real social contract between the people and their rulers, there can be no social contract between juveniles and teachers.

One writer, Bracebridge Hemyng, explored at length the boy's potential to understand ideas of democratic right and to oppose corporal punishment as an infringement of this right. *Eton School Days* (1864) and its sequel *Butler Burke at Eton* (1865) are about a boy's journey to becoming a responsible, rational citizen and about his conscientious resistance to corporal punishment at school.[125] Hemyng was an old Etonian and former lawyer who wrote part of Mayhew's *London Labor and the London Poor*, as well as producing so-called 'penny dreadful'-style literature, including the *Jack Harkaway* series, which begins with a school story. Among school story writers, Hemyng is probably the most open to the idea of adolescent boys expressing their own opinions about education and his hero spearheads a campaign to reform and democratize Eton's disciplinary system. He argues in this book that, although most boys and masters are caught up in a culture where relationships are defined in terms of competition and violence, it is possible to educate boys who are capable of reason and who do not need to be beaten.

Butler Burke is, initially, another example of 'everyboy'. He gets into trouble as soon as he arrives at Eton by hitting another boy with a cricket stump in a fight – a 'barbarous and unmanly' act that overshadows his early school career.[126] However, after negotiating a series of moral trials, he becomes more responsible. He is helped by his cousin Purefoy, a studious and effeminate boy who spends his free time reading in his 'prettily furnished' room.[127] With Purefoy's encouragement, Butler Burke – 'a believer in muscular Christianity, after the creed of Kingsley'[128] – grows from fighting boy into thinking adult. This is not easy, because Burke's Eton is a world in which relationships are negotiated either through physical violence or through sport and where discipline is maintained through the threat of the rod. Burke's earliest friendship is with Chorley (the boy he hit with a cricket stump) and in this relationship fighting is frequent and verbal intercourse practically non-existent. In detailing the dynamics among Burke's peer group, Hemyng, unlike

---

123 Spencer 1966, p. 135.
124 Runciman 1883, p. 483.
125 Chandos 1984 (p. 140) describes the former work as a 'documentary account', which suggests that he has evidence that it is at least partly biographical.
126 Hemyng 1870, p. 25.
127 Ibid., pp. 39–40.
128 Ibid., p. 230.

Hughes, avoids romanticizing combat with heroic allusion, preferring to present it with squalid realism. Burke's face in one fight, we are told, 'was covered with blood which flowed from his nostrils, and he gasped for breath as if some of the blood had gone down his throat and half choked him'.[129] Eventually, Burke gets an opportunity to re-learn how to relate to others. When some of Purefoy's money is stolen, the boys assume the culprit is Burke and form a lynch mob to duck him in the river, like in 'the Middle Ages'.[130] Meanwhile, the masters impotently stand by to let the boys do what they will. It is left to the rational Purefoy to defend Burke's innocence by putting 'the different links of evidence together' to form a case for Burke's defense that he presents to the housemaster.[131]

Purefoy, a talker rather than a fighter, insists that boys are inherently capable of reason. He argues for Burke in the theft case 'with the ability of a Nisi Prius lawyer addressing a jury'.[132] Purefoy's level of moral maturity excels that of the other boys. When a schoolfellow dies, Purefoy shows Burke how to cope emotionally and intellectually. Burke complains that boys cannot deal intellectually with such matters and Purefoy replies: 'Why not boys as well as men? What's the difference between them? They are both thinking, reasoning beings, and capable of sinning; if so, they are able to repent, and prepare themselves for death'.[133] It takes time, however, for Burke to learn how to talk rather than to fight problems out and he undergoes a kind of martyrdom as a major step in the learning process. After Purefoy has secretly revealed to a master that Chorley, not Burke, stole his money, Chorley's widowed and heartbroken mother appears, horrified that her only son might be rusticated and lose his reputation. Burke consequently agrees to take the blame publicly until Chorley can leave school inconspicuously and retreats to Purefoy's study, where he spends the rest of the term reading books. The initial reason Burke makes this outstandingly selfless decision is because he is introduced to Chorley's sister, Constance, a 'fairy' with whom he instantly falls in love and who 'twisted him round her finger [...] not with diplomatic art and *finesse*, but with the convincing eagerness of a frank outspoken nature'.[134] Burke's relationship with Constance (with whom he spends all his holidays) continues to flourish throughout the two books. Hemyng seems to suggest here that one way to draw boys out of the kind of male relationships that foster violence and competition is to encourage them to form relationships with girls. The desire to impress girls counterbalances the desire to maintain caste among male counterparts. Hemyng is one of the very few male authors to suggest that schoolboys embark on close friendships with girls and to suggest also that such friendships might be favorable to discipline and rational growth.

---

129 Ibid., p. 80.
130 Ibid., p. 169.
131 Ibid., p. 178.
132 Ibid., p. 135.
133 Hemyng 1865, p. 322.
134 Hemyng 1870, pp. 145, 147.

Hemyng's narrative is also rare in that is depicts a boy who actively protests against corporal punishment inflicted by masters. There are two episodes in which Burke is unjustly sentenced to be flogged. In the first volume, some pheasants' eggs are stolen from the living quarters of Burke's housemaster. The innocent Burke, again prime suspect, is told that if he does not confess, he will be flogged. Again, the masters feel justified in flogging him, even though the case is not watertight, because they feel that all boys are morally corrupt and benefit from a beating whether or not it is deserved. Hemyng (confident that his boy readers will understand his legalistic prose) remarks that 'the theory of government was jealous suspicion, and that in the subject every representation was *prima facie* made with a purpose and felonious ends'.[135] It seems that Eton, like other schools that employ a Hobbesian-style disciplinary regime, is out of step with national democratic feeling. In the second of the two books, another miscarriage of justice happens when Burke is falsely accused of knocking a woman's eye out by throwing stones. This time, the Head decides to flog him. Burke, like 'one of [Charles] Kingsley's ancient heroes',[136] takes an uncompromising stance and runs away from school, refusing on principle to be flogged when there is no evidence of guilt. In effect, he goes on strike. Again, in making the decision to strike Burke demonstrates that he is capable of the highest level of moral reasoning on Kohlberg's scale; he makes his decision not on pragmatic grounds or under social pressure, but according to the well-reasoned moral principle that proper evidence should be presented before a punishment takes place. On the other hand, when Burke is aware that he has willfully and deliberately broken the rules, he willingly submits to a flogging. Like most anti-flogging writers, what Hemyng objects to is the indiscriminate use of corporal punishment, rather than corporal punishment per se. The majority of writers sympathize with boys who are flogged because of misunderstanding, or academic failure, or because of reasoned disagreements with school policy. The writers discussed here never argue that flogging is an inappropriate response to deliberate provocation of teachers, bullying or willful violence, though most, like Farrar, show boys guilty of such offences being expelled, rather than beaten.

Hemyng subscribes to liberal/democratic views on the abolition of corporal punishment. '[W]hile people are charitably inclined, and wish to abolish corporal punishment in the army and in the navy,' he remarks, 'they may just as well probe the evil to its foundation, and lift up their voices against flogging in public schools.'[137] When one group in society has fewer human rights than other groups, it signals deeper fractures in the body politic. Hemyng equates corporal punishment with another human rights issue, slavery. 'If slavery is the "peculiar institution" of the dis-United States', he insists, 'so is flogging the "peculiar institution" of the public schools'.[138] Teachers who support corporal punishment are out of step

---

135 Ibid., p. 21.
136 Hemyng 1865, p. 110.
137 Ibid., p. 129.
138 Ibid., p. 128.

with the humanitarian trends of the times. Burke's housemaster, Mr Wynne, who clearly knows that Burke is innocent after the stone-throwing episode, nonetheless upholds the headmaster's right to flog indiscriminately. He remarks: 'You boys now-a-days think much more of a switching than we ever did. Come – come, you must listen to reason; [...] I cannot have you running away like this; if my most promising boys leave me, what is to become of the house?'[139] Hemyng, however, implies that boys have evolved since Wynne's youth, as have ideas of justice and reason. No longer do boys take unquestioning obedience as a matter of course; they want dialogue with masters and parents.

After making a stance against corporal punishment and returning to school victorious, Burke begins to search for a political voice. Towards the end of the second book, he discusses the ethics of both flogging and political activity with his friend Montrose, the son of a Tory MP. When Burke explains his ideas about corporal punishment, Montrose comments: 'Fellows kick up a shindy about being flogged, but they flog sailors and they flog soldiers; why shouldn't they flog schoolboys?' He also remarks that boys who do not like flogging should 'go somewhere else', ignoring the fact that no anti-flogging schools exist. Burke replies that this argument 'does not prove that the rules are just or expedient'. He then criticizes Montrose's Tory philosophy for preserving tradition at the expense of progress.[140] The boys go on to discuss whether it is the duty of the citizen to support reform, to advocate *laissez-faire* or to protect the status quo. A reasoned discussion of what it is to be a citizen thus grows out of the corporal punishment debate. In becoming mature civic subjects, therefore, the first step for boys is for them to question the rationale behind the discipline they experience at school, in particular the principle of corporal punishment.

The democratic citizenship argument was only one arm of the anti-flogging debate. As Chapter 3 showed, F.W. Farrar believed that corporal punishment prevented aesthetic sensibility and emotional literacy from developing. An anti-flogging public school story written by 'E.P.' the year before *St Winifred's*, *Solomon's Precept: Or the Power of the Rod* (1861), concentrates exclusively on various types of violence in school and the way it destroys creativity and sensibility. This text, which gives little clue as to who wrote it or in what circumstances, may well have been a direct response to *R v. Hopley*, since we are told that the headmaster of the school concerned had once flogged a pupil to death. E.P.'s protagonist, Carew, is initially sent to public school because his parents fear that his habit of reading too much will damage his health. The school regime is based on the 'hardening-theory' of education, which deprives young people of physical and aesthetic comfort in order to repress unruly desires and instill an ability to withstand life's knocks.[141] In this system, wrongdoers are punished with indiscriminate flogging, which E.P.

---

139 Ibid., pp. 110–11.
140 Ibid., p. 269.
141 E.P. 1861, pp. 52–63.

considers to be a lazy, quick fix means of discipline.[142] Order is maintained by the 'impolitic' use of 'fear' and there is no attempt to address individual needs; all are treated 'alike'.[143] Because of the incessant public flogging, the boys lose 'all sense of pain',[144] the more so because they are forced to watch each other being flogged (a common practice in schools, designed to deter offenders). E.P. compares this practice to the public execution of 'reformers', 'Catholics' and 'witches', indicating that school discipline looks back to pre-Enlightenment times. The Headmaster not only neglects his boys' intellectual growth but also shows contempt for their intellect by beating them about the head, which damages some mentally.

The lack of verbal communication between boys and masters is also a cause for concern. Because nobody talks rationally to the boys, their language degenerates into obscenity. One 'revolting spectacle of youth' has a 'disgusting and blasphemous nature'. Another uses 'filthy discourse'.[145] Successive beatings brutalize them and their speech and bodies also become 'filthy'.[146] Devoid of creative outlet, the boys enthusiastically read 'anatomical studies' and dismember insects for entertainment.[147] The corporal punishment regime, demonstrates E.P., magnifies the physical at the expense of the intellectual.[148] If a boy develops criminal or immoral tendencies and if his body holds undue sway over his mind, it is because, by beating him and not talking to him, adults have neglected his intellectual capabilities. Carew's Headmaster assumes that every boy is by nature criminal or immoral and, in a vicious spiral, actually ends up making innocent boys into monsters. This is ironical, remarks E.P., since real criminals are dealt with rationally, while boys are 'treated in every respect worse than convicts and felons' in conditions unacceptable among 'reformatories or gaols'.[149]

Carew alone strives to retain his creativity. He entertains the Headmaster, his wife and their visitors with a puppet theatre and they prophesize he 'will be a great artist one day'.[150] Like Scheherezade, he tells nightly stories to the other pupils ('The Forty Thieves', 'Sinbad' and 'The Persian Prince') to ward off their bullying.[151] To E.P., literary creativity promotes good relationships. However, a system predicated on violence and fear puts creativity at risk and Carew degenerates when he is forced to watch other boys being beaten. His confidence drops, he begins to fail and he finally gets beaten himself and becomes the 'fool of the school'.[152]

---

142 Ibid., p. 35.
143 Ibid., pp. 44–45.
144 Ibid., pp. 36–38.
145 Ibid., pp. 69–71.
146 Ibid., p. 77.
147 Ibid., p. 105.
148 Ibid., p. 134.
149 Ibid., pp. 140–41.
150 Ibid., pp. 94–95.
151 Ibid., p. 102.
152 Ibid., p. 135.

In the end, the Headmaster notices the deterioration in Carew's behavior and modifies his teaching methods. E.P. excuses him, saying he was prey to a short temper and 'conservative obstinacy'.[153] This 'happy ending' seems contrived and problematic. The creative Carew is an anomaly – an 'Ishmael'[154] – and none of his peers show artistic potential. Other boys take it for granted that violence at school is natural and acceptable. Only Hadman – a 'mad fellow', brain-damaged by a water-pump in early life – makes an effort to protest ('not unreasonably') when he is beaten.[155] Violence is so much the accepted norm that it takes an exceptional individual to break the cycle. There is also a further problem with the claim for rational education here. Although E.P. insists (somewhat vaguely) that 'reason' can overcome disciplinary problems at school,[156] Carew himself was not originally a placid, creative boy. He was an unruly infant, a 'juvenile performer', who had tantrums in Oxford Street and was a 'poisonous influence'.[157] It was not rational education but typhus that made him 'more governable'.[158] It seems that the only hope of changing school culture is to rely on freak accidents to produce exceptionally gifted boys, who can expose the faults of the system. E.P. never really commits himself to the idea that some boys might be born with a sense of rationality and without disruptive instincts.

While E.P. and Bracebridge Hemyng set great store by the political and aesthetic potential possessed by boys, they fail to outline any systematic way in which these skills might be harnessed by the education system. Other commentators doubted, moreover, whether much of the adolescent population even possessed these skills, or whether they were the preserve of a small number of exceptional boys. Many disputed the extent to which adolescents were capable of the kind of rational thought needed to negotiate complex moral situations. Evangelicals in particular questioned the extent to which juveniles could understand abstract ideas of right and wrong, follow moral arguments, or control their own behavior. Some commentators felt that young people did not choose consciously to err, but were passively driven by their inherent lack of mental balance. A.R. Craig referred to bad behavior as a 'disease' and to 'punishments' as 'remed[ies]'.[159] He urged schoolmasters to diagnose the 'origins' of misdemeanors (especially quarrels) and to set about 'organizing' and 'balancing' young people's minds.[160] Although Craig opposed flogging, he seems to have believed that reasoned persuasion was not an option with young people and he continued to promote fear as a major component of discipline. The fear to be engendered was not to be a fear of the

---

153 Ibid., p. 138.
154 Ibid., p. 93.
155 Ibid., pp. 81, 114.
156 Ibid., p. 5.
157 Ibid., pp. 2–5.
158 Ibid., pp. 6–7.
159 Craig 1844, p. 14.
160 Ibid., pp. 26–27.

rod nor of any earthly power, but the fear of damnation.[161] Unlike the assertive, autonomous Butler Burke, Craig's juvenile is driven back to the earliest stages of moral development.[162]

Another major problem with allowing boys to think for themselves was that they might come up with the wrong moral conclusions. The presence of reasoned moral dissent among the young may have been an especially difficult challenge for Evangelical parents and teachers who had been brought up in the 1830s but who were dealing, in the 1860s, with a more skeptical, Darwinian generation. H.C. Adams's *Schoolboy Honor* (1861) is another anti-corporal punishment text that grapples with ideas of non-violent social control. The central problem is the question of how a master can secure unquestioning obedience from boys without resorting to the rod, since only a 'bad ruler' governs by 'brute force'.[163] Rejecting continental-style 'surveillance' (partly because it is impractical), the hero master of 'Halminster College' has no disciplinary force to rely on other than the boys' own sense of 'honor'. Their peculiar moral code, however, means that 'honor', to them, does not always entail obedience. As Adams remarks, their concept of 'honor'

> taught them to abhor meanness, cowardice, and treachery; to reject everything that was coarse and ungentlemanly; to be obliging and good humored to their schoolfellows; respectful to such of the masters as dealt with them kindly and justly; and observant of such rules as seemed reasonable, and not very troublesome to obey. But as for obeying, simply because a thing was ordered, or avoiding anything simply because it was forbidden, either by divine or human law – these formed no items in their code of morals.[164]

This 'Schoolboys' Creed' is a 'dangerous heresy' and revolves around this concept they call 'honor'. A man who acts on his honor, they agree, is a man who 'would not lie or cheat'.[165] The boys disagree fundamentally with the masters over the meaning of the concept of honor, because they see honor in terms of honoring a mutually binding social contract, while the masters see honor in terms of obedience to a superior. As one boy comments: 'I do not see that I have made any compact with the masters which I am bound in honor to maintain. Nor do they trust to my word of honor that I will keep to their rules'.[166] Masters only appeal to a boy's honor, the boy explains, when they are not on hand personally to supervise behavior.

The problem at Halminster is not that boys cannot reason, but that their ethical reasoning is based on the context of each moral decision and the impact

---

161 Ibid., p. 29.
162 Ibid., p. 31.
163 Adams 1861, p. 362.
164 Ibid., pp. 78–79.
165 Ibid., p. 9.
166 Ibid., p. 10.

it makes on their relationships rather than being based on a moral code learned from their masters. In this sense, strangely, the boys resemble the girls in Carol Gilligan's study into gender-specific perceptions of morality. This study sought to counter Lawrence Kohlberg's assertion that the development of moral maturity requires an individual to subordinate the claims of personal relationships first to 'rules' and then to 'universal principles of justice'.[167] Gilligan found that when considering moral scenarios, girls were more likely to consider the impact of the decisions on the relationships between parties involved, whereas the boys were more likely to apply abstract principles. While Kohlberg had dismissed those who failed to move on from prioritizing relationships to applying abstract principles as immature, Gilligan argued that the de-valuing of relationships in the moral reasoning process was a result of an overly individualistic, patriarchal upbringing.

In *Schoolboy Honor*, the master Holford similarly privileges overarching (mainly Biblical) principles over personal allegiances and the boys question the validity of this moral stance. At one point, for example, they debate whether it is worse to break school rules by entering 'low' public houses, or to break a promise to meet one's friends in the pub.[168] Finally, the boy at the centre of the dilemma opts to please his friends rather than obey the rules. This preference for friendship over abstract principle is not a mere case of blind conformity; the boys consciously decide that their allegiance to each other overrides their allegiance to the school status quo. They also apply abstract moral reasoning to the dilemma, and point out that sometimes in order to obey one universal imperative (that it is wrong to break a promise), one must sometimes disobey other absolute principles, such as the idea that it is wrong to go to the pub. When confronted with two equally valid moral choices, personal allegiances swing the decision one way or another. The bonds between boys are stronger than the bonds between boys and masters, so a promise to a boy in this case takes precedence.

A debate on moral principles later in the book reinforces this point. When the pious Austen declares that it is always wrong to lie, another boy responds by again appealing to a hierarchy of allegiances:

> [S]uppose you were a Yankee, and an unlucky nigger who had just escaped from his master, came and got you to hide him, and his master came up afterwards, and asked if you had seen him, and if you knew where he was. If you were to say you wouldn't tell him, it would be just the same thing as handing the poor wretch over to the nigger-driver to be beaten into punkin [*sic*] sauce, as the Yankees say, and you would break your promise to him into the bargain.[169]

---

167 Gilligan 1993, p. 18.
168 Adams 1861, p. 115.
169 Ibid., p. 175.

Here, a promise made to a fugitive slave is weighed against the imperative never to lie.[170] The personal sympathies of the boys lie with the slave (with whom they have developed a relationship and with whom the Yankee has a political bond) rather than with the owner and this clinches the decision.[171]

The problem with the boys' reasoning, for Holford, is that it fails to pay enough respect to the systems of social hierarchy that uphold the status quo. It will not do for boys to put each other's demands before those of teachers. Holford, therefore, needs a non-violent way of making the boys subordinate their private allegiances to each other to follow his own absolutist Evangelical principles. He does not, therefore, institute a democratic disciplinary system like the one at Rugby, but rather tries to push the boys back to the 'pre-conventional' mode of moral reasoning that operates on fear. Holford terrorizes his students into obedience by using his school sermons to manipulate their sense of fear, particularly their fear of disease and the physically repulsive. By awakening their fears, he hopes to instill a respect for proper hierarchical order. For example, in one sermon he discusses an event in 2 Kings where Elisha is visited by the Syrian general Naaman. Naaman comes to Elisha to be cured of leprosy, but does not give Elisha's servant, Gehazi, the customary reward that a host's servants are entitled to receive.[172] Gehazi remains empty-handed because Elisha has refused all money from Naaman, the healing having been done for the glory of God. Wanting his rightful reward, Gehazi runs after the departing general and lies to him, saying that Elisha needs some money to buy clothes for somebody. Naaman obliges, but Elisha later smites Gehazi with leprosy as a punishment. The moral is that although Gehazi should reasonably have had what he was owed, it was Elisha' right as his superior to deny him it, for whatever (undisclosed) reason he chose. However unjust Elisha's behavior was, Gehazi had no right to lie. Holford tells the boys to remember that to obey an order from a person in authority is an obligation, even if they feel 'that unreasonable restrictions were laid upon them'.[173] There is no two-way social contract at school. A teacher is not obliged to reason with a boy, or to disclose the rationale behind rules and prohibitions, even though the boy must remain scrupulously honest in his dealings with the adult. The only way to reinforce such a message is with a threat. Therefore, Holford discourses at length

---

170 Interestingly, Kohlberg presented subjects in one of his studies with a very similar conundrum ('whether it was right to break the law and aid slaves to escape before the Civil War'). See Kohlberg 1981, p. 158.

171 It should be remembered that even some supposedly enlightened social commentators such as Carlyle, Ruskin and Kingsley were against abolition at this time. Nowadays, this moral dilemma would be easier to solve, given the consensus against slavery as a fundamental evil; such a consensus did not exist in Adams's day. Levy 2001 discusses this at length.

172 2 Kings v: 20–27.

173 Adams 1861, p. 203.

on the moral leprosy which [disobedience] must inevitably produce – a leprosy, he said, more terrible than that of Gehazi, which gradually ate away the physical organs, until the death of the body ensued; but the leprosy of a perverted conscience corrupted by slow degrees all that was sound in the spiritual nature, till it reached the vitals of the soul, and it perished for ever.[174]

In terms of citizenship education, Holford wants school to operate not by nineteenth-century standards of civil government, but according to Biblical feudalism, a system that can only operate on fear.

Fear – specifically a fear of divine retribution – is also crucial to the resolution of *Schoolboy Honor*'s main moral episode. The protagonists, close friends Austen and Cole, get mixed up in an incident where a gamekeeper is accidentally shot at with an illicitly held firearm. This takes place when an Irish boy, O'Grady, challenges Cole to a shooting match in local woods. A gamekeeper happens upon them and Cole, vaulting a fence to escape, accidentally sets off his gun. The shot does not hit the keeper, but he trips with surprise when the gun fires and is injured. Austen, the more pious of the two boys, is not present, having gone back to school for 'lock-up' (when the register is taken at the end of the day, to ensure all pupils are inside). Nonetheless, he becomes the prime suspect when his flask, borrowed without permission by Cole, is found at the scene of the incident and the other boys cover for each other by refusing to give any information to the authorities. The process of discovering the truth is relevant to the pedagogical message of the book. Although this is a criminal matter, a police officer who arrives to investigate the case is informed by the Head that he has no business at the school. Instead, the Head explains that internal enquiries will be undertaken by an old boy who is a lawyer and if no culprit is found matters will be handed over to the police. If the lawyer, assisted by a committee of house captains, discovers the culprit, the school, not the police, will see justice done.[175] The state, evidently, has no role in the discipline and punishment of adolescent boys. The adolescent does not belong to wider civic society and it has no business with him; he is not, therefore, a true civic subject with rights and responsibilities. On the contrary, adolescent discipline is the business of priestly schoolmasters, undertaken not according to the conventions of civil society, but through the rigors of religious discipline.

Adams uses an act of God to resolve the shooting mystery. Cole's mother becomes dangerously ill and he promises God that he will make a full confession of his crime if his mother is spared.[176] She recovers and Cole rushes to Holford who tells him that: 'God's Providence [...] made use alike of your mother's danger

---

174 Ibid., p. 204. In *Tom Brown* Tom, Arthur and East also discuss the story of Naaman, but this time they use the text to explore ideas of principle and compromise. They each interpret the story in a different way, and, unlike Adams, Hughes avoids imposing a definitive reading of the text. See Hughes 1857, pp. 243–45.

175 Ibid., pp. 229–32.

176 Ibid., p. 311.

and recovery, to awaken your conscience to a sense of your own sin and of His mercy'.[177] By using this kind of providential resolution to a moral question, Adams deploys the same method of discipline as his character Holford, appealing to a fear of divine retribution to drive home a disciplinary message. At a time when adolescents frequently lost parents, the suggestion that one might kill one's mother through one's misdeeds would have been a particularly strong lever for an author or clergyman to use. Adams uses this kind of religious manipulation not once but twice. When Austen tries to attend his 'immoral' drinking party, Adams drives home his disciplinary message (that boys should obey adults rather than fulfill commitments to other boys) by using natural justice as part of the plot. Late for the engagement, and returning up the river by boat from a sailing expedition, Austen capsizes in a strong current and, almost drowning, loses consciousness. After he is rescued, he sinks into a delirium, 'not owing to the exhaustion of fever, but to mental disquietude'.[178] During convalescence, he confesses to Holford that before the accident he had been about to do something wrong. After this confession, he submits himself entirely to Holford's influence and becomes a model boy. Holford, the non-flogger, has an easy job here – the river current, which beats Austen into moral submission, does his disciplinary work for him. Adams, for all his non-violent rhetoric, does not refute the idea that juvenile discipline must be done by force. He merely puts discipline into the hands of God.

Paradoxically, Adams seems conscious of the flaws in Holford's authoritarian stance even while repeating Holford's pedagogical methods in his own writing, but he persists in order to reinforce the status quo. Other commentators were also disturbed by the impact on social hierarchy that might occur were boys to exercise a democratic sense of reason. Unlike Adams, however, many suggested that violence was the only way to discipline the young. In the same year that Butler Burke made his statement against corporal punishment, 'Bouncing Boys' in *All the Year Round* (1865), lamented the decline of the traditional boy, who had 'all the complaints of infancy', 'over-ate' and 'robbed orchards'. The writer recalls that relations between boys and the adults in the past used to be naturally and healthily violent: 'I can quite understand how the schoolmasters of the period could not keep their hands off him. The whole physical development of him was a standing invitation to the cane'. He complains that the modern boy is 'morally and physically repulsive to the cane'. One cannot 'flagellate a boy who writes, edits, prints and publishes a newspaper'. Modern boys, moreover, who spend their leisure hours playing with sophisticated new technology, no longer have the chance to test themselves in the normal rough-and-tumble of childhood. This is bad because it gives the working classes and their 'active, energetic, well-educated progeny' a physical and economic advantage.[179] 'Youthful Prodigies' in *Chambers's Journal* (1870) remarked that mental over-development in youth could lead to the brain's

---

177 Ibid., p. 313.
178 Ibid., p. 125.
179 'Bouncing Boys' 1865.

'vital springs [...] drying up'.[180] *Once a Week*'s 'The English Boy of the Future' (1862) complained that, in peacetime, education had made children 'wiser', 'puzzled with questions' and 'crammed with knowledge'. The author recalls a time when mothers encouraged fighting and boys played at volunteers, wishing they 'had been born a generation earlier', during the Napoleonic wars.[181] The wartime environment, says the writer, kept young people fit and disciplined. Now, the only outlets for juvenile energy were poaching, rioting and violent sports.[182] Later, in 1882, the *Saturday Review* complained that 'there are schools in which the elder boys [...] are really absorbed in modern controversies about evolution, religion, and the descent of man from the ascidian'.[183] This over-emphasis on intellectual matters, it said, endangered the race. All these writers assumed that young people were at their most natural in a state of conflict and violent repression – essentially, they believed that naughtiness and punishment were healthy and that brainwork was not.

Later Victorian storywriters often revisit the idea that incessant physical conflict is a natural state for boys. In *Bully, Fag and Hero, or In Playground and Schoolroom*, by C.J. Mansford (1896), the *laissez faire* public school returns with a vengeance. To Mansford, who wrote for magazines such as *Boys' Realm* and *Chums*,[184] violence is an innate part of boyhood behavior and a necessary bloodletting process. Mansford's hero, Bob Challenge, starts fighting the moment he arrives at school and continues right the way through the book, never learning any other way to settle differences. The Headmaster of Challenge's school leaves the boys alone to sort out their own problems. Unlike earlier Heads, he shows no interest in moral ideas and dismisses his boys' naughtiness as 'prank[s]' ('Boys will be boys'[185]). Mansford has no time for the idea that boys should be encouraged to talk problems out and he reverts to the idea that fighting is by far the best way for boys to communicate. Claudia Nelson and Joseph Bristow have both identified the late-Victorian trend to encourage the young to be combative or even 'naughty' as having its roots in a Darwinist concern for the nation's physical wellbeing and for national competitiveness on the world stage. As Bristow remarks, Social Darwinism clashed with the ideas of Arnoldian Christians and as a consequence popular representations of boyhood 'veered precariously between violence and virtue'. The 'pluck' and 'vigor' that had precipitated the school rebellions that had horrified polite society were now signs of evolutionary fitness.[186] Thus, some authors urged that in order to safeguard both race and empire, '"feminine" servility' must be abandoned. As a result, many late-Victorian narratives feature episodes

---

180 'Youthful Prodigies' 1877.
181 'The English Boy of the Future' 1862, p. 203.
182 Ibid., p. 204.
183 'Boys' 1882, p. 492.
184 Kirkpatrick 2000, p. 227.
185 Mansford 1897, p. 157.
186 Bristow 1991, p. 60.

of naughtiness where authority is 'successfully challenged, even if loyalty to the school is required at the end of the day'.[187]

The idea of treating young people as rational subjects and of preparing them to be active democratic citizens was, therefore, unwelcome to some adults, both for political and probably also for more personal reasons. Although writers such as Hemyng and Farrar promoted a model of the reading and debating rather than the fighting boy as the ideal citizen for the future, others felt that encouraging too much debate might upset the 'natural' hierarchical order, both between generations within the family itself and between classes in wider society. Literature had its own role in enforcing these hierarchies and it was adopted as a key ideological tool and as a disciplinary strategy that obviated the need both for barbaric physical punishments and for the European panoptical systems so inimical to British sensibilities. The heirs of paternalism decided to make literature itself into a virtual disciplinary institution, without walls, or 'spies', or officers, where obedience would be produced not by constraint or through pain, but by emotional persuasion. I will explain how this was done after briefly showing how popular juvenile literature was transformed in the later nineteenth century from a social menace into an instrument of control.

During the Victorian period, with the reading population growing and a flourishing mass-publishing industry, an idea flourished that popular literature was spreading subversive ideas among the young. Whole literary genres were perceived to have a mass effect for good or ill and Evangelicals suggested that cheap but edifying literature could be an antidote to the dangerous effects of popular pulp fiction. I will spend most of the rest of this chapter, therefore, examining how school stories specifically written for the lower classes could be deployed to spread disciplinary – and, ultimately, anti-democratic – ideologies. At the centre of the problem lay the 'Penny Dreadful', a diverse genre dating from the 1830s and 1840s, originating from the gothic novel and the *Newgate Calendar*.[188] This category included pulp publications sold by costermongers, cheap sensation novels and penny magazines from the Newsagents' Publishing Company (which appeared in the 1860s).[189] Often featuring narratives of adolescent insurrection, penny dreadfuls capitalized on growing juvenile literacy.[190] John Springhall has written informatively about how the Victorian economy increased wage-earning opportunities for working-class boys, producing a ready audience for the dreadfuls.[191]

A typical 'dreadful' narrative was Harrison Ainsworth's 1839 novel, published in *Bentley's Miscellany*, about Jack Sheppard (1702–1724), the runaway apprentice

---

187 Ibid., p. 69.
188 Springhall 1998, p. 11.
189 Ibid., p. 42.
190 Rose (1991) remarks that in 1842–1853, around 57 per cent of juvenile offenders could read to some degree, increasing to 70 per cent in 1891, although in some areas it could be as low as 24 per cent (pp. 196–97).
191 Springhall 1998, p. 46.

and jail-breaker.[192] Many school stories by Evangelicals, in particular those published in magazines such as the *Boys' Own Paper*, were attempts by upper-middle-class Evangelicals to produce what Edward Salmon called an 'antidote' to this literature. Moralists alleged that the dreadfuls unbalanced the mind and incited the young to crime. For example, Salmon claimed that one youth had been maddened by reading and killed his father and brother. Another, addicted to Harrison Ainsworth, had chloroformed and robbed his master.[193] In contrast to the penny dreadfuls, which portrayed adolescence as a time of independence, rebellion and self-realization, most school stories represented juveniles as dependent, conforming to an agenda set by adults and restricted within set physical and intellectual parameters. Penny dreadful authors, however, had their own take on the school story. One of the most popular 'dreadfuls' was Bracebridge Hemyng's *Jack Harkaway* series, the first volume of which, *Jack Harkaway's Schooldays*, was published by Edwin J. Brett in *Boys of England* in 1871. According to Springhall, at its peak *Harkaway* sold 250,000 copies per week and 'would have been seen by [...] at least one in five of all 10–19 year-old boys'.[194] I have already demonstrated how Hemyng encouraged self-empowerment among upper-class readers and below I will show how he adapted similar ideas for working-class readers, using *Jack Harkaway* as an example of what moralistic public school writers were fighting against.

Many of the plot elements of *Jack Harkaway's Schooldays* are hackneyed reworkings of traditional school story motifs. Jack saves a younger boy from drowning, vanquishes the school bully and has boots thrown at him for praying before bedtime. However, like many 'penny dreadfuls', the story is also a wish-fulfillment fantasy, because Jack eventually discovers that he is the son of rich, generous parents. Jack, adopted by the unfeeling Mr and Mrs Scratchley, is sent away to the cheap, second-rate Pomona House school because he is 'precocious' and impossible to discipline (one objection to his behavior is that he bites and kicks whenever Scratchley tries to beat him[195]). Unlike conventional school heroes, who are commonly depicted as small and, often, childlike, Jack is big enough to challenge adults physically and has learned to fight by 'milling' with donkey boys on Hampstead Heath.[196] Indeed, another reason why he needs to be sent away is that mixing with independent, working boys has made him less pliable by adults. When he gets to Pomona House he is too old and experienced to internalize school values, but is 'clever enough to see that he must conform to the rules'.[197] He is intelligent and enjoys learning, but objects to the self-interestedness of the Headmaster, who uses his position to inflate his social status.

---

192 Howarth 1973, p. 36.
193 Salmon 1886, p. 256.
194 Ibid., p. 87.
195 Hemyng 1880, pp. 5–6, 23.
196 Ibid., p. 31.
197 Ibid., p. 27.

Hemyng's message is an empowering one for his readers: educate yourself and beware of those who would exploit you. The plot revolves not around what values Jack is taught at school, but around his discovery of his true identity. Mistreated at school, he runs away. During his escape, he hides in a shed and overhears some men planning to rob a house belonging to Lady Mordenfield, the mother of a fellow-pupil. Jack foils the plan and later discovers that Lady Mordenfield is really his mother and that she was tricked into a (bigamous) marriage with the now dead Lord Mordenfield by relatives who told her that her rightful husband, Jack's father, was dead. It turns out that Jack's foster parents were paid to look after him and to hide his identity. When Jack returns voluntarily to school after making his discovery, he is put in chains as a punishment and the other boys riot in protest. The head of the sixth form, Collinson, who has organized the protest, refuses to be caned as a punishment, snatches the cane from the Head and breaks it.[198] The boys then hold a barring-out and tar and feather a captured teacher.[199] The headmaster's wife sides with the boys, commenting:

> Look at your severity. It is disgusting. Would such things be tolerated at Eton or Harrow? Their demands are perfectly reasonable, and I am glad to see the boys are not the sneaks, and the hypocrites and poor soulless things you have tried to make them.[200]

Lord Mordenfield, Jack's half brother, gets crushed during the barring-out and conveniently dies, leaving Lady Mordenfield free to return to Jack's father. Jack's parents can then settle down to a conventional married life and Jack goes to Shanghai to learn how to behave properly and earn a living.

Jack Harkaway disrupts ideas of 'appropriate' relationships between adults and juveniles. The Headmaster, who should be a fatherly Arnoldian figure, reminds everyone of Dickens's Pecksniff, particularly when he disingenuously exclaims 'I love my boys [...] and I think they look upon me as a father'.[201] Jack's strategy for surviving in school is to befriend the Headmaster's wife, a beautiful woman of 'between thirty and forty' – something of a *femme fatale* who can be a 'firm friend' but also 'cruel'.[202] In one episode, after she has nearly caned Jack to death for accidentally throwing a stone at her, he is confronted by her begging him for forgiveness. Jack replies 'If you would only give me one kiss, it would make me so happy'[203] and tells her he would like her to mother him. Jack resembles pre-Victorian characters such as Gil Blas and Tom Jones in his ability to develop and exploit his own sexuality to gain power in relationships with older women. He also resembles earlier heroes from fairy tales and the changelings and foundlings

---

198 Ibid., p. 162.
199 Ibid., p. 173.
200 Ibid., p. 169.
201 Ibid., p. 37.
202 Ibid., p. 34.
203 Ibid., p. 61.

of popular folklore in his search for his 'true' parents. Hemyng uses this complex mixture of influences to expose the insecurity of Victorian ideas about relationships between generations, particularly the idea that education and parenting are founded on the disinterestedness of adults and the innocence of the young.

This kind of plot was calculated to annoy moralistic commentators. In his prescriptive survey of young people's reading and morality, *Juvenile Literature as It Is* (1888), Edward Salmon commented that juveniles who read this kind of subversive pulp literature were liable to land up in jail.[204] Salmon, who gives the impression of being rather sheltered, blames popular literature for many social ills, demonstrating a blindness towards the environmental causes of crime shared by many commentators on popular literature.[205] Actual statistics fail to support his claim that reading penny dreadfuls caused boys' behavior to deteriorate. Springhall points out that there was, in fact, a decrease in juvenile larceny rates during the late nineteenth century, when the penny dreadful was most popular.[206] Anxiety about penny dreadfuls, he remarks, had more to do with 'a rise in the conscious regulation of working-class boys: encapsulated in compulsory schooling; a fixation with uncontrolled, high-earning 'boy labor'; and the rise of adult-organized youth movements'.[207] The real motives behind supposedly 'wholesome' school stories such as those that appeared in publications such as the *Boys' Own Paper*, which were supposed to be an antidote to the influence of the dreadfuls, seem to have been more to do with enforcing the social and political status quo and stemming political reform than with preventing crime.

Consequently, few 'public school' stories tackled issues such as poverty or educational exclusion, one exception being G. Griffith's *The Life and Adventures of George Wilson* (1854), a pre-*Tom Brown* story that protests against the fact that the rich hypothecate educational endowments originally intended for the poor. Griffith describes how George Wilson, a scholarship boy, arrives at the King Edward VI School in Birmingham, is immediately introduced to the head in the flogging room and told that he must not mix with wealthier students.[208] Griffith, documenting George's battle against vested interests, argues for a free, egalitarian education system, embracing the commercial, professional and aristocratic worlds.[209] Juvenile delinquency is a consequence, he explains, of society's failure to educate the poor to succeed in the marketplace and prisons and workhouses will not solve the problems educational inequality has brought about.[210] Post-*Tom Brown* school stories practically never associate delinquency with poverty in this way.

---

204 Salmon 1888, p. 191.
205 Bristow 1991 remarks on this tendency, p. 16.
206 Springhall 1998, p. 72.
207 Ibid., p. 93.
208 Griffith 1854, p. 62.
209 Ibid., p. 12.
210 Ibid., pp. 128, 131.

Juvenile Literature as It Is demonstrates the belief that the public school literature was a powerful disciplinary tool, especially when delivered through organs such as the *Boy's Own Paper*, patronized, as Salmon put it, 'chiefly by the sons of working men, the future masters of the political situation'.[211] Public school stories, Salmon explained, were a good way of introducing moral values to those who, with the extension of suffrage and political reform, were set to have increasing social power as they matured. Through these stories, writers had a chance to instill national discipline through ideology without resort to physical force or violence. The school in literature, Salmon commented (in Benthamite vein), is 'a manufactory of character', not just for the fictional characters portrayed, but also for readers. In *Tom Brown*, Hughes 'thrashes the bully' and protects the weak, becoming 'a sort of captain for a boys' army'; in addition, such literature instills the cultural values of 'sweetness and light' against the forces of social disorder. Indeed, Salmon found no limit to the influence school stories could have on juvenile psychology and even warned writers not to include morbid death scenes (like Farrar's) since they could prove 'fatal' to the 'weakly-minded child'.[212] In an earlier essay, 'What Boys Read' (1886), Salmon had analyzed the way boys related to books. He argued that boys saw fictional characters as real people and that they inevitably identified with and emulated them.[213] This was the key to teaching morality. Good authors, like good teachers, he explained, strive not to impose their own doctrines too obviously. Every book should have a hero whose simple and transparent morality will make values obvious to readers while keeping the authorial voice as unobtrusive as possible.[214] There is no room in Salmon's agenda for debating moral or social complexity. Merely disguising the authorial voice makes it easy to instill morality without attracting attention to it and, therefore, without giving an opportunity for dissent. Salmon also, incidentally, recommends that the state should rigidly control the publication of juvenile literature, remarking that 'the matter seems of such vital moment in the social economy of the masses as to justify [such] high-handed action'.[215]

Salmon praises Thomas Hughes, but it is clear that he has no intention of working-class boys absorbing the complexities of *Tom Brown* that were revealed in Chapter 2. Ironically, *Tom Brown*, if read carefully enough, is antithetical to the aims of those concerned with de-politicizing the lower classes. Talbot Baines Reed's *The Fifth Form at St Dominic's*, which appeared in the *Boys' Own Paper* in 1881 is more typical of what was offered to the working classes and demonstrates how the school story could be employed to encourage political quietism in the young. I will, therefore, for the remainder of this chapter, discuss this text as an example of the a-political public school story. Reed (1852–1893), a non-public

---

211 Salmon 1888, p. 185.
212 Ibid., pp. 84–91.
213 Salmon 1886, p. 249.
214 Ibid., p. 250.
215 Ibid., p. 257.

school educated reporter at the *Leeds Mercury*, regularly contributed to the *Boys Own Paper*.[216] According to Isabel Quigly, *St Dominic's* set the format for many subsequent fictional schools, such as the Greyfriars of the Billy Bunter stories.[217] *St Dominic's*, promoting public school ideals to the *BOP*'s mostly non-public school audience, however, strips the school story of the analytical, moral and political debate that had been present throughout its history so far. The narrative is divided into plot and sub-plot. The main plot concerns older adolescents, the eponymous Fifth Form, and contains a melodramatic crime and detection scenario common in school stories. This provides a safe, simple moral lesson for readers without going into issues of power or debating the intricacies of morality. A scholarship exam paper is stolen, and the hero, Oliver Greenfield, is wrongly blamed. He suffers silently, despising public opinion and showing no emotion when reviled by peers. The true culprit, a sixth former named Loman, needs the scholarship because he has fallen prey to a confidence trickster and has been drawn into a spiral of debt. Desperate for money, he steals the exam paper, fails to win the scholarship anyway and runs away. Caught in a gothic thunderstorm while running away (another handy piece of natural justice), he catches rheumatic fever and, during the sickness, he reconciles himself with God and the world finally determines to become a better boy.[218] The final page mentions that he eventually becomes a lawyer.

Alongside the moralistic narrative about the older boys runs a 'comedy' narrative involving the 'Fourth Junior', which includes Greenfield's younger brother, Stephen. The story of the battle between the junior boys' two warring factions, the 'Tadpoles' and the 'Guinea Pigs', is evidently designed to appeal to a younger audience. This plot division has ideological implications. The fags fight among themselves and hold a strike against the fifth form not because of any specific, principled grievance, as in *Tom Brown*, but because Oliver Greenfield has scolded them for being noisy during a party. Reed does not represent their rebellions as part of their wider development towards political maturity, as Hughes had done with Tom, but merely as aimless high spirits. The fags are, moreover, infantilized; it is hard to imagine any real thirteen- or fourteen-year-old boy joining a faction called the 'Tadpoles' or the 'Guinea Pigs'. The leader of one of these factions, Bramble, is not, as Tom is, flexing his muscles against a significant enemy in preparation for future political activity; he is an egotistical but academically weak bully who thrives on power and who is ruthlessly put down by the Headmaster in a class examination. In the absence of any democratic structures for either younger or older pupils in the school, the boys have no role in choosing the course of their own education or in forming the moral atmosphere of the school. They are merely required to conform to a pre-determined status quo. The Head cautions Bramble that 'the best way for little boys to get on is not by giving themselves ridiculous airs,

---

216 Howarth 1973, p. 51. Reed's work includes *The Adventures of a Three Guinea Watch* (1883), *The Master of the Shell* (1894) and *The Cock-House at Fellsgarth* (1893).
217 Quigly 1984, p. 77.
218 Reed 1887, p. 312.

but by doing their duty steadily in class, and living at peace with one another, and submitting quietly to the discipline of the school'.[219] For Reed, self-empowerment and self-assertion are anti-social. Like Farrar, he prioritizes personal emotional bonds over political development. For example, at the beginning of the book, Stephen Greenfield goes on strike with the other fags after having been mildly abused by senior pupils. However, he reviews his priorities on a summer boating holiday with his brother and a fifth-form friend, Wraysford. There is an accident and Stephen and Wraysford almost drown together, an event that joins them in a 'bond which had stood the test of life and death'.[220] Walter then cheerfully submits to being Wraysford's fag, forgetting his previous radicalism; peace is maintained by a miniature version of the paternalist governance so beloved of Ruskin and Matthew Arnold.

Other than the main characters, Reed presents most of the St Dominic's boys as primarily comical figures. One narrative subtext in *St Dominic's* involves a magazine published by a boy named Pembury, who devotes himself to writing because he is lame and cannot join in sports. Rather than being published by a professional printer, the magazine is pinned to a door, like 'Luther's manifesto'.[221] It does not attempt to develop a mature critical voice, but concentrates on trivializing and objectifying younger boys and on making a scurrilous running commentary on the theft case. The fags, it says, are a disgusting contamination in the school, who should be forcibly washed and submitted for scientific study.[222] Pembury is not the only boy who writes; literary creativity is encouraged at the school, particularly composing poetry for exams, but their mainly satirical output displays none of the self-exploratory power that the *St Winifred's* boys show. The Head advises Pembury to concentrate on 'the broad round of humor and pure fun' and to use the magazine 'to try to make common cause over the whole school, and unite all the boys in common cause for the good of St Dominic's'. It certainly should not, he says, 'separat[e] off one set from another, and mak[e] divisions between class and class'.[223] All the other leisure-time activities at St Dominic's are similarly unchallenging. The boys have the facilities for developing mature democratic roles, such as the magazine and a debating club, but never confront issues important to the outside world. Reed thus promotes conformity and obedience to the status quo not by threats or overt propaganda, but by presenting readers with an unproblematic, a-political, inward-looking, light-hearted fantasy world. Lower-class boys were invited to look upon this lifestyle as desirable and idealistic. The model of citizenship it presents is one of passive obedience, with an emphasis on duty rather than rights, and on emotional bonds rather than political consciousness.

---

219 Ibid., pp. 139–40.
220 Ibid., p. 151.
221 Ibid., p. 140.
222 Ibid., p. 217.
223 Ibid., p. 142.

The *BOP* and *St Dominic's* were targeted at non-public school readers. The *BOP* of 1881, where *St Dominic's* was first published, give clues as to its readership through lists of subscribers to the Paper's lifeboat fund. They range from the (presumably) middle-class E.J. Woodhouse of Ropley Vicarage through to Benjamin H. North of Staffordshire Industrial School.[224] They also include a smattering of girls. Most, however, are boys at state schools or private day schools. Reed's story must have been popular, because one donor to the magazine's lifeboat appeal signed himself 'A Dominican' and others as 'Two Guinea-Pigs'.[225] These boys clearly identified with the characters in the story and, in a way, considered themselves to be part of the community they were reading about. Indeed, the editor of the *BOP*, G.A. Hutchinson, wanted *St Dominic's* to be as inclusive as possible, and remarked that

> though the story is one of school life, its interest is by no means limited to school or college walls. Boys of all sorts and conditions – ay, and their parents too – will follow its fortunes with unflagging zest from the first page to the last.[226]

As I have argued elsewhere, the *BOP* set itself up as a kind of ersatz public school.[227] The magazine's year began in October and it attempted to foster a sense of community through pages like *The Boys' Own Club Room*, which invited questions and held competitions. It also propagated public school values through advice pages, by publishing public school stories, by printing full-color pull-outs of public school uniforms and badges and by including photographs of school treasures. It even had its own motto: *'quicquid agunt pueri nostri farrago libelli'* ('All the doings of boys will be the subject of our pages'[228]). However, although it claimed to offer boys high levels of participation, it very rarely published anything written by a boy. Even advice columns post the answer to each question without showing the question itself. Indeed, one piece of advice, to 'Confucious' [*sic*] reads 'we do not take amateur contributions'.[229] In the end, the *BOP* gives the same message as *St Dominic's*: working-class boys should read and learn, but they have no right to a voice.

The *BOP*'s class-centered approach is highlighted further when contrasted with evidence that Lorinda Cohoon has provided on American boys' periodicals from the 19th century. It emerges from Cohoon's work that, although race and gender

---

224 *Boys' Own Annual* (1882–1883), pp. 31, 144.
225 Ibid., pp. 423, 231.
226 Preface to Reed, *The Fifth Form at St Dominic's* (1887 edition), pp. 5–6.
227 See Holt 2002. Another magazine which offered the ersatz public school to frustrated state school boys was the *Captain*, 'A Magazine for Boys and Old Boys,' whose editor assumed the pseudonym of 'The Old Fag' (thanks to Claudia Nelson for this information).
228 A corruption of Steele's motto for the *Tatler* (from Juvenal *Satires* I, vv. 85–86), substituting *pueri* for *homines*.
229 Ibid., p. 144.

featured as factors for discrimination,[230] American works took it for granted that all social classes of male reader should be participating as democratic citizens, something that cannot be said for British works, which seem actively calculated to stifle readers' urges to be involved in national life. It is true, of course, that some American writers were divided opinion over citizenship and the purpose of education, 'with Whigs believing the right kind of education would "improve" problem areas and contain potentially revolutionary dissenters, and Democrats arguing that knowledge could be used to prevent injustices'.[231] However, when Cohoon talks about American perdiodicals and their encouragement of 'entrepreneurial skills', their drive to absorb trades union membership into ideas of democratic citizenship and their 'critique' of the European leisured-class scorn for labor,[232] it becomes evident that this is a far cry from British texts with their 'virtual' public schools, where citizenship is a spectator sport, rather than something all are invited to participate in.

What really separates public school literature for working and lower-middle class readers from literature for upper-class boys, then, is that the former aims to produce passive rather than active citizens. It does this by cultivating their emotional attachment to the status quo rather than by teaching them the art of independent decision-making. As Peter Musgrave has already remarked, school stories aimed at a non-public school audience had little in common with books aimed at public schoolboys.[233] In the twentieth century, of course, George Orwell complained bitterly in *Boys' Weeklies* (1940) that the descendants of *St Dominic's* produced for working-class readers in cheaper magazines such as *The Magnet* – stories such as Frank Richards's *Billy Bunter* series – ignored contemporary socio-political issues. When Orwell called for a politically literate boys' paper to be established, Frank Richards rebuffed him. He insisted that a 'writer for young people should still endeavor to give his young readers a sense of stability and solid security, peace of mind' and that boys should not be 'disturbed and worried by politics'.[234]

The trouble was that working-class juveniles did want to be bothered with politics. The years 1889 and 1911 saw nationwide school strikes, emanating from Scotland and spreading to Wales. The strikers' demands included the abolition of corporal punishment and the improvement of physical conditions in school. In 1892 pupils held anti-Tory riots in Headington Quarry, near Oxford.[235] Again, in 1914, children struck in support of two Christian Socialist teachers at Burston County Council school in Norfolk. The local gentry had attempted to expel the

---

230 Cohoon 2006, p. xvii.
231 Cohoon p. 15.
232 Cohoon pp. 25, 31, 39.
233 Musgrave 1985, pp. 224–25.
234 Ibid., 225, quoted from *Horizon* (1940).
235 Rose 1991, p. 181. Rose describes several instances of working-class resistance to physical bullying by teachers.

teachers for union activity, for questioning the right of the local rector to sit, unelected, on the parish council and for protesting about poor physical conditions at the school.[236] Their alternative 'strike school' lasted for the next twenty-five years.[237] Literature was purposely deployed to discourage this kind of activity. For example, Jacqueline Rose argues that literary education in schools was part of the 'linguistic-educational policy of the state',[238] a form of social conditioning that encouraged readers to internalize the values that underpinned the social hierarchy. With this aim in mind, mid-Victorian school stories were re-issued for state school pupils well into the twentieth century, encouraged by government initiatives such as the Newbolt Report (discussed in Chapter 6, below), which recommended literature as an antidote to political radicalism. The 1910 and 1912 Board of Education reports recommended *Tom Brown* as a standard text for state school use but, as a book with many complex references, it would have required a willing adult to explain the political nuances to pupils. Although lower-class juveniles were supposed to admire Tom, the book also represented a world they might yearn for but would never enter. Like many modern-day visitors to stately homes or readers of glamour magazines, they were kept in a state of admiration, aspiration and guaranteed disappointment, too sentimentally attached to the world they read about to challenge the values that kept them out.

The public school narrative, therefore, had a complex relationship to ideas of discipline that were, in turn, inextricably bound up with ideas of citizenship. Liberals, particularly Evangelicals, used the public school genre in the 1860s as a way of exploring, through debates on discipline, how repressive and violent social structures damaged the character and made the individual unfit as a citizen in an increasingly democratic country. In doing this, they resisted not only corporal punishment but also the implementation of the 'mechanistic' disciplinary systems favored by continental educational institutions, which were thought to violate ideas of 'Britishness'. The male adolescent was an important figure in the disciplinary debate, because he was considered to be in the process of developing both his reasoning faculties and the skills that would make him into an active citizen. As increased state education brought working-class readers into the picture, however, the school story as a vehicle for disciplinary debate began to diverge into two distinct categories. One category of school story was aimed at older, upper-class adolescents, promoting political and social awareness and preparing its readers to join a political and legislative elite. For characters in these narratives, questioning the power relationships behind disciplinary structures at school was a major step on the road to autonomy. These texts could also be used as manifestos for disciplinary reform and often argued vociferously against corporal punishment. The other kind of text was designed for working-class boys and was itself part of the disciplinary mechanism that aimed to stem unrest and protect the status quo.

---

236 See Higdon 1984.
237 Rose 1991, p. 182.
238 Rose 1994, p. 121.

Here, the adolescent was not an emergent citizen but an introverted and often burlesque figure preoccupied by his personal moral universe but not engaged with bigger social problems. Although books such as *St Dominic's* were, in a way, part of a liberal agenda, in that they were part of a movement to control young people by persuasion rather than by violence, they were reactionary in presenting politically inactive role models. In the years that followed, school stories for lower-class juveniles continued to follow this path, utterly detached from the enormous social and democratic changes affecting the lives of real young people. In the next chapter, I will discuss how elite public school literature dealt with new sociological concepts of adolescence at the turn of the century and how, in spite of growing democracy, upper-class boys continued to dominate progressive debate on the nature of adolescence.

Chapter 5

'It's not Brutality ... It's Boy; Only Boy': Public Schools and Adolescence at the Turn of the Century

> In school life at any rate, the Rule of Force and the Survival of the Fittest are no mere barren catch-words of philosophy.[1]
> —Desmond Coke, *The Bending of a Twig* (1906)

The end of the Victorian period and the early twentieth century brought dramatic changes in the way juveniles were perceived by writers and commentators. Under the influence of the new discipline of sociology, contemporary debate increasingly saw adolescence as a key event in the growth of maturity. Stanley Hall's 1904 treatise, *Adolescence: Its Psychology and its Relations to Physiology, Anthropology, Sociology, Sex, Crime, Religion and Education*, was both a turning point and a culmination of interest in adolescence. This surge in interest enthused a new generation of public school authors to reassess the genre, a process that led some, at least on the surface, to reject what had gone before completely. In Kipling's *Stalky* (1899), 'Eric' is a byword for Victorian priggery. Desmond Coke's *The Bending of a Twig* (1906) also demolishes earlier school stories for their lack of veracity by describing a boy whose father is not a public school man preparing to enter Shrewsbury by reading *Eric*, *Tom Brown*, *St Dominic's* and even *Stalky* itself. The boy makes an utter fool of himself at school by aping the behavior of these stories' heroes. In this chapter, I will discuss how sociological theories at the turn of the century dealt with adolescence and how public school writers and commentators responded to these developments. First, I will outline the aims of the 'National Efficiency' movement, which sought to apply Social Darwinist principles to education, and describe turn-of-the century approaches to adolescence used by sociologists. I will then show how a number of boys' writers responded to this movement and consider in particular the role of fatherhood and other male relationships in constructing ideas of eugenically responsible citizenship at this time.

Much of the re-interpretation of adolescence was spearheaded by Social Darwinists, who were beginning to apply the eugenic educational ideas first introduced by Herbert Spencer in the 1860s. During the pre-First World War

---

1   Coke 1906, p. 242.

period these ideas were enthusiastically adopted by the 'National Efficiency' movement, which set about observing young people's lifestyles with the same assiduity that commentators on crime had employed several decades before. Geoffrey Searle has described National Efficiency as a 'cohering ideology'; a 'technocratic and militaristic' movement supported by prominent figures across the political spectrum, from Fabians such as H.G. Wells to Baden-Powell and more conservative figures.[2] These thinkers, fearful of the growing military and political strength of Germany and surprised by the rapidity of Japanese industrial and military development, sought to draw attention to the turn-of-the-century downturn in Britain's economic and colonial performance, of which Britain's successive embarrassments in the Boer wars was symptomatic. They blamed this downturn on poor racial hygiene, a school system that neglected science and a pervading atmosphere of individualistic disregard for the greater national good. Specifically targeting the young as bearing most responsibility for stopping this decay, devotees of National Efficiency proclaimed that a sound scientific training and an education founded on Samurai-style self-denial and self-discipline were the key to preventing further national degeneration.[3] Among initiatives designed to address problems of indiscipline and military weakness were the founding of school cadet corps and the publication of Baden-Powell's *Scouting for Boys* (1908). Education Acts, which organized state schools under local authorities in 1902,[4] provided free meals in 1906 and introduced school medical inspections in 1907, also responded to the perceived emergency and were aimed at improving the physical and mental development of the lower classes.

The National Efficiency agenda was described in detail in *Essays on Duty and Discipline* (1910), a series of papers on the subject collected by the president of the Church Army, Lord Meath (1841–1929) and endorsed by Kipling and Baden-Powell. Meath warned that the twentieth century might become the 'century of the child',[5] with young people indulged so much that they cared little for the future of the race. The former headmaster of Harrow, J.E.C. Welldon (1854–1937), complained of the 'growth of indiscipline among children of all classes'.[6] He declared that 'Men and women, boys and girls, are becoming soft'. The answer was

---

2   Searle 1990, p. xx.

3   Alfred Stead's *Great Japan: A Study in National Efficiency* (1906) is a good example of the interest shown in Japan's prodigious industrial growth as a lesson to the supposedly degenerate west. *Scouting for Boys*, with its frequent references to the Japanese and their healthy, disciplined lifestyles, echoed the eugenicist idealization found in Stead's work. Influential works inspiring the National Efficiency movement included *National Life from the Standpoint of Science* (1900), by the eugenicist Karl Pearson, which develops ideas put forward by Francis Galton's *Natural Inheritance* (1869) in a racially supremacist context. This work takes the Boer War as its starting point.

4   Searle 1990, p. 207.

5   Brabazon 1910, p. 2.

6   Ibid., p. 36.

to '*to cultivate a certain hardness of character*' or 'fortitude' in the young.[7] T.H.M. Home worried that boys would become the 'waste product' of the nation.[8] What emerges from this discourse is the fact that the focus of moral reform in education had moved away from crime and religious matters towards a preoccupation with biological 'sin' – behavior that made the individual unfit to fulfill the duties of soldiering and fatherhood. The supposedly 'objective' findings of eugenicists, who confidently asserted exactly how young people might achieve maximum physical potential for the benefit of the nation, also led to new perceptions of citizenship that prioritized the race over the individual. Welldon, citing Aristotle's insistence that the citizen exists to 'serve the State, to honor the State, to live and, if need be, to die for the State', argued that 'Individualism, if it means the rights of individual men and women, counts for little or nothing'. In short, 'The state is everything'.[9] Citizenship did not mean taking an active role in democratic processes or in working for social change but required absolute obedience, in thought as well as in action, to authority.

The National Efficiency movement's ideas on adolescent education can be traced back to Herbert Spencer's *Education: Intellectual, Moral and Physical* (1861), a scheme for providing young people with a physical and mental training to help them survive in a Darwinist world. Here, Spencer criticized both male and female education for supplying nothing more than decorative accomplishments. Education, he said, should teach young people how to do a specific number of activities, which he listed in order of importance:

> 1. those activities which directly minister to self-preservation; 2. those activities which, by securing the necessaries of life, indirectly minister to self-preservation; 3. those activities which have for their end the rearing and discipline of offspring; 4. those activities which are involved in the maintenance of proper social and political relations; 5. those miscellaneous activities which fill up the leisure part of life.[10]

'Self-preservation', the highest educational priority, was about learning how to exercise, avoid disease and respond properly to feelings of tiredness, lack of fresh air and so on.[11] Young people owed it to posterity to observe a strict physical regimen, since it is 'physical sins – partly our forefathers' and partly our own – which produce [...] ill-health, [and] deduct more from complete living than anything else'.[12] The next most important discipline to learn about was science, which included sociology. Spencer was particularly concerned about the lack of scientific information given to young people as future parents. Any antiquary looking back

---

7 Ibid., p. 47.
8 Ibid., p. 5.
9 Ibid., p. 41.
10 Spencer 1966, p. 9.
11 Ibid., p. 14.
12 Ibid., p. 16.

on Victorian education would, he remarked, conclude that it was a *'curriculum for their celibates'*.[13] To Spencer, parenting needed to be taught by experts. He denigrated 'ignorant nurses' and 'prejudiced [...] grandmothers' and implied that only properly qualified male professionals are fit to decide how children should be raised.[14] Spencer also suggested that young people should be taught citizenship through 'Descriptive Sociology':[15] the study of the laws of human nature. Students would learn how governments evolved, how customs, traditions and superstitions are formed and about the daily lives of people through history.[16]

However, Spencer paid scant attention to the role of play, art or other imaginative or creative activities in forming future citizens. To Spencer, play was essentially for improving the body, not the mind, and art, though important, failed to count as 'a fundamental requisite to human happiness'.[17] By spending too much time on cultural activities, he commented, the current educational system 'neglects the plant for the sake of the flower'.[18] Another of Spencer's insistences is that child development is determined by evolutionary laws and cannot be understood without 'a knowledge of these laws'.[19] The individual, he insisted, should not deviate from the developmental norm and those who do (for instance, by taking part in activities unsuited to their age) may become rebellious or even die.[20] Psychologists, educationalists and members of the National Efficiency movement all used and adapted these ideas of Spencer's for their own ends.

Between the 1890s and the First World War much of the writing done on adolescence came from two groups. One group, which claimed a scientific basis for its work, was focused around the American psychologist and Social Darwinist G. Stanley Hall. Like Herbert Spencer, these commentators discussed adolescence in terms of immutable laws governing mental and physical development and attributed most psychological and behavioral changes to incipient sexuality. They often depicted adolescents as having little individual volition and being blindly led by their biological drives. The way their investigations were conducted – by compiling and devising supposedly 'scientific' categories under which boys of every conceivable type could be classified – had a lot to do with the ambitions of researchers themselves. As Hugh Cunningham points out, educationalists had been promoting their subject as a 'science' since the 1870s, and psychology was a 'new' subject at the turn of the century. Practitioners of both disciplines were 'most urgently engaged in a process of professionalization'.[21] Competing for

---

13 Ibid., p. 25.
14 Ibid., p. 26.
15 Ibid., p. 36.
16 Ibid., p. 35.
17 Ibid., p. 38.
18 Ibid., p. 39.
19 Ibid., p. 29.
20 Ibid., p. 31.
21 Cunningham 1992, p. 199.

funds and authority, both groups sought a methodology that would render their work as 'scientific' as possible, using paper tests and questionnaires whose results were analyzed to offer what was claimed to be hard, 'objective' information on trends and categories, which could be used in the formation (and justification) of a range of social policies.[22] In response, some 'serious' fiction writers used juvenile literature, including the public school story, to debate the social impact of scientific approaches and theories. Sometimes, they cooperated in the scheme of propagating social Darwinist ideology; often they challenged the behavioral, political and gender norms that sociologists, psychologists and educationalists were trying to establish.

The 1890s seem to have fostered a renewed interest in youth as a subject of literary and sociological debate. On October 21, 1899, *The Academy* announced that 'the boy' had just been 'discovered' and was 'about to be widely exploited in fiction'. This discovery was thanks to two books, Rudyard Kipling's *Stalky & Co.* and Eden Phillpotts's *The Human Boy* (both of 1899), the first works 'soberly aimed at adults' to study the 'true' nature of boys. These works, *The Academy* says, are a fresh departure. Although grown men may enjoy *Tom Brown* because it lets them sentimentally relive their past through fiction, a more objective documentation of boyhood life is needed. Phillpotts's narrative is particularly valuable, the writer argues, because it presents the 'sternness of genuine realism'.[23] For example, Phillpotts classifies his boys according to the types of mental pathology they present ('the bucolic, the manic, the criminal, the senile, the various feminines'). Such an emotionally detached psychological study may be beneficial in developing new methods of discipline. However, *The Academy* is skeptical about whether a truly comprehensive analysis of boyhood is possible. Boys have a peculiar logic of their own, 'Boy-lore', which 'borders on the incredible' and is mystical and supernatural.[24] They also have an 'instinct' for detecting and exploiting the difficulties of those in authority and for confounding adults with their diplomatic skills. The boy 'is always a great statesman' and 'It is his statesmanship, coupled with the plethora of unemployed teachers, that makes many schools into a battlefield of diplomacy'. If writers exposed the hidden abilities of boys, there would be a public disturbance 'compared to which the original reception of Ibsen was an ecstatic welcome'.[25] *The Academy* does not say

---

22 Cunningham remarks that 'even at the time critics thought [much of this information] was of dubious value' (p. 200). For example, Stanley Hall claimed, bafflingly, that 'girls [...] have from six to fifteen times as many ideals as boys' (Hall 1925, vol. II, p. 391). Kidd remarks that 'Hall was known for his use of lengthy questionnaires and his obsessive compilation of pop-ethnographic data without analysis' (p. 55). Much of this information gathered by Hall and his ilk (for example, work on the concept of IQ) was used to enforce existing class, race and gender structures.
23 'Boy, Only Boy' 1899, pp. 457–58.
24 Ibid., p. 457.
25 Ibid., p. 458.

exactly why boys are so threatening, but emits a vague sense of moral panic and the feeling that a more effective control of the young is necessary.

Phillpotts's approach of classifying adolescents into behavioral and sociological 'types' followed a more general trend in the study of psychology and behavior during the *fin de siècle* period. I will discuss these ideas further, and the resistance they provoked among various writers, later in the chapter. However, it is worth briefly mentioning *The Human Boy* and its 'anthropological' approach to adolescence. *The Human Boy* (originally published as short articles in J.K. Jerome's *The Idler*), unlike previous works on adolescence, is not about the development of one individual through his school career. Instead, each chapter, supposedly 'written' by a different boy, describes an 'amusing' incident in school life. Rather than tracing the ways in which individual boys or groups learn citizenship and problem-solving skills, Phillpotts concentrates on the trivialities of daily life. With the exception of one Jewish boy, Gideon, the characters employ little abstract thought and seem obsessed with their bodies and with the petty romances they enact with the Headmaster's daughters. The first chapter mentions voices breaking, facial hair emerging and acne.[26] Later, 'Tin Lin Chow', the son of a Chinese Mandarin, attempts suicide after a failed love affair,[27] demonstrating how an emergent sense of sexuality unbalances the mind. In order to add a sense of veracity to his text, Phillpotts explains in his introduction that 'probably half' of the stories were 'elaborations' of events from his own schooldays and that he made the boys 'tell their own stories and so avoided any danger of the adult vision creeping in'.[28] However, although his aim is to produce a cool-headed, unsentimental depiction of adolescence, he deals in racial as well as age-related stereotypes in order to situate the British adolescent culturally and historically. The melodramatic Tin Lin Chow, coming from 'the birthplace of civilization',[29] is emotionally backward in the eyes of his schoolfellows, while Gideon, with his shrewd, usurious investment schemes, is ahead of them intellectually, but morally degenerate. Here, the process of recapitulation, in which boys passively follow the developmental paths set out in ancient history by their forbears, is the motivating factor in determining behavior. There seems to be little scope for the individual to initiate social change, or to demonstrate intellectual originality.

Those who chose to take a 'scientific' approach to the study of adolescence commonly followed the example of G. Stanley Hall, professor of psychology and pedagogy at Clark University, whose epic 1904 work, *Adolescence*, became an internationally recognized authority. The work was a multidisciplinary fusion of psychological, anthropological, historical and literary ideas – an often confused attempt to cover the subject of adolescence in as encyclopedic a manner as possible. Although Hall's work made few direct references to the public school

---

26 Phillpotts 1930, pp. 11–15.
27 Ibid., p. 313.
28 Ibid., p. viii.
29 Ibid., p. 314.

system, it was welcomed by commentators who wished to reform English upper-class education. Hall focused almost exclusively on male youths in secondary and higher education, because 'Student life', as he remarked, 'is perhaps the best of all fields [...] for studying the natural history of adolescence'.[30] Kenneth Kidd describes Hall as part of a social, scientific and literary movement that he terms 'boyology' – a cultural trend that used a combination of popular myth and biological essentialism to fashion an essentially conservative ideology of male development which emphasized the importance of all-male communities in adolescent development, getting back to nature and to 'natural', essentialist ideas of masculinity and excluding women and 'feminine' influences from the environment of the boy.[31] Female development was relegated by Hall to separate chapters, and working-class life to a section on 'Juvenile Faults, Immoralities and Crimes'. This tendency to dwell disproportionately on upper-class boys was followed by the sociologists who adapted Hall's work to a British context.

In his work, Hall demonstrated what Patricia Meyer Spacks has called 'the extremes of utterances on adolescence from the eighteenth century to the present'.[32] Although at times he took a rigidly Social Darwinist approach, he drew extensively on Classical and European history, literature and philosophy. Influenced by Benjamin Jowett, Hall identified himself with the pedagogues of Ancient Greece. Socrates, he said, like all good teachers, knew the secret of education. '[T]o love boys' he explains, 'is the key [...]. All who strive are lovers; and the only true love is of knowledge and virtue [...] which is so impersonal and pure that wisdom-love is a kind of dying.'[33] To the romanticist in Hall, adolescents possess a kind of genius because they reject the prosaic adult world. He cites J.S. Mill's discovery of Wordsworth and rejection of Utilitarianism as an example of adolescent consciousness overriding the urges of material necessity.[34] In adulthood, this genius is lost – especially in males, who must reconcile themselves to the everyday business of making a living.[35]

Hall explains that adolescence is the key to understanding both the future and the past. It is something like an evolutionary 'missing link', during which time the individual revisits a stage of human development the race has forgotten about:

> Just as the well-matured adult [...] has utterly lost all traces and recollection of the perturbations of the storm and stress period [...] so the race must have gone through a long heat and ferment, of which consciousness, [...] was lost, partly because growth was so rapid.

---

30 Hall 1925, vol. II, p. 399. 'Student life' here means 'boarding-school life'.
31 See Kidd 2004, *passim*.
32 Spacks 1981, p. 229.
33 Hall 1925, vol. I, p. 519.
34 Ibid., p. 567.
35 Ibid., p. 547.

We catch glimpses of this past in the 'grotesque myths and legends of races' and in the behavior of adolescents.[36] If we examine the adolescent, we can discover how we evolved and devise measures to prevent ourselves degenerating. However, while adolescence can teach us about the nature of progress in the very long term, Hall rejects the idea that the individual boy, growing into maturity, can play a significant role in his country's development, because progress works on a phylogenic not an ontogenic level. Although he admits that adolescents have a 'spontaneous tendency to develop social and political organizations', he explains that they should avoid radicalism, and learn to 'feel the force of conventionalities, the truth of highly saturated creeds, the value of established institutions'. This policy is necessary because the inherent mental instability of the adolescent means that

> There is especial danger that temperament or environment will destroy this balance and precipitate the mind for life into one or another of these camps where extreme views are so easy and simple, and moderate ones so hard and complex.[37]

The adolescent is a delicate organism and the 'Heraclitic fire of life' is easily affected by environment.[38] Because of his nervous fragility, no matter how strong he may seem, the adolescent needs 'protection, physical care and moral and intellectual guidance',[39] not over-stimulation with political fervor.

Hall's response to adolescence is, therefore, mixed. The Platonic and romantic parts of him admire the young. The social Darwinist in him, meanwhile, sees them as a useful resource, but an unstable one that needs to be controlled. Moreover, like other commentators of the period, Hall is disturbed by the fact that adolescents seem somehow to evade adult attempts to make a comprehensive study of the adolescent mind, since, according to him, they communicate on an entirely different level to adults. Citing W.A. White's *The Court of Boyville* (1899), he remarks: 'There is a wall around the town of Boyville [...] impenetrable when its gates have once shut upon youth. An adult may peer over the wall [...] but finds [...] himself banished among the purblind grown-ups'.[40] Hall's adult, shut forever outside 'Boyville', is a desperate figure: desperate to study the adolescent, desperate to recapture his 'genius' and desperate to control.

Hall's authentic adolescent subject lives divorced intellectually, morally and economically from the adult world, which is problematic. Because Hall cherishes an ideal of youth unfettered by economic and material constraints, he denies the authenticity of any adolescent experience found outside wealthy homes and elite schools. He also worries that labor may damage the motor functioning of

---

36 Ibid., vol. II, p. 73.
37 Ibid., pp. 397, 87.
38 Ibid., vol. I, p. 33.
39 Ibid., p. 47.
40 Ibid., pp. 535–36.

working-class juveniles,[41] but fails to discuss how the working environment might contribute to adolescent development or identity. A working-class teenage breadwinner, who might have a relatively mature understanding of labor and financial issues, would be an unnatural anomaly to Hall. Hall's stance here is one that must have been increasingly easy for sociologists to adopt, given that child protection, education and employment legislation were taking more and more teenagers out of the adult sphere. Classing the adolescent as an inhabitant of an entirely separate moral and intellectual sphere, incomprehensible to those accustomed to adult reason and logic, must have also given sociologists a convenient excuse for ignoring any adolescent voice that contradicted their own proclamations.

In *The Adolescent* (1911), the American educational psychologist and colleague of Hall, John Willis Slaughter, develops Hall's basic anthropological ideas to show how boarding school practices resemble rituals performed by 'primitive' man. In aboriginal societies, he explains, adolescent boys are 'taken from the company of the women and initiated into the mysteries known only to the men, the instruction being carried on by the old men of the group'. In this seclusion, boys undergo trials, some of them violent. If a boy performs well 'he is henceforth regarded as a man and is capable of possessing a wife and becoming the head of a family'. Examinations are the modern-day equivalent of these tests and the wise tribal elders have become schoolmasters and university professors. Thus, to Slaughter, anthropology gives credence to the idea that adolescence is a phenomenon peculiar to males; indeed, he proclaims, it is all about becoming 'male'.[42] Slaughter uses this theory to reinforce a highly gendered conception of citizenship. Since 'citizenship' entails the right to have a family, it follows that a 'citizen' is one deemed physically and socially fit to be a father.

Slaughter's idea of citizenship is much less individualistic than those of previous writers, although adolescence still plays a role in social change. He explains that although many adolescents desire to be active citizens in a traditional sense, they fail to see how limited the effect of individual political activity can be. He remarks that

> Every adolescent is a reformer, and the world probably advances through the utilization of the ideals and energies of successive generations of youth. Older persons perhaps desire reforms, but they are too well aware how little they can accomplish and are correspondingly deficient in courage, but the adolescent possesses in a high degree the ability to 'rush in where angels fear to tread'.[43]

Adolescents rush headlong at problems expecting to make a heroic individual impact on society. Although their individual efforts are too small to be significant,

---

41 Ibid., pp. 170–71.
42 Slaughter 1911, p. 2.
43 Ibid., p. 8.

however, their energies combine to bring about change that is constant and gradual.[44] Social change, like evolutionary change, happens at such a slow rate that the individual's impact on the process is unnoticeable. Slaughter's work shows how, under the influence of Social Darwinism, the narrative of adolescent citizenship loses the highly individualistic idealism of Coningsby or Tom Brown.

British educationalists, who were overwhelmingly male and middle or upper class, also willingly adopted Hall's bias towards privileged schoolboys. Few discussed more average adolescents. F.H. Hayward's *Day and Evening Schools* (1910) was an exception, but even this text claimed that public schools were a good model on which to design state schools and maintained that *Tom Brown*, although fifty years old, still set an ideal standard for adolescent education.[45] Revolutionary experiments in progressive education – for instance, J.H. Badley's Bedales (1893) or A.S. Neill's Summerhill (1921) – also focused on the tiny minority who found boarding school education affordable and desirable. Even the socialist Victor Gollancz, in his 1918 manifesto advocating the transformation of public schools 'into instruments by means of which a genuine and complete democracy may be achieved',[46] made no mention of including poorer boys, or girls. Coming at a time of expanding state education, this emphasis on the public schoolboy as the 'authentic' adolescent seems illogical. After all, at the turn of the century, more adolescents were in education than ever before (470,876 over-twelves in 1895),[47] and in 1902 the Balfour Education Act made provision for endowed grammar schools and county secondary schools. There is an explanation, however, for the obsession with public school tradition. Working-class adolescent identities, when formed outside the pale of middle-class control, were often viewed with distaste by those in authority. Stephen Heathorn has shown that the new state secondary schools borrowed traditions from older public schools in order to instill a sense of identity among those whose forefathers had experienced quite different kinds of adolescence.[48] Indeed, this policy went into every sphere of education. Alec Waugh's former teacher at Sherborne, S.P.B. Mais, remarked in his autobiography that after reading Mark Benny's *Low Company* he had discovered that even the Borstal system had been based on the public schools.[49]

---

44 Ibid., p. 89.
45 Hayward 1910, pp. 241, 225, 479. It is possible that the privileged schoolboy model of growing up was even more pervasively influential than I have suggested. Kidd cites Sarah Winter's suggestion that, in Freudian theory, 'the schoolboy became the model subject of psychoanalysis: learned, ambitious, professionalized, and ambivalent about male bonds'. Thus the Oedipus Complex itself is a theory founded in anxieties brought about by the 'all-male Gymnasium'. See Kidd 2004, p. 10.
46 Gollancz 1918, p. 5.
47 Armytage 1965, p. 186.
48 See Heathorn 1996, 107.
49 Mais 1937, p. 37.

One of the first works to apply the ideas of Stanley Hall to an English context was Cyril Bruyn Andrews's *An Introduction to the Study of Adolescent Education* (1912). Andrews initially expressed an interest in state education, saying that state schools would always be a matter 'of public interest' and remarking that 'the education in a State school can never be very far behind the most modern and sane views on adolescence'.[50] However, state education was not Andrews's highest priority; it remained 'behind' the schooling of the elite, not in the forefront of change. He felt that the adolescence of the 'Directing Classes' attracted less political interest than it deserved and so, in his analysis, practically ignored state schools and girls' education. Andrews declared that the public schoolboy was 'in far greater danger during adolescence than his poorer brother', because 'lilies fester worse than weeds'.[51] The botanical metaphor makes a clear eugenic point: public schoolboys are a superior species who will degenerate if left to their own devices and they need extra attention and protection from parents, teachers and sociologists. Unlike the poor, who thrive and proliferate abundantly, they are difficult to raise (and possibly even to breed). To make matters worse, public schools hide boys out of sight where inspectors and sociologists cannot get their hands on them. They are, therefore, 'more potent for good or evil' than day schools,[52] which are subject to constant government monitoring.

Andrews's primary concern is adolescent sexual behavior. He insists, although without providing evidence, that 'sexual pathology' (which he never properly defines) is endemic in the system[53] and he diagnoses all other behavioral problems as being rooted in sexual development. Society, he claims, has been too prudish to investigate 'the real atmosphere in which our boys and girls live', to combat adolescent disease and delinquency,[54] or to find the roots of discipline problems. Because adolescent problems are essentially biological, education should move closer to scientific disciplines such as 'physiology, psychology, and mental pathology' and psychologists and doctors should be more involved in schools.[55] Andrews's adolescent is a passive vessel of biological impulses, who scientists can study in the interests of the race but who has little to offer society in terms of individual thought. The figure of the virtuous Arnoldian boy, struggling manfully with the most profound moral questions, is an outdated fantasy to Andrews, because the strength of biological drives makes adolescents irrational and morally powerless. The boy, an amoral tool of his own biology, should therefore be protected from 'evil passions' by being placed in a totally safe environment where his decisions are made for him, because if he is forced to make his own moral

---

50 Andrews 1912, p. 6.
51 Ibid., p. 8.
52 Ibid., p. 7.
53 Ibid., pp. 79–117.
54 Ibid., pp. 2, v–vi.
55 Ibid., p. 20.

decisions it will create a 'civil war' between his body and his mind.[56] Because boyhood morality is a biological problem, moreover, the traditional guardians of young people (especially unmarried masters and parents) should defer to psychologists,[57] whose role in school life is more important than those of the schoolroom, playground and chapel.

The belief that biology dominates the mind of the adolescent above all else had serious ramifications for citizenship education. Andrews ostensibly follows a typically Arnoldian line on citizenship, remarking that boys should enjoy 'almost complete self-government' because they live in a democratizing world where 'liberty of action and toleration of thought are manifesting themselves in no uncertain way'.[58] He explains, for example, that pupils should make their own rules and run a miniature market economy to sell their own products. However, the boys in Andrews's ideal system are less autonomous than it initially appears, because their 'independent' choices are conditioned by their education in social science, economics and eugenics. They learn about the 'trading instincts' of human beings and about self-help and economic advancement and they study how to become legislators by learning 'sociology and the social aspects of psychology and physiology'.[59] The scientific and economic ideas they learn are non-negotiable absolutes. Their 'liberty' does not extend to the freedom to question these ideas or to experiment in developing their own beliefs. School discipline, moreover, depends on the idea that, in the interests of racial and economic success, certain 'scientific' rules cannot be broken. Andrews warns that 'nature dislikes being abused' and that 'if she is continually offended, [she] loses power to reassert herself'.[60] Ironically, Andrews, as a disciplinarian, follows the rhetorical approach of earlier Evangelicals, who had argued for an ostensibly liberal educational regime but who had backed up their moral agendas with religious threats. Andrews merely replaces religious threats with scientific threats. Indeed, Herbert Spencer also proposed that, as a form of discipline, science could rival the very harshest Christian doctrine:

> Instead of the rewards and punishments of traditional belief, which people vaguely hope they may gain, or escape, in spite of their disobedience; [...] there are rewards and punishments in the ordained constitution of things; [...] the evil results of disobedience are inevitable [and] the laws to which we must submit are both inexorable and beneficent.[61]

Physical (especially reproductive) degeneracy was the new damnation and biological sin had replaced the multiplicity of Christian sins that occupied Hughes

---

56 Ibid., pp. 10, 35.
57 Ibid., pp. 29–32.
58 Ibid., pp. 90, 16.
59 Ibid., pp. 99, 24.
60 Ibid., p. 66.
61 Spencer 1966, p. 52.

and Farrar. To the eugenic age, sin was bad not because it offended God but because it weakened the race. Nonetheless, however much the moral vocabulary of educationalists had changed, the Puritanism and prurience of fifty years before had shifted in emphasis rather than disappearing. Although, as Claudia Nelson has observed, the late Victorians, stimulated by the Darwinian imperative, had jettisoned the mid-Victorian Evangelical/Malthusian unease at the very existence of sexuality and intimate relationships,[62] the paranoia that surrounded boys' private behavior largely remained in place, justifying an intense and intrusive scrutiny and control of every part of their lives.

Educational rhetoric may have changed, therefore, but the basic concerns of educationalists had not. Although Social Darwinist principles initially seem remote from the ideals that governed 1830s Rugby, some 'revolutionary' theorists still sought legitimacy by alluding back to Thomas Arnold. The introduction to J.W. Slaughter's book was by Joseph Findlay (Professor of Education at Manchester[63]), who had edited Arnold's writings fourteen years before. Findlay stressed the continuity between Slaughter's ideas and Arnold's. He remarked that, although Arnold 'knew nothing of formal psychology', his recognition of stages of adolescent growth foreshadowed later work, while 'his description of the uncontrolled "barbarian" society of a boarding school' resembled Slaughter's analysis of hooligan gangs.[64] He explains that Arnold, like G. Stanley Hall, felt an urgent need to address the problems of adolescent behavior, and that his warnings made one 'tremble for the future of our race'.[65] Slaughter and Arnold differed, however, in one way:

> Arnold was always desirous of 'hastening' his pupils though the early years of adolescence, anxious to raise them, with precocious seriousness, to a higher level of 'moral thoughtfulness'. [...] but it may be doubted whether the type of manhood produced is always of the finest: whether God and Nature are really at strife in the way this theory would presuppose.[66]

What Findlay's analysis reveals is that although the rhetoric and rationale had changed, adults were in the same state of panic regarding adolescence as they had been throughout the previous century. In the remainder of this chapter, I will consider how 'serious' public school fiction writers at the end of the nineteenth century dealt with new debates on degeneracy, heredity, citizenship, fatherhood and sexuality as they were emerging. I will first show how some writers accepted and promoted the National Efficiency ideal and the social scientific agenda and then how some tried to resist what they felt to be dangerous trends emerging in

---

62 Nelson 1989, pp. 541–42.
63 Armytage 1965, p. 198.
64 Slaughter 1911, p. xi.
65 Ibid., p. xii.
66 Ibid., p. xi–xii.

science, politics and gender ideology – trends that were to find fullest expression in the sociological works I have just discussed. I will also show how ideals of rational liberal education and active citizenship were put under threat by those who saw unequivocal obedience and conformity to one specific idea of male citizenship as fundamental to national superiority.

The first text I will consider here, Robert Massie Freeman's *Steady and Strong* (1891), is enthusiastically Spencerian in its approach to education – more so, indeed, than subsequent works. To Freeman, the priority of education is the cultivation of a healthy body, which requires a wholehearted devotion to sport. As I mentioned in the previous chapter, sport had taken on a fresh relevance in public schools during the later half of the nineteenth century, and J.A. Mangan has already described in detail how schools used sport as part of a scheme to develop the kind of physical and mental fortitude thought to be needed by colonial administrators and soldiers.[67] In this regime, the Arnoldian ideal of the Christian gentleman lost out to single-minded toughness and an unquestioning belief in British supremacy and racial superiority. This obsession with sport and fitness, however, was not just founded in imperialist ambition; it also came from a fear of degeneration. Darwin's *The Descent of Man* (1871) had warned that 'natural selection acts only in a tentative manner' and that 'individuals and races may have acquired certain indisputable advantages, and yet have perished from failing in other characters'.[68] Evolutionary 'superiority' could not be taken for granted, and there was a chance that Nature would choose socially undesirable individuals (for example, the working classes) to survive rather than the elite. Writers such as Freeman, therefore, took it upon themselves to teach how Social Darwinist principles could best be harnessed in defense of the status quo.

The setting for *Steady and Strong* is Loretto School at Musselburgh ('Chudleigh Abbey'), which Mangan discusses at length in *Athleticism in the Victorian and Edwardian Public School*. Loretto was the brainchild of H.H. Almond, who bought it in 1862 to fulfill his dream of athleticizing the Scottish upper classes who, he thought, were too scholastic and obsessed by bourgeois commercialism for their own good.[69] Influenced by Ruskin, Kingsley and, above all, Herbert Spencer, Almond dedicated himself to 'the scientific training of the young human animal', implementing German-style exercise systems and encouraging team games to encourage group loyalty and prevent egotism.[70] Mangan remarks that Almond was preoccupied 'with physical health rather than social control, or even morality'[71] and demonstrates in detail how he rigidly controlled boys' time and enforced conformity.

---

67 Mangan 2000, p. 136.
68 Darwin 1871, p. 178.
69 Mangan 2000, pp. 48–49.
70 Ibid., pp. 50–53, 55, 58, 56.
71 Ibid., p. 58.

At the beginning of *Steady and Strong*, the degenerate Reginald Owen, 'dark, almost sallow, as if from ill health',[72] is sent to Chudleigh Abbey, a school where athleticism is as important as academic work. At Chudleigh, there is a hysterical fear of physical illness and weakness. Windows are permanently ajar and masters and boys obsessively remove their coats, complaining that rooms are too warm. The cane is the only punishment, because other kinds of discipline require indoor work. Universal natural laws are used to justify the school's regime and physical health has replaced religion as the root of morality. As Freeman's headmaster comments: 'we pay the most careful attention to the laws of health and bodily exercise' because 'sound mental and sound moral training are largely bound up with sound physical training'.[73] Gradually, Reginald grows strong and Freeman (unlike earlier writers whose physical descriptions are sparing) documents his improvements in detail. His measurements are recorded when he arrives at school and readers are kept informed of the progress of his vital statistics, to such an extent that Freeman's text sometimes resembles a prescriptive manual, detailing not only the exercises and regimen necessary to achieve a desirable standard of physical health but dictating a norm to which readers should aspire. Indeed, Freeman's approach rather prefigures the early chapters of Hall's *Adolescence*, which carefully detail the average vital statistics of 'normal' adolescents and classify height and strength in terms of 'inferiority' and 'superiority'.

However, Freeman's Headmaster does not accept Spencer's ideology wholesale. Spencer believed that because the laws of survival were good for progress, well-meaning social reformers, including educationalists, should limit their interference in young people's development and let nature do its work. A *laissez-faire* system such as might have appealed to Spencer was thinkable in 1861 when Spencer was writing, but, as I showed earlier, the late-Victorian climate was turning towards stricter control of the young. Chudleigh's Head interferes in every aspect of his students' lives and there is no arena at Chudleigh for boys to practice independent decision-making. In the 1890s, it was taken for granted that teachers would take formal responsibility recreation and sport, but in *Steady and Strong* the Head attempts to control even supposedly spontaneous activities; he even goes so far as to tell the boys when to bully each other ('if a fellow bungles at games from not trying or playing up, I recommend the head of his side to thrash him'[74]). Although it is claimed that at Chudleigh 'there's no spying, or supervision, or poking of masters' noses into everything', the Head seems to be everywhere and 'if any headmaster was likely to have an intimate acquaintance with all his boys, it was the headmaster of Chudleigh'.[75] The boys even have elocution lessons to control the way they speak. To ensure further that the boys have no opportunity to take their own wayward paths, the curriculum is 'calculated to promote healthy

---

72 Freeman 1891, p. 9.
73 Ibid., pp. 32–33.
74 Ibid., p. 33.
75 Ibid., pp. 51, 211.

fatigue' and the boys have no individual hobbies since they collapse exhausted into bed in the early evening (a policy used at the time to prevent 'immorality').[76]

In earlier narratives with a Darwinian influence – for example, *St Winifred's* – boys fought against Nature unaided by adults. To become a hero, a boy had to make critical decisions for himself in this battle. In *St Winifred's*, the muscular Walter saves the drowning Kendrick without the benefit of an organized training regime. Boys became fit and healthy by rambling in the countryside or in casual sport and masters focused on spiritual and creative development. Sometimes, for instance in *Butler Burke*, the system even allowed weak boys to die. However, in *Steady and Strong* nothing is left to chance. The boys never even glimpse danger, but are kept safe until they are fit and old enough to encounter the outside world in complete safety. Their most pressing concern is football, which has no relation to life-and-death struggles in the real world, but which is treated with the same gravity that Farrar gives to eternal salvation. Chudleigh aims to cheat the genetic lottery. It is no longer permissible for boys like *Tom Brown*'s George Arthur to sit back and accept that they are not of the Darwinian elect. Indeed, by making the puny Reginald grow into a paragon of strength, Freeman shows that every adolescent can and *must* become one of the 'fit'.

Freeman, obsessed with the body, rejects the tradition of rational liberal education. As the previous chapter showed, Bracebridge Hemyng and other writers who believed that moral progress depended on rational debate had emphasized the educational importance of verbal dialogue over physical competition. At Chudleigh, fighting is back on the agenda. The Head advises that when boys have a quarrel, they should 'pommel each other's persons, then shake hands and be friends – not wound each other's hearts with spiteful and bitter words'.[77] Freeman seems to assume that disagreement between boys is never a matter of principle, but the fault of an animal bad temper that can be purged through physical activity. There is no suggestion that by arguing, debating, or just plain talking, boys might achieve a better understanding of their world or evolve ways of dealing with difficult issues. In this preoccupation with the body, Freeman stigmatizes verbal and intellectual skills. Chudleigh's bad boy is Fletcher, who edits the school paper. Fletcher is 'out of keeping with the [...] tone of the school', 'sneer[ing] inwardly at many of the Head's little rules, and [...] inclined to ridicule the Head himself as an eccentric old enthusiast'. His sins include late nights, playing cards and wearing 'stick-up collars' in the holidays.[78] While for Farrar, Hughes and others writing had been a symbol of boyhood autonomy and critical thought, it is dangerous for Freeman, since every utterance carries a potential for dissent. In the absence of opportunities for independent dissent, the preparation the boys receive for the decision-making aspects of citizenship seems to be minimal.

---

76 Ibid., p. 52. Hime 1899 advocates exhausting boys in this way.
77 Freeman 1891, p. 140.
78 Ibid., p. 51.

The main drama of the book begins when Reginald imprudently buys some faulty fishing tackle and lands himself in debt to the local moneylender. The worry the debt causes him disrupts his academic work and spoils his physical health. The less control Reginald has over his money, the lower his energy levels on the football field become and the worse his play. While Reginald plays, the loan shark looks on from the edge of the pitch, intent on winning a sweepstake he has on the game, like a kind of economic vampire who uses the boy's innocence to drain him of money. Reginald's inability to manage his money is linked, therefore, to his inability to manage his own health. His problems with the loan shark are eventually solved when the lawyer father of his friend, Cartwright, points out that, since Reginald is a minor, he has no legal responsibility for his own debts. While the debt issue is hanging over him, Reginald shows no understanding of his rights and, unlike earlier school story characters, fails to show any ability to handle adult matters. Indeed, according to Freeman, adolescents in general are vulnerable because of their lack of understanding of their rights and obligations, leading unscrupulous individuals to exploit 'the legal ignorance of youths and young men'.[79] However, instead of counseling boys to learn their rights (as Hemyng might have done), Freeman merely reminds them to obey orders. Unable to take a role in solving their own problems, Freeman's boys show no prospect of becoming civic subjects at all.

In particular, Chudleigh boys lack the financial independence of earlier boys such as Tom Brown, who gambled, borrowed, made unwise financial decisions and were left to learn from the consequences. Before the mid-Victorian period, learning to control money seems to have been a fundamental though unofficial aspect of education. Accounts of early Victorian Eton, for example, celebrate its flourishing sub-economy, where boys traded and bartered with semi-official tradesmen. According to C.F. Johnstone, one tradesman, Spankey, was 'looked up to as a perfect oracle'.[80] For Freeman, however, financial and physical vulnerability go together. The image of the adolescent as a sanitary and economic liability fits in with the National Efficiency idea that imperfectly controlled adolescents were responsible for national degeneration. Money, health and youth all need strict control. Indeed, Freeman compares the role of the schoolmaster to that of the banker, because both need to be vigilant for the tiniest signs of instability. The banker's job is to minimize his losses, while 'the object of the schoolmaster is to save the boy whose moral condition he is watching'.[81]

Freeman's choice of debt rather than the more traditional theft as a main plot motif is significant, considering the perceived link between school discipline and national economic performance. Economics, of course, had always been a factor in education. The Victorians had a system of payment by results.[82] The 1862 Code of Grants was set up to make sure money was spent properly, and school inspectors

---

79 Ibid., p. 219.
80 Johnstone 1870, p. 39.
81 Freeman 1891, p. 213.
82 Armytage 1965, p. 120.

were sent to examine children. Schools received money when children performed well and were fined for each failure.[83] However, as the debate over Eton finances provoked by 'Paterfamilias' (see Chapter 3) showed, many adults wanted to believe that children and adolescents were blissfully free from mundane economic concerns, a romantic idea endorsed by Stanley Hall. It is ironical that, although adolescents were deemed not to understand money properly, early twentieth-century school stories raise the subject of the economics of education in a way that had not happened before. H.A. Vachell's *The Hill* (discussed below) makes an unprecedented allusion to school fees. One housemaster cautions his students: 'How about work, eh? Lot o'slacking last term. Is it honest? You fellows cost your people a deal of money'.[84] *The Hill* also features a debt episode, in which a boy called Beaumont-Greene, whose father has made a fortune from the 'Imperishable Whaleskin Boot', starts gambling and ends up in debt to the school villain, Scaife. He then forges a note from his father requesting a thirty-pound loan from a Harrow tradesman and is expelled. In contrast, *Stalky* mocks the hypocrisy of those who believe that young people are romantically detached from debt, profit and usury. Stalky's buffoonish housemaster, Prout, remarks that 'money-lending [...] made youth cold and calculating, and opened the door to all evil'.[85] He then upsets the school by 'unearthing, with tremendous pomp and parade, the natural and inevitable system of small loans that prevails among small boys'.[86] The boys themselves are fully aware that the school itself is not a haven from the economic world, but 'a limited liability company payin' four per cent',[87] with parents among the shareholders. Thus, while in *The Hill*, education is dissociated from the profit motive with parents paying selflessly to educate their sons (who in turn repay in duty), in *Stalky*, education is a business like any other, where even parents, supposedly the most disinterested people in society, profit. Kipling's boys are aware of the self-interest underlying the provision of education and make their own financial arrangements, pawning, dealing in goods and borrowing, in order to become less dependent on adults. In particular, they buy food, which is insufficiently provided at school due to a drive to maximize profits.[88] In *The Hill* and *Steady and Strong*, however, the boy economy is not only wrong but downright dangerous.

The boys in *Steady and Strong*, unable to act like responsible citizens financially or in any other way, seem to exist outside any kind of social or political context. If they are being trained for leadership in the empire, Freeman does not show how. We are given no clue as to the point of all the physical and moral training and it seems that Freeman expects his readers to take it on trust that Chudleigh's education is meaningful to the wider world. In fact, only a tiny number of writers, focusing

---

83 Ibid., p. 124.
84 Vachell 1928, p. 189.
85 Kipling 1987, p. 105.
86 Ibid., p. 107.
87 Ibid., p. 186.
88 Kipling 1937, p. 23.

on the most elite public schools, actually explain what a National Efficiency-type regime might mean for society. *The Hill: A Romance of Friendship* (1905) by H.A. Vachell (1861–1955) is one work that explores adolescence in the context of imperial politics. Superficially, *The Hill* is about a triangular relationship that develops between three Harrow boys: John Verney, son of a parson and nephew of an explorer, Henry Desmond, the son of an aristocrat and Scaife, son of a *nouveau riche* Liverpool merchant. Verney and Scaife compete throughout the story for the attention of Desmond, seen as an ideal by both of them, Verney admiring his sense of *noblesse oblige* and Scaife coveting his social and political power. The book describes how Scaife tries to tempt Desmond to gamble and visit nefarious places in London and shows Verney fighting to protect his friend's integrity. The events happen during the lead-up to the Boer War and end with Desmond, shaken by his own moral failure at school, joining the war, heading an offensive and dying for his country, while Scaife joins up out of love for Desmond, but survives. Finally, Desmond's father, an MP, takes Verney on as his protégé, and in the sequel, it is heavily implied that Verney marries Desmond's sister.[89]

At face value, Vachell's story seems to be nothing more than the soft face of militarist propaganda – an elaboration of Henry Newbolt's *Vitae Lampada*, where war is a romantic extension of field sport (Desmond charges at the front 'as if he were racing for a goal'[90]). However, under its sentimental façade, *The Hill* is a deeply political book in which the proper civic education of adolescent boys at public school becomes the be-all and end-all for national survival. Vachell's decision to have Henry Desmond die shortly after the 'awful slaughter on Spion Kop'[91] is deeply significant. Spion Kop (January 29, 1900) followed closely after 'Black Week', which saw a series of dismal military failures, at Stormberg (December 10), Magersfontein (December 11) and Colenso (December 15). Black Week marked an all-time low in public confidence in Britain's military capabilities and led to the dismissal of Desmond's General, Redvers Buller, as Commander in Chief of Troops.[92] Desmond dies while fighting at the unsuccessful battle of Vaalkrans (February 5–7), a preparation for attacking the Boer stronghold of Ladysmith (Vachell explains 'It seemed that a certain position had to be taken – a small hill[93]'). Desmond does not survive to see victory at Ladysmith (February 28).

According to Geoffrey Searle, in the public mind Black Week and Spion Kop were the final confirmation of what economists, scientists and military reformers had warned would happen. British industry, they said, was flagging and standards in education were behind those of Britain's competitors, most notably Germany. In consequence, weaponry was out of date, leaders were behind in their understanding

---

89 See Vachell 1911.
90 Vachell 1928, p. 311.
91 Ibid.
92 See Judd 2002, pp. 128–29 and *passim*.
93 Vachell 1928, p. 311.

of modern warfare and soldiers were too unhealthy to fight properly.[94] Vachell, in addition, observes that commanders in the Boer Wars had failed to plan campaigns responsibly ('For the hundredth time in this campaign too few men were detailed for the task'[95]). As Searle explains, these military failures added momentum to the eugenics movement, which had been gathering force since Francis Galton had founded it in the 1880s.[96] Governments responded to the perceived crisis in national health with initiatives such as free school meals and medical examinations at Local Authority schools, which were implemented after the recommendation of the Interdepartmental Committee on Physical Deterioration of 1904.[97] However, while it was easy for the government to tackle eugenic issues among the poor, it was more difficult to tackle 'unfitness' among the upper classes. Public school writers, therefore, seem to have taken the task upon themselves.

Vachell develops the eugenic themes of fitness and inheritance and demonstrates how the public school elite is responsible for maintaining the wellbeing of the nation. He had been at Harrow under Edward Bowen, an intellectual version of Loretto's H.H. Almond, who had promoted organized games.[98] Bowen, master of The Grove house, was a Social Darwinist, but also an anti-militarist and egalitarian who had contributed to Farrar's *Essays on Liberal Education*.[99] When Verney arrives at Harrow in the late 1890s (towards the end of Bowen's career), the school is in poor shape. The house he enters ('The Manor' – formerly the highest-achieving house) is known as 'Dirty Dick's' because the housemaster had once said that 'one bath a week was plenty'.[100] It is 'showing considerable signs of decay', bolstered by the boys' 'Tory' affection for 'Tradition'[101] and on his arrival the *nouveau riche* Scaife makes things worse by introducing excessive drinking and gambling. However, the boys are physically healthy and their parents seem committed to making them as fit as possible. The family of Lord Esme Kinloch has even broken with tradition by sending their son to Harrow rather than Eton, because their doctor says the tough atmosphere at Harrow will strengthen his weak constitution.[102] The problem for Vachell is how best the eugenic fitness of the house might be revived.

In Scaife, Vachell presents a picture of ultimate evolutionary success; that is, if success is measured in material terms. He is the kind of 'Admirable Crichton who appears [at Harrow] now and again in every decade',[103] a superb sportsman

---

94 Searle 2002, pp. 195–96.
95 Vachell 1928, p. 311.
96 Searle 2002, p. 198.
97 Armytage 1965, p. 201.
98 Mangan 1982, p. 28.
99 Ibid., p. 31.
100 Vachell 1928, p. 9.
101 Ibid., p. 47.
102 Ibid., p. 30.
103 Ibid., p. 219.

whose grandfather pulled himself out of poverty using natural quick-wittedness and became a wealthy Liverpool merchant. Scaife is exceptionally vigorous because his father and grandfather had to struggle to survive in their youth. Vachell remarks that

> Scaife [...] tackled problems which many men prefer to leave alone. Here heredity cropped up. Scaife's sire and grandsire were earning their bread before they were sixteen. Of necessity they faced and over-came obstacles which the ordinary Public Schoolboy never meets till he leaves the University.[104]

Scaife is all the more powerful because he is unrestrained by moral scruples: 'Old Adam was strong in him. He liked, craved for, the excitement of breaking the law'.[105] He comments: 'I am a sinner. And my governor is a sinner, a hardened sinner. His father made our pile by what you would call robbery'[106] (Scaife's father has insider-knowledge about the war, which suggests he is an arms dealer). Through Scaife, Vachell shows that Darwinian selection cares little for morality. Although Vachell's own athleticist tutor Bowen, like Spencer and Almond, had insisted that Darwinism would work for the intellectual and spiritual good of the community,[107] Vachell, much more skeptical, suggests that, under unrestrained natural selection, lawlessness thrives.

As the Scaife family rises in success, society's traditional rulers are losing their grip on power. Henry Desmond's father is a Cabinet Minister, which would make him part of Lord Salisbury's Conservative administration of 1895–1902. He subscribes to the One Nation Conservatism that persisted in parts of the Salisbury regime and under Salisbury's successor, Balfour, and which brought about landmark reforms such as the 1902 Education Act.[108] A devotee of Lord Shaftesbury, he believes that 'extreme poverty' can be 'wiped out of England' without disrupting the traditional order (Shaftesbury was 'no leveler, save of foul rookeries').[109] However, the future looks gloomy for the Desmonds. Vachell remarks that Desmond senior is the man who is 'supposed to have the peace of Europe in his keeping'[110] – a bad prospect, considering his government's failures in South Africa. Furthermore, Desmond junior, who is not terribly bright, has no inclination to follow his father into politics. Indeed, it seems as if the Desmond family is heading for intellectual burnout. Their over-expenditure of energy in the political world over many generations has caused a gradual falling-off of wealth

---

104 Ibid., p. 147.
105 Ibid., p. 120.
106 Ibid., pp. 106–7.
107 Mangan 1982, p. 25.
108 Armytage 1965, p. 186.
109 Vachell 1928, p. 166.
110 Ibid., p. 37.

and mental power,[111] something that signals the presence of evolutionary entropy. Other aristocratic families are going the same way. The father of the effeminate Esme Kinloch, although a good and conscientious aristocrat, is 'not clever' like his friends, and 'not even good-looking [...] *undistinguished*, in fine, in everything save rank and wealth'.[112] What Desmond does inherit, however, is a sense of *noblesse oblige* and a desire to care for those who cannot compete in the race for survival. One Sunday evening, walking with Verney, he stops to assist a starving woman and child in the street, despite his friend's self-centered objection that they will be late for chapel.[113] Here, Desmond is displaying virtues which, Vachell implies, could disappear if the present elite die out and others take over.

The answer to Britain's problems lies with Verney, the son of minor gentry. His uncle (and namesake) is an explorer and much-revered old Harrovian – an heroic Carlylean specimen of mental and physical perfection who exerts himself in documenting and enlightening benighted parts of the globe. His nephew imagines him 'scaling heights, cutting a path through impenetrable forests, wading across dismal swamps [...] seeking the hitherto unknowable and irreclaimable, [and] introducing order where chaos reigned supreme'. Verney junior is overjoyed to share his heredity and meditates the fact that he has 'blood of his blood, his, his, his'.[114] Unlike the Desmonds, the Verneys are rising on the evolutionary scale and stand out, along with the Scaifes, as the potential rulers of tomorrow. The battle for Desmond's love fought out between Verney and Scaife is, therefore, a political allegory. Mental entropy has made it necessary for the ruling class to graft itself onto stronger stock and choose suitable heirs to preserve its values. Desmond must choose either Verney or Scaife and forge an alliance. In presenting Scaife as a moral and physical temptation to Desmond and as a love rival to Verney, Vachell shows how seductive new money and Social Darwinist success are to the ruling elite when they are choosing political allies.

In the end, however, it is art not eugenic fitness which confirms Verney's fitness to be the Desmonds's political heir. Echoing Matthew Arnold, Vachell maintains that the qualities that fit a man to rule cannot be acquired merely through rigorous practical and scientific education or physical training. The qualities needed by rulers are mystical, spiritual and indefinable and Desmond and Verney recognize them in each other. When Desmond realizes how much Verney cares for him, they both experience an epiphany: 'For the moment they stood alone, ten thousand leagues from Harrow, alone in those sublimated spaces where soul meets soul unfettered by flesh'.[115] Scaife, who, although himself 'cynic and unclean, recognized God in Henry Desmond', attempts to observe and copy these qualities, but fails because

---

111 Ibid., p. 35.
112 Ibid., p. 99.
113 Ibid., pp. 150–51.
114 Ibid., p. 2.
115 Ibid., p. 94.

he has no 'soul' and can only 'pretend to attain' Desmond's social ideals.[116] Verney demonstrates his moral superiority through his intense emotional reactions to art, literature and music. In a chapter headed 'Revelation', Verney sings a treble solo at a school concert and in doing so both wins the esteem of a renowned Field Marshal and cements his relationship to Desmond, impressing them by his response to the music and his 'clear, sexless notes'.[117] Scaife, on the other hand, is unable to produce an emotional response to either art or nature.

Vachell, therefore, presents yet another view of adolescent education and its role in social evolution. At public school, new blood in the evolutionary battle mixes with those who were dominant in the past and competes for the right to take responsibility for future government. Unlike Freeman, however, Vachell does not believe that evolutionary fitness is achievable for all. The Boer War is not a sign of overall national decay but a sign that it is time for the old elite to hand over power. War wipes the old blood out during late adolescence (presumably before they can breed even more degenerate offspring) and makes room for the new. Natural selection alone cannot be relied on, however, to protect civilized values, because it is an amoral force. Since adolescence is where the coming civic elite is recruited, schools must greet change not with Spencerian science, but with a program of artistic and literary education, because statesmanlike qualities cannot be measured on a purely material scale.

Freeman's idea that Spencerian education was the best way to produce a race of healthy, ideal-standard citizens equipped to survive in the Darwinian world was not, therefore, shared by all. Most 'serious' school storywriters agreed, however, that the *fin de siècle* was, in some way, a turning point in the evolution of the race. Adolescence was supposedly the place where racial changes became most visible and where the individual reached extremes of fitness and degeneration. Freeman and Vachell are optimistic about these changes, but other writers echo F.W. Farrar's concern that 'Nature' has no regard for humility, intellect or aesthetic sensibility. In particular, some are troubled by the implications of the Darwinian outlook for those who fail to conform to standard ideas of masculinity. For example, Howard Sturgis's Eton-based *Tim* (1891) and James Welldon's *Gerald Eversley's Friendship* (1895), both of which I will discuss shortly, explore extremes of male identity. The protagonists of these books are sensitive and intellectual, but also physically inadequate and effeminate. They develop one-sided romantic attachments to popular and athletic, but rather insensitive, boys and ultimately do not achieve the goals that Darwinists associate with success (Tim dies and Gerald Eversley becomes a confirmed bachelor). Both writers use the figure of the effeminate boy to criticize the model of male adolescent citizenship promoted by Social Darwinists and it is on this aspect of these works that I will concentrate for the next part of this chapter.

---

116 Ibid., pp. 33, 75, 95.
117 Ibid., p. 130.

There are a number of theoretical perspectives from which these school 'romances' can be read. Isabel Quigly interprets *Tim*, *Gerald Eversley* and *The Hill* simply as homosexual love stories in which overt sexuality is repressed because of its social unacceptability. Although '*explicit* sexuality [and] the *admission* of sexual feelings [...] is missing', she remarks, 'love is the books' whole reason for existing and provides their plot, action and interest'.[118] This viewpoint is somewhat confirmed by Havelock Ellis's *Sexual Inversion*, which lists *Tim* as a novel that 'deals largely with school-life and boys in order that the emotional and romantic character of the [homosexual] relations described may appear more natural'.[119] Other works beg rather different interpretations. The exploration of male relationships in *The Hill* seems to provide a classic demonstration of the mechanisms queer theorists have identified at work in elite communities of men. Vachell shows clearly how homoerotic bonds facilitate the strengthening of the governing class, and how families exchange women in order to cement their relationships. Vachell celebrates the bonds that underlie political allegiances, and gives an example of one way in which homoerotic feeling can be stimulated in his lavish depiction of the emotional surge that the Field Marshal and Desmond experience while listening to Verney's disembodied singing voice. As might be expected, for Vachell, homoerotic bonds are strictly limited to platonic, upper-class male relationships.

However, relationships that transgress over class boundaries or which tip over from the platonic into the physical are strictly proscribed. Vachell gives few details about the relationship between Desmond and Scaife, but it is clearly felt to be 'inappropriate' – homosexual, as opposed to homoerotic. His failure to explain more specifically how 'appropriate' relationships differ from 'inappropriate' relationships imparts a mystique to male friendship, in which understanding of 'appropriate' conduct is exclusive knowledge possessed only by the initiated upper classes. The Desmond–Verney–Scaife dynamic provides a good example of the way in which, as Kosofsky-Sedgwick puts it,

> the continuum of male homosocial bonds has been brutally structured by a secularized and psychologized homophobia, which has excluded certain shiftingly and more or less arbitrarily defined segments of the continuum from participating [...] in the complex web of male power over the production, reproduction, and exchange of goods, persons, and meanings.[120]

Vachell's implication is that only upper-class men know how to forge close, non-sexual relationships with other men and that the dangers of associating with men who do not intuitively understand the delimitations of male friendship justify the exclusion of the working classes from the prerogatives of citizenship. Adolescence,

---

118 Quigly 1984, p. 9.
119 Ellis 1931, p. 339.
120 Sedgwick 1990, p. 185.

as a period in which sexual preference becomes most strikingly apparent, is a particularly important phase, because a boy's behavior towards other men at this juncture helps to reveal whether his heredity is good or bad. As Richard Dellamora has observed, homophobia may protect gendered privilege, but there is a class dynamic to it that is often ignored by middle-class oriented queer theorists.[121]

The categorization of men according to sexual preference here performs as yet another means of determining whether a man is fit to enjoy the status of full citizenship and has a further impact on the way the male democratic subject is conceived in two crucial ways. It is obvious that in Scaife's case, homosexuality is a sign of something wrong: the lack of an indefinable moral and aesthetic quality needed to enter the ruling classes. But Vachell's definition of homosexuality is so vague that readers must inevitably be left worrying whether they and their friends might, too, be wandering unknowingly into deviance. Vachell aims to make any boy who is not entirely confident in himself somewhat vulnerable to self-doubt, engendering what Sedgwick calls the 'acute *manipulability*, through the fear of one's own "homosexuality," of acculturated men'.[122] Thus Vachell's work performs as a brake on the democratic process by undermining the confidence of all boys, not just overtly homosexual ones, in their own moral ability to participate in national affairs. In his portrayal of Scaife, Vachell grafts the qualities deemed to be innate to the *nouveau riche* onto the figure of the pervert in an attempt to create an aversion to the idea of introducing working-class blood into the political system.

However, there is another, much simpler reason why the experience of same-sex physical desire might be seen to preclude boys from proceeding to full citizenship. In her chapter on Henry James's story 'The Beast in the Jungle', Sedgwick suggests that James's sense of 'homosexual panic' was engendered by 'the male *compulsion to desire* women'.[123] This, she explains, led him to attempt a relationship with Constance Fenimore Woolson; it failed and the ensuing feeling of emptiness led him to create the homosexual protagonist of 'The Beast', a man 'to whom nothing on earth was to have happened'.[124] As I will suggest below, however, the emptiness associated with an inability to desire women is more than just a reaction to the stigmatizing operations of homophobia or 'compulsory heterosexuality'. In the period in question, heterosexuality was considered to be a prerequisite to embarking on fatherhood, and fatherhood, in a eugenic age, lay at the very foundation of the male citizen's identity.[125] In the following sections I

---

121 See Dellamora 1990, pp. 10–12 for a critique of Sedgwick's over-reliance on middle-class oriented literature.
122 Sedgwick 1990, p. 186.
123 Ibid., p. 198.
124 Ibid., p. 201.
125 Of course, the desire for children is hardly unique to heterosexuals. Given James's touching depictions of childhood and seeming affection for children, it would be surprising if the 'nothingness' he supposedly felt at his inability to be heterosexual had nothing to do with being childless. Queer theorists often underestimate the importance, to many people,

will explore issues of fatherhood and citizenship as they pertain to the adolescent development of identity, taking into consideration work by H.O. Sturgis, J.E.C. Welldon and, perhaps surprisingly, Rudyard Kipling.

H.O. Sturgis – an Old Etonian, friend of James, Forster, Wharton and Santayana[126] and author of *Tim* – was proud of his sexuality and famous for deconstructing gender norms. He copied feminine mannerisms and took up embroidery and other ladylike hobbies to show, as F. Kirchhoff puts it, 'that a man could do anything a woman could do, and that, by implication, all gender labeling of behavior was arbitrary'.[127] His school story *Tim*, set some time before the 1890s, describes how an imperialist, chauvinistic society, preoccupied with the Darwinist idea that 'real' men hunt, fight and communicate in monosyllables, fails to accommodate those who cannot fit into normative gender roles. Sturgis undoubtedly celebrates Tim's orientation as making him morally superior to other men and women. However, he also expresses an underlying fear that this orientation is the product of an evolutionary flaw that renders his hero 'useless' to society. Tim's father disappears to India while he is a small child and his mother has absconded in 'disgraceful' circumstances.[128] While in India, the father, a 'tall yellow-faced gentleman, with grizzled hair and whiskers', nurtures a fantasy about the athletic, racially-perfect 'pink-and-white Briton' he thinks is waiting for him at home.[129] Tim, with his poor heredity, is puny and effeminate, but he develops a strong attachment to the local squire's grandson, Carol, older than himself and a model of traditional masculine hardiness. Their relationship begins after Carol accidentally shoots Tim while hunting game. When Tim is eight, his father arrives home unexpectedly on a day when Carol has come to play. Convinced that his son must be the physically superior boy, he embarrasses himself by 'straining [Carol] passionately to his heart'.[130] Carol, disgusted, repulses him and the crestfallen father banishes him from the house. Tim and his father are then forced to coexist in mutual dislike. Carol goes to Eton and Tim later follows and continues his devotion to him there. At the end of the novel, Carol gets engaged and Tim dies. He has never been physically strong and his inability to cope with the mental pressures of the 'real world' kills him.[131]

Tim defies 'masculine' norms. He cannot bear hearing or seeing animals being shot, reads fairy tales instead of factual literature, likes wildflowers, plays house in the woods and is emotionally sensitive to the point of telepathy. Carol is a 'boyish boy', who collects birds' eggs, plays cricket, builds a telegraph system

---

of having children – something that can have a major influence on life choices and ideas of personal fulfilment, regardless of sexual orientation.

126 For the relationship between *Tim* and Sturgis's second novel *All That Was Possible* and Forster's *The Longest Journey* see Thomson 1968.
127 Kirchhoff 1990, p. 427.
128 Sturgis 1891, p. 31.
129 Ibid., pp. 10, 54.
130 Ibid., p. 54.
131 Ibid., p. 244.

and is concerned with the factual, everyday world. For Carol, the most important boyhood rites of passage are getting his first gun and going to Eton.[132] Because he hunts and drinks wine, he sees himself as a 'formed' youth and Tim as a child.[133] In contrast, Tim's sensibility and distaste for struggle mark him out as a non-survivor. As his doctor observes, 'Things will affect him more than other people all his life; what would be nothing to an ordinary person might kill him'.[134] His squeamishness about death and killing resembles the 'morbidity' that Sally Shuttleworth detects in Hardy's Little Father Time, a condition Victorian psychologists identified as an inability to witness the normal workings of nature without suffering acute mental anguish.[135] When Tim follows Carol to Eton he finds that the whole educational system is founded on the idea that boys thrive on struggle. Tim's contemporaries at school spend most of their time doing 'naughty' things, and Tim's father hopes that he will be able to make a bond with him when he runs home for sympathy after getting into scrapes. However, the only 'bad' qualities displayed by Tim at school are 'purely negative, sins of omission, absence of qualities decreed to be necessary to salvation by the *Vehm-gericht* of collective boyhood through many generations'.[136] Because he has no desire to struggle, Tim has no way of forming relationships either as a boy or as a son.

What Sturgis shows, however, is that boys have the potential to be more than a collection of biological drives geared to a Darwinist end and that not all boys operate according to physical drives derived from evolutionary and survival mechanisms. When Carol, looking back on his schooldays, excuses his barbarism by commenting that 'boys *are* brutes', Sturgis remarks bitterly, 'Oh, high new standpoint from which to look back and speak of "boys"!'[137] Tim feels excluded by contemporary narrow definitions of masculinity. When his nurse casually comments that he 'never was much of a boy for his dinner', Tim starts to think 'that he was not "much of a boy" for anything'.[138] Because, as a male, he falls outside the parameters of 'normality', there is no provision for him. He has his own intellectual strengths but, because these qualities are not recognized as part of the adolescent boy's make-up, they are neglected and fester. Sturgis, however, implies that upper-class male culture was not always so geared towards the survival of the fittest. One of the traits Tim admires in Carol before he goes to Eton is his *noblesse oblige*; for example, as a child, he saves money to buy a crutch for a disabled local boy and carries firewood for the neighborhood 'crone'.[139] However, these are the values of Carol's grandfather's generation and Carol abandons them at Eton. Tim,

---

132 Ibid., pp. 17, 54.
133 Ibid., p. 27.
134 Ibid., p. 40.
135 Shuttleworth 2002, p. 135.
136 Sturgis 1891, pp. 140–41.
137 Ibid., p. 181.
138 Ibid., p. 43.
139 Ibid., p. 38.

in contrast, is 'old-fashioned',[140] seemingly of a past age when characters such as Hughes's George Arthur and Hemyng's Purefoy had a niche in school and society. Modern schools, in contrast to those of the past, encourage a crude ethic of self-interest. Thus, when Tim first arrives at Eton and begs Carol to protect him, the older boy, fearing he will lose face, rejects him, declaring that the rule of the school is 'Layssy fair' (a doctrine learned from a master and only half understood by Carol).[141] Nonetheless, Carol learns through watching Tim suffer that, as his fag-master, he owes him protection. Thus, although he is not a proactive character in any meaningful sense, Tim's presence is nonetheless beneficial to his community, because his weakness stimulates the *noblesse oblige* of others and because he demonstrates that men can have relationships based on something other than competition.

Tim is attracted exclusively to males and, in a classic Uranian gesture, reflects that no woman could ever love Carol more than he does.[142] Even if he did not die prematurely, his lack of interest in women might preclude him from fatherhood, which, at this time, plays so large a role in the construction of the ideal citizen. Heterosexuality is at a high premium here and Carol makes an economically and socially advantageous alliance with a girl who promises him heirs, affluence and power. As Chapter 2 remarked, Thomas Hughes's construction of the ideal man as a father (or at least a potential father) before anything else had involved the abjection of boys who preferred same-sex relationships, a process which relied on the idea that their 'deviance' made them socially useless. In a sense, *Tim* can be seen as a re-writing of the *Tom Brown* narrative from the point of view of a George Arthur figure, with the supposition that the Arthur really does have the potential to become a 'Molly'. Unlike Hughes, however, Sturgis stresses the social value of the effeminate. Both Tim and Arthur, as effeminates, function as catalysts in domesticating and civilizing a rumbustious older boy and in this sense they are vital to society. After Arthur has played his role in transforming Tom, Hughes assumes that he would then wish to be transformed himself into a 'boyish' boy. Sturgis objects by depicting what might happen if Arthur could not accomplish this 'boyshness'. Similarly, Hughes takes it for granted that boys are capable of changing the way they express their gender affinities and insists that it is their duty to conform. Sturgis, in contrast, shows that the post-*Tom Brown* educational world, which only admits one way of expressing maleness, provides no legitimate arena in school or in juvenile literature for boys who are innately unsuited to normative expressions of masculinity.

Sturgis rejects the idea that intense physical activity must be central to the schoolboy narrative, but the problem is that there is nothing else for a boy to do at school and no other activities or hobbies through which he might express or develop his own identity. For example, there is no avowedly homoerotic

---

140 Ibid., p. 105.
141 Ibid., p. 92.
142 Ibid., pp. 158–59.

subculture, nobody to introduce Tim to art or literature that expresses the desire he feels and no niche in which he might find a social role. Sturgis was at Eton during the time of the Uranians William Johnson Cory and Oscar Browning in the 1860s and 1870s and Tim receives support from a master who seems to know about his proclivities but who 'was necessarily obliged, for many reasons, to ignore much of what he knew'.[143] Sturgis mentions this fact in a chapter headed with a quotation from Cory's poetical work *Ionica*,[144] making the context obvious to the initiated. However, he remarks that it is unwise to reveal too much about individual masters, because the danger of them being identified and persecuted is too great. Indeed, Sturgis may have felt that things had deteriorated for homosexual boys since his time at school. Certainly, according to Shane Leslie, Edmond Warre, the Head of Eton between 1884 and 1905, was an ardent athleticist who had no time for unathletic boys.[145]

Perhaps Sturgis was hoping that his work would pave the way for 'potentially homosexual' boys to find a creative outlet and maybe it is partly thanks to him that such an outlet was permitted a couple of decades later, in Cyril Connolly's time. During the First World War, when Connolly was at Eton, there was a distinct subculture for those who did not like athleticism. Discussing the teaching of Classics, Connolly explains that

> the potentially homosexual boy was the one who benefited, whose love of beauty was stimulated, whose appreciation was widened, and whose critical powers were developed; the normal boy, free from adolescent fevers, missed both the perils and the prizes; he was apt to find himself left out.[146]

Sturgis was certainly aiming to fulfill a need in attempting to create a space in which non-normative masculinities could be explored. This need was later articulated by Havelock Ellis and J.A. Symonds in *Sexual Inversion*, where they had emphasized the necessity of enabling 'the invert' 'to be healthy, selfrestrained and selfrespecting', rather than trying to 'convert him into the mere feeble simulacrum of a normal man'.[147] They argued for a cultural validation of homosexuality as an end in itself and provided a list of books that describe same-sex relationships, including Sturgis's *Tim*. By creating this reading list, they were affirming the existence of the kind of subculture to which Tim, by virtue of his isolation, has no access. Indeed, the small sub-genre of school stories exploring 'alternative' masculinities and sexualities that appeared in the wake of *Tim* and which included *The Hill*, Welldon's *Gerald Eversley's Friendship*, A.W. Clarke's

---

143 Ibid., p. 116.
144 Ibid., p. 115.
145 Leslie 1922, p. 231. See Chapter 6 below.
146 Connolly 1983, p. 235.
147 Ellis 1931, p. 338.

Jaspar Tristram (1899) and E.F. Benson's *David Blaize* (1916), is evidence of a shared need to develop such a cultural understanding.

In *The History of Sexuality*, Michel Foucault discoursed at length on the nineteenth century's production of 'categories' of sexuality, which functioned as a means by which medico-legal authorities could exercise power over the individual by legislating on the 'normalization or pathologization'[148] of desires, a strategy they inherited from priests. Inquiring into details of individuals' private lives, late-nineteenth-century medical discourse borrowed the confessional strategies of religion, justified by the idea that sexuality was

> a domain susceptible to pathological processes, and hence one calling for therapeutic or normalizing interventions; a field of meanings to decipher; the site of processes concealed by specific mechanisms; a focus of indefinite causal relations: and an obscure speech [...] that had to be ferreted out and listened to.[149]

As I have shown, psychologists and educationalists clearly saw sexual desire as a particularly sensitive point in the adolescent consciousness – both as a kind of portal through which the adolescent might be emotionally manipulated and, through its connection to reproduction and racial hygiene, as something that justified 'experts' interfering in the private lives of adolescents (something I will return to in the next chapter). Foucault catalogues a list of experts in the fields of 'medicine, psychiatry, and pedagogy' such as 'Campe, Salzmann, and especially Kaan, Krafft-Ebing, Tardieu, Molle, and Havelock Ellis', who created 'an indefinite record of [...] people's pleasures' as part of the Victorian scheme to create a comprehensive map of sexuality.[150]

However, it is questionable whether all these efforts were aimed at imposing an external framework of reference onto human subjects (which could be interpreted as potentially oppressive), or whether some researchers were operating with other priorities. Ellis, for example, implemented a seemingly much more liberating scheme of allowing the subjects he interviewed to represent themselves according to the framework of understanding they had built up over the years either alone or as members of groups of like-minded individuals.[151] Krafft-Ebing's mechanical categorization of sexual pathology is very different to Ellis's careful transcription of interviews with homosexual subjects. Ellis specifically resists the classification

---

148 Foucault 1990, p. 105.
149 Ibid., p. 68.
150 Ibid., pp. 63–64.
151 Letting individuals speak for themselves was not unknown among Victorian researchers, sociologists and social reformers. For example, the Commissions on children's employment specifically sought to record children's experiences in their own words. Whether this could be interpreted as a particularly (Lockean, democratic) British way of conducting analytic procedures would be a good subject of study, offering, perhaps, another perspective on Foucauldian analyses of nineteenth-century social structures.

of homosexual subjects into 'categories' after the style of Krafft-Ebing and others and, indeed, concluding that it 'seemed best [...] to attempt no classification at all',[152] leaves them mostly to speak for themselves. Rather than being a part of the potentially repressive cataloguing of desire, therefore, Ellis's work has the potential to encourage self-representation and thus a democratization of gender identity; an idea that seems to be embraced by writers such as Sturgis and, as I will show below, J.E.C. Welldon. Richard Dellamora has remarked (following Foucault) that with 'medicalization [...] homosexuality began to speak in its own behalf, to demand that its legitimacy or "naturality" be acknowledged'.[153] Cold and oppressive medicalization can stimulate in response revelatory acts of self-expression. Thus Sturgis, working practically alongside Ellis, produces not a work of confession but an act of self-exploration and vindication which, rather than seeking to develop rigid and confining categories of identity, breaks categorizations down. Remarking on Sturgis's use of *In Memoriam* as a linguistic marker suggesting homosexual sentiment in *Tim*, Frederick Kirchhoff comments that:

> If Tennyson uses the language of courtship and marriage to characterize his love for Hallam, he does so because the unexpectedness of his figures emphasizes the uniqueness of the relationship. In contrast, Sturgis uses this language to deny the difference between romantic love between men and women and romantic love between schoolboys. The result is a novel at once conventional and, for that reason, disquieting.[154]

Tim, a liminal figure, indeterminate in age, sexuality or gender, destabilizes notions of category and distinction and the conventional premises on which the bourgeois world was understood. Indeed, it is arguably the specific liminality of the adolescent that provides authors with the means of resisting the repressive encroachment of externally socially imposed structures of identity.

Attacking cultural constructions of masculinity, however, did not necessarily bring about positive answers to the question of how society could be persuaded to accept male effeminacy as a valid way of life. Tim is essentially a victim. As Ross Posnock remarks, he presents no viable alternative to bourgeois heterosexuality and he fails to evolve as a character; Sturgis describes him as one of those 'happy people' who 'never grow up but are boys and girls at heart all their lives'.[155] Education is an irrelevance to him, particularly since his intellectual and emotional faculties, as G.H. Thomson remarks, seem to be mature even during childhood.[156] Perhaps Sturgis created such a tragically impotent character because he felt the only way to de-stigmatize homosexuality was by eliciting sympathy, rather as Gaskell and Hardy elicited sympathy for the single mother with the implausibly

---

152 Ellis 1931, p. 89.
153 Dellamora 1990, p. 2.
154 Kirchhoff 1990, p. 428.
155 Posnock 1991, pp. 82–83.
156 Thomson 1968, p. 426.

whiter-than-white characters of Ruth and Tess. Certainly, he left it up to others to develop the theme and to find some way of understanding the role of male–male desire and 'effeminacy' in adolescent society.

'Liminal' adolescent sexuality was perceived by some sociologists, however, as socially useful, providing certain parameters were observed – parameters which somewhat complicate theories about the role of homoerotic desire in holding together bonds of male interest. Sociologists observed that adolescent sexual orientation could be somewhat flexible and some were anxious to harness the potential for romantic relationships between boys in order to teach them how to create the mutually supportive social bonds necessary for adult life. Stanley Hall suggested that same-sex relationships should be institutionalized, arguing that 'attachments for elders or for well-developed specimens of the same sex' encouraged imitation in the younger party and responsibility in the elder.[157] Physical attraction, he explained, inevitably existed between boys, but there should be a moratorium on sexual activity 'til maturity is complete, on into the twenties', when legitimate relationships with the opposite sex could be entered into.[158] What Hall had in mind, presumably, was not, in contemporary jargon, homosexual 'inversion', but the 'artificial homosexuality' that Ellis and Symonds described in *Sexual Inversion* as one of the 'traditions' of the older public schools. This tradition existed, they remarked, because 'school life largely coincides with the period during which the sexual impulse frequently tends to be undifferentiated'.[159] This 'artificial homosexuality' is close to the 'homosociality' that Linda Dowling has described being instituted by Benjamin Jowett in his Oxford tutorials as 'a vehicle for intensifying reciprocal bonds of masculine interest, affection, and obligation'.[160] However, it differed significantly in that commentators reserved this relationship for boys, avoiding the inclusion of masters (whose role was to be married and contributing to the population). In some spheres, therefore, adolescent homoerotic behavior was tolerated as far as it had a Utilitarian purpose in furthering the strength of the race by promoting Platonic masculine bonds. When it frustrated this aim, by resulting in non-reproductive sexual behavior, it became taboo. Boys who persisted in this behaviour and grew into mature 'congenital inverts' were deemed not to play a useful part in the furtherance of the race, even if they felt able to marry, because, as Havelock Ellis remarked, they were deemed to come from 'neurotic and failing stock'.[161]

Whatever sociologists might have thought, there seems to have existed a paranoia about 'inappropriate' sexual conduct that saw the demise in some schools of the kind of male–male relationships hitherto essential to the kind of civic education I described in earlier chapters. Masters at older schools were, perhaps,

---

[157] Hall 1925, vol. II, p. 107.
[158] Ibid., pp. 120–21.
[159] Ellis 1931, p. 192.
[160] Dowling 1994, p. 35.
[161] Ibid., p. 198.

conditioned by their own upbringing in a public-school environment to be tolerant of homoeroticism. The eugenic fear of homosexuality, however, seems to have been a greater cause for concern at newer schools, who tended to see it as a crime against racial hygiene, and they vigorously policed boys' private behaviour in the effort to prevent same-sex relationships. Alec Waugh remarked in 1922 that educators who were concerned about morality and racial health had fostered

> the athletic cult as a preventative, in the belief that the boy who is keen on games will not wish to endanger his health, and that the boy who has played football all the afternoon and has boxed between tea and lock-up will be too tired to embark on any further adventures.[162]

Cyril Connolly (1903–1974), at prep. school just before the First World War, was taught that literature encouraged homosexuality: 'I was warned to be careful, my literary temperament rendering me especially prone to "all that kind of poisonous nonsense"'.[163] Some commentators remarked on the atmosphere of hysteria in schools and blamed it on the lives masters led, remote from 'normal' adult existence. During the First World War at Rossall, S.P.B. Mais was reprimanded for allowing younger and older boys to mix in his rooms, something that was forbidden. Mais saw this interdiction as an over-reaction and remarked that 'There is a good deal of difference between passionate friendship and an act of unnatural intercourse'.[164] Mais said that masters were obsessed with boys' private lives because they were themselves sexually repressed 'and in consequence fostered [immorality] just as a man who walks in daily fear of influenza is always more liable to fall a victim to it than the man who never thinks about it'.[165] The solution, he explained, was to ask masters to marry or leave.

Alec Waugh, himself expelled from Sherborne for alleged indecency, complained in *Public School Life* (1922) that educators were too preoccupied by adolescent sexuality.[166] He remarked that 'although people speak glibly enough of immorality in Public Schools, it is extremely doubtful whether they realize of what exactly that immorality consists'.[167] In 'trying to reduce love to an exact science',[168] commentators had denied the variety of same-sex experiences which

---

162 Waugh 1922, p. 254.
163 Connolly 1983, p. 193.
164 Mais 1937, p. 44.
165 Ibid., p. 57.
166 Waugh's point rings true to the present day; with the present emphasis on psychosexual interpretations of literature and on sexuality in general, it is easy for commentators to neglect other aspects of adolescent life in their debates – for example, issues such as politics, work and play. By concentrating too heavily on sexuality, we fall, in a way, into Stanley Hall's trap and fail to engage with adolescents as emergent citizens in a more rounded sense.
167 Waugh 1922, p. 127.
168 Ibid., p. 133.

existed. Citing Ellis, he argued against the external imposition of sexual identities on boys by educators and experts:

> Havelock Ellis collected at the end of certain volumes of his psychology authenticated histories of men whose development he claimed to be normal, but whose histories were as different from one another as apples are from plums. In the face of such evidence it is dangerous to dogmatize on the gradual discovery of the sexual impulse by public school boys during adolescence.[169]

Again, he suggested that the constant barrage of warnings boys received about homosexuality merely served to encourage them to experiment further. Because boys were constantly warned about 'romantic friendship' in sermons, their curiosity was 'quickened'. If their interest had not been thus aroused, their relationships would have remained nothing more than deep, intense friendships.[170] Waugh added that the all-male environment of school was far from being the 'natural' state of affairs that anthropologists claimed it was, explaining that the lack of contact with girls left boys confused and with no option but to form relationships with each other. Many other authors tried to insist that adolescent sexuality existed mainly in the adult imagination, or that the idea was planted in boys' minds by hysterical or deviant adult men. In *Stalky*, Beetle is 'genuinely bewildered' when Mr Prout gives him a lecture warning him against indulging 'the baser side of youthful imagination'.[171] In *The Hill*, it is the outsider Scaife, influenced by his working-class father and grandfather, who introduces the idea of homosexuality to his upper-class contemporaries. Scaife is also the one who judges other men's relationships in terms of the sexual. Verney's uncle is unmarried and Scaife suggests that this is because he is homosexual, when it is in fact for other reasons. Vachell seems to be arguing that, in a world where male behavior is measured primarily in sexual terms, friendship and 'life-style choices' are often judged by overly narrow criteria. Shortly, I will show how this over-sexualization of adolescence also led to a further lack of confidence in inter-generational male relations.

Another problem with male relationships seems to have been linguistic. In an age obsessed with categorization, there was simply no way to describe subtle differences between relationships. Vachell calls the story of Verney and Desmond's relationship a 'romance of friendship' and a 'romance of the struggle for good and evil',[172] taking refuge in chivalric and allegorical terms. In *Gerald Eversley's Friendship*, discussed below, J.E.C. Welldon even describes love between father and son in terms of romantic love ('Does a lover need to be told in words how he is loved? Nay, love is a fire, it cannot burn and glow unfelt'[173]). Welldon explains that

---

169 Ibid., p. 131.
170 Ibid., p. 249.
171 Kipling 1987, p. 111.
172 Vachell 1928, p. 310.
173 Welldon 1895, p. 208.

it is impossible to describe human relationships accurately, because language does not easily distinguish between the physical and the spiritual: 'it is natural to human language to express the spiritual in terms of the sensuous; are not conception, apprehension, religion itself, terms of the senses?'[174] The absence of subtle enough language may be why many of the boys in later-nineteenth-century books, unlike mid-century boys, avoid discussing friendship altogether. Kipling copes with the language problem in *Stalky & Co.* by comparing the threesome of Stalky, Beetle and M'Turk to a long-established marriage. This move at first sight seems to have been deliberately (and paradoxically) deployed to de-eroticize their relationship. The three live, eat and survive together and address each other in rather Pooterish terms as 'dear' and 'duckie'. When Beetle comes home after disappearing to read alone, Stalky greets him 'like a wife welcoming her spouse from the pot-house' ('Readin' again').[175] They also take gendered roles within the threesome; for example, Beetle is 'the house-keeper'[176] who makes their famous 'brews'. Kipling used the same metaphor in his autobiography, commenting that he and his friends fought among themselves 'regular an' faithful as man an' wife', but presented a united front against the outside world.[177] They even use a music-hall song about baby minding ('Arrah, Patsy, mind the baby') to communicate secretly during their exploits in India.

This was not the only time Kipling touched on the knotty issue of how to discuss male friendship. Claudia Johnson has shown how in Kipling's story 'The Janeites' (1924), a 'club' of soldiers develop a fascination with the works of Jane Austen and the everyday trivialities described therein and how they use references to the works both as an escape from their wartime situation and as a source of secret code.[178] Like Kipling's boys, the soldiers are searching desperately for an emotionally neutral language in which to relate to each other, and Austen seems to offer them a common point of reference that will provide this neutrality and that will, at the same time, serve as a 'restorative to sensitive men', offering them comfort through its emphasis on stability and order. Because they believe Austen's work to be passionless, the men deem it to be a 'safe' mode of communication. However, Johnson argues that the very fact that the men have chosen supposedly 'passionless' works of literature to share suggests that they are afraid of intimate relationships and are trying to avoid contemplating what intimacy might actually mean to them, as individuals or as a group of close comrades. In the atmosphere of homophobic paranoia prevalent in Kipling's day, the Janeites' fear, and Kipling's insinuation, is that they are 'not masculine enough'.[179] In *Stalky* the boys avoid thinking deeply about issues of intimacy by communicating through burlesque.

---

174 Ibid., p. 265.
175 Kipling 1987, p. 226.
176 Ibid., p. 247.
177 Kipling 1937, p. 27.
178 Johnson 2000, p. 33.
179 Ibid., p. 34.

The nursery-tea lifestyle with the overweight Beetle presiding as mother (doubling up as Widow Twankey for their pantomimes) is humorously comfortable, but it also performs as a mask that hides the fact that openly expressed intimacy – not specifically heterosexual or homosexual intimacy, but also parent–child and sibling intimacy – looms as a troubling and confusing monster behind the scenes.

One way some authors dealt with boys' relationships seems to have been to transpose a stereotyped model of male–female relationships onto male–male relationships. They often divide boys as though they belong to two 'genders', an idea acquired, perhaps, from commentators such as Slaughter, who argued that in tribal societies adolescent boys endured rigorous ordeals to decide who assumed 'men's' roles in society and who were sidelined with the women, or from the concept of sexual 'inversion', the understanding of homosexuality as a misalignment of sexual identification. The heroes of Sturgis, Welldon and Vachell are sensitive to aesthetics, have strong verbal abilities, communicate well with adults and are 'monogamous' in terms of friendship, retaining intense affection for one other boy throughout their schooldays. The objects of their affection are less academic, athletic, sometimes prone to trouble and have a promiscuous tendency to abandon close friendships once somebody more physically fit and attractive arrives. Adolescence is the place where boys discover on which side of this binary divide they belong.

J.E.C. Welldon's story *Gerald Eversley's Friendship* (1895) is another work that attempts to understand male identity by dividing boys on a binary paradigm. Welldon (1854–1937), Headmaster of Harrow from 1881 to 1895, was a former Etonian, a Classicist who nevertheless campaigned against compulsory Classics, and eventually became Bishop of Calcutta.[180] J.A. Mangan devotes several pages to Welldon, whom he describes as 'the public school headmasters' most eloquent, persistent and opinionated spokesman on the schools and imperialism'.[181] Mangan represents Welldon as a racial supremacist and an anti-intellectual who promoted games at the expense of all else in the interests of maintaining British imperial dominance. Perhaps this is overly harsh, since Welldon did take the trouble to point out that although the conformist, athletics-oriented curriculum was well suited to the 'majority of boys', 'many boys of highest temper and keenest feeling have derived not benefit but injury from their school'.[182] *Gerald Eversley* shows a rather reflective side to Welldon, albeit with a heavily patrician outlook. The narrative has all the components of traditional school stories: a false accusation, a serious illness and an epic football match, but it is a plea for greater tolerance of different kinds of masculine temperament in school.

Gerald Eversley (echoing Sturgis's Ebbersley) is the son of an emotionally inadequate, old-fashioned vicar. When he goes to school, sometime in the mid-1860s,[183] he becomes deeply attached to Harry Venniker, son of an athletic,

---

180 See *Dictionary of National Biography*, Mangan, *Imperialism*, p. 112.
181 Mangan 1986, p. 33.
182 Welldon 1895, p. 77.
183 Ibid., p. 75.

paternalistic aristocrat. Eversley's regard for Venniker amounts to 'hero worship', a devotion that does not exceed women's love but strives towards it – 'a sentiment of which he could give, or did give, no account to himself'.[184] Gerald, like Tim, shuns violence, finding the sight of shot birds 'sicken[ing]' and lacking the desire to 'wag[e] war against the masters', something that astonishes Venniker.[185] He also cries openly and avoids the misogyny endemic among his contemporaries.[186] Gerald's housemaster Brandison, a 'Radical',[187] practices social engineering by placing the athlete and the intellectual together. Welldon explains that 'boys of widely different characters and antecedents, by being placed together, did each other good, [...] the shy scholar becoming more a man of the world, and the athletic aristocrat imbibing a qualified love of learning'.[188] While Freeman was suggesting that conformity to a eugenic norm would protect racial health, Welldon makes his own Darwinist point, insisting that diversity, as much as fitness, is essential to racial success. Indeed, to Welldon, the suppression of 'eccentricity or individualism' in school is an evolutionary sin. Welldon echoes Henry Maudsley's claim that the 'tincture of originality' is the root of progress when he remarks that 'science teaches that the progress of the species depends upon the preservation and improvement of varieties'.[189] He suggests that schools have failed to contribute significantly to social progress because they have suppressed variation. Welldon's effeminate boy, who nonetheless carries strong social convictions, contrasts both with the athleticist, who has 'no special sense of a vocation or mission in life', and with his conservative father, who cannot tolerate political, economic or religious 'ideas'.[190] Welldon demonstrates that conventional masculine values, bred into the ruling elite through a rough-and-tumble education, are not the only values that contribute meaningfully to human evolution. The public school system, 'The modern bed of Procrustes',[191] must learn to accommodate difference for the sake of the race. Welldon underlines this idea by making the Venniker family one of poor health. Despite his athleticism, Harry becomes ill (ironically, after a triumphant football match) and his sister and mother are sickly. No matter what scheme of physical training is undertaken, heredity and chance mean that the athletic body is not always reliable and it seems foolish that schools concentrate all their energy on producing healthy bodies rather than a range of different abilities.

Welldon also demonstrates how a too-radical belief in Darwinist principles can be destructive to the mental stability of the individual. When Gerald leaves school, he has a breakdown, prompted by a Tennysonian discovery of Darwinism

---

184 Ibid., p. 114.
185 Ibid., p. 14.
186 Ibid., p. 12.
187 Ibid., p. 80.
188 Ibid., p. 84.
189 Shuttleworth 2002, pp. 144, 76.
190 Welldon 1895, pp. 33, 29–30.
191 Ibid., p. 73.

for which neither his public school education nor his Evangelical upbringing has prepared him. He loses his religious faith, shocked at the realization that Nature is 'a wild battling of forces, ruthless, inexplicable, working out good – such good as exists – by agonies of evil',[192] a worldview inevitably reinforced by the 'savage' school environment. He then becomes alienated from his Evangelical father, a believer in Providence and predestination, and rejects the logical inconsistencies of his father's beliefs. For example, Gerald issues a Malthusian condemnation of his father's carelessness in producing more children than he can adequately care for:

> Mr Eversley held that children were 'an heritage and gift that cometh of the Lord;' he had been known to say that, where God sent the mouths, He would send the bread to feed them. The theory can hardly be said to be justified by experience. Gerald resented and condemned it. He argued that the parent was responsible for his children's welfare here and hereafter [...] his father ceased to be any more his friend, and became to him as a stranger.[193]

When Gerald discovers that his father is not perfect, he feels suicidal and, like Jude Fawley (who appeared the same year), echoes Job's lament, 'let the day perish wherein I was born'.[194] Indeed, Welldon's despair is very much a mirror of Hardy's, since both are concerned that, in a Darwinian scheme, sensitive and creative individuals tend to die off, while the less sensitive survive. A lack of confidence in God's authority here goes hand-in-hand with a lack of confidence in fathers and with the whole system of bringing up boys. There is no institutional structure, educational or otherwise, in which men might help each other to face these issues, especially when schools are dominated by typical sporting men such as Venniker and his father, who are incapable of holding a conversation on emotional or intellectual matters.

A fracture in the relationship between father and son is, as I have shown, a commonplace aspect of school literature. However, now Darwinism exerts a further pressure on this relationship, it is even harder for the son to find security in other male relationships. Spiritual relief is provided for Gerald by Venneker's charitable mother, who teaches that 'There is no mistake in religion so great as that of being too logical'.[195] Welldon adds that 'Logical contradictions are an absurdity in human things; in divine things they are sometimes the only possible expressions of truth'.[196] The interesting point here lies not in Welldon's somewhat bemusing theology but in his view of the role of gender in education. Individuals who are not public school educated, such as Venniker's mother, and who do not see the world through the framework either of traditional classical logic or of

---

192 Ibid., p. 255.
193 Ibid., p. 260.
194 Ibid., p. 274.
195 Ibid., p. 257.
196 Ibid., p. 258.

scientific positivism, offer answers to some problems where public school men have none. Like Hemyng, Welldon is one of the few boys' authors to go against anthropological orthodoxy and suggest that women have a role in educating males. Venniker's mother and sister Ethel share Gerald's dislike of hunting and his interest in social charity. Their home has been 'divided by Nature into two sections as well as into two sexes'.[197] Gerald finds his mental equal in Ethel who, 'whether by native generosity of character or [...] by inheritance of thought and principle from her mother', is able 'to enter into some degree of sympathy with some of his views which would be treated as heretical in the majority of country houses'.[198]

Gerald regains his faith when he falls in love with Ethel, who dies before the pair can marry. Quigly interprets this scenario as a deflection of homosexual impulses; Gerald's love for Venniker is projected, for prudery's sake, onto his sister, whose death conveniently gets the homosexual Gerald out of marriage. However, the situation is more complex. Gerald identifies with Ethel, Venniker's mother and the female sphere, and the novel seeks to assert the value of that sphere by presenting women as acceptable intellectual partners for men. Welldon is not involved in a process of creating a male homosocial hegemony that keeps women out; he is attempting to escape the overly unilateral way in which boys are educated. He also argues that National Efficiency needs to embrace people with a variety of different identity standpoints in order to maximize its success and shows that biological parenthood is not the only way of serving the race. When Ethel dies, Gerald, after almost attempting suicide, instead decides to immerse himself in 'civic beneficence and charity', benefiting mankind in other ways than by raising a family of his own and emulating his favorite teacher, Mr Selby, who, it is implied, did something similar.[199] A childless man may attain the full citizenship, he implies, by finding substitute children, in the form of students or objects of charity.

One of the biggest problems for the concept of education for elite male citizenship posed by these works is that fathers can, seemingly, do nothing right, no matter how many children they produce or how sporting, aristocratic, or intellectual they are. Indeed, it seems that even while Social Darwinists were putting a heavy stress on parenthood as the supreme goal of the citizen, the role of the father was less secure than ever.[200] Spacks suggests that late nineteenth-century adults had their confidence in their social and economic strength sapped 'by the overpowering presence of mass media and massive corporations', which left them

---

197 Ibid., p. 277.
198 Ibid., p. 280.
199 Ibid., pp. 353, 118–19.
200 The large output of the leading turn-of-the-century eugenicist Caleb Williams Saleeby is a good example of how pressure was placed on young people and couples to ensure their families were evolutionarily 'fit'. Saleeby's *Parenthood and Race Culture: An Outline of Eugenics* (London: 1909) condemned the complacency of those who took parenthood as it came, and who failed to apply proper eugenic principles to family life.

feeling less equipped to manage 'the pressure of business and professional life'.[201] Middle-class jobs, increasingly concentrated in companies or large bureaucratic systems rather than in smaller businesses, limited the overall importance of the individual worker. Fathers continued to lose authority and respect.

Insecurities felt by non-public school fathers who were educating their sons at public school were particularly keen. Eby comments on how the *nouveaux riches* anxiously pushed their children to achieve sporting honors at school as 'certificates of membership into the English elite caste [...]',[202] to achieve a social status that fathers could not bestow. Upper-class fathers were also in trouble, attacked by C.B. Andrews and his ilk for being more interested in traditional Classical education than in training their children scientifically.[203] Lower-class fathers, he informed them, were less complacent and their sons, with the benefit of a modern education, would soon be challenging the hegemony of the rich:

> The poor man wishes his son to obtain a better training than himself [...] and to be a better man than his father. He therefore seeks for the latest and most useful education system that he can find. The rich man, perfectly satisfied with his education, desires his son to receive an education exactly similar.[204]

Stanley Hall said that an adolescent's highest aim should be to make himself worthy of his father.[205] However, in a rapidly evolving society where each generation is supposed to improve on the achievements of the last, a father's own backwardness and failure to maintain proper eugenic hygiene may endanger his son. Hall remarked that: 'we suffer for the sins of our forebears or mid-parents back to Adam, or the amphioxus or even amoeba'.[206] This science was supported by thinkers such as Francis Galton, Henry Maudsley and Constantine Hering who, as Sally Shuttleworth observes, believed that 'Though individuals die their offspring carry on the memory of all the impressions their ancestors acquired or received'.[207] Thus we hear, for example, that Tim's father is an orphan unaccustomed to parental love, and that the burden of heredity from grandparents and parents cumulates in Tim, who cannot be a parent at all. Shuttleworth comments that, during the late-Victorian period, heredity was commonplace in 'discussions of the ailments of modern life [...] in periodicals, newspapers and books'.[208] The discourse of heredity was disturbing because it challenged the very nature of individual identity

---

201 Spacks 1981, pp. 81–82.
202 Eby 1987, p. 118.
203 Andrews 1912, p. 5.
204 Ibid., p. 18.
205 Hall 1925, vol. I, p. 521.
206 Ibid., vol. II, p. 309.
207 *Natural Causes and Supernatural Seemings* (1886), quoted in Shuttleworth 2002, p. 137.
208 Ibid., p. 137.

and the ideas of self-determination which Victorian liberals cherished so much. It also changed ideas of adolescent development. Tom Brown gradually distanced himself from his father during adolescence and went off to create his own identity and role in society. Tim's parents, in contrast, weigh down his chances of asserting individual initiative. Education is powerless to remedy his predicament.

Indeed, it seems that there was a distinct problem in finding suitable individuals to bring up the next generation of citizens. If the father was in trouble, the schoolmaster, *in loco parentis*, was in even greater trouble, partly because of the growing atmosphere of homophobic panic. Some 'serious' school stories throw suspicion on adult men who have too much interest in boys. Turn-of-the-century works rarely feature characters such as Thomas Arnold or Farrar's Mr Percival, who had a disinterested (perhaps 'motherly') involvement in education. Perhaps this arose because gender roles were becoming less flexible. S.P.B. Mais complained that suspicions of abuse ran so rife at Rossall that teachers were allowed to spend no more than ten minutes alone with a boy.[209] Again, there seems to have been no way of conceiving of male relationships in any way other than as either competitive or exploitative. After the First World War some writers saw the wholesale slaughter on the battlefield as the logical result of an unhealthy idealization of the boy. In Ernest Raymond's *Tell England* (1922), adults at a pre-war school, both male and female, stand by the cricket pitch voyeuristically watching 'the flannelled figures of the players, with their wide little chests, neat waists, and round hips, [which] promised fine things for the manhood of England ten years on'.[210] One member of staff remarks to a colleague, 'don't you think this generation of boys is the most shapely lot England has turned out?'[211] The boys are viewed as though they are animals at an auction. The adults justify their attitude by arguing that the country's wellbeing lies in the boys' physical fitness. When the hero, Rupert Ray, goes to war, a recruiting officer tells him that the nation's wealth is its youth: 'She's solvent with you, and bankrupt without you'.[212] In Raymond's interpretation, the adolescent boy is a commodity bred not to fulfill his own private goals, but to be of use to others. This commodification and objectification is an abuse of adult power.

In a culture where women had begun to find a voice and to fight against objectification, the boy, unable to answer on his own terms, seems to have become a new object of fantasy for grown men. Indeed, in their supposed mysteriousness, boys were often compared to women. S.P.B. Mais remarked that: 'Boys are as queer as women, but not so unaccountable' and Kipling has Stalky describe himself as a '*femme incomprise*' – a 'misunderstood woman'.[213] Martha Vicinus has even suggested that in the *fin de siècle*, the adolescent boy became a kind of *femme fatale* figure. Culturally, the adolescent was an 'indeterminate character' onto whom

---
209 Mais 1937, p. 44.
210 Raymond 1926, p. 50.
211 Ibid., p. 51.
212 Ibid., p. 167.
213 Mais 1937, p. 41, Kipling 1987, p. 295.

adults could project a variety of 'desires and emotional needs'.[214] Vicinus identifies two 'types' of adolescent *femme fatale*: the 'fragile, ethereal' figure (resembling Tim) and a figure similar to Kipling's Stalky – an 'arrogant untamed rule-breaker [...] other-worldly [...] knowing more than the man' but 'more innocent than he first appeared'.[215] Boys were an ideal 'other'; different from the self, but familiar, since every man had once been one. For those who felt too daunted by the demands of citizenship and mature family life, the fantasy of remaining an adolescent, or remaining among adolescents, seems to have been particularly appealing, a fantasy that Rudyard Kipling explored the full in *Stalky & Co.*

It is a paradox that Kipling, who was capable of contributing to an authoritarian piece of 'National Efficiency' propaganda such as Meath's *Essays in Duty and Discipline*, should have explored so persuasively in *Stalky & Co.* (1899) the capacity of adolescents to reject 'adult' values. Indeed, Kipling, more than any other author discussed here, sees adolescence almost as an end in itself. *Stalky* is the ultimate fantasy of boyhood biting back against adult abuse, a declaration of the power of adolescence to save the Empire from the kind of predatory, exploitative, bourgeois adult values. Published sporadically in magazines,[216] *Stalky* comprises a series of semi-autobiographical short stories describing life at the United Services College, a private school for prospective soldiers. Each story presents the Stalky group (Lionel Corkran, a.k.a. Stalky, the future soldier-hero, the literary Beetle, based on Kipling himself and the Ruskinian M'Turk, heir to an Irish estate), with a 'problem'. Most show the boys disciplining adults or teaching them some kind of a lesson by using lateral thinking and diplomatic skills. The boys' power within their community derives from their ability to upset traditional conceptual frameworks.

In Chapter 1, Lionel Corkran acquires the name 'Stalky', a word applied, we are told, to anybody who is deft and cunning and who uses counter-intuitive logic. In this chapter, local farmhands catch some College boys tormenting cows and lock them in a barn while Stalky & Co. watch from a distance. Stalky descends in the manner least expected, frees the boys from *inside* the barn, contrives to ingratiate himself with the farmhands and ends up getting a cream tea from the farmer's wife. Stalky here operates behind the scenes – a *deus ex machina*, omnipresent and unseen. He not only provides a 'miraculous' answer to the problem, but diplomatically resolves the conflict situation (making peace between the school and the farmer). His is an upside-down approach; he does the opposite to what is expected. In doing so, he reverses relationships based on power and strength,

---

214 Vicinus 1994, 91.
215 Ibid., 93.
216 The Stalky Stories appeared in *Cosmopolis*, *McClure's*, *The Windsor*, *Nash's*, *Pall Mall*, *Metropolitan*, *The Strand* and *The London* magazines, plus *Hearst's International*, between 1897 and 1929. The first book, containing all but four chapters ('Stalky' (1898), 'Regulus' (1917), 'The United Idolaters' (1924), 'The Propagation of Knowledge' (1926), and 'The Satisfaction of a Gentleman' (1929)) was published in 1899. See Quigly's textual notes to Kipling 1987, pp. xxvix–xxx.

challenging the assumptions about relationships between adolescents and adults. The boys turn their apparent weakness and vulnerability to their advantage in their battle against a society run for the convenience of adult men. For example, when they climb into Farmer Toowey's barn, they exploit their small physique ('It was in no sense a lawful path, but twelve inches square is all that any boy needs'[217]). Smallness here becomes a way of defeating superior size and strength and an overturning of Darwinian assumptions. If the phrase 'survival of the fittest' traditionally conjures up the idea of the largest, most brutal male in the group wielding domain over others, Kipling provides an alternative; minimal size, lateral thinking and diplomatic skill – surprisingly old-fashioned, Tom Brownian (maybe even feminine) qualities, successfully undermining the status quo.

Stalky & Co. also capitalize on their uncertain, liminal social position. In 'In Ambush', a local landowner, Colonel Dabney, accuses them of trespassing, a situation dealt with by M'Turk. M'Turk is heir to an Irish estate, although Stalky has beaten his accent out of him. Both as an Irishman and as a schoolboy, M'Turk occupies a vulnerable position, open to racial harassment, denied his national identity and deprived of the 'viceroy' status he enjoys at home.[218] In dealing with Dabney, however, M'Turk uses his repressed dialect to create a sense of fellow feeling and equality ('It was the landed man speaking to his equal – deep calling to deep – and the old gentleman acknowledged the cry'[219]). He then demonstrates a good grasp of legal ideas by citing trespass law.[220] After M'Turk has impressed Dabney by his mature landowner's rhetoric, the boys take advantage of their youth, befriending Dabney's lodgekeeper and his wife, who spoils them like children ('little dears'[221]), giving them cream teas and a stuffed badger. As adolescents with the reasoning powers of adults but the bodies of children (the opposite combination to that which Arnold feared) they can capitalize on both assets.

Through *Stalky*, Kipling questions the aims of education, debating how adolescence relates to adulthood and the needs of race and Empire. Stalky & Co. view male adulthood and adult roles with suspicion. Adults are the 'hard and unsympathetic peasantry', hypocritical school governors and teachers, *Eric*-fixated maiden aunts and the odd bumbling, incompetent politician or retired army officer, all of whom the boys lampoon. They see biological parenthood, especially in teachers, as repulsive. Beetle comments: 'I've met chaps in the holidays who've got married House-masters. It's perfectly awful! They have babies and teething and measles and all that sort of thing right bung *in* the school'.[222] The only parent mentioned is Stalky's father ('the guv'nor'), an anti-aesthete with some connection to India, who never appears, but gives Stalky a 'long Indian

---

217 Ibid., p. 17.
218 Ibid., p. 35.
219 Ibid.
220 Ibid., p. 32.
221 Ibid., p. 43.
222 Ibid., p. 120.

cheroot' during the holidays, which makes the boys sick.[223] The one adult the boys look up to is 'the Prooshian Bates', the Headmaster, 'father-confessor and agent-general' to all past pupils, 'a most delightful and comprehending uncle'.[224] Bates displays an extraordinary capacity for self-sacrifice when he sucks fluid from the lungs of a boy with diphtheria,[225] displaying healing qualities that contrast with the nausea-inducing behavior of Stalky's father. Bates has a lot in common with other unmarried uncle-figures in juvenile fiction (for example the Indian Uncle in E. Nesbit's *The Treasure Seekers* or Arthur Ransome's Captain Flint), who have no wife or children and are free from adult economic responsibilities. He is similar to what U.C. Knoepflmacher describes as the 'hybrid figure' common in Victorian (and later) children's fiction, the adult who can behave or think like a juvenile and who mediates between the adult and juvenile worlds.[226] He understands the mores of both the adult and juvenile worlds and helps the young to deal with adults without betraying other young people. According to Knoepflmacher, some authors saw themselves as hybrid figures, 'mediating' between the generations.[227] Kipling, appearing in *Stalky* as the adolescent Beetle, clearly shares this mediating role. This role is nurtured by Bates, himself modeled on Kipling's real-life headmaster Cormell Price, who was connected to the Arts and Crafts movement and encouraged Kipling's writing.[228] Bates undermines the imperialist authoritarianism supported by the USC by tacitly allowing the boys to defy members of staff who are keen to promote conformity and school patriotism. He also conspires with the boys to dupe and manipulate the ex-military school governors, who uphold the values of keeping up appearances, 'expediency' and 'fear of consequences'.[229]

Bates also seems very much like Kidd's figure of the 'boy worker', the expert in 'boyology' who 'increasingly comes to supplant the father as the figure of authority and expertise' in educationalist projects to study the boy and in youth-work activities such as Scouting.[230] Kidd suggests that the boy worker came to the fore because the pressures of family life in industrialized cultures had caused a sense of Oedipal crisis between boys and fathers.[231] But, from a eugenic standpoint, there is a huge problem with Bates as a 'boy worker' and that is that, as a role-model, he fails to present the image of mature manhood held by Hall and others to be desirable; that of the fertile father. He remains a child in many ways, as do Stalky & Co. Putting him up as a role model represents a departure from the ideas of adolescent development Kipling had promoted in his other much more

---

223 Ibid., pp. 228, 182.
224 Ibid., pp. 188, 190, 253.
225 Ibid., p. 192.
226 Knoepflmacher 1983, p. 501.
227 Ibid., p. 498.
228 Moss 1982, p. 7.
229 Kipling 1987, p. 258.
230 Kidd 2004, p. 14.
231 Ibid., p. 15.

influential book on growing up. Claudia Nelson has written about how Kipling's earlier *Jungle Book* stories 'end with a tale to which sexuality is central', with Mowgli realizing he must relinquish his 'sterile and childish' bachelor life with the animals and obey nature's command that all must grow up and reproduce.[232] *Stalky* is much more resistant to the reproductive calls of nature and Kipling seems to have begun to question the Darwinian imperative, possibly finding a crisis in his own sense of fatherhood following the stress of his daughter's death; indeed, Kipling's fatherhood is completely absent in the semi-autobiographical *Stalky* narrative. At the end of this chapter, I will suggest more reasons why Kipling rejects adult prerogatives in favor of keeping his boys single and childless well into manhood.

There is a deep gulf in *Stalky* between the education Bates gives and the 'official' imperialist education advocated by the governors and masters. The masters try to instill a sense of common identity and group loyalty in a way typical of the 'newer' public schools described in Chapter 4. Stalky's house-master, Prout, does this in a relatively simple way, constantly referring to the 'honor' of the house and punishing Stalky & Co. for not playing properly.[233] The boys' main adversary, King (a former student of Jowett's at Balliol[234]), is more skilled at manipulating popular feeling in order to inculcate conformity and obedience. In 'An Unsavory Interlude', King goads his house members to brand Stalky's house as unclean.[235] The aim is to provoke inter-house conflict, impelling the prefects in Stalky's house to insist on more solidarity and forcing Stalky's group to abandon their individualistic stance against games and other conformist activities. King's house, buoyed up by a sense of commonality based on hatred of an opposing house, willingly play along, while the 'democracy' of Prout's House convene to decry the dishonor. Prefects visit Stalky & Co. to demand solidarity, but get a Rabelaisian comeback ('Stalky puffed out his cheeks and squinted down his nose in the style of Panurge, and all he said was, "Oh, you abject burblers"').[236] Stalky's intriguing use of the world 'abject' implies that he understands the psychological processes by which an individual or a group can be coerced when it refuses to conform to normative standards of behavior. Instead of being intimidated, the boys hide a dead cat under the eaves of King's dormitory, where it decomposes and reeks. The 'stink' and contamination is now no longer imaginary or rhetorical but literal. The boys transfer the school's feeling of communal revulsion back onto King and hound him with references to plague and leprosy.[237] They have learned how to resist the psychological mechanisms that socialize the young into accepting the status quo.

---

232 Nelson 1989, pp. 544–45.
233 Kipling 1987, p. 73.
234 Ibid., p. 237.
235 Ibid., p. 74.
236 Ibid., p. 76.
237 Ibid., p. 87.

Indeed, Kipling questions the value of education and socialization *per se*. Herbert Spencer had insisted that the first aim of education was to teach the young to survive. Kipling's adolescents do not need adults to survive. They are already adept at surviving in the outside world, to the extent of hunting and foraging for food. Even in matters of morality, as the Chaplain comments, 'Boys educate each other [...] more than we can or would dare'.[238] Although the masters consider the boys to be fundamentally anarchists,[239] what they actually lack is not an understanding of morals but an acceptance of arbitrarily determined social convention. They ignore their snobbish housemaster when he forbids them to mix with social 'inferiors' ('farmers and potwallopers'[240]) and refuse to accept that there are different rules for adults and juveniles. They are overjoyed when Prout is accused of trespassing when, thinking they are out of bounds, he pursues them over Colonel Dabney's land, causing Dabney to quote Juvenal's phrase '*Quis custodiet ipsos custodes*'.[241]

Stalky and his companions do not need a moral education – they are already scrupulously moral. They do not steal (although they 'borrow'), or swear, or get drunk, or have physical relationships, and they evolve a scheme of sharing money and property (referred to as 'communism') which avoids any one of them ever falling into debt and ensures all three have equal access to material goods. They are also exquisitely sensitive to vulgarity, and are offended by the rhetoric of a jingoistic visiting MP because 'the reserve of a boy is tenfold deeper than the reserve of a maid' and the MP had 'profaned the most secret places of their souls with outcries and gesticulations'.[242] While writers such as Hall insisted that boys had an imperfectly formed sense of morality akin to that of the 'savage', moreover, Kipling suggests that the morality of both boys and colonized peoples is superior to white adult morality. Radha Achar observes that in Kipling's imperialist worldview, colonized peoples exhibited a 'childhood innocence serving as a prototype of primitive communism'. Such social values contrasted with the ethics of white, masculine adulthood, which 'sanctif[ied] in the name of such values as competition, achievement, control and productivity – new forms of institutionalized violence'.[243] Kipling favors characters such as the anti-materialist Lama in *Kim* (1901), who is 'uneducated but wise, superstitious but spiritual, womanly but pacific'.[244] Morally, boys seem to need moral education from adults as little as the East Asians in 'The Buddha at Kamakura' need it from imperialists. This display of cultural relativism is an unexpected stance, to say the least, from a supporter of the National Efficiency movement.

---

238 Ibid., p. 138.
239 Ibid, pp. 113–14.
240 Ibid., p. 25.
241 Ibid., p. 45.
242 Ibid., p. 218.
243 Achar 1987, p. 47.
244 Ibid., p. 52.

Kipling has attracted criticism as an exponent of imperialism and, since an imperial agenda lay behind the National Efficiency project, it is worth making a short comment about the role of imperialism in school stories here. Very few of the 'higher brow' school stories give the Empire any more than a cursory mention, *Stalky* being the most notable exception. Even in *Stalky*, explicit demonstrations of imperialist proselytizing, such as the speech made by the 'Jelly-bellied Flag-flapper',[245] are considered to be in poor taste. Occasionally, boys from colonized groups appear in lower-brow books, such as the identical twin Indian boys, 'Curry' and 'Chutney' in C.J. Mansford's *Bully, Fag and Hero* (1897), who practice Voodoo and guerrilla warfare.[246] Like many Irish characters, for example Kipling's M'Turk, they are celebrated for their 'pluck', and their subversiveness serves to keep the establishment on its toes. C.D. Johnstone's biographical account of Eton from the 1870s mentions an Irish boy who was not 'of bad disposition', but who was flogged more than anyone else because of his 'island blood', warm temper and contempt for punishment and written work,[247] a theme that had also been present in Fitzgerald's *Schooldays at Saxonhurst* and which various authors revived from time to time in fiction.

Most surprising, perhaps, though, is that as deeply committed an imperialist as James Welldon did not make more of the Empire in his work. One explanation for this may lie in the analogy that describes public school as a 'miniature world', and the boy as a 'savage'. Schoolboy savagery was an idea central to recapitulation theory, which, as Kenneth Kidd has shown, played a prominent role in constructing ideas of 'boyhood' in the late nineteenth and early twentieth century. This 'biopolitical narrative of general ontogenetic-phylogenetic correspondence'[248] was a theory promoted as a biological 'fact' and therefore as incontrovertible proof of the specific gendered attributes of young males, unassailable by feminists, effete males or any other body who chose to challenge prescribed norms. Kipling had his own role to play in this movement, having popularized the idea of the 'feral' boy brought up by animals rather than parents in *The Jungle Book*, creating a mythology that was drawn upon in the Boy Scout movement and in other all-male, back-to-nature style schemes of inducting boys into male citizenship.[249] The Scouts, created by a public school man worried about the development of non-public school boys, were in many ways another kind of ersatz public school and a way in which a public-school oriented experience of growing up was constructed as the norm for male development. Being a public schoolboy and being a savage were natural, instinctive states for boys and it logically followed that this instinctive understanding would extend to an understanding of real-life colonial 'savages', whose nature was similarly determined by the inevitable workings of biology and

---

245 Kipling 1987, p. 220.
246 Mansford 1897, p. 42.
247 Johnstone 1870, p. 87.
248 Kidd 2004, p. 16.
249 Ibid., pp. 7–8, 87.

evolution. Thus Stalky & Co. demonstrate an instinctive ability to manage and communicate with servants, the Devonshire 'peasantry' and others who might be identified as being at a lower stage of development to mature, upper-class males.

If schoolboys (particularly younger ones) were developmentally equivalent to 'savages', who express 'the germ of morals [rather] than morality itself',[250] and the public school the environment in which 'savage' behaviour was most in evidence, it follows that an education in such an institution automatically familiarizes its inmates an understanding of the colonial subjects they were destined to govern. Each school has an 'internal geography', which attributes varying degrees of racial difference to specific bodies of boys. Thus, for example, the fags in George Melly's school are described as existing at 'the outposts of civilisation'. They were 'barbarians' who made 'fiery sorties' into the realms of older (presumably, more civilized boys) 'after the manner of gallant Turks at Silistria'.[251] Melly creates a microcosmic empire where 'inter-racial' tensions exist between different stages of the adolescent evolutionary process from 'savage' to civilization. H.C. Adams's *Schoolboy Honour* also associates adolescence with racial evolution. To new boys, 'Mumbo Jumbo is scarcely a more awful personage in the eyes of the negroes of Africa, or the overseer in those of their brethren in South Carolina, than the head boys of a public school to the raw youngsters recently arrived there'.[252] The comparison of boy to the 'savage' in most of these scenarios is usually flattering to neither. Kipling transforms this equation. For him, the adolescent boy – particularly when born in an imperial outpost – is, along with the colonial subject, an invigorating source of new ideas and new ways of dealing with problems. Adolescence and colonial subjectivity have a social value in themselves rather than being stages on the way to complete mature citizenship, and have the potential to introduce fresh ideas and approaches to social problems.

Indeed, *Stalky* suggests that becoming an adult is to relinquish the intelligence of boyhood: to live one's life keeping up appearances and conforming to the status quo. In the last chapter, Stalky is shown behaving as an adult in India just as he did at school, playing with identity and undermining hierarchical structures. Indeed, school dominates India so much that Kipling almost seems to turn the 'school as little world' analogy on its head: the school is not a little world – the Empire is a big school, full of people waiting to be trained in the ways of school so that one day they might grow up into English gentlemen. Stalky and his friends are successful in India because of the comradeship they built at school, mainly in the pantomimes they created (the song they use as a private code is a composition made by Beetle for one of their dramas, 'Aladdin now has got a wife'). However, there is an irony in this. *Aladdin*, like many fairy tales, is a narrative about a young person's self-actualization. The hero struggles with the adult world and the power status quo in order to achieve what is rightfully his: wealth, a position as head of a family and

---

250 Brabazon 1910, p. 75.
251 Melly 1854, p. 95.
252 Adams 1861, p. 33.

power over his own life. When he has achieved it, the pantomime ends. In *Stalky*, the boys achieve none of these things (whatever their real-life counterparts did). India allows them not to grow up. It is a place where, in Kipling's view, adolescent values are still held, where adolescent traits are necessary for survival and where the pantomime never ends. Although the boys may be willing to trade adult privileges in order to avoid the hypocrisy and banality of maturity, however, their bodies cannot cope. The boy who played Aladdin becomes 'a baldish, broken-down captain of Native Infantry, shivering with ague'.[253] Abanazar has a 'face [...] like white glass, and [... fragile] hands'.[254] Only the almost-mythical Stalky can cope with the pace. Those who wish to survive must reconcile themselves to enjoying adolescence vicariously, as Bates does through his teaching and Beetle through his writing. Bourgeois maturity is the price they pay for this survival.

In refusing to allow all adolescents to progress to adulthood, and in seeing the whole of life in terms of school, Kipling follows many other writers discussed in this book. Indeed, the more prominent the Social Darwinist agenda became, the more likely boys in literary works seem to have been not to attain the 'privileges' of adult citizenship; marriage and social and political power. Various critics have offered explanations for this. Quigly suggests boy death is simply a way of 'pickling the perfect specimen at his moment of perfection', a way for authors and their characters to avoid controversial adult matters like sexuality and economic responsibility.[255] Cecil Degrotte Eby, analyzing popular literature in the run-up to the First World War, suggests that there might have been a wider cultural trend in which adolescence became an 'end in itself' and adulthood became something better avoided or rejected.[256] He suggests that Britain was undergoing a process of national psychological regression, remarking that 'English sensibility was shifting from the values traditionally regarded as adult to those of adolescence'.[257]

Indeed, some earlier commentators also held this view. Cyril Connolly's *Enemies of Promise* (1938), a chronicle of his years at prep. school and Eton, accused Kipling's generation of deliberately stunting the emotional development of his own generation. Connolly developed a 'Theory of Permanent Adolescence', which *Enemies of Promise* describes as

> the theory that the experiences undergone by boys at the great public schools, their glories and disappointments, are so intense as to dominate their lives and to arrest their development. From these it results that the greater part of the ruling class remains adolescent, school-minded, self-conscious, cowardly, sentimental, and in the last analysis homosexual.[258]

---

253 Ibid., p. 279.
254 Ibid., pp. 279–80.
255 Quigly 1984, p. 240–41.
256 Eby 1987, p. 96.
257 Ibid., p. 97.
258 Connolly 1983, p. 271.

Connolly blames this failure to grow up and face the realities of adulthood on the romantic perceptions of youth and childhood that predominated when he was young. Romanticists, he says, hold that 'truth is beauty and beauty truth, that love is stronger than death, the soul immortal and the body divine'.[259] Romanticists need constant mental and emotional stimulation, have unrealistic, childish yearnings and behave like spoiled children. Maturity, on the other hand, 'is the quality that the English dislike most'.[260] Connolly cites a few examples of 'mature' versus 'immature' individuals. In politics, Marx and Freud are mature. Disraeli is 'boyish'.[261] Eliot and Valéry are mature, while De la Mare, Housman and Tennyson are romantic. Modernism embraces all the ideas Connelly regards as 'mature': atheism, a frank attitude towards sexuality and an acceptance that root-and-branch political change is necessary. Permanent adolescents, however, reject change out of hand, believing that 'Human beings [...] are perpetually getting above themselves and presuming to rise superior to the limitations of their nature', something that invites punishment from a 'jealous God'.[262]

Connelly saw romanticism and 'permanent adolescence' as ideological constructs purposely designed to preserve the status quo and said that permanent adolescents were always employed in bureaucratic positions.[263] The ideology of the unashamedly profit-making, 'Spartan' and obsessively anti-homosexual private schools was upheld by their literature curriculum.[264] Connolly read *Vice Versa*, the *Gem* and the *Magnet* before attending private school, then Carlyle's *French Revolution*, which was advocated by the school authorities. Connolly summarizes the official curriculum thus:

> Chaucer begat Spenser, Spenser begat Shakespeare, Shakespeare begat Milton, Milton begat Keats, Coleridge, Shelley, Wordsworth, and they begat Tennyson who begat Longfellow, Stevenson, Kipling, Quiller-Couch, and Sir Henry Newbolt. There are a few bad boys we do not speak about – Donne, Dryden, Pope, Blake, Byron, Browning, Fitzgerald [...] and Oscar Wilde who was a criminal degenerate.[265]

Literature was not there to be criticized but to be used as a 'romantic escape' and none of the teachers embraced the ambiguities of interpretation.[266] Good poetry was either 'funny' or made one 'want to cry', because laughing and crying were cathartic and purged the emotions. However, 'because poetry was associated with emotional excess, night and unhappiness', Connolly 'felt disgusted with it by day

---

259 Ibid., p. 183.
260 Ibid., p. 185.
261 Ibid., p. 272.
262 Ibid., p. 273.
263 Ibid., p. 276.
264 Ibid., p. 175.
265 Ibid., pp. 181–82.
266 Ibid., p. 181.

as by a friend in whom when drunk one has unwisely confided'.[267] The system taught boys to limit their involvement with socially radical literature by teaching them to feel disgusted with the emotional content.

If Connolly was right, and maturity really was the quality the English hated most, a complete U-turn in cultural perceptions not only of adolescence but also of adulthood must have occurred between Arnold's time and Kipling's. This change prompts us to question why adulthood had become so unappealing. Connelly thought permanent adolescence was a conspiracy to prevent progress, but the situation was probably more complex than that. To Thomas Hughes, Percy Fitzgerald and others, adulthood, at least for upper-class males, meant the attainment of proper citizenship. The man, having spent his boyhood at public school developing his own social and political ideology, finally acquired the power to influence his rapidly evolving society in whatever way he saw fit. Marriage and fatherhood were an integral part of this citizenship. To turn-of-the-century 'realists' such as Stanley Hall, however, maturity was an acceptance of the economic and scientific realities of the world. It was a realization that 'life is not all joy and that the individual must be subordinated and eventually die'[268] (a realization which, he explained, caused suicidal tendencies among young people). According to his analysis, people had become afraid of adulthood because they had awoken to the existence of certain incontrovertible scientific truths.

The fundamental difference between mid- and late-Victorian attitudes seems to be that whereas for the former adulthood signaled the attainment of individual power, for the latter it meant the opposite: an acceptance that individual power and autonomy were limited. A variety of social and cultural changes might explain such feelings. Some doubtless felt that large bureaucratic and corporate machines were impinging on their autonomy, or took a Darwinist view that progress was not the fruit of individual effort but the result of slow, collective evolution. Competition for influential social positions was stronger than before. The number of individuals entering secondary education had never been higher. With graduates of numerous public and grammar schools competing for political stardom, public school men no longer had the virtual guarantee of political influence they might have taken for granted sixty years earlier. As secondary education became less of an elite privilege, the adulthood it was designed to usher was, accordingly, becoming less illustrious. As one educationalist put it, in a more democratic future, every (male) individual would have a tiny share of power, but no great influence.[269] Nonetheless, school hierarchy structures were still based on the monitorial system, originally designed to give boys the experience they needed to wield the authority that was the birthright of the aristocracy and squirearchy. Thus, individuals who enjoyed an important status at school might never again find themselves with such power again. Although the upper classes probably underestimated the amount of power

---

267 Ibid., pp. 182–83.
268 Hall 1925, vol. I, p. 384.
269 S.R. James in Norwood 1909, p. 316.

they retained, the fact remained that adolescence had become for many a glorious prelude to nothing.

At the turn-of-the-century therefore, adolescence maintained its hugely symbolic status, especially among Social Darwinists who saw it as a crucial time both for individual and social evolution. Since these thinkers were mostly public school men themselves, they tended to view the public schoolboy as the normative adolescent and to orient their educational programs around a public school model. They were convinced that science gave them authority over the population at large and used it to justify their desire to intervene in people's private everyday lives – especially when those people happened to be young.[270] A handful of writers strongly opposed the Social Darwinist scheme, arguing that prescribed models of male behavior were detrimental to both individual and race. They suggested that an obsession with eugenic fitness was leading to a disturbing overemphasis on physical prowess and on the goal of parenthood. Social Darwinist ideology also problematized the adolescent narrative in new ways. Concerns about degeneration and the supposed manifestations of degeneration – in particular, homosexuality – led believers in Social Darwinism to focus to a ridiculous and intrusive extent on youth sexuality at the expense of all other aspects of juvenile life. The preoccupation with heredity and eugenically correct fatherhood made them to cast doubt on the integrity of the kind of male relationships that had so far been central to the narrative of adolescence, including those between father-figures and sons. Some authors – Kipling, for example – portrayed male adults as predatory, perverse and exploitative and rejected maturity altogether. Maturity for turn-of-the-century public schoolboys, more often than not destined for desk jobs, no longer held the glory it had offered to Tom Brown's generation, who went on to become the movers and shakers of the empire. Social change and new sociological theories obviously called for new, more relevant types of adolescent narrative to be developed, to supersede the *Tom Brown* model. However, despite the continuing obsession of educational commentators with the public schools, it seems it was becoming ever harder to produce a coherent and representative narrative of adolescence using a single-sex public school setting. In the next chapter I will show how, during the chaos of war, public school writers reacted to the changing demands growing democracy was making on public school concept of citizenship. I will also show how some public schoolboys themselves finally found a voice with which to reply to those who, for more than a century, had held them under such intense scrutiny.

---

[270] The question remains as to whether their attempts resulted in as doubtful a success as the earlier attempts at implementing systematic social coercion described in Chapter 4. For example, Britain never had an overt eugenic program like the ones implemented in Scandinavia, Germany or the USA and movements such as the Boy Scouts never evolved into instruments of social control like the Hitler Youth. Further research might profitably determine how 'Lockean ideas of liberty' at work in the nineteenth century continued through the early twentieth century.

Chapter 6

The Death of an Ideal

Although public school stories, novels and biographies are being written to the present day, it is probably fair to say that the strain of 'serious' boys' school stories I have discussed in this book effectively ended after the First World War. It is worth briefly recapping here the fundamental components of these narratives. These texts tend to have a strong political element to them, making connections between the adolescent sphere and the political world, and portraying adolescent life as being about far more than introspective concerns. They also contain some kind of agenda for educational reform – they are not merely historically descriptive works or catalogues of private experience, but dynamic contributions to social and educational debate. Finally, they predominantly involve boys (both fictional and real) who become members of the ruling classes; boys whose parents have private incomes and who go on to become members of the legislative and governing elite. Among them there are lawyers (Butler Burke, Percy Fitzgerald), politicians (John Verney, George Melly), army officers (Harry East, Stalky), philanthropists (Tom Brown, Gerald Eversley) and, of course, writers. It goes without saying that in every biographically-based work, somebody inevitably grows up to be a writer. In this chapter, I will discuss some of the last examples of this genre that appeared during and in the aftermath of the First World War and suggest why the developmental pattern for the 'ideal' citizen promoted by public school literature fell into disuse. This period was significant as the time when the idea of civics education was rapidly gaining currency and I will compare the type of civic education advocated by educationalists with that described in literature. I have included in this debate one work written by an adolescent, Alec Waugh's *The Loom of Youth* (1917), and some commentaries on it written by schoolboys, as rare examples of boys being invited to reflect on their own situation as developing citizens.

During and after the First World War the entire thrust of the school genre changed. Indeed, from the postwar period onwards, the political and pedagogical confidence of writers was so shaken that it is often hard to identify any coherent message at all. Shane Leslie's *The Oppidan* (1922), which deals with Eton in the period before the First World War under the Headmastership of the reforming philathlete Edmond Warre, is emblematic of this loss of sense of direction. In his narrative, Leslie deliberately avoids presenting any kind of a goal-oriented pedagogical scheme. His aesthetic, nihilistic hero, Peter, is killed in the Eton fire of 1903, thus realizing his greatest ambition, which is to die at school. Leslie explains that, in the aftermath of war, tragedy is the mandatory ending for novels (especially those involving boys).[1] There will, therefore, be no happy, successful maturity for his hero. The novel will not be about a 'normal' boy, either, because normal boys' lives are too dull, and because 'Disorder [...] is the more attractive theme' to novelists.[2] In a Modernist climate, an 'everyboy' such as Tom Brown is not worth reading about; the literary adolescent must be something problematic, marginal and, essentially, pathological.

Leslie's Eton is a huge degenerating edifice, slowly being torn down and modernized, despite the protests of staff and boys. Peter loves the buildings, 'strung together at no particular time, and with certainly no consistent plan'.[3] His 'house' (the 'gin palace') is inadequately built, faces the graveyard, and is staffed by women from a penitential home. By page six, Peter, taking the Eton entrance exam, already entertains suicidal thoughts ('It was comforting to have [the graveyard] to fall back on in case of failure'[4]). Peter's favorite teachers, who try to resist Edmond Warre's modernizations, share in the degeneracy. The classics master had 'died to all outside the world of Eton'.[5] The English teacher, Lamb, is an inconspicuous 'simple, smiling personage'. His opinions on literature are that 'Scot was nice and Stevenson nicer but Milton was nicest'.[6] The history master, Jenkinson, a 'tall invalid',[7] is compared to Socrates in his asceticism. Hailed as a brilliant historian, teacher and poet, and as 'a midwife of consummate skill [...] who knew how to deliver the boyish mind of its adolescent enthusiasms', he is driven into 'exile' by the athleticists.[8] Peter learns from Jenkinson the phrase 'those whom the gods loved died young'.[9] Under him, Peter reads the *Phaedo*, which teaches that death, either a 'timeless sleep' or an opportunity to meet past heroes, is a desirable goal. From this point, Peter decides to die at Eton and to believe that death is 'an absolute good'.[10]

Peter's great enemy is Warre's National Efficiency-style athleticism, which subordinates intellect to the proper training of the body. Warre, remarks Leslie caustically, reduced everything to the principle of having healthy bowels:

> Form and knowledge cannot procure athletic success, unless there are reposing within many yards of clean white gut, unworn by overstrain, untarnished by hereditary diseases. Upon his guts, the most primitive and insensitive of his organs, an Etonian depends to carry him through the lung-tearing ordeal of rowing or steeplechasing.[11]

---

1   Leslie 1922, p. xii.
2   Ibid., p. ix.
3   Ibid., p. 5.
4   Ibid., p. 6.
5   Ibid., p. 20.
6   Ibid., p. 33.
7   Ibid., p. 54.
8   Ibid., p. 85.
9   Ibid., p. 103.
10 Ibid., p. 264.
11 Ibid., p. 79.

In this scheme, books are 'vermin' proscribed by the school's 'Mosaic code', and no boy will claim one as his own.[12] Academic boys are unclean and their only use is to help athletic boys cheat in class.[13] Intellectuals (*'saps'*) are not even allowed into the debating society. Ironically, however, although Warre is a modernizer, his anti-intellectualism has left him ignorant of technological advances. He follows standard 'modern' public school practices (founding, for instance, an army corps), and is adept with 'oar and rifle and pen', but is 'heedless of the machine-gun and the typewriter'[14] and leaves his students similarly clueless. When the Boer War casualty lists come in, it is clear that his exclusive concern with physical cultivation has been fatal to the next generation.

Looking for a niche, Peter, who has a strong taste for Pre-Raphaelitism and Medievalism, becomes an Anglo-Catholic. He and his friends believe that modernity, with its emphasis on the material, betrays the principles of Eton's founder (Henry VI), who would be shocked by modern attitudes to adolescent education. One boy remarks, 'I am afraid the Governing Body think that Eton boys, like niggers, have no souls'.[15] Indeed, modernity has obscured the soul of the adolescent and Peter looks to art and pre-Reformation history as a way of rediscovering it. He reads Swinburne and produces a satirical magazine called the *Insider*, 'not printed, but hectographed and distributed to the initiated'.[16] However, Peter, although supposedly a socialist, has no intention of carrying his mission to rediscover the adolescent soul outside Eton. He has made his mind up to die at Eton, which he does, due to supernatural causes. Peter's dead father, formerly an archaeologist, has left him some Egyptian mummy's heads and a charm that depicts the god of death, half of which belongs to Peter and half to his sister.[17] Peter does not know his sister, but, by chance, she happens to give her part of the charm to his friend Socston, who she meets at a party.[18] Peter obtains the fragment from Socston and glues the two sides together, bringing, it seems, a curse upon himself. He subsequently dies in his sleep, stifled by smoke when the boarding house catches fire. His death is highly aesthetic but totally undramatic. There are no flames, just a 'rose of smoldering fire' and 'no mark of fire on the body, only a slight smell of smoke'. While the other boys calmly save each other, Peter merely 'did not rise'.[19]

At the end of the book, Leslie reflects on the prospects for Peter's generation, who were 'doomed to pass through some far-off and fiery harvest, of which the

---

12　Ibid., p. 80.
13　Ibid., p. 81.
14　Ibid., p. 65.
15　Ibid., p. 236.
16　Ibid., p. 237.
17　Ibid., p. 278.
18　Ibid., p. 331.
19　Ibid., p. 357.

first fruits had been mysteriously reaped before their eyes'.[20] According to Leslie, fundamental flaws in civic education at Eton (and presumably at other schools) brought the war about. Eton failed, he says, to follow Disraeli's 'Young England' scheme, and ceased to produce luminaries such as Fielding, Shelley or Swinburne. Rather than stimulating fresh political ideas, it taught its pupils how to maintain the status quo through 'diplomacy, statecraft and consulship'.[21] Eton, he says, had a policy of tolerating diversity of opinion, but in reality 'diversity' meant that although individuals had a right to hold opinions, they were expected to keep quiet about them. Masters who made their principles known were assiduously expelled: the 'Oxford Renaissance' was suppressed and the socialist J.L. Joynes was sent away 'for his sympathy with the Irish cause', as was his brother-in-law Henry Salt for his Humanitarianism and vegetarianism.[22] Leslie claims that the 'liberalism' of Eton is, in reality, a brand of consensus politics achieved by stifling debate. No longer a 'nursery of Statesmen',[23] Eton ignores modern political thought. Leslie fears that Eton will be taken unawares by science and democracy and forced under state control, 'with her Head Master appointed by each incoming Government, with H.G. Wells as Chairman of her Governing Body, and the Chapel [...] given over to [...] clouds of chemical work'.[24]

Leslie blames the war on the National Efficiency movement, which stifled political dissent in school by focusing boys' attention unduly on physical fitness. However, the adolescents in his text can find few other causes to champion. One alternative to National Efficiency, in Leslie's view, is a decadent devotion to aesthetics, where boys turn their backs on pressing everyday questions and favor death over the prospect of facing the practicalities of adult life outside school. Another is Wellsian scientism, which promises to promote technology but neglects history, art and religion. All three alternatives disempower the adolescent and leave the public school story writer with no room to prescribe a course for the future. Like Eton's decadent literature teachers, Leslie seems to have nothing to teach his readers, other than the idea that 'those whom the gods love die young'.

What had also died, however, was the concept of adolescence on which 'serious' public school literature depended. The First World War, and the lead up to it, was, of course, a turning point in many ways for the whole of society. The 'Indian Summer' of the Edwardian upper classes, described so vividly by writers such as L.P. Hartley, was perhaps itself a kind of 'social adolescence'. Like Stalky, desperately trying to ward off adulthood in India, the upper classes were living off borrowed time, and would eventually have to justify their existence through paid employment. The private incomes that had enabled them to dedicate themselves solely to what are now considered to be leisure-time activities such as philanthropy,

---

20 Ibid., p. 365.
21 Ibid., p. xi.
22 Ibid., p. 231.
23 Ibid., p. 246.
24 Ibid., p. xii.

amateur natural history, amateur lawmaking, politics and unremunerated scholarly and artistic activities were disappearing. Gone also were the old-style, unpaid parliamentary careers documented by Trollope and Disraeli. The shabby-genteel protagonists of Orwell, Maugham and Samuel Butler – educated for the old status quo but without the means to sustain an amateur career or the wherewithal to thrive in business or the professions, – are products of this period. Increasing democratization also made the elite socialization process described by the public school narrative irrelevant. The demand for qualified professionals meant that education had to be more utilitarian in focus, meaning that adolescence could no longer be conceived of as a time to be devoted to freedom, experimentation and aesthetic indulgence. Even in the Victorian period, the lives of Stalky & Co were already overshadowed by exams, and J.E.C. Welldon was remarking gloomily that 'Learning, alas! Will someday be smothered by its own children, examination, competition, the calculation and publication of results'.[25] The 'permanent adolescence' of moneyed adults who refused to grow up could remain as a literary ideal, but was nowhere near a reality, and although writers such as Kipling were aware of this, it took the mechanical butchery of the First World War to really drive the point home. The remainder of this chapter will suggest how Waugh's nihilistic view of adolescent life and education arose, demonstrating how ideologies of public school adolescence were affected by new ideas of citizenship that were developing under the pressures of war.

The lead up to the war had produced specific ideas of how young people should be educated for citizenship. Widening democracy brought demand for changes in the way adolescents were educated as citizens and the formal teaching of civics, proposed a century and a half before by Joseph Priestley, began to be taken seriously. Some thinkers suggested that citizenship and statesmanship should be taught in the formal curriculum. Few, however, were willing to go as far as H.G. Wells, who demanded that political education take place in every secondary school, or F.H. Hayward, who argued that state schools should 'urge' socialism, teach the 'Rights of Man' and carry out experiments in proportional representation and women's suffrage.[26] Civics was a major concern of *The Higher Education of Boys in England* (1909), by Cyril Norwood (educationalist and future Head of Harrow) and Arthur H. Hope, who owed much to Stanley Hall. Norwood and Hope broke relatively new ground by suggesting that all boys be educated in the same state-controlled system. A state system was, they said, the best way to extend citizenship to all male subjects (presumably they ignored girls because non-voting women were not proper citizens). Their scheme was superficially democratic, but anti-individualistic. Breaking down 'caste' in schools would mean that 'the subordination of self to the community will perhaps, as in the Greek City-state, become the rule and not the rare exception'.[27] In one chapter, C.J.

---

25 Welldon 1895, p. 109.
26 Wells 1924, pp. 122, 53, Hayward 1910, pp. 362–63.
27 Norwood 1909, p. viii.

Hamilton remarked that 'The plea for the teaching of Civics [...] is today one of the commonest cries to be heard in the education world', something that 'is suggestive of an attitude of mind, with regard to the school and its functions, which is almost wholly new'.[28] Democracy, he explained, had brought about a need to educate the electorate to exercise their newly found powers wisely. The problem was how to implement this education. For example, civics could not be taught through History, as had been previously thought, because there was a risk of political bias from the teacher. Instead, a sense of civic responsibility had to be taught through clubs, sports, lessons on the political process, economics and social science.

This brand of 'citizenship' was founded on community loyalty rather than active political participation. It seems, paradoxically, that as civics gained recognition as a part of formal education, boys were losing their right to work out how to solve social problems for themselves, as they had done during their leisure time in the past, by trial and error and through play. In the same book, S.R. James warns against 'Self-Government among the Boys'. He remarks that it has recently been fashionable to introduce democratic ideas into school discipline. Some schools have decided 'to abolish the autocracy of the Headmaster and to govern through a Council of the Staff', giving boys 'a much larger share in their own management'. This degree of autonomy is granted in the belief that boys will 'go forth to govern themselves' in adulthood. This is 'a pestilent heresy', since in a democracy men only 'exercise at rare intervals under the Septennial Act an infinitesimally fractional part of sovereignty'. It is more important that boys learn to obey, since democracy is sustained 'by self-discipline and self-sacrifice', instilled by lessons in 'unquestioning obedience to orders'.[29]

As far as the actual education of boys went, it seems that the less elite a school was, the less autonomy boys had in fashioning themselves as citizens. S.P.B. Mais, who wrote several books on his experiences in public school education, remarked that at the first (minor public) school he taught in, Rossall (founded 1844), boys were discouraged from thinking about politics:

> I tried to stir up enthusiasm in the School Debating Society but, as boys were never allowed to discuss any subject that directly affected their own lives, it was scarcely surprising that debates were ill-attended or that the speakers relied on the type of facetiousness that one associates with the Oxford Union.[30]

At wartime Sherborne, however, Mais was allowed to give the pupils autonomy:

> I decided to let my form practice the art of self-government. They appointed their own captain of form, and allocated various offices, from the Keeper of the Marks to the Keeper of the Classroom. I did less and less teaching with the quite certain result that

---

28 Ibid., p. 411.
29 Ibid., p. 316.
30 Mais 1937, p. 50.

they learnt more and more. They learnt the art of speaking in public. Everyone had to deliver one lecture a week on any topic he liked.[31]

After the war, Mais arrived at the conclusion that it was better for teachers minimize their interference in the learning process. He commented in his autobiography that

> Boys left on their own quite often acquire a passionate desire to make galvanometers out of sardine tins. We schoolmasters spoil our whole game by over-zeal and over-teaching. [...] All that education too often does is to twist [a boy] from being a responsible, reasonable citizen into a games-playing oaf.[32]

Wartime works on citizenship show widely conflicting attitudes towards how the young should be educated and I will here discuss some of the extremes. Mais started the war with a far different idea of how adolescent citizenship could be formed than that expressed in the works cited above, sharing Norwood's view of citizenship as 'self-discipline and self-sacrifice'. In *A Public School in War Time* (1916), he described his work leading the Officer's Training Corps at Sherborne and the way he used English literature and debating to prepare boys to become soldiers. Initially, Mais followed Vachell, Kipling and Stanley Hall in suggesting that the war would put an end to national degeneration. Hall praised Arnold and the 'great English schools' for working against degeneration by cultivating competitive aggression.[33] He suggested that military 'ideals', and perhaps even war itself, could be a form of 'psycho-physical education' that would counterbalance the aesthetic tendencies of the young with sound physical training.[34] The young were better off dead, he insisted, than falling into academic 'stagnation'.[35] Mais, in turn, suggested combining aesthetic and military ideals. War and literature could operate in symbiosis: the 'tribulation' of war and the threat of early death would teach boys to value the 'solace' of literature, which would bring about an 'unbelievable' artistic 'renaissance'.[36] The visionary state of mind which would be produced when art and war were placed side by side would not only eliminate the 'ennui' of ordinary education, but would prevent 'secret vices'.[37]

Mais explained that he introduced his students to literature through the work of Rupert Brooke, whose aesthetic patriotism encouraged them willingly to contemplate self-sacrifice to a much greater extent than 'all the teaching in

---

31 Ibid., pp. 71–72.
32 Mais 1940, pp. 69–70.
33 Hall 1925, vol. I. p. 217.
34 Ibid., p. 222.
35 Ibid., p. 221.
36 Mais 1916, p. 4.
37 Ibid., p. 38.

the world' could do.[38] Mais criticized intellectual and overly rational boys, who he associated with 'Decadence, the Pre-Raphaelites, Shelley, Keats, and De Quincey'.[39] Single-minded scholars, he remarked scornfully, did nothing but return from Oxford with their Firsts in Greats to 'vomit the undigested masses of the classics [... on] boys of a later generation'.[40] Posing aloof from 'the herd', they were unfit for leadership.[41] Only the experience of war and suffering enabled, and entitled, an adult to teach literature:

> Having endured the horrors of war, he will, to use a phrase of Carlyle's, have cleared his mind of cant [...] boys will believe [him] all the more readily when they see from his face that his statements are [...] fundamental facts learnt only by dreadful experience; his theories, having been purified seven times in the fire, will carry an air of verisimilitude.[42]

Once it was deployed in the interests of war, literature would be sanitized. In turn, literature itself would sanitize war's ugliness. When battle and literature came together, they would create a kind of golden mean,[43] purging the nation of the self-interest and materialism that caused the war in the first place. In short, Mais's idea was that war was an opportunity for a kind of intellectual and cultural spring clean. In later years, he distanced himself from his role in the OTC at Sherborne, stating that it was not by choice but 'by command of the War Office' that he had become involved in 'training younger men to die'.[44] Perhaps, like Kipling, Mais had initially believed that this would be a Stalky war, fought with cunning and tactics, rather than wholesale mechanical slaughter. Certainly, the shock of his students' deaths led him to develop other, quite radical, educational ideas, as I will show later.

A completely different plan for democratic education was produced at the end of the war in the form of Victor Gollancz's *Political Education at a Public School* (1918). While he was a master at wartime Repton (1916–1918), Gollancz encouraged pupils to take an interest in political and aesthetic debate. He believed that by denying boys creative self-actualization, the classical curriculum turned them into 'highly efficient intellectual slave[s]', and he argued that allowing them free debate on socio-economic and political issues would enable them to view the adult world critically, making them 'master[s]' of discourse, ready to enter a full citizenship of 'liberty and discipline'.[45] In particular, Gollancz advocated that students be encouraged to criticize the Northcliffe press, which he believed to be

---

38 Ibid., p. 6.
39 Ibid., p. 84.
40 Ibid., p. 92.
41 Ibid., p. 85.
42 Ibid., p. 116.
43 Ibid., pp. 86–87.
44 Mais 1937, p. 62.
45 Gollancz 1918, pp. 16–17, 21.

the greatest enemy of democracy. Gollancz suggested that having boys run their own independent periodical press was central to a democratic education: 'The educational value of such a paper seems to us to be threefold; for its readers, for its contributors, and for the body politic in which it exists'.[46] As a community-building activity, he hoped that publishing would come to rival athletics. Most schools, of course, already had their own papers but, as Mangan remarks, these were frequently merely a 'vehicle of institutional propaganda to indoctrinate the reader' into the pervasive, athleticist, conformist status quo.[47] Gollancz believed, however, that given the right kind of press, public schools could potentially be national repositories of liberal values, with the boys educated with a view to becoming leaders working for socialistic progress. Unlike Stanley Hall, he also argued that boys are perfectly able to understand political issues:

> The boy of from seventeen to nineteen is perfectly capable of understanding the connection between capital and diplomacy in the nineteenth century, of criticizing Plato's Republic, and of forming a judgement as to the respective merits of Christian and Nietzchean ethics; and very much younger boys can grasp the meaning of social and ethical principles when expressed in their simplest forms. Even economics, which grown men find so boring, exercise over many boys an intense fascination.[48]

After establishing evening classes in political education at Repton, however, Gollancz was dismissed, having been accused of being a 'traitor' and a 'pacifist' and of 'undermining the authority of the teachers by encouraging the boys to ask questions and by working with the boys in a spirit of open enquiry'.[49] He went on to found the Left Book Club, hoping to educate the populace through another route.[50]

Gollancz was one of the first to contemplate the idea of having overt political education at school, and he transformed the idea of the public schoolboy as a member of the clerisy into the idea of the critical boy as guardian of civilized values against the Northcliffe press. Even while these ideas were evolving, though, a new trend in schoolboy literature was developing which gave a far more pessimistic view of the kind of citizenship values boys were acquiring at public school. The twenty-five-year-old Arnold Lunn set out to describe in realistic and unromantic terms the way elite adolescents at Harrow learned not to facilitate inclusive government, but to manage, coerce and control the populace. Public school stories had never explored this part of civic education before. Lunn (1888–1974) began a brief trend in 'authentic' youth writing that set out to undermine the schemes adults had been setting out for the improvement of adolescent civic education. Debunking the 'myths' about elite adolescent social training propagated by Vachell in *The Hill*,

---

46 Ibid., p. 79.
47 Mangan 1986, p. 70.
48 Ibid., pp. 15–16.
49 Brown 2000, p. 41.
50 McCulloch 1991, pp. 108–11.

he aimed to produce a narrative of adolescence that was not driven by pedagogical motives. This narrative would, he believed, present a far more authentic view of public school adolescence than any so far written. Lunn's book shocked readers, not for its political import but partly because he broke taboos by openly showing that teenage boys had a physical interest in women and by suggesting that to discuss sex is not unclean (indeed, the only thing the boys consider 'really indecent'[51] is when adults intrude upon their private physical feelings). This prurient emphasis on the part of Lunn's critics undoubtedly deflected attention from the tough message it carried – that there was no prospect of any adult writer ever again creating a credible and educational narrative about adolescent life.

The Harrovians (1913), based on Lunn's schoolboy diaries, challenged many contemporary sociological assumptions about adolescence. The aim was to present the harsh reality of school life stripped of romanticism, something that both scandalized and enthused readers. Lunn proclaimed that the gospel of Harrow taught:

> Blessed are those who bear as marked a resemblance to the Pharisee as possible by discussing the tone of their House on every possible occasion. Blessed are those that learn to kill the young men of other countries with the greatest possible dispatch.[52]

Christ, he says, would not have survived at public school. Lunn imagines a housemaster telling Him to fit in and 'not to lecture [His] elders on their supposed lapses from virtue'.[53] However, although Lunn follows earlier writers by condemning the public schools' overemphasis on athleticism and neglect of scholarship, he does not view the education provided at Harrow as being without certain political uses. In terms of providing an education that seeks to consolidate the power of the elite in an increasingly democratic age, Harrow is very effective. In Lunn's eyes, politics shows no respect for aesthetic temperament or sensibility, and the Harrow system adequately supplies the qualities needed by leaders: emotional and physical resilience and a Machiavellian ability to control and persuade.

Lunn's protagonist, Peter, is a misfit because he is an intellectual with little aptitude for games, who spends his early time at Harrow trying merely to survive and avoid trouble. He is brighter than average and eventually becomes a prefect, at which point he has to learn how to overcome his own unpopularity and how to control his subordinates. Peter's education for governance happens in a prewar atmosphere, with educators busy toughening boys up for the coming conflict. Peter and his friends discuss the ideologies peddled by the National Efficiency movement, in particular the idea that boys should have their more violent instincts nurtured and channeled into soldiering. They read an essay entitled 'The Public School Spirit', a so-called 'contribution to political science' that suggests how

---

51 Lunn 1913, p. 151.
52 Ibid., p. 139.
53 Ibid., p. 140.

schools could produce better citizens. The article says that if schools put more emphasis on 'playing the game' and less on intellectual acquisition, they would be able to combat the trend in 'Art for Art's sake' that is mentally and physically enfeebling the young.[54] The essay complains that the demise of general bullying has made modern boys too 'gentle', an idea Peter's unsympathetic guardian echoes when he writes to him:

> I sometimes wonder whether schools to-day lack something of that rough-and-ready discipline of my generation. There is a growing tendency to molly-coddle boys. Fighting seems to have died out; perhaps it is as well, but there was a good deal to be said for their simple English way of settling things with bare fists.[55]

On the contrary, however, there is a more than adequate amount of violence and conflict at Lunn's Harrow. This violence is not, though, the systematic conflict of the Regency public schools, where boys supposedly honed their political instincts by ganging up against self-interested masters. Lunn does not believe that boys can learn the principles of democratic citizenship by co-operating with their peers, and the boys in his books seem to be oblivious of the idea of mutual support. Rather than campaigning against the system, dissatisfied boys merely bully other boys. The social structure is a chain of violence:

> A boy spends his life in propitiating those who can kick him and kicking those who feel the need of propitiating him. He expects no mercy, and he gives no quarter in the rough warfare of school life. That is why school is such an excellent training for real life.[56]

Political indifference at Lunn's Harrow is mainstream. Even 'Small weak minorities never hang together'.[57] Anybody who calls for change is accused of socialism and warned that Harrow will become a board school if reform is allowed.[58] The boys' only attempt at social cohesion is to force clever boys into helping less academic boys to cheat, ensuring an equal academic outcome for all. Peter refuses to cooperate with cribbing and mark doctoring, not for ethical reasons but because of 'pure cussedness, helped out by an Irish love for being in a minority'.[59] Being alone against mass opposition teaches him 'moral independence'.[60] Lunn, in fact, suggests that it is useful for schools to cultivate resentment and indulge rebellion, but not for democratic purposes. Rebels make good leaders, because 'rebellion and the power to suppress rebellion spring from the same faculty, the defiance

---

54 Ibid., p. 67.
55 Ibid., p. 76.
56 Ibid., p. 207.
57 Ibid., p. 238.
58 Ibid., p. 70.
59 Ibid., p. 91.
60 Ibid., p. 239.

of authority and the firm exercise of authority are kindred tastes'.[61] The mob culture prevalent at school gives more intellectually able boys valuable practice in controlling public opinion and order.

Peter, who lives for books, as 'All people with imagination do',[62] is not naturally inclined to join in school 'ragging'. However, instead of opting out and taking a back seat in the race for survival like the misfit protagonists of the 1890s, he discovers a new kind of political education by becoming a school prefect. Lunn explains that the advantage of the old-style violent, repressive monitorial regime that well-meaning writers had earlier deplored is that it 'provided a valuable moral training for the boy whose official position was not broad-based upon the people's will'.[63] When Peter, unpopular and rather sensitive, becomes a prefect, he has to cultivate an enjoyment of aggression that enables him to wield authority in an aimlessly violent atmosphere. He 'whop[s] quite as much as he need have' and enjoys an 'intoxicating sense of power'.[64] Administering discipline becomes an art form. Peter exercises 'subtle[ty]' and 'craft' in manipulating rules to his own ends.[65] He also discovers that the most satisfying form of discipline consists of mental cruelty, since 'it's much more amusing to beat folk with one's brain instead of one's fists'.[66] Lunn half-sardonically remarks that the ruthlessness that the 'naturally sensitive' Peter develops through being an outsider 'is a startling tribute to the moral value of a Public School training'.[67] Indeed, Peter's training is best described as 'Machiavellian'. During Peter's career Lunn quotes Machiavelli's advice that leaders should cultivate the art of conspicuously exhibiting good qualities in order to win public acclaim, while being able to change them to 'the opposite [...] when the necessity arises'.[68] Civic education for the elite is here geared towards producing manipulative despots, rather than enlightened statesmen.

Peter spends most of his time at school un-learning the popular romantic beliefs about juvenile psychology promoted by most commentators on adolescence. Initially, he expects that, during his school career, he will experience some kind of moral or spiritual epiphany. He looks forward to significant adolescent rites of passage (for example, confirmation), meditating on how he, like the heroes of traditional school stories, will undergo a moral renaissance ('People would realize that he had changed – that was all'[69]). However, no Damascene revelation befalls him. He has been fooled by the romantic notion that adolescents have preternatural spiritual and aesthetic powers, and he has unrealistic expectations of himself.

---

61 Ibid., p. 251.
62 Ibid., p. 231.
63 Ibid., p. 236.
64 Ibid., p. 235.
65 Ibid., p. 266.
66 Ibid., p. 289.
67 Ibid., p. 239.
68 Ibid., p. 90.
69 Ibid., p. 160.

Although, says Lunn, writers like to portray marginalized boys as visionaries, most boys who are 'kicked are not Shelleys'.[70] Indeed, the intellectual boy 'is apt to be priggish if he can read poetry or write English with enjoyment'.[71] School plays the utilitarian role of teaching the minority who do possess artistic pretensions that creativity is an impediment to individual and collective survival. A school should 'transform an inefficient artist into a humdrum useful member of society'. It will 'teach the lesson that the brilliant individualist is often a nuisance in the game of life', and 'relieve the overcrowded literary market by transforming a bad poet into an indifferent civil servant'.[72] Schoolboys find intellectual pretension repulsive and beat it out of others. At Lunn's Harrow, one boy who interprets Shakespeare from a 'psychological' standpoint is accused of 'physical uncleanliness' by other boys and punished with a ritual bath.[73] Lunn says this measure was justified, since the boy had demonstrated unwarranted egotism.

Adolescent sensibility, which both the *Bildungsroman* and the public school narrative had generally deemed essential to development, has now become an obsolete quality. The vestiges of moral idealism Peter initially retains are soon smothered. When the school authorities turn water hoses on hunger marchers protesting outside the school, Peter, inspired by Lord Shaftesbury, writes a letter to 'The Harrovian' in protest. The editor refuses to print the letter because it might offend old boys. Peter learns that the scheme of consolidating the power of the elite in a democratizing age requires not the cultivation of specific civilized values and individual conscience, but the sacrifice of personal opinions in the interests of contingency, however ugly or unpleasant this may be. Education here is not about developing ideals, but about learning how to adapt to one's environment, something which the majority of adolescents are naturally fitted to do. Most of Lunn's boys conform unquestioningly to the prevailing atmosphere in society and follow whatever rituals are current in their environment, because they are ritual creatures. They lack 'frankness and sincerity'[74] in matters such as religion, because external conformity means more to them than inner conviction. Most even regard football – 'playin' up and all that tosh' – as a waste of time.[75] Abstract principle is absent from such an environment and the traditional public school narrative, as a manifesto for political and pedagogical change, is irrelevant.

Lunn's book stimulated a sudden enthusiasm for authentic writing by schoolboys themselves. There were several more reasons why schoolboy writing had a minor boom at this time. The unexpected severity of the war and the guilt it engendered probably motivated adults to get boys' ideas down on paper before they were killed on the battlefield. *The Harrovians* had also encouraged the belief that

---

70 Ibid., p. 44.
71 Ibid., pp. 243–44.
72 Ibid., p. 45.
73 Ibid., p. 244.
74 Ibid., p. 143.
75 Ibid., p. 33.

the world of boys was impenetrable to adult eyes and that only boys themselves could give a reasonable account of it. S.P.B. Mais was moved to remark that all literature about boys by adults was 'romantically impossible and hopelessly out of date',[76] and that adults should stick to writing from an adult point of view. Lunn's bleak Machiavellian universe must also have caught the attention of liberal educationalists, who would have been anxious to find out why boys were seemingly developing forms of proto-fascism at school, despite efforts by sociologists to 'civilize' them. For a brief period, therefore, a level of credence was given to boys' writing that had not existed before. Stanley Hall had believed that adolescent boys were 'dumb-bound, monophrastic, inarticulate, and semi-aphasic'.[77] He had remarked that juveniles should not be allowed to write for themselves, because to teach written skills before oral skills are fully developed 'violate[s] the great law that the child repeats the history of the race'. Young people, he said, should not be expressing their own thoughts but listening to what adults have to say, since they 'do not learn to write by writing, but by reading and hearing'.[78] He also had little confidence in their ability to think critically, and explained that adolescents should be encouraged to make emotional, rather than intellectual, responses to what they read, since 'critical notes' and examinations are potentially 'harmful'.[79] Hall even recommended that adults prevent young people from reading books that were too exciting, because 'When left to develop according to chance, the tendency is often toward a selection of books which unfit one for every-day living'.[80] Too much critical thought and too much literary excitement too young, he warned, would irreparably damage reproductive and mental health. However, it seems that the war allowed a brief respite from this resistance towards young people's critical abilities which, although it soon subsided, produced a handful of texts that give a rare insight into the way adolescents themselves viewed their situation.

Alec Waugh's *The Loom of Youth* (1917) was the first public school novel written by an adolescent. It was published with the encouragement of S.P.B. Mais, who, shocked by the war, had begun to search for a more boy-centered approach to education.[81] Waugh (1898–1981) was seventeen and at Sandhurst when this semi-autobiographical novel was written. He had been expelled from Sherborne ('Fernhurst') a year earlier, after being accused of homosexuality, an event he dealt with in his book, to the outrage of the press and the public school establishment.[82] The Head of Winchester called it 'devilish, sensual, unthinkable, destructive of and mocking at all ideals [...] Baudelaire and bawd [...] incredibly untrue and yet

---

76 Mais 1916, p. 131.
77 Hall 1925, vol. II, p. 454.
78 Ibid., p. 462.
79 Ibid., p. 475.
80 Ibid., p. 477.
81 Musgrave 1985, p. 183.
82 See *Dictionary of National Biography*.

[...] clearly a photograph'.[83] It is remarkable that *The Loom* caused such offense. Waugh's references to boyhood affairs amount at most to four pages and there is nothing explicit. Moreover, earlier and much more open accounts of homosexuality written by adults, such as E.F. Benson's *David Blaize* (1916), had attracted no such attention. Here is the offending passage, where one of the protagonist's seniors, about to be expelled for an illicit relationship, comments:

> Who made me what I am but Fernhurst? [...] Fernhurst made me worship games, and think that they alone mattered, and everything else could go to the deuce. I heard men say about bloods whose lives were an open scandal, 'Oh, It's all right, they can play football.' I thought it was all right too.[84]

The other boys show little interest in this boy's 'crime'. They are indifferent to homosexuality, which they view as a private matter. It matters far more to them that the expelled boy is their best footballer and that when he goes they lose matches. In the book as a whole, politics, especially war politics, is a far more important issue. The fact that media critics again chose to focus on homosexuality rather than Waugh's critique of social and political issues is yet another instance of a general tendency to view adolescents solely in terms of their sexuality. This attitude annoyed Waugh. Later, in *Public School Life* (1922), a manual written specifically *for* boys, Waugh stated with ire that it was high time educationalists and the media left 'boy-friendship' alone and stopped trying to make private relationships into an 'exact science'.[85] He defended boys' fundamental right to privacy and criticized the amount of surveillance to which they were subjected.

Whatever critics may have thought of *The Loom*, it was the work's literary and political emphasis that interested its editor, Thomas Seccombe.[86] Seccombe reads in *The Loom* 'a sublime contempt for all the fatted calves of nineteenth-century altars'. Waugh, he says, displays a 'therapeutic energy in regard to the seamy problems in literature'[87] and throws down a challenge to the predatory, warmongering adult world. According to Seccombe, teachers, as servants of an exploitative state, use the literary canon, with its sentimentalized images of adolescence, to make young people pliable to the demands of the military machine. The Royal Military College, where Waugh wrote his book and where Seccombe himself was Professor of History, is 'the Devil's Own training camp',[88] devoted to seducing boys onto the battlefield by engaging their emotions through literature and aesthetics. Waugh's work is valuable because it de-romanticizes boys' lives.

---

83 Quoted in Quigly 1984, p. 199.
84 Waugh 1917, p. 60.
85 Waugh 1922, pp. 124 and 134.
86 Quigly 1984, p. 202. Seccombe (1866–1923) was sub-editor of the *Dictionary of National Biography* and a literary critic. See *Dictionary of National Biography*.
87 Waugh 1917, p. 10.
88 Musgrave 1985, p. 183, Waugh 1917, p. 11.

Seccombe commends the 'objective reality' of *The Loom*, which contrasts with Farrar, Kipling and the 'calculated falsity of Talbot Baines Reed',[89] which are all part of the general conspiracy to coerce and control the young. Not only do boys have an exclusive right to comment on their own lives, they also have a 'Divine Right' to comment on adult affairs such as imperial politics and economics.[90] Seccombe condemns 'the "do as you are told" tradition of coercive discipline' which dominates education and politics, and holds up the newly liberated writing boy as the antidote to war and its causes: anti-intellectualism, athleticism, Smiles, Cobden, '"Free" trade' and 'Volunteer theory'.[91]

Alec Waugh's main educational point in *The Loom* has become a commonplace tenet among critics of Victorian and early twentieth-century public schools. The public school system, he declares, 'loves mediocrity'. Most of its products are

> nonentities, the set who drift through their six years, making no mark, hurting no one, doing little good. Finally they pass out into the world to swell the rout of civilized barbarians whom it 'hurts to think' and who write to the papers, talk a lot about nothing and then die and are forgotten.[92]

Waugh's hero, Gordon Carruthers, begins his school career as a philistine with hidden artistic potential. While at Fernhurst, he reads *The Harrovians*, which shocks him so deeply that he hopes it portrays 'the exceptional, not [...] the average boy'. Waugh explains that *The Harrovians* describes 'the life of a Public School boy stripped of all sentiment, crude and raw' and is 'the finest school story written'.[93]

Gordon, however, is not content to revel in Lunn's dystopianism, but desperately tries to re-invest adolescent culture with aesthetic value as a defense against the economic materialism of contemporary society. Indeed, Waugh himself writes of how he longs for the restoration of the public school ideal of 'innocence and beauty', which has been lost to 'a generation that was being taught to blind itself to the higher issues of life'.[94] He laments the fact that the modern public school system is designed to make nothing more than pliable drones. The average public school graduate 'has learnt to do what he is told; he takes life as he sees it and is content'.[95] The academic curriculum, revolving around meaningless tasks, trains boys to avoid work and to defend their own inactivity and incompetence:

---

89 Ibid.
90 Ibid., p. 12.
91 Ibid., pp. 13, 15.
92 Ibid., p. 30.
93 bid., p. 153.
94 Ibid., p. 155.
95 Ibid., p. 141.

It was a greater effort to pit one's brains against a master long trained in spotting tricks than against some dull-headed scholar. The Public School system, at any rate, teaches its sons the art of framing very ingenious theories with which to defend their faults; a negative virtue, perhaps, but none the less an achievement.[96]

These boys, replete with 'negative virtues', will become acquiescent, passive citizens, unlikely to challenge the status quo in any way. Waugh, however, wants boys 'trained to take their proper place in the national struggle for a right and far-sighted civilization',[97] and he debates whether cultural education can have a role in encouraging active citizenship.

Waugh uses the 'loom' metaphor to describe the psychological changes which occur during adolescence, a period of 'ferment' that exists between the blind obedience of childhood and the principled observance of law in adulthood.[98] In early adolescence, the individual's entire moral universe collapses. In the following years, the 'unraveled [...] threads' of his moral consciousness are gradually rearranged, until 'out of the disorder of conflicting ideas and emotions the tapestry is woven on the wonderful loom of youth'. During the youth's 'apprenticeship' at public school, all his 'jumbled' ideas miraculously come together to form a coherent, aesthetically pleasing view of society and morality. This is maturity. Exceptional and 'dangerous' boys, however, who have 'a personality' and who may not be able to find such moral consistency in the world, have a potential to become heroes. Such a boy might either 'dash himself to pieces fighting for a worthless cause' or, 'More likely [...] be like Byron, a wonderful, irresponsible creature, who at one time plumbed the depths, and at another swept the heavens – a creature irresistibly attractive because he is irresistibly human'.[99] Gordon, who is one of these exceptional boys, becomes 'a mixture between Don Juan and Puck', a 'hedonist' and a devotee of art for art's sake, but searching for a righteous cause.[100]

In Waugh's view, conventional ideas of civic maturity, which is synonymous with passivity and mediocrity, are instilled through a wrong-headed, Arnoldian-style literary education. Masters promote the values of Tennyson, Browning and Wordsworth, which, Gordon complains, encourage boys to 'drift on with low aims, with nothing to help us to live differently from cattle'.[101] 'It is all very well' remarks Gordon, 'for a middle-aged man to worship Wordsworth and calm philosophy'.[102] Adults force the young to abandon idealism and to devote themselves to the mediocre aims of survival and comfort. Consequently, Gordon

---

96 Ibid., p. 43.
97 Ibid., p. 141.
98 Ibid., p. 89.
99 Ibid., p. 90.
100 Ibid., pp. 135, 84.
101 Ibid., p. 152.
102 Ibid., p. 147.

rejects the poetry of 'mature thought' for Swinburne and 'the poetry of revolt', castigating the system for attempting to blunt his sensibilities by 'offer[ing] him mature philosophy instead of colour and youth'.[103]

Gordon's favorite teacher, Ferrers – based on S.P.B. Mais – encourages a more active involvement with literature and with political and social thought. Ferrers's educational philosophy is that 'A master must get to the boy's level'.[104] A journalist himself, who writes 'a great deal about Public Schools to the various London papers', his curriculum centers around discursive writing and he sets his boys to write on topics such as 'Poetry is in the first instance the outpouring of a rebel'.[105] The boys consider a good master to be one who loathes the idea of 'maturity' and refuses to become 'mature' himself (rather like Kipling's Bates). They remark of Ferrers: 'He's a boy still; he can see our side of the question, and he knows what footling idiots half of the common room are'.[106] Maturity is defined as a self-deception in the mistaken idea that there is a set order to the world. Ferrers, we are told, had realized that 'the world is not in sympathy with men of ideas who do not prophesy smooth things'. Since he could not return to youth, he had decided he would 'spend his life in company with high hopes and smiling faces'.[107]

The problem with Ferrers is that he is more interested in deconstructing the cultural and intellectual ideas than in building a forward-looking agenda. At one point in the book he participates in a school debate and tells the boys about how Mackenzie's *Sinister Street* 'smashes up everything [and] shows the shallowness of our education',[108] but he gives no idea of how a smashed up system might be rebuilt. One older boy remarks that Ferrers is a 'revolutionary' when 'A gradual change is what is needed'.[109] However Gordon, who is fourteen or fifteen, enthusiastically adopts Ferrers's ideals and reiterates 'Byron's sweeping confession of faith, "I have simplified my politics into an utter detestation of all existing governments"'. Waugh comments that Gordon

> had yet to read the essay in which Matthew Arnold says that 'Byron shattered, inevitably shattered himself against the black rock of British Philistinism.' He was at present so full of hope. The Poetry of Revolt colored his imagination to such a degree that he saw himself standing alone and triumphant amid the wreck of the world he had overthrown.[110]

---

103 Ibid., pp. 147, 152.
104 Ibid., p. 206.
105 Ibid., pp. 239, 220.
106 Ibid., p. 99.
107 Ibid., p. 183.
108 Ibid., p. 171.
109 Ibid., p. 174.
110 Ibid., p. 179.

Gordon is stuck in a 'Jekyll and Hyde' situation, with one 'soul-side [...] for the world' and one 'for art – and Ferrers',[111] and discovers that Ferrers's anarchic individualism cannot help him find a political or social mission. Waugh comments that if Gordon had read Arnold's *Rugby Chapel*, 'he might have recognized himself in the pilgrim who had saved only himself, while the world was full of others [...] who were "bringing their sheep in their hand"'.[112] In his haste to destroy all previous ideas and systems, Ferrers dismisses the progressive elements of Arnoldianism and Muscular Christianity that might potentially be of use.

When he realizes that war is imminent, Ferrers at last feels he has discovered his cause, proclaiming that war will purge England of vulgarity and 'old outworn traditions', and bring about an 'Elizabethan'-style reawakening after a hundred-year 'slumber'.[113] Gordon, however, is not anxious to join the war himself. After a brief period of moral anarchy and a homosexual relationship, he decides 'with Sophocles that "Not to be born is best"'[114] and begins to think that Ferrers's principles are no better than those of militarists who disenfranchise the young and use them as pawns in battle. Gordon's friend explains to him that the literature Ferrers uses to inspire his boys is all part of the seductive 'tinsel of war'. The older generation will benefit from the Philistinism and Commercialism war encourages, while the young will be 'sacrificed'.[115] Unable to conceive of any way to protest against the war and with 'no philosophy', Gordon chooses a 'final surrender' to Catholicism,[116] which offers him the option of approaching life from an aesthetic, religious viewpoint instead of an intellectual one, and enables the deferral of moral responsibility to a higher authority.

The Loom of Youth, therefore, portrays the evolution of a nihilist. The war has finally broken the bonds between adults and adolescents and the latter no longer trust the former to have their interests at heart. Even creative disciplines such as literature, which had been hailed by Farrar and the liberal educationalists as the antidote to an authoritarian and alienating classical curriculum, had been used to coerce boys. The war, breaking bonds of trust between adults and adolescents, turns young people into the ultimate deconstructionists. The fate of Waugh's generation is to 'analyze its emotions, dissect its pleasures, till in the end it finds nothing left',[117] which is probably why *The Times Literary Supplement* described the book as 'destructive rather than constructive'.[118] This kind of conclusion must have made it very difficult for any adult ever to contemplate writing the old, didactic, reforming style of public school story again.

---

111 Ibid., p. 223.
112 Ibid., p. 241.
113 Ibid., pp. 255, 257.
114 Ibid., p. 285.
115 Ibid., p. 293.
116 Ibid., p. 307.
117 Ibid., p. 328.
118 July 26 1917, quoted in Musgrave.

Waugh's book offered little to those hoping to find a new direction for education in terms of civics and citizenship. Now that he had opened the way for boys to comment on their education, however, two boys did come forward to suggest how schools could improve. Martin Browne's *A Dream of Youth* was published a year after *The Loom* as 'An Etonian's reply to "The Loom of Youth"'. Shortly after Browne's book, there also appeared *The Heart of a Schoolboy* by the pseudonymous Jack Hood, in similar vein. Both pose as apologists for the public school system, dutifully defending the institutions to which they belong, but in actuality use their platform to suggest changes that could benefit the system rather than to refute Waugh.

For Browne, as for most of the writers I have discussed, school is a miniature state that exists inside the more menacing English state apparatus, protecting its inhabitants from the exploitations of the outside world. Browne commends the public school system at its best for striking an ideal balance between 'law' and 'personal freedom'.[119] This freedom is 'the agent which produces the character of the leader'. It is also 'the very root of all true education'; 'Only if he is free, as far as is possible for his safety,' argues Browne, 'can a boy develop himself'.[120] Such freedom can only be achieved if the school is independent of the government. The 'Lycée' system of the continent, run by the state, destroys liberty and promotes conformity. 'If the Public Schools be accused of producing too uniform a type,' asks Browne, 'how much more must a system of the *Lycée* character do so?'[121] The problem with state schooling, according to Browne, is that it would interfere with the political impartiality of schools and with the growth of new initiatives for stimulating training in citizenship and political awareness. Browne comments that

> There has been a great deal of stir in the school of late, in every direction, both among masters and boys. The foundation of the Political Society for debate, with a paper attached to it, shows the interest evinced in contemporary problems by quite a large number both of boys and masters.[122]

Browne seems concerned that if too much is known in the outside world about these innovations, they will be thwarted. 'To speak in detail of her educational reform', he remarks, 'might injure a work carried on by quiet steps; suffice it to say that it goes forward'.[123]

Superficially, Browne addresses all the usual criticisms which critics of the public school system had been making since the early Victorian period: lack of work ethic, conflict between boys and masters and the inadequacy of the curriculum. Browne agrees that Classics produces 'mental stagnation' and 'repression of

---

119 Browne 1918, p. 24.
120 Ibid., p. 23.
121 Ibid., p. 24.
122 Ibid., p. 26.
123 Ibid., pp. 26–27.

youthful energy of spirit', but argues that it nonetheless teaches the fundamentals of civil society, because Rome is the 'parent of all civilized European nations'.[124] Sciences, although valuable, he says, do not 'bring out human character'[125] and therefore are of secondary use in the inculcation of citizenship. Political, economic and labor relations, however, are fundamental fields of study.[126] He remarks

> That boys are interested in these matters is amply proved by the intense enthusiasm for such classes where they have been started, and by the foundation of such societies as the 'Eton Political Society', and of such papers as *A Public School Looks at the World* (from Repton) and *The Eton Review*.[127]

Hiding under a superficial conservatism and pretending to hold the official line against Waugh, Browne constantly reiterates his call for political education and intellectual freedom in schools.

Browne, and later Hood, present an entirely new take on moral education. Browne argues that all boys are 'good chaps at heart' and that any 'sordid immorality' that exists is not to be blamed on them.[128] Schoolboy 'immorality', he scolds his audience, 'is primarily your fault!' He continues: 'if you treat the state of national morals which has lately been revealed with the prudish cowardice so far characteristic of your dealings with it, you cannot expect anything very much better from the Public Schools'.[129] In blaming problems in schoolboy morality on adults, Browne does something that very few school commentators and writers do. Most writers tend to see the adolescent as an isolated entity, generating his own problems and immoralities. Hardly anybody suggests that boys who have witnessed 'immorality' or violence in the home may be responsible for introducing it to school. Browne resents the emphasis placed on boys and schools as being responsible for the nation's ills. He asks, 'Are all parents perfect? Do not immoral men and women ever have sons whom they send to Public Schools?' Then he explains that 'some boys do inherit bad qualities (besides physical imperfections) from their parents, as well as good ones'.[130] He remarks, moreover, that boyhood 'immorality', whether of the subversive social and political type encouraged by the Penny Dreadfuls[131] or of the more explicit sexual type, is a phenomenon blown out of proportion by a media that thrives on sensation. In the preface to Hood's book, E.A. Burroughs, a Fellow of Hertford College, Oxford, makes the same point:

---

124 Ibid., pp. 30, 38.
125 Ibid., p. 37.
126 Ibid., p. 42.
127 Ibid., p. 43.
128 Ibid., p. 61.
129 Ibid., pp. 59–60.
130 Hood 1919, p. 7.
131 Ibid., p. 10.

what is complained of is the fault neither of the Public School system, nor of magisterial negligence, nor of special depravity in boys of this class, but mainly of our common British public opinion on sexual questions. The public tolerates in society and everywhere else, and encourages through the theatre, the cinema, and the press, a tone which it is then shocked to find reflected in the Public Schools.[132]

Browne argues that 'immorality' could be dramatically reduced in schools if boys were better educated about matters of reproduction, from a woman's point of view. Such an education, he says, would improve their regard for women. He asks that boys be given information and, following that, privacy and trust: 'Give a boy all the information and help he wants, and then trust him, as the natural thing for a gentleman, to keep his honor, and you are absolutely safe with him'.[133] The latent chivalry inherent in boys can then be brought out, he says, by the 'thought of the future wife and children'.[134] Having more contact with women connected to school would also improve things, since school 'is a very soulless existence, with no love and no homely feeling in it'.[135]

Hood's *The Heart of a Schoolboy* (1919) was also written when the author was seventeen. E.A. Burroughs, Hood's editor, dwells in his introduction on how the book's '*naïveté*' is a 'guarantee' that it is 'the work of a real boy'.[136] The charm of adolescent work is that it has an authenticity of utterance that adults cannot reach:

> it is pleasant to be reassured by one who is still at school that the romantic and idealistic side is indeed so strong, though often so inarticulate, at what we grown-ups are apt to call 'the awkward age.' The moral is that, instead of taking a boy's inexpressiveness as a reason for not trying to express ourselves to him, we should rather go the further to meet him ... – and *don't* play down to what might seem to be his only line of interest because about the others he is still too confused and self-conscious to talk.[137]

Hood, like Browne, plays up his modesty, conservatism and fidelity to the status quo: 'I have no claim' he says, 'higher than any other to write'.[138] He is writing, he says, because no adult critic has defended the public schools against the accusations of Waugh.[139] Hood's initial condemnation of Waugh, however, soon abates. His chapter 'Romanticism', which deals with poetry, quotes Waugh favorably. The real focus of Hood's attack is the popular media, whose noxious influence could be countered if schools nurtured boys' critical faculties so that they

---

132 Ibid., pp. xii–xiii.
133 Browne 1918, pp. 74–75.
134 Ibid., p. 69.
135 Hood 1919, p. 75.
136 Ibid., p. ix.
137 Ibid., pp. ix–x.
138 Ibid., p. 4.
139 Ibid., p. 2.

could defend themselves against attacks on the school system and on boyhood morality in general. Cloaking his call to be allowed a public voice by quoting Newbolt's *Vitae Lampada*, he argues that it is only 'fair play' to allow boys to fight back against the moral slurs directed at them.[140] 'Britannia' (the name Hood gives to public opinion and the popular media) corrupts boys with 'trashy novels' and turns 'gold to dross',[141] but all the while calls on the state to regulate boys' behavior more closely. The establishment, economically wedded to the media, allows the circulation of corrupting literature even while condemning the young for reading it. The most important thing in education, therefore, Hood remarks, is the development of taste, which is eroded by mass culture.[142] Hood asks for instruction in modern art, literature and music as an antidote, commenting that public schools must clean up their act before a Labour government gets in and cleans it up for them.

Hood also defends adolescents against biological reductionism. The boy is not a 'soulless animal' but is essentially a poet, hidden under 'an exterior perhaps rough or timid or "ordinary"'.[143] This comment is a veiled attack on sociologists, educationalists and politicians interested in National Efficiency as well as against those who favor more state control of the public schools. Hood conveys a sense that scientists overemphasize the physical aspects of adolescence at the expense of the aesthetic and spiritual and suggests that there is a danger of the state using these theories in the reform of public schools. He seems to be aware of the work of writers such as C.B. Andrews and bitterly opposes it. Andrews had favored state control of education as the best way to put scientists in charge and to train boys according to theories of bodily development and sexual 'feeling'.[144] Hood condemns this all-prevailing emphasis on 'immorality' and the scientific obsession with bodily health, especially those that try to instill morality through fear by using threats of physical degeneration. Such approaches are counterproductive, since if adults warn boys that something is physically dangerous, they will be all the more likely to do it:

> If we funked anything dangerous, we should never look ourselves in the face again. If they would tell us that God has entrusted us with a power to keep for the future, that would make all the difference. *If a boy is trusted he always rises to the trust.*[145]

Hood's argument is essentially a plea for autonomy. If a boy is left alone, he will behave. Browne makes the same point.[146] In any case, he explains, boys nowadays

---

140 Ibid., p. 29.
141 Ibid., pp. 37, 49.
142 Ibid., p. 37.
143 Ibid., pp. 34–35.
144 Andrews 1912, pp. 42–43.
145 Hood 1919, p. 51.
146 Browne 1918, p. 74.

can see behind the manipulative attempts of adults to instill morality using religion or science. From the moment a boy first observes the disparity between the Bible and science – both of which he is told to respect, but which are fundamentally opposed – he will inevitably ask 'Is it all a great hoax to keep me straight?'[147] Hood's plea is clear; he wants moral and civic education to be a dynamic, two-way process, a conversation between boy and master in which each listens to the other and in which the boy's rational faculties are respected. It is time, he argues, to abandon the process of emotional manipulation that currently dominates the educational field.

In this brief moment of history when boys had an opportunity to express themselves publicly, therefore, they were clear about what they wanted. They felt humiliated by the way in which social science treated them and resented the idea that their private lives should be judged on different terms from those of adults. They wanted to be engaged in public debate and to be educated in political ideas, and they were deeply critical of the popular press and its impact on educational attitudes. Victor Gollancz wholeheartedly adopted their ideas in his manifesto for political education in public schools and S.P.B. Mais argued that boys should have more autonomy in their education. But for various reasons, the schemes dreamed of by Mais and Gollancz never materialized. The postwar period saw no great outpouring of adolescent literary effort to show educationalists the way of the future. There are a number of reasons why the envisaged revolution never happened. Many boys may simply not have had the willpower to carry on campaigning after seeing so many of their generation die. Cyril Connolly, for instance, said that Eton boys, encouraged by adult freethinkers, developed a decadent culture of art for art's sake type of aestheticism as a reaction to National Efficiency and the war, rejecting any engagement with national affairs. Thus, when Brian Howard, the model for Anthony Blanche in Evelyn Waugh's *Brideshead Revisited*, published a decadent magazine entitled *The Eton Candle*, 'those suspect old Etonians, Aldous Huxley, [and] Osbert and Sacheverell Sitwell', as well as Max Beerbohm, contributed.[148]

There were other reasons why political expression among the young was actively discouraged. With the likelihood of a Labour government being elected just over the horizon, moves were made to stifle political activism in the state school population. Lloyd George's government scored a goal for reactionary literary education when, in 1921, it commissioned a Departmental Committee chaired by the public school poet Henry Newbolt to write a report into English teaching in state schools. The Newbolt Report proposed that the canon of English Literature should be used as a way of training potentially revolutionary working-class secondary school students to develop a sentimental, protective attachment

---

147 Hood 1919, p. 80.
148 Connolly 1983, p. 265. Esmond Romilly also published *Out of Bounds: The Education of Giles Romilly and Esmond Romilly* in 1935 while running a refuge for public school recusants, but he was definitely not given a warm welcome by the established system.

to the status quo.[149] The *Times Educational Supplement* hoped literary study would quell 'the disquieting symptoms which are to be discerned in our modern society'[150] by instilling a sense of nationhood through the common shared cross-class values of literature. English Literature was again to be used as a means of instilling quietist values in the young, in the tradition of Martineau, Farrar, and Talbot Baines Reed.

The literature of adolescence seems, therefore, to have lost much of its potential to be a force for creating active citizens. To the modern day, literature about adolescent life has a tendency to replicate the nihilism of Waugh and Leslie and the dystopian Lunn, who themselves reiterated the fatalistic, introverted pessimism of Farrar's *Eric*. Major late-twentieth-century works still tended to portray adolescents as socially dysfunctional, a-political or fascistic, preoccupied with their own private (often sexual) affairs and self-destructive. Anthony Burgess's *A Clockwork Orange*, Colin McInnes's *Absolute Beginners*, J.D. Salinger's *The Catcher in the Rye* and perhaps also William Golding's *Lord of the Flies* spring to mind. Burgess's anarchic Alex even goes through the same sudden reformation of character when he reaches adulthood as Farrar's naughty boys do. Film has joined in this trend, most notably with Peter Weir's *Dead Poets' Society* (1989). Echoing Farrar, this film offers English Literature as an antidote to an illiberal curriculum but again, the consequence of self-actualization is death and boys fail to find a way of resisting the educational choices made for them by self-interested adults. The most overwhelmingly popular recent narrative of adolescence, J.K. Rowling's *Harry Potter* series, takes the schoolboy protagonist out of the real world entirely, seeking supernatural, rather than rational, answers to problems. The liberal tradition of adolescence as a time when rational, civic and political thought seems to have been lost. In a post-Freudian world dogged by global conflict, in which reason itself seems always to be prey to the irrational, perhaps adults feel too insecure about their own sense of reason to investigate the reasoning powers of the young. This despair is perhaps most painfully demonstrated in *Lord of the Flies*, where Piggy and Ralph long for rational 'grown-ups' to save them, not realizing that the adult world is engaged in a conflict little more reasonable than the one happening among the boys. Few grown-ups, though, have been as willing to admit that adults have deficient rational faculties, preferring to classify irrationality as the preserve of the young.

Conclusion

In the course of this book, I have shown how the ideas of adolescence depicted in public school literature were formed under the influence of numerous, often competing, ideologies. Of all the concerns that adults expressed about adolescent

---

149 See Bhattacharyya 1991, pp. 4–19 and King 1987, pp. 14–37.
150 King 1987, p. 17.

education and the needs it was supposed to fulfill, however, two seemingly contradictory ideas emerge as dominant themes. The first idea is that adolescents somehow hold the key to social progress. For writers such as Thomas Hughes, adolescence was where the ideas which would eventually grow into the political philosophies of the next generation began to germinate. A couple of generations later, adolescence began to be seen as a crucial stage in the eugenic progress of the race. The other idea present in most of the work I have discussed here is a sense of a deep need to control adolescents in the interests of creating social stability. The young are a focus of political unease and those wishing to defend the status quo explore a variety of control mechanisms by which dissent among the young can be suppressed. Public school writers often struggle to balance the need for adolescents to have free space to experiment with the (perceived) necessity of controlling them and the balance often tips towards the principle of control. Hughes's *Tom Brown*, which places a great deal of trust in the ability of boys to evolve progressive social ideas without intensive adult interference, is often perceived to be the ur-text of the public school story. However, later authors rarely portray boys as having the freedom to indulge in the kind of socio-political play enjoyed by Hughes's boys. It is the quietist, inward-looking world of F.W. Farrar, where boys who rebel or show initiative meet a tragic and salutary end, which authors of adolescent narratives seem inclined to replicate even to the present day.

Arguably, the model of citizenship promoted by public school writers changed through the course of the period discussed here. Citizenship went from an active paradigm, based on the idea that the individual adolescent was training to fight for his political beliefs in the real world, to a passive model, where duty and obedience were the priorities. One reason for this withdrawal from ideas of active citizenship was probably that the proportion of young people spending their adolescence in full-time education rather than in work was increasing, prompting fears that hitherto powerless sectors of the community might demand a share in the political process. Another reason was that the middle classes, having achieved the power and status they desired in the early Victorian period (in other words, having implemented 'progress'), wished, in the later nineteenth century, to consolidate their power base rather than to facilitate further dramatic change. In effect, the function of adolescence changed. It was no longer an experience reserved for a tiny elite who needed to learn how to run the country, but a process through which a larger number of young people (although still a minority) were educated to maintain the national and imperial status quo. The adolescent boy himself therefore became, in ideological terms, an essentially different creature from what he had been before; in particular, it could no longer be suggested that he was inherently political or revolutionary. By the time of Stanley Hall, the myth had evolved that the adolescent was inherently naïve, unable to understand the economic and social intricacies of the adult world and blinded by the overpowering process of his or her own physical development. Adults who believed that adolescents were essentially irrational could therefore feel justified in dismissing any ideas young people had which ran contrary their own. In the most conservative narratives of adolescence, the Promethean boy who attempts to initiate himself prematurely into adult mysteries faces physical and mental destruction. Originality and creativity, the roots of progress that were celebrated by most early and mid-nineteenth-century writers, became dangerous qualities.

Perhaps it is partly because ideas of radical progress were deemed inflammatory that the serious boys' public school novel, which laid so much stress on aesthetic and political development, fell out of fashion towards the 1920s, leaving only popular, comic private school stories behind. Frank Richards, author of *Billy Bunter*, a good example of the comic, uncontroversial private school story, said he hoped that, thanks to his work, any potential Chekov reading *The Magnet* (the paper in which *Bunter* was published) would turn into a 'Bob Cherry':[151] harmless, naïve, and socially impotent. Thus, as the British school system expanded to embrace a greater social mix and co-education gradually became the norm, but the boys' school story ossified into facile, a-political *Billy Bunter*-ism. To be sure, the girls' school story came into its own as the boys' school story faded and could be said to have addressed empowerment and citizenship issues, but it continued to focus, as the boys' works had done, on a small privileged elite. Moreover, citizenship for women in the real world involved working alongside men and competing for political power in a system devised by men, not escaping into a male-free bubble. The single-gender 'little world' of school no longer reflected the real-world political arena. When all is said and done, the combination of real inclusivity and a commitment to political citizenship issues has practically eluded the school story as a genre.[152]

The adolescent relationship to citizenship remains fraught with contradictions. Although adolescence is, in many ways, a prelude to mature citizenship, adolescents are still often understood as being somehow essentially anti-social. When I asked various acquaintances to suggest which ideas they associated with the adolescent period, they invariably alluded to crime, rebellion, violence, promiscuity, drugs, alcohol and depression. Adolescents were thought to be self-absorbed and introverted and to display the opposite qualities to those associated with conscientious citizenship. The belated introduction in 2002 of formal citizenship classes to the UK National Curriculum seems not to have changed this general view. The contrast between the nascent democratic subject envisaged by campaigners for citizenship education and the 'abject' adolescent of the popular imagination was spectacularly displayed in 2003 during British demonstrations

---

151 Richards 1940, p. 355.

152 There is one possible exception. In 1978, Phil Redmond launched the BBC's *Grange Hill*, a long-running series about a London comprehensive school which has dealt with issues such as drug abuse, disability and sexuality and which is probably the most widely received 'school story' of the post-*Tom Brown* age. It could be argued, however, that *Grange Hill* continues to concentrate on personalist 'youth' issues rather than exploring active citizenship, but this would be a topic for a different book. Musgrave 2000 also mentions works by E.W. Hildick and Geoffrey Trease as dealing with state schools (p. 270).

against the Iraq War. Many journalists viewed adolescent protests against the war with cynicism, unable to believe that a younger generation which is supposed to be self-absorbed and preoccupied by private issues could have sincerely-held views on the subject. The *Daily Telegraph* commented that 'By protesting, [teenagers] could play truant while at the same time feeling safely rebellious, vaguely political and fashionably"aware"'.[153] David Hart, of the National Association of Head Teachers, implied that young people did not know enough about the subject to have an opinion by remarking that they 'might benefit more from learning about the causes of war than by demonstrating against it'.[154] The protesters were anxious to refute the claim that they were not making a reasoned stance and found it ironical that they were required to take lessons in citizenship while being denied the prerogatives of citizens. Seventeen-year-old Kierra Box, organizer of 'Hands Up For Peace', complained that adults try to focus the attention of young people away from political ideas and onto personal issues. She remarked:

> The educational establishment pushes you all the time: 'You should be interested in having debates about sex, about drugs, because that's what we need you to be aware of. You must be informed about these young people's issues'. But then there was the firemen's strike, the teachers' pay dispute, tuition fees and the war, all of which are far more relevant to our lives. Yet we're told to ignore all of that, and just concentrate on not getting pregnant, not taking an overdose and getting a job with good prospects.[155]

Latterly, there has been a backlash among some educationalists against the idea that young people lack the intellectual skills to cope with politics, something that demonstrates how changeable our understanding of juvenile consciousness is. Liz Wood has remarked that even small children are capable of making complex decisions and that 'benign and patronizing learning environments' deny them the active citizenship that is their right.[156] Jean Rudduck comments that the 'bracketing out' of children's voices from social and political processes 'is founded upon an outdated view of childhood which fails to acknowledge children's capacity to reflect on issues affecting their lives'.[157] Moreover, as Adrian Furnham and Barrie Gunter remark, there has actually been very little research done on the development of political awareness.[158] Ironically, what research has been done may not actually promote the political participation of the young. Recently, in *The Primal Teen: What the New Discoveries About the Teenage Brain Can Tell Us About Our Kids* (2004), Barbara Strauch has used neuroscience to argue that teenagers' brains

---

153 'Children's crusade' 2003.
154 See BBC News, March 21 2003, available on http://news.bbc.co.uk/2/hi/uk_news/education/2869147.stm
155 Brooks 2003.
156 Liz Wood in Holden 1998, p. 33.
157 Quoted in Holden 1998, p. 17.
158 Funham 1983, p. 28.

are still developing and are incapable of what adults would recognize as rational thought.[159] The debate will no doubt continue.

Adolescence has developed during the last two centuries into an enormously powerful metaphor for general social progress or decay. It is hard, therefore, to know which of society's commonly held impressions of adolescence are imaginary, which are based on objective observations of adolescent behavior and which are based on adults' (often faulty) memory of their own adolescent years. The struggle to represent the 'real' adolescent subject is one constant battle that links the Victorian period with our own. Repeated efforts by sociologists and authors to gain a deep knowledge of adolescent behavior and to document adolescent life with accuracy has rarely, however, involved adults seeking information from boys and, even more rarely, from girls. In a brief period at the beginning of the twentieth century, upper-class male adolescents were allowed to speak for themselves. That liberty, however – the result, probably, of guilt and pity felt by adults towards young men on whom a monstrous ordeal had been inflicted – turned out to be very short lived. Adolescent publication, at least in terms of work that challenges the social and educational status quo, seems to have gone the same way as 'homes fit for heroes' and all the other good things promised in the aftermath of the First World War.[160] It failed to materialize in the social and economic tumult of the 1920s. Perhaps, however, critical writing by young people will one day make a comeback and young people will finally be allowed to contribute to the educational debate and make their needs and opinions felt in a truly two-way educational process, whether this be through fiction or autobiography (as in the early twentieth century), or through open debate. In 2002, 13-year old Luke Jackson, who has Asperger Syndrome, published the brilliant *Freaks, Geeks and Asperger Syndrome: A User Guide to Adolescence*[161], a work which tackled complex issues surrounding the treatment of one specific adolescent group by society and the educational system. But then again, Jackson is very gifted and possibly the very reason he is given space to speak is that he is exceptional (at the time of writing his book, he had a reading age of over eighteen[162]). There is no knowing what kind of social change or hiatus would have to occur in order for the rest of the adolescent population to have their opinions sought. But until we solicit these opinions, our understanding of adolescence will remain as it has been since writing about adolescence began: an adult fantasy built from half-recollected memories and founded on adult needs.

---

159 Strauch 2003.
160 It has been pointed out to me that the *Eragon* books by Christopher Paolini are by an adolescent, about adolescents and for adolescents, but, since they are fantasy works that offer fantasy answers to problems, they cannot really be seen as hard social criticism.
161 Jackson 2002.
162 Newnham 2002.

Bibliography

Primary Sources

'*Adam Bede*', *Blackwood's Edinburgh Magazine*, 85.522 (April 1859), pp. 490–504.
Adams, H.C., *Schoolboy Honour: A Tale of Halminster College* (London: Routledge, 1861).
Adams, H.C., *Wykehamica: A History of Winchester College and Commoners, from the Foundation to the Present Day* (Oxford: James Parker, 1878).
Adams, W. and H.C., *The Cherry Stones, or Charlton School: A Tale for Youth* (London: F. and J. Rivington, 1851).
'Against Boys', *Chambers' Edinburgh Journal*, 39 (March 7, 1863), pp. 145–47.
A.L.O.E. (C.M. Tucker), *The Young Pilgrim: A Tale Illustrative of 'The Pilgrim's Progress'* (London: T. Nelson and Sons, 1858).
Andrews, C.B., *An Introduction to the Study of Adolescent Education* (London: Rebman, 1912).
Anstey, F., *Vice Versa: A Lesson to Fathers* (London: Smith, Elder and Co., 1905).
Armstrong, R.A., *Our Duty in the Matter of Social Purity* (London: Social Purity Alliance, 1885).
Arnold, M., *Democratic Education* (Ann Arbour: University of Michigan Press, 1962).
Arnold, T., *Sermons Preached in the Chapel of Rugby School* (London: B. Fellowes, 1833).
Arnold, T., *Introductory Lectures on Modern History* (London: B. Fellowes, 1843).
Augustine, *Confessions*, Books I–IV, ed. G. Clark (Cambridge: Cambridge University Press, 1995).
Ballantyne, R.M., *The Coral Island* (Ware: Wordsworth Classics, 1993).
Barnett, M.G., *Young Delinquents* (London: Macmillan, 1913).
'B. Bouverie' (W. Gladstone), *The Eton Miscellany* (Eton: 1827).
Benson, E.F., *David Blaize* (London: Hodder and Stoughton, 1916).
Benson, A.C., *Fasti Etonenses: A Biographical History of Eton* (Eton: Ingalton Drake, 1899).
Bentham, J., *Chrestomathia* (Oxford: Oxford University Press, 1983).
Blunden, E., Youngman Carter, P., Bennett, E. and Morpurgo, J.E. (eds), *The Christ's Hospital Book* (London: H. Hamilton, 1953).
'Bouncing Boys', *All the Year Round*, 14 (August 5, 1865), pp. 38–40.
'Boy Monsters', *All the Year Round*, 19 (1868), pp. 193–95.
'Boy, Only Boy', *The Academy*, 57 (October 21, 1899).
'Boys', *Saturday Review*, 53 (April 22, 1882), p. 492.

Brabazon, R. (Lord Meath) (ed.), *Essays on Duty and Discipline: A Series of Papers on the Training of Children in Relation to Social and National Welfare* (London: Cassell, 1910).
Brinsley-Richards, J., *Seven Years at Eton, 1857–1864* (London: R. Bentley and Son, 1883).
Brookes, J., *Manliness: Hints to Young Men* (London: John Blackwood, 1859).
Brooks, L., 'Kid Power', *The Guardian* (April 26, 2003), p. 42.
Brown, H.S., *Manliness and Other Sermons* (Edinburgh: Oliphant, 1889).
Browne, M., *A Dream of Youth* (London: Longmans, 1918).
Butler, S., *The Way of All Flesh* (London: J.M. Dent, 1946).
Caird, J., *Christian Manliness: A Sermon* (Glasgow: James Maclehose, 1871).
Carlyle, T., *On Heroes, Hero Worship and the Heroic in History*, ed. C. Niemeyer (Lincoln: University of Nebraska Press, 1966).
Carlyle, T., *Past and Present* (London: Chapman and Hall, 1843).
'Children's Crusade', *Daily Telegraph* (March 22, 2003).
Churchill, R.E.H., *The Praying School-Boy: A Brief Memoir of Robert Ernest Houghton Churchill by His Stepmother* (London: Elliot Stock, 1869).
Clarendon Commission, *Report of Her Majesty's Commissioners Appointed to Inquire into the Revenues and Management of Certain Colleges and Schools and the Studies Pursued and Instruction Given Therein* (London: 1864), vol. 2.
Cobbett, W., *Advice to Young Men, and (incidentally) to Young Women in the Middle and Higher Ranks of Life* (London: The Author, 1829).
'Coelebs' (E.A. Carlyon), 'Peoples Boys', *Macmillan's Magazine*, 23 (March 23, 1871), pp. 432–35.
Coke, D.F.T., *The Bending of a Twig* (London: Humphrey Milford, 1906).
Coleridge, A.D., *Eton in the Forties, by An Old Colleger* (London: Richard Bentley, 1896).
Coleridge, J.T., *Public School Education: A Lecture* (London: John Murray, 1860).
Coleridge, S.T., *On the Constitution of the Church and State*, ed. John Colmer (Princeton: Princeton University Press, 1976).
Connolly, C., *Enemies of Promise* (London: Andre Deutsch, 1983).
Cowper, W., 'Tirocinium: Or, A Review of Schools', in H.S. Milford (ed.), *The Complete Poetical Works of William Cowper* (London: H. Milford, 1913).
Craig, A.R., *Strictures on the Practice of Corporal Punishments in Schools, and the Means of Preventing them by a Course of Moral Discipline* (London: Simpkin and Marshall, 1844).
Cust, L., *A History of Eton College* (London: Duckworth 1899).
Darwin, C., *The Descent of Man, and Selection in Relation to Sex* (London: John Murray, 1871).
Day, S.P., *Juvenile Crime: Its Causes, Character and Cure* (London: J.F. Hope, 1858).
(?Day, Thomas), *The History of a Schoolboy* (London: John Stockdale, 1788).
Dickens, C., *Great Expectations* (London: Collins, 1976).

Disraeli, B., *Coningsby* (Harmondsworth: Penguin, 1989).
The Dying School Boy: By His Tutor (London: 1863).
Edgeworth, M. and R.L., *On Practical Education*, 3 vols (London: J. Johnson, 1801).
Edgeworth, M., *The Parent's Assistant* (London: J. Johnson, 1800), vol. 6.
Eliot, G., *The Mill on the Floss* (Oxford: Oxford University Press, 1996).
Ellis, H., *Studies in the Psychology of Sex: Volume II, Sexual Inversion* (Philadelphia: Davis, 1931).
E.L.P, *Schoolboy Morality: An Address to Mothers* (London: Social Purity Alliance, 1888).
'The English Boy of the Future', *Once a Week*, 7 (August 16. 1862), pp. 203–8.
E.P., *Solomon's Precept: Or the Power of the Rod. A Tale of the Flogging System* (London: 1861).
Farrar, F.W., *On Some Defects in Public School Education* (London: 1867).
Farrar, F.W. (ed.), *Essays on a Liberal Education* (London: Macmillan, 1868).
Farrar, F.W., *In The Days of Thy Youth: Sermons on Practical Subjects Preached at Marlborough College, from 1871 to 1876* (London: 1876).
Farrar, F.W., *Social and Present-Day Questions* (London: Hodder and Stoughton, 1891).
Farrar, F.W., *The Young Man Master of Himself* (London: J. Nisbet, 1896).
Farrar, F.W., *The Bible and the Child: The Higher Criticism and the Teaching of the Young* (London: J. Clarke, 1897).
Farrar, F.W., *Eric: Or, Little by Little*, 6th ed. (London: A. and C. Black, 1899).
Farrar, F.W., *St Winifred's: Or the World of School* (London: Ward, Lock, 1910).
Farrar, R., *The Life of Frederic William Farrar* (London: James Nisbet, 1904).
Faulkner, R., *The Grave of Emma Vale at Havering Bower* (London: 1859).
A Few Words of Advice to a Public School Boy by an Assistant Master (London: 1846).
Figgis, B.J., *Manliness, Womanliness, Godliness* (London: 1885).
Findlay, J.J., *Arnold of Rugby: His School Life and Contributions to Education* (Cambridge: Cambridge University Press, 1897).
Firth, J. D'E., *Winchester College* (London: Winchester Publications, 1949).
Fitzgerald, P.H., *School Days at Saxonhurst: By 'One of the Boys'* (Edinburgh: 1867).
Freeman, R.M., *Steady and Strong; Or, a Friend in Need* (London: Griffith and Farran, 1891).
Gilkes, A.H., *Boys and Masters: A Story of School Life* (London: Longmans, 1887).
Goethe, J.W. von, *Wilhelm Meisters Lehrjahre* (München: Deutscher Taschenbuch Verlag, 1981).
Gollancz, V. and Somervell, D., *Political Education at a Public School* (London: Collins, 1918).
Griffith, G., *The Life and Adventures of George Wilson, a Foundation Scholar* (London: 1854).

Hall, G. Stanley, *Adolescence: Its Psychology and its Relations to Physiology, Anthropology, Sociology, Sex, Crime, Religion and Education* (New York: D. Appleton, 1925).
Hayward, F.H., *Day and Evening Schools; Their Management and Organisation, with Special Reference to the Problems of Adolescent Education* (London: Ralph, Holland, 1910).
Hazelwood, J.E., *The Knight of Purity: Some Thoughts for Schoolboys* (Leeds: Inchbold and Beck, 1888).
Hemyng, B., *Butler Burke at Eton* (London: 1865).
Hemyng, B., *Eton School Days, or Recollections of an Etonian*, 2nd edn (London: 1870).
Hemyng, B., *Jack Harkaway's Schooldays* (Chicago: Donohue, c.1880).
'The Hill', *Times Literary Supplement* (April 28, 1905), p. 137.
Hime, M.C., *Schoolboys' Special Immorality* (London: J. and A. Churchill, 1899).
Hitchman, F., 'Penny Fiction', *Quarterly Review*, 171 (1890).
Hood, J., *The Heart of a Schoolboy* (London: Longmans, 1919).
Hope, A.R. (A.R.H. Moncrieff), *Schoolboy Stories* (Edinburgh: W.P. Nimmo, 1888).
Hopkins, T.M., 'Corporal Punishment in Schools', *Westminster Review*, 152 (1899), pp. 460–63.
Hughes, T., *The Manliness of Christ* (London: Macmillan, 1879).
Hughes, T., *Tom Brown at Oxford* (London: Macmillan, 1897).
Hughes, T., *Tom Brown's Schooldays* (Oxford: Oxford University Press, 1989).
Hunt, L., *Essays and Sketches*, ed. R. Brimley Johnson (London: Oxford University Press, 1912).
Ingle, J., *The Decease of a School-Fellow: A Warning to the Living* (London: Ely, 1858).
Jermyn, H., *The Adolescence of Aubrey* (London: Mills and Boon, 1913).
Johnstone, C.F., *Recollections of Eton, by an Etonian* (London: 1870).
Joyce, J., *A Portrait of the Artist as a Young Man* (Harmondsworth: Penguin, 1968).
'Judicious Kicking', *Saturday Review* (November 23, 1872), pp. 660–61.
Kilner, D., *First Going to School: The Story of Tom Brown and His Sisters* (London: Robert J. Kirkpatrick, 1995)
Kingsley, C., *True Words for Brave Men* (London: 1870).
Kingsley, C., *Health and Education* (London: 1874).
Kingsley, C., *Words of Advice to School-Boys* (London: Simpkin, 1912).
Kipling, R., *Something of Myself* (London: 1937).
Kipling, R., *The Complete Stalky & Co.*, ed. I. Quigly (Oxford: Oxford University Press, 1987).
Kipling, R., *Kim* (Oxford: Oxford University Press, 1998).
Laborde, E.D., *Harrow School: Yesterday and Today* (London: Winchester Publications, 1948).

Lamb, C., *Elia and The Last Essays of Elia* (Oxford: Oxford University Press, 1987).
'Leading Strings', *The Spectator*, 70 (April 22, 1893), pp. 517–18.
Leslie, S., *The Oppidan* (London: Chatto and Windus, 1922).
Locke, J., *Some Thoughts Concerning Education*, in J. Locke, *Works of John Locke* (London: H. Woodfall, 1768), vol. IV.
Lunn, A., *The Harrovians* (London: Methuen, 1913).
Mais, S.P.B., *A Public School in War Time* (London: John Murray, 1916).
Mais, S.P.B., *All the Days of My Life* (London: Hutchinson, 1937).
Mais, S.P.B., *Diary of Public Schoolmaster* (London: Lutterworth Press, 1940).
Malthus, T.R., *An Essay on the Principle of Population: Or, A View of its Past and Present Effects on Human Happiness* (London: J. Johnson, 1803).
Mansford, C.J., *Bully, Fag and Hero, or In Playground and Schoolroom* (London: Jarrold and Sons, 1897).
Markby, T., 'Public Schools', *Contemporary Review* (1867), pp. 149–75.
Marshall, B., *George Brown's Schooldays* (London: Constable, 1946).
Martin, W., *The Hatchups of Me and My Schoolfellows* (London: 1858).
Martineau, H., *The Crofton Boys* (London: G. Routledge and Co., 1856).
Matthews, W., *Adolescence* (Cambridge: 1911).
Melly, G., *School Experiences of a Fag* (London: 1854).
Mill, J., *Schools for All* (Bristol: Thoemmes, 1995, reprint of 1812 edition).
Moncrieff, R.H., *A Book About Dominies: Being the Reflections and Recollections of a Member of the Profession* (Edinburgh: W.P. Nimmo, 1867).
Mudie's Library, *List of Standard and Recent Works in Circulation* (London: 1891).
'Muscular Christianity', *Tait's Edinburgh Magazine*, 25 (1858), pp. 99–102.
Neill, A.S., *Summerhill: A Radical Approach to Education* (London: Victor Gollancz, 1962).
Neuman, B.P., 'Take Care of the Boys', *Fortnightly Review*, 70 (September 1898), pp. 410–21.
Newcomb, H., *Youth and its Duties* (London: 1872).
Newman, F.W., 'Corporal Punishments, and Penal Reformation', *Fraser's Magazine*, 71 (February 1865), pp. 154–65.
Nichols, J., 'The Boy Bishop. – Eton Montem. – Salt Bearers', *Gentleman's Magazine* (June 1814), pp. 537–39.
Norwood, C. and Hope, A.H., *The Higher Education of Boys in England* (London: Murray, 1909).
Observations on the Offensive and Injurious Effect of Corporal Punishment or the Unequal Administration of Penal Justice and in the Pre-Eminent Advantages of the Mild and Reformatory over the Vindictive System of Punishment (London: 1827).
Oldfellow, O. (B.B. Bockett), *Our School: Or, Scraps and Scrapes in Schoolboy Life* (London: 1857).
Orwell, G., 'Boys' Weeklies', in S. Orwell and I. Angus (eds), *The Collected Essays, Journalism and Letters of George Orwell* (London: Secker and Warburg, 1968), vol. I.

'Our Modern Youth', *Fraser's Magazine*, 68 (1863), pp. 115–29.
Oxenden, A., *Emily Nigh or the Sufferer at Rest* (London: 1860).
Paget, S., *Adolescence* (London: Constable, 1917).
'Pain. – Corporal Punishment &c.', *Family Herald* (November 17, 1879), pp. 460–61.
Palmer, E., *Thoughts on Public Schools: A Sermon, Preached at Sutton's Hospital in the Charter-House* (Oxford: 1875).
Parker, E., *Eton in the 'Eighties* (London: Smith, Elder and Co., 1914).
Paterfamilias (M.J. Higgins), *Papers on Public School Education in England, in 1860, Reprinted from the 'Cornhill Magazine' and the 'Edinburgh Review' by Paterfamilias* (London: Smith, Elder and. Co., 1865).
Phillpotts, E., *The Complete Human Boy* (London: Hutchinson, 1930).
Priestley, J., *An Essay on a Course of Liberal Education for Civil and Active Life* (London: Routledge 1992, facsimile of 1765 edition).
'The Public-School Boy', *The Spectator*, 90 (January 17, 1903), pp. 655–69.
'Public Schools', *Fraser's Magazine* (1864), p. 663.
'Public Schools', *Meliora*, 7.26 (1865).
'Public Schools Commission', *Christian Remembrancer* (1865).
'Public School Education', *Fraser's Magazine* (1868), pp. 301–19.
'Public Schools in 1887', *Athenaeum*, 3116 (1887).
'Public Schools in 1888', *Athenaeum*, 3169 (1888).
'Public Schools in 1889', *Athenaeum*, 3221 (1889).
'Public Schools in 1891', *Athenaeum*, 3326 (1891).
'Public Schools of England – Eton', *Edinburgh Review*, 51.101 (April 1830), pp. 65–80.
'Public Schools. – Report of the Commission', *Fraser's Magazine* (1864), 657.
Raymond, E., *Tell England: A Study in a Generation* (London: Cassell, 1926).
Reed, T.B., *The Fifth Form at St.Dominic's* (London: Religious Tract Society, 1887).
Reed, T.B., *The Master of the Shell* (London: Religious Tract Society, 1925).
Religious Tract Society, *The Boys' Own Annual* (London: Religious Tract Society, 1883).
Richards, F., 'Frank Richards Replies to George Orwell', *Horizon*, 5 (May 1940), pp. 346–55.
Richmond, E., *Boyhood to Manhood: A Plea for Ideals* (London: Longman, 1899).
Romilly, Esmond, *Out of Bounds: The Education of Giles Romilly and Esmond Romilly* (London: H. Hamilton, 1935).
Rosevear, W.T., *Christian Manliness and Sympathy* (London: H. Stone, Hamilton, Adams, 1872).
Rousseau, J.J., *Émile*, trans. B. Foxley (London: J. Dent, 1993).
Runciman, J., 'Corporal Punishment in Schools', *Macmillan's Magazine*, 48 (October 1883), pp. 481–84.
R. v. Hopley, 2 F&F 202, 175 ER 1024, Assizes, July 23, 1860.

'R v. Hopley', *The Times* (July 24, 1860).

Salmon, E.G., *Juvenile Literature as It Is* (London: H.J. Drane, 1888).

Salmon, E.G., 'What Boys Read', *Fortnightly Review*, 45 (February 1886), pp. 248–59.

Salt, H.S., *The Nursery of Toryism: Reminiscences of Eton Under Hornby* (London: A.C. Fitfield, 1911).

Salt, H.S., *The Flogging Craze: A Statement Against Corporal Punishment* (London: G. Allen and Unwin, 1916).

Slaughter, J.W., *The Adolescent* (London: Swan and Sonnenschein, 1911).

Smith, J.C., *Carthusian Worthies* (Oxford: Shakespeare Head Press, 1940).

Southey, R., *The Flagellant* No. 2 (London: 1792).

Spateman, T., *The School-Boy's Mask Design'd for the Diversion of Youth and their Excitement to Learning* (London: J. Roberts, 1742).

Spencer, H., *Education: Intellectual, Moral and Physical* (Osnabrück: Otto Zeller, 1966, reprint of 1890 edition).

Starr, L., *The Adolescent Period: Its Features and Management* (London: H.K. Lewis, 1915).

Stephen, J. F., '*Tom Brown's Schooldays*. By an Old Boy', *Edinburgh Review* (1858), pp. 172–93.

Sturgis, H.O., *Tim* (London: Macmillan, 1891).

Tanner, L.E., *Westminster School: A History* (London: Country Life, 1934).

Trench, M.C., *Little Richard: Or, Notes on the Life and Death of a Dear Boy, By His Mother* (London: 1861).

Trollope, A., 'Public Schools', *Fortnightly Review*, 2 (1865), pp. 476–87.

Tucker, W.H., *Eton of Old: Or Eighty Years Since, 1811–1822, by an Old Colleger* (London: Griffith, Farran and Co., 1892).

Vachell, H.A., *John Verney* (London: Murray, 1911).

Vachell, H.A., *The Hill* (London: John Murray, 1928).

'A Visit to Rugby', *Blackwood's Edinburgh Magazine*, 91.559 (May 1862), pp. 537–64, 559.

Ward, E., *Boys and their Rulers; Or What We Do at School* (London: N. Cooke, 1853).

Watson, W.C., *The War, the Church, and the Adolescent* (London: J. Bale, 1915).

Waugh, A., *The Loom of Youth* (London: G. Richards, 1917).

Waugh, A., *Public School Life: Boys, Parents, Masters* (London: W. Collins, 1922).

Webster, F.A.M., *Our Great Public Schools: Their Traditions, Customs and Games* (London: Ward, Lock, 1937).

Welldon, J.E.C., *Gerald Eversley's Friendship* (London: Smith, Elder and Co, 1895).

Wells, H.G., *A Year of Prophesying* (London: T.F. Unwin, 1924).

Wesley, J., Journal no. 9 in *Journals and Diaries*, ed. W.R. Wardin *The Works of J.J. John Wesley*, vol. 20 (Nashville: Abingdon Press, 1991), vol. III (1743–1754).

Wesley, J., Sermon 94 (1772), in *Sermons*, ed. A.C. Oulterin *The Works of John Wesley*, vol. 20 (Nashville: Abingdon Press, 1986), vol. III, pp. 74–114.
Whitely, W., *Catalogue of Whiteley's Circulating Library* (London: 1909).
Wilkinson, R., *The Prefects* (Oxford: Oxford University Press, 1964).
Wolley, T.L., *Juvenile Delinquency: The Social Problem of the Day, Its Prevention Easier than Its Cure* (London: 1854).
Wordsworth, W. *Poetical Works*, ed. by T. Hutchinson and E. de Selincourt (Oxford: Oxford University Press, 1969).
Worsley, H., *Juvenile Depravity* (London: independently published, 1849).
Worsley, T.C., *The Flannelled Fool* (London: Hogarth, 1985).
Yonge, C.M., *What Books to Lend and What to Give* (London: National Society's Depository, 1887).
'Young England', *The Saturday Review* (April 28, 1883).
'Youthful Culture', *Chambers' Edinburgh Journal*, 15 (1851).
'Youthful Prodigies', *Chambers' Edinburgh Journal*, 54 (September 15, 1877).

Secondary Sources

Abrahamson, J., 'Still Playing it Safe: Restricted Realism in Teen Novels', in R. Bator (ed.), *Signposts to Criticism of Children's Literature* (Chicago: American Library Association, 1983), pp. 319–23.
Abrams, Philip, 'Rites de Passage: The Conflict of Generations in Industrial Society', *Contemporary History*, 5.1 (1970), pp. 175–90.
Achar, Radha, 'The Child in Kipling's Fiction: An Analysis', *The Literary Criterion*, 22.4 (1987), pp. 46–53.
Adams, James Eli, *Dandies and Desert Saints* (London: Cornell University Press. 1995).
Alaimo, Kathleen, 'Childhood and Adolescence in Modern European History', *Journal of Social History*, 24.3 (1991), pp. 591–602.
Alderson, David, *Mansex Fine: Religion, Manliness and Imperialism in Nineteenth-Century British Culture* (Manchester: Manchester University Press, 1998).
Allen, Dennis, 'Young England: Muscular Christianity and the Politics of the Body in *Tom Brown's Schooldays*', in D. Hall (ed.), *Muscular Christianity: Embodying the Victorian Age* (Cambridge: Cambridge University Press, 1994), pp. 114–32.
Allen, Peter, 'Christian Socialism and the Broad Church Circle', *Dalhousie Review*, 49.1 (1969), pp. 58–68.
Allsop, Kenneth, 'A Coupon for Instant Tradition: On *Tom Brown's Schooldays*', *Encounter* (November 25, 1965), pp. 60–63.
Anstruther, Ian, *Dean Farrar and 'Eric': A Study of* Eric, or Little by Little *and its Author, Dean Farrar, Together with the Complete Text of the Book* (Bury St Edmund's: Haggerston Press, 2002).

Appleyard, J.A., *Becoming a Reader* (Cambridge: Cambridge University Press, 1990).
Armytage, Walter, *Four Hundred Years of English Education* (Cambridge: Cambridge University Press, 1965).
Avery Gillian, *Nineteenth Century Children: Heroes and Heroines of English Children's Stories 1780–1900* (London: Hodder, 1965).
Avery, Gillian, *Childhood's Pattern: A Study of the Heroes and Heroines of Children's Fiction 1770–1950* (London: Hodder and Stoughton, 1975).
Bakhtin, Mikhail, *Rabelais and His World*, trans. H. Iswolsky (Cambridge, MA: MIT Press, 1965).
Bailey, Steven, 'Living Sports History: Football at Winchester, Eton and Harrow', *Sports Historian*, 15 (1995), pp. 34–53.
Beatty, C.J.P. ,'Thomas Hardy and Thomas Hughes', *English Studies*, 68.6 (1987), pp. 511–18.
Behlmer, George, *Child Abuse and Moral Reform in England 1870–1908* (Stanford: Stanford University Press, 1982).
Bergen, Doris, and Fromberg, Doris (eds), *Play from Birth to Twelve and Beyond: Contexts, Perspectives and Meanings* (London: Garland, 1998).
Berry, Laura, *The Child, the State and the Victorian Novel* (Charlottesville: University Press of Virginia, 1999).
Bhattacharyya, Gargi, 'Cultural Education in Britain: from the Newbolt Report to the National Curriculum', *Oxford Literary Review*, 13.1–2 (1991), pp. 4–19.
Bilger, Audrey, *Laughing Feminism: Subversive Comedy in Frances Burney, Maria Edgeworth, and Jane Austen* (Detroit: Wayne State University Press, 1998).
Boas, George, *The Cult of Childhood* (London: Warburg Institute, 1966).
Boehrer, Bruce, '*Epicoene*, Charivari, Skimmington', *English Studies*, 75.1 (1994), pp. 17–33.
Bradley, Ian, *The Call to Seriousness: The Evangelical Impact of the Victorians* (London: Cape, 1976).
Brake, Laurel, *Subjugated Knowledges: Journalism, Gender and Literature in the Nineteenth-Century* (Basingstoke: Macmillan, 1994).
Bratton, Jacqueline, *The Impact of Victorian Children's Fiction* (London: Croom Helm, 1981).
Bristow, Joseph, *Empire Boys: Adventures in a Man's World* (London: HarperCollins, 1991).
Buckley, Jerome, *Season of Youth: The Bildungsroman from Dickens to Golding* (Cambridge. MA: Harvard University Press, 1974).
Buckton, Oliver, '"An Unnatural State"; Gender, "Perversion" and Newman's *Apologia Pro Vita Sua*', *Victorian Studies*, 35.4 (1992), pp. 359–83.
Burton, D.L., 'Pap to Protein? Two Generations of Adolescent Fiction', in R. Bator (ed.), *Signposts to Criticism of Children's Literature* (Chicago: American Library Association, 1983), pp. 310–18.

Butler, Marilyn, *Maria Edgeworth: A Literary Biography* (Oxford: Clarendon Press, 1972).

Carpenter, Humphrey, *Secret Gardens: A Study of the Golden Age of Children's Literature* (London: Allen and Unwin, 1985).

Chandler, Timothy, 'Emergent Athleticism: Games in Two English Public Schools, 1800–60', *International Journal of the History of Sport*, 5.3 (1988), pp. 312–29.

Chandler, Timothy, 'Games at Oxbridge and the Public Schools, 1830–80: The Diffusion of an Innovation', *International Journal of the History of Sport*, 8.2 (1991), pp. 171–204.

Chandos, John, *Boys Together: English Public Schools 1800–1864* (London: Hutchinson, 1984).

Chitty, Susan, *Playing the Game: A Biography of Sir Henry Newbolt* (London: Quartet, 1997).

Chorley, Katharine, *Arthur Hugh Clough: The Uncommitted Mind: A Study of his Life and Poetry* (Oxford: Clarendon Press, 1962).

Clark, Beverly, *Regendering the Public School Story: Sassy Sissies and Tattling Tomboys* (New York: Garland, 1996).

Cohen, David, *The Development of Play* (London: Routledge, 1987).

Cohoon, Lorinda, *Serialized Citizenships: Periodicals, Books and American Boys, 1840–1911* (Lanham, Maryland: Scarecrow Press, 2006).

Cunningham, Hugh, *The Children of the Poor: Representations of Childhood since the Seventeenth Century* (Oxford: 1991).

Curtis, Stanley and Boultwood, Myrtle, *A Short History of Educational Ideas* (London: University Tutorial Press, 1966).

Danahay, Martin, *A Community of One: Masculine Autobiography and Autonomy in Nineteenth-Century Britain* (Albany: State University of New York Press, 1993).

Darton, Harvey, *Children's Books in England: Five Centuries of Social Life* (London: British Library, 1999).

Davidoff, Leonora and Hall, Catherine, *Family Fortunes* (London: Hutchinson, 1987).

Davin, Anna, 'What is a Child?', in A. Fletcher and S. Hussey (eds), *Childhood in Question: Children, Parents and the State* (Manchester: Manchester University Press, 1999).

Davis, Cynthia Buffington, 'Dr Arnold's Public School Ideal: Victorian Muse and Motif' (University of Virginia Thesis, 1981).

Davis, David, *Slavery and Human Progress* (Oxford: Oxford University Press, 1984).

Dellamora, Richard, *Masculine Desire* (Chapel Hill and London: University of North Carolina Press, 1990).

Dingley, R.J., 'Beetle's Responsibility: The Ending of *Stalky & Co.*', *Kipling Journal*, 58.230 (1984), pp. 9–17.

Dixon, Bob, *Catching them Young I: Sex, Race and Class in Children's Fiction* (London: Pluto Press, 1977).

Dixon, Bob, *Catching them Young II: Political Ideas in Children's Fiction* (London: Pluto Press, 1977).
Dowling, Linda, *Hellenism and Homosexuality in Victorian Oxford* (London: Cornell University Press, 1994).
Eby, Cecil Degrotte, *The Road to Armageddon: The Martial Spirit in English Popular Literature, 1870–1914* (Durham, NC: Duke University Press, 1987).
Edirisingha, Palitha and Holford, John, *Citizenship and Governance Education in Europe: A Critical View of the Literature* (Surrey: University of Surrey, 2000).
Ezell, Margaret, 'John Locke's Images of Childhood', in R. Ashcraft (ed.), *John Locke: Critical Assessments* (London: Routledge, 1991), pp. 231–45.
Faber, Richard, *Young England* (London: Faber, 1987).
Ferguson, Frances, 'Reading Morals: Locke and Rousseau on Education and Inequality', *Representations,* 6 (1984), pp. 66–84.
Findlay, Joseph, *Arnold of Rugby: His School Life and Contributions to Education* (Cambridge: Cambridge University Press, 1897).
Foucault, Michel, *Discipline and Punish*, trans. Alan Sheridan (Harmondsworth: Penguin, 1991).
Gagnier, Reginia, *Subjectivities: A History of Self-Representation in Britain 1832–1920* (Oxford: Oxford University Press, 1991).
Gathorne-Hardy, Jonathan, *The Public School Phenomenon, 597–1977* (London: Hodder and Stoughton, 1977).
Gibson, Ian, *The English Vice: Beating, Sex and Shame in Victorian England and After* (London: Duckworth, 1978).
Gillis, John, *Youth and History: Tradition and Change in European Age Relations 1770–Present* (London: Academic Press, 1974).
Ginsburg, Michael, 'The Case against Plot in *Bleak House* and *Our Mutual Friend*', *English Literary History*, 59 (1992), pp. 175–95.
Glowczewski-Barker, Barbara, 'Growing up and Sexual Identity: A Cross-Cultural Approach', *Anthropological Forum*, 7.1 (1994), pp. 7–29.
Goodheart, Adam, 'The Last Island of the Savages', *The American Scholar*, 69.4 (Autumn, 2000), pp. 13–44.
Goodlad, Lauren, *Victorian Literature and the Victorian State: Character and Governance in a Liberal Society* (Baltimore: Johns Hopkins University Press, 2003).
Griffin, Christine, *Representations of Youth: The Study of Youth and Adolescence in Britain and America* (Cambridge: Polity, 1988).
Gruggen, George and Keating, J., *Stonyhurst: Its Past History and Life in the Present* (London: Kegan Paul, 1901).
Hall, Donald, *Fixing Patriarchy: Feminism and Mid-Victorian Male Novelists* (Basingstoke: Macmillan, 1996).
Hall, Donald, 'On the Making and Unmaking of Monsters: Christian Socialism, Muscular Christianity, and the Metaphorization of Class Conflict', in D. Hall (ed.), *Muscular Christianity: Embodying the Victorian Age* (Cambridge: Cambridge University Press, 1994), pp. 45–65.

Hanawalt, Barbara, 'Historical Descriptions and Prescriptions for Adolescence', *Journal of Family History*, 17.4 (1992), pp. 341–51.

Harrington, Henry, 'Charles Kingsley's Fallen Athlete', *Victorian Studies*, 21 (1977), pp. 73–86.

Harrington, Henry, '"Muscular Christianity" and Brutality: The Case of Tom Brown', *The Victorian Newsletter*, 65 (1984), pp. 26–29.

Hartley, A.J., 'Christian Socialism and Victorian Morality: The Inner Meaning of *Tom Brown's School-Days*', *Dalhousie Review*, 49 (1969), pp. 216–23.

Heathorn, Stephen, '"For Home, Country and Race": the Gendered Ideals of Citizenship in English Elementary and Evening Continuation Schools, 1885–1914', *Journal of the Canadian Historical Association*, 7 (1996), pp. 105–24.

Higdon, Thomas, 'The Burston Rebellion' (Dissertation, Trustees of Burston Strike School, 1984).

Hilton, Boyd, *Evangelicalism in the Age of Atonement: The Influence of Evangelicalism on Social and Economic Thought, 1795–1865* (Oxford: Clarendon Press, 1988).

Hinde, Andrew, *England's Population: A History Since the Domesday Survey* (London: Arnold, 2003).

Holden, Cathie, and Clough, Nick, '"The Child Carried on the Back does not Know the Length of the Road": The Teacher's Role in Assisting Participation', in C.

Holden and N. Clough (eds), *Children as Citizens: Education for Participation* (London: Jessica Kingsley, 1998), pp. 13–27.

Hollingworth, Brian, 'The Mother Tongue and the Public Schools in the 1860s', *British Journal of Educational Studies*, 22.3 (1974), pp. 312–24.

Holt, Jenny, 'The Textual Formations of Adolescence in Turn-of-the-Century Youth Periodicals: The *Boy's Own Paper* and Eton College Ephemeral Magazines', *Victorian Periodicals Review*, 38.1 (2002), pp. 63–88.

Houghton, Walter, 'Victorian Periodical Literature and the Articulate Classes', *Victorian Studies*, 22 (1979), pp. 389–412.

Howarth, Patrick, *Play Up and Play the Game: The Heroes of Popular Fiction* (London: Eyre Methuen, 1973).

Humphries, Stephen, *Hooligans or Rebels?* (Oxford: 1981).

International Herald Tribune (September 2, 1999).

Jamieson, J., 'F.W. Farrar and Novels of the Public Schools', *Journal of Education Studies*, 16.3 (1968), pp. 271–78.

Jobe's Dictionary of Mythology, Folklore and Symbols (New York: 1961).

Judd, Denis and Surridge, Keith, *The Boer War* (London: John Murray, 2002).

Keating, Peter, *The Haunted Study: A Social History of the English Novel 1875–1914* (London: Secker and Warburg, 1989).

Kidd, Kenneth, *Making American Boys: Boyology and the Feral Tale* (Minnesota: 2004).

Kincaid, James, *Child-Loving: The Erotic Child and Victorian Culture* (London: Routledge, 1994).

King, Noel, '"The Teacher Must Exist Before the Pupil": The Newbolt Report on the Teaching of English in England, 1921', *Literature and History*, 13.1 (1987), pp. 14–37.

King, Terry, *The Politics of Corporal Punishment* (Sheffield: Sheffield City Polytechnic, 1987).

Kirchhoff, Frederick, 'An End to Novel Writing: Howard Overing Sturgis', *English Literature in Transition*, 33.4 (1990), pp. 425–41.

Kirkpatrick, Robert, *The Encyclopaedia of Boys' School Stories* (Aldershot: Ashgate, 2000).

Knoepflmacher, Ulrich, 'The Balancing of Child and Adult: An Approach to Victorian Fantasies for Children', *Nineteenth Century Literature*, 37.4 (1983), pp. 497–530.

Knowles, Kenneth, *Strikes – A Study in Industrial Conflict* (Oxford: Blackwell, 1952).

Kohlberg, Lawrence, *The Philosophy of Moral Development* (2 vols, San Francisco: Harpur and Rowe, 1981), vol. 1.

Kosofsky-Sedgwick, Eve, *Between Men: English Literature and Male Homosocial Desire* (New York: Columbia University Press, 1985).

Lawson, Philip, *The East India Company: A History* (London: Longman, 1993).

Leeson, Robert, *Reading and Righting* (London: Collins, 1985).

Leinster-Mackay, D.P.,'Victorian Quasi-Public Schools: A Question of Appearance and Reality or an Application of the Principle of the Survival of the Fittest?', *British Journal of Educational Studies*, 29.1 (1981), pp. 54–68.

Leinster-Mackay, D.P., 'Private or Public Schools: The Educational Debate in *Laissez-Faire* England', *Journal of Educational Administration and History*, 15.2 (1983), pp. 1–6.

Lesník-Oberstein, Karin, *Children's Literature: Criticism and the Fictional Child* (Oxford: Clarendon Press, 1994).

Levy, David, *How the Dismal Science Got Its Name: Classical Economics and the Ur-Text of Racial Politics* (Ann Arbor: University of Michigan Press, 2001).

Lister, Ian, 'Citizenship and Citizenship Education in Britain', in O. Ichilov (ed.), *Citizenship and Citizenship Education in a Changing World* (London: Woburn Press, 1998), pp. 254–66.

Jackson, Luke, *Freaks, Geeks and Asperger Syndrome: A User Guide to Adolescence* (London: Jessica Kingsley, 2002).

Kennedy, Kerry, *Citizenship Education and the Modern State* (London: Falmer Press, 1992).

Mack, Edward, *Public Schools and British Opinion Since 1860: The Relationship between Contemporary Ideas and the Evolution of an English Institution* (New York: Columbia University Press, 1941).

Mack, Edward, and Armytage, Walter, *Thomas Hughes: the Life of the Author of Tom Brown's Schooldays* (London: Ernest Benn, 1952).

Magraw, Roger, *A History of the French Working Class* (Oxford: Blackwell, 1992).

Magure, J., 'Images of Manliness and Competing Ways of Living in Late Victorian and Edwardian Britain', *British Journal of Sports History*, 3 (1986), pp. 265–87.

Mangan, James, 'Play Up and Play the Game: Victorian and Edwardian Public School Vocabularies of Motive', *British Journal of Educational Studies*, 23.3 (1975), pp. 324–35.

Mangan, James, 'Images of Empire in the Late Victorian Public School', *Journal of Educational Administration and History*, 12.1 (1980), pp. 31–39.

Mangan, James, 'Social Darwinism, Sport and English Upper Class Education', *Stadion*, 7.1 (1981), pp. 93–116.

Mangan, James, 'Philathlete Extraordinary: A Portrait of the Victorian Moralist Edward Bowen', *Journal of Sport History*, 9.3 (Winter, 1982), pp. 23–40.

Mangan, James, *The Games Ethic and Imperialism: Aspects of the Diffusion of an Ideal* (Harmondsworth: Penguin, 1986).

Mangan, James, 'Images of Manliness and Competing Ways of Living in Late Victorian and Edwardian Britain', *British Journal of Sports History*, 3 (1986), pp. 265–87.

Mangan, James, *Athleticism in the Victorian and Edwardian Public School: The Emergence and Consolidation of an Educational Ideology* (London: Frank Cass, 2000).

Martin, Maureen M., '"Boys who will be Men": Desire in *Tom Brown's Schooldays*', *Victorian Literature and Culture* (2002), pp. 483–502.

Martini, Fritz, '*Bildungsroman* – Term and Theory', in J. Hardin (ed.), *Reflection and Action: Essays on the Bildungsroman* (Columbia: University of South Carolina Press, 1991), pp. 1–25.

Marshall, John, *The Old Poor Law 1795–1834* (Basingstoke: Macmillan, 1985).

Mason, Michael, *The Making of Victorian Sexuality* (Oxford: Oxford University Press, 1994).

Matthews, John, 'Literature and Politics: A Disraelian View', *English Studies in Canada* x.2 (June 1984), pp. 172–87.

May, Jill, *Children's Literature and Critical Theory: Reading and Writing for Understanding* (Oxford: Oxford University Press, 1995).

May, Margaret, 'Innocence and Experience: The Evolution of the Concept of Juvenile Delinquency in the Mid-Nineteenth Century', *Victorian Studies*, 17 (1973), pp. 7–29.

McCallum, Robyn, *Ideologies of Identity in Adolescent Fiction: The Dialogic Construction of Subjectivity* (New York, 1999).

McCrum, Michael, *Thomas Arnold Head Master: A Reassessment* (Oxford: Oxford University Press, 1989).

McCulloch, Gary, *Philosophers and Kings: Education for Leadership in Modern England* (Cambridge: Cambridge University Press, 1991).

Money, Tony, *Manly and Muscular Diversions; Public Schools and the Nineteenth-Century Sporting Revival* (London: Duckworth, 1997).

Moss, Robert, *Rudyard Kipling and the Fiction of Adolescence* (London: Macmillan, 1982).

Mulhauser, Frederick (ed.), *Correspondence of Arthur Hugh Clough* (Oxford: Clarendon Press, 1957), vol. II.
Musgrave, Peter, *From Brown to Bunter: The Life and Death of the School Story* (London: Routledge and Kegan Paul, 1985).
Muuss, Rolf, *Theories of Adolescence* (New York: McGraw-Hill, 1996).
Neill, Alex, 'Locke on Habituation, Autonomy, and Education', in R. Ashcraft (ed.), *John Locke: Critical Assessments* (London: Routledge, 1991), pp. 246–65
Nelson, Claudia, 'Sex and the Single Boy', *Victorian Studies*, 32 (1989), pp. 525–50.
Nelson, Claudia, *Boys Will Be Girls: The Feminine Ethic and British Children's Fiction, 1857–1917* (New Brunswick, NJ: Rutgers University Press, 1991).
Nelson, Claudia, *Invisible Men: Fatherhood in Victorian Periodical 1850–1910* (Athens, GA: University of Georgia Press, 1995).
Neubauer, John, *The Fin-de-Siècle Culture of Adolescence* (New Haven: Yale University Press, 1992).
Neuman, B.P., 'Masturbation, Madness, and the Modern Concepts of Childhood and Adolescence', *Journal of Social History*, 8.3 (1975), pp. 1–27.
Newnham, David, 'It's Fun Being Weird', *Times Educational Supplement* (August 16, 2002).
Newsome, David, *Godliness and Good Learning* (London: Murray, 1961).
Norton, Rictor, *Mother Clap's Molly House: The Gay Subculture in England 1700–1830* (Stroud: Chalford Press, 2006).
Norton, Rictor, *The Myth of the Modern Homosexual: Queer History and the Search for Cultural Unity* (London: Cassell, 1997).
O'Gorman, Francis, 'Victorian Natural History and the Discourses of Nature in Charles Kingsley's *Glaucus*', *Worldviews: Environment, Culture, Religion*, 2 (1998), pp. 21–35.
O'Gorman, Francis, 'Charles Kingley's Costruction of Natural History', in J. John and A. Jenkins (eds), *Rethinking Victorian Culture* (New York: St Martin's Press, 2000), pp. 146–61.
Ong, Walter, *The Presence of the Word* (New York: Simon and Schuster, 1967).
Pearce, R.D., 'The Prep. School and Imperialism: The Example of Orwell's St. Cyprian's', *Journal of Educational Administration* (1991), pp. 42–53.
Peck, John, *War, the Army and Victorian Literature* (Basingstoke: Macmillan, 1998).
Pickering, Samuel, *Moral Instruction and Fiction for Children, 1749–1820* (London: University of Georgia Press, 1993).
Pickering, Samuel, Jr., 'The "Race of Real Children" and Beyond in *Tom Brown's Schooldays*', *The Arnoldian*, 11.2 (1984), pp. 36–45.
Pilkington, Ace, '*Stalky & Co.*: Kipling's School in the Absurd World', *Encyclia*, 63 (1986), pp. 126–32.
Pollock, Linda, *Forgotten Children: Parent-Child Relations from 1500–1900* (Cambridge: Cambridge University Press, 1983).
Posnock, Ross, 'Genteel Androgyny: Santayana, Henry James and Howard Sturgis', *Raritan*, 10.3 (1991), pp. 58–84.

Protherough, Robert, 'The Figure of the Teacher in English Literature 1740–1918' (University of Hull thesis: 1980).
Protherough, Robert, 'Shaping the Image of the Great Headmaster', *British Journal of Education Studies*, 32.3 (1984), pp. 239–50.
Quigly, Isabel, *The Heirs of Tom Brown: The English School Story* (Oxford: Oxford University Press, 1984).
Rapple, Brendan, 'Dean Frederic William Farrar (1831–1903): Educationalist', *British Journal of Education*, 43.1 (1995), pp. 57–74.
Rich, Paul, *Chains of Empire: English Public Schools, Masonic Cabalism, Historical Causality, and Imperial Clubdom* (London: Regency, 1991).
Rich, Paul, *Elixir of Empire: English Public Schools, Ritualism, Freemasonry and Imperialism* (London: Regency Press, 1993).
Richards, Jeffrey, *Happiest Days: The Public Schools in English Fiction* (Manchester: Manchester University Press, 1988).
Richardson, Alan, 'From *Émile* to *Frankenstein*: The Education of Monsters', *European Romantic Review*, 1.2 (1991), pp. 147–62.
Robison, Roselee, 'Victorians, Children and Play', *English Studies*, 64.4 (1983), pp. 318–29
Rose, Jacqueline, *The Case of Peter Pan, or the Impossibility of Children's Fiction* (Basingstoke: Macmillan, 1994).
Rose, Lionel, *The Erosion of Childhood: Child Oppression in Britain 1860–1918* (London: Routledge, 1991).
Rosen, David, 'The Volcano and the Cathedral: Muscular Christianity and the Origins of Primal Manliness', in D. Hall (ed.), *Muscular Christianity: Embodying the Victorian Age* (Cambridge: 1994), pp. 17–44.
Scott, Carole, 'Kipling's Combat Zones: Training Grounds in the Mowgli Stories, *Captains Courgeous*, and *Stalky & Co.*', *Children's Literature*, 20 (1992), pp. 52–68.
Scott, P.G., 'The School Novels of Dean Farrar', *British Journal of Educational Studies* (1971), pp. 163–82.
Searle, Geoffrey, *The Quest for National Efficiency: A Study in British Politics and Political Thought 1899–1914* (London: Ashfield, 1990).
Searle, Geoffrey, '"National Efficiency" and the "Lessons" of the War', in D. Omissi and A.S. Thompson (eds), *The Impact of the South African War* (Basingstoke: Palgrave, 2002), pp. 194–211.
Shaffner, Randolph, *The Apprenticeship Novel: A Study of the* Bildungsroman *as a Regulative Type in Western Literature* (Frankfurt am Main: Peter Lang, 1984).
Shore, Heather, *Artful Dodgers: Youth and Crime in Early 19th Century London* (Woodbridge: Boydell, 1999).
Shrosbree, Colin, *Public Schools and Private Education: The Clarendon Commission 1861–64 and the Public Schools Acts* (Manchester: 1988)
Shuttleworth, Sally, '"Done because we are too menny": Little Father Time and Child Suicide in Late-Victorian Culture', in P. Mallett (ed.), *Thomas Hardy: Texts and Contexts* (Basingstoke: Palgrave Macmillan, 2002).

Smith, Bonnie, 'The Adolescent Road to Historical Science', *History of Education Quarterly*, 33.4 (1993), pp. 563–77.
Smith, Jonathan, 'Philip Gosse and the Varieties of Natural Theology', in L. Woodhead (ed.), *Reinventing Christianity: Nineteenth-Century Contexts* (Aldershot, Hampshire: Ashgate, 2001), pp. 251–62.
Smith, Olivia, *The Politics of Language 1791–1817* (Oxford: Clarendon Press, 1984).
Spacks, Patricia Meyer, 'Us or Them', *Hudson Review*, 31 (1979), pp. 34–52.
Spacks, Patricia Meyer, *The Adolescent Idea: Myths of Youth and the Adult Imagination* (London: Faber, 1981).
Springhall, John, *Coming of Age: Adolescence in Britain 1860–1960* (Dublin: Gill and Macmillan, 1986).
Springhall, John, *Youth, Popular Culture and Moral Panics: Penny Gaffs to Gangsta-Rap, 1830–1996* (Basingstoke: Macmillan, 1998).
Stanley, Arthur Penrhyn, *The Life and Correspondence of Thomas Arnold, DD*, 2 vols (London: John Murray, 1882).
Steedman, Carolyn, *Strange Dislocations: Childhood and the Idea of Human Interiority 1780–1930* (London: Virago, 1995).
Stewart, D.H., '*Stalky* and the Language of Education', *Children's Literature*, 20 (1992), pp. 36–51.
Strachey, Lytton, *Five Victorians* (London: Reprint Society, 1942).
Strauch, Barbara, *The Primal Teen: What the New Discoveries About the Teenage Brain Can Tell Us About Our Kids* (New York: Doubleday, 2003).
Sussman, Herbert, *Victorian Masculinities: Manhood and Masculine Poetics in Early Victorian Literature and Art* (Cambridge: Cambridge University Press, 1995).
Sutton-Smith, Brian and Kelly-Byrne, Diana, 'The Idealization of Play', in P.K. Smith (ed.), *Play in Animals and Humans* (Blackwell, Oxford: 1984).
Swales, Martin, 'Irony and the Novel: Reflections on the German *Bildungsroman*', in J. Hardin (ed.), *Reflection and Action: Essays on the* Bildungsroman (Columbia: University of South Carolina Press, 1991), pp. 46–68.
Sweeney, Simon, *Europe, the State and Globalization* (Harlow: Pearson, 2005).
Terasaki, Hiroaki, *Igirisu Gakkou Taibatsu-Shi: 'Iistobouno no Higeki' to Rokku-Teki Kouzuoe* (*The History of School Corporal Punishment in England: The 'Eastbourne Tragedy' and the Lockean Labyrinth*) (Tokyo: University of Tokyo Press, 2001).
Thomson, George, 'E.M. Forster and Howard Sturgis', *Texas Studies in Literature and Language*, 10 (1968), pp. 423–33.
Tosh, John, 'Authority and Nurture in Middle-Class Fatherhood: The Case of Early and Mid- Victorian England', *Gender and History*, 8.1 (1996), pp. 48–64.
Tosh, John, *A Man's Place: Masculinity and the Middle-class Home in Victorian England* (New Haven: Yale University Press, 1999).
Trevelyan, George, *English Social History* (London: Londmans Green, 1942).
Usborne, Richard, 'A Re-reading of "Tom Brown"', *Spectator*, 197 (August 17, 1956).

Vance, Norman, *The Sinews of the Spirit: The Ideal of Christian Manliness in Victorian Literature and Religious Thought* (Cambridge: Cambridge University Press, 1985).

Vicinus, Martha, 'The Adolescent Boy: *Fin de Siècle Femme Fatale*?', *Journal of the History of Sexuality*, 5.1 (1994), pp. 90–114.

Wakeford, John, *The Cloistered Élite* (London: Macmillan, 1969).

Wallbank, M.V., 'Eighteenth Century Public Schools and the Education of the Governing Elite', *History of Education*, 8.1 (1973), pp. 1–19.

Watson, Ian, 'Victorian England, Colonialism and the Ideology of *Tom Brown's Schooldays*' *Zeitschrift fur Anglistik und Amerikanistik*, 29 (1981), pp. 116–29.

White, Hayden, *Tropics of Discourse* (Baltimore: 1978).

Worth, George, 'Of Muscles and Manliness: Some Reflections on Thomas Hughes', in J.R. Kincaid and and A.J. Kuhn (eds.), *Victorian Literature and Society* (Columbus: Ohio State University Press, 1984), pp. 300–314.

Websites

http://news.bbc.co.uk/2/hi/uk_news/education/2869147.stm
http://www.andaman.org/BOOK/reprints/goodheart/rep-goodheart.htm
http://www.isle-of-man.com/manxnotebook/fulltext/wi1931.htm
http://www.readingschool.reading.sch.uk/school/schoolhistory/index.php

Index

Abrahamson, J., 12
Abrams, Philip, 18, 108
Academy, The, 11, 161–62
Adams, H.C., 21, 26, 67, 121, 140, 141–44, 204
   Schoolboy Honor (1861), 4, 140, 204
Adams, J.E., 29–30, 31
Adams, W., 92
   The Cherry Stones (1842), 56–57
Addison, Joseph, 33
adolescence
   as controlled, 8, 197
   defined, 1, 2–3, 115
   and genius, 18, 48, 163
   as metaphor for social and national change, 9, 81–82
   and permanent adolescence, 198–99, 204, 205, 206, 208, 213
   and puberty, 8
   recapitulation theory, 203
   as stage, 17, 18, 57–58, 116, 225
adolescent development, 47
adult-adolescent bond, 144, 227
adulthood, 56
   adolescent view post WWI, 199, 204, 205, 206–208
   Victorian vs. turn-of-the-century views, 207–208
aesthetics, 102, 212, 215
Ainsworth, Harrison, 146–47
Alaimo, Kathleen, 114
Alderson, David, 106–107
All the Year Round, 144
Allen, D.W., 64
Allsop, Kenneth, 17, 59
Almond, H.H., 170
Andrew, Cyril Bruyn, 167–68, 196
   An Introduction to the Study of Adolescent Education (1912), 167
Anglican religion, 29, 106–107
Anstey, F., 11
   Vice Versa, 3, 11

anthropology, 165
anti-determinism, 47
anti-domestic ideology, 38–39, 42, 49
apprenticeships, 17
Ariés, Philippe, 17
Aristotle, 33, 159
Arnold, Matthew, 46, 106, 119
Arnold, Thomas, 2, 5, 13, 15, 20–21, 22, 28, 29–30, 38–39, 50, 79, 81, 107, 129
   followers of, 29, 34, 67–68
   'On the Discipline of Public Schools' (1835), 129
   as reformer, 29, 43–46
   repulsion of adolescent bodies, 52–53, 56, 131
   sermons, 29, 44, 52
Arnold, Thomas; *see also* Hughes, Thomas, *Tom Brown's Schoolboy*, fictional Arnold
Arnold-Foster, H.O., *The Citizen Reader* (1885), 1–2, 7
Arnoldian manliness, 68
asceticism, 33, 35
Athenaeum, The, 116
audience, 2, 3, 4, 5, 12, 13, 23
Augustine, *Confessions*, 53, 56
Austen, Jane, 191
autobiography, 20, 22, 34
autonomy, 26, 53, 131, 214–15, 232, 234

Baden-Powell, *Scouting for Boys* (1908), 158, 158n3
Baden-Powell, J., 158
Badley, J.H., *Bedales* (1893), 166
Bagehot, Walter, 31
Bakhtinian ideas, 10, 24
Balfour Education Act (1902), 166
Ballantyne, R.M., 89, 93
   The Coral Island, 88, 93
barring out, 39
Bator, R., *Signposts to Criticism of Children's Literature*, 12

behavior
  bad behavior, 48, 139–40, 167–68, 190
  contrast of home and school, 3
  during free time, 37
  and gender labeling, 182
  growth of adolescent body and, 52
  for new male civic subjects, 82
  normal and deviant in public school literature, 10
  pre-Victorian era crisis and school rebellion, 25–26
Behlmer, George, 119, 123
Benny, Mark, *Low Company*, 166
Benson, A.C., 31, 122–23
Benson, E.F., *David Blaize* (1916), 186
Bentham, Jeremy, 74–75, 131
  Chrestomathia ('Useful Learning' 1815–1817), 131
Berry, Laura, 114
Berry, Linda, 54
Bible, the, 57–58, 95, 96, 107, 141
  as the statesman's manual (Farrar), 107
Biblical feudalism, 141, 142–43
Bildungsroman English version, 66–67, 76, 77–78, 99–100, 110–11, 221
Bildungsroman European tradition, 18, 20, 99–100
birching, 127
Blackwood's, 11, 83
Board of Education, 155
boarding schools, 3, 10, 165
body; *see also* recapitulation theory
  and diversity, 193–95
  growth and amoral behavior, 52–53, 95, 99
  modern body, 55
  permanent adolescence and, 205
  pre-Darwinian, 172
  repulsion of over-sized athletic body, Arnold, 53
Boer Wars, 176, 179
'Bouncing Boys' (1865), 144
Bowdler, John, 28–29, 50
Bowen, Edward, 83, 176
Box, Kerra, 236
Boy Scout movement, 200, 203, 208n270
boy worker, Kipling, 200–201
boy-lore, *The Academy* (1890s), 161–62
boyology, 163

Boys of England, 147
Boys' Own Paper, 4, 56, 147, 150, 153–54
Boys' Realm, 145
Brighton Observer, The, 126
Brinsley-Richards, James, 30
Bristow, Joseph, 108, 145
Britain
  character building philosophy, 18
  Indian Rebellion, 75
  laissez-faire policies, 75
  turn-of-the-century world position, 158
  'Young England movement', 35, 36
Britain educational system, and punishment, 118, 119
British government, 7
  George administration, 232
British male citizens, superiority of, 89
Brockett, B.B., *Our School: Or, Scraps and Scrapes in Schoolboy Life* (1857), 120
Brooks, Rupert, 215–16
Brougham, Henry, 29
Browne, Martin, 228–30
  A Dream of Youth (1918), 228
brutality in schools, 32–33, 69, 71
Buckeridge, Anthony, *Jennings* stories, 11
Buckley, J.H., 66–67, 76, 90
Burgess, Anthony, *A Clockwork Orange*, 84, 233
Burkean concept, 107
Burroughs, E.A., 229–30
Burton, D.L., 12
Byron, Lord, 37, 226
  Manfred, 90

Caird, John, 96
Cancellor, Reginald, 125–27
cannings, 30, 32
careers, public school story genre and, 5
Carlyle, Thomas, 31, 75, 80, 107
  Past and Present, 75, 80
  Sartor Resartus (1833), 31
Chambers's Journal, 'Against Boys' (1863), 116
  'Youthful Prodigies' (1870), 144–45
Chandos, John, 34, 55, 69, 70
change, 165–66
character development reform, 119
Charterhouse, 10

Cheltenham, 10
child abuse, 119
child labour, 114, 114n1, 115
childhood
    and citizenship entitlements, 115
    education, 47
    and identity, 22–23
    innocence and morality, 12, 52–53, 55, 96
    mid-century definition, 115
    regression and Romantic literature, 22
    as stage, 12, 47
childlessness, queer theorists on, 181n125
childlikeness, 96
children
    identity, 75–76
    substitute children and citizenship, 195
Children Act, 115
Christian ideals, citizenship education for, 5–6
Christian Socialists, 107
Christianity, 73–74, 91
    Muscular Christianity, 73
Christians, and effeminacy, Hughes on, 73–74
Christ's Hospital, 10, 50–52, 51n206
Chums, 145
Cicero, 33
citizen, 5, 33, 133, 159
citizenship
    defined, 6, 179
    Descriptive Sociology, 160
    eugenics and, 159
    goals prior to 1944 Education Act, 7, 172
    history of, 6–7
    male-gendered conception, Slaughter, 165
    Marshall on, 6
    new, Priestly, 44–45
    for non-public school boys, 203–204
    and public school story genre, 2–3, 4, 227–28, 234–35
    on social consensus, Farrar, 11
    and stage of adolescence, 17
    training in free time, 35, 79
City of London School, 10
civic education
    Arnold on, 5
    and boys' loss, 214
    brief history, 7–8
    as cause of war, Leslie, 211–12
    defined, 8, 167–68
    early nineteenth century, 1–2, 5–6
    and elite, 19
    pre WWI, 213–15
    in schools, 213–14, 225
    WWI and changes in society, 212–13
    WWI wartime literature and, 215–16
civic education reform, 44–45
clan mentality, 62–63
Clarendon Commission (1861), 10, 37
Clarendon Commission (1861–1864), 105–106, 114–15, 118, 123, 127
Clark, Beverly, 38
Clarke, A.W., *Jaspar Tristram* (1899), 185–86
class
    careers, 2, 5
    education, 3
    mid-century, crime rate, 116
Co-operative movements, work of Arnold, 29
Cobbett, William, 42
    Advice to Young Men (1829), 48
Code of Grants (1862), 173–74
codes, symbolic codes, 122
Cohen, David, 79
Cohoon, Lorinda, 153–54
Coke, Desmond, *The Bending of a Twig* (1906), 157
Coleridge, A.D., 21, 40, 119, 122
colonial subjects, 22, 204, 211, 221
combative learning, 30, 31–32, 34, 36–37, 41, 182
Committee of Privy Council on Education, 114
competition, 103
conformity, 51, 67, 129
Connolly, Cyril, 185, 205, 232
    Enemies of Promise (1938), 205–206
Corn Law debates, 28; see also *R* v. *Hopley*
corporal punishment
    alternatives, 1860s, 124
    conspiracy of silence of ex-students, 127
    defense of, 128–29, 134
    laws, 124, 124n70, 125–26, 134

obstinacy as basis for, 130
opposition to, 124, 127, 132–34, 136–37, 138, 139–40
by peers, 132
as topic in schools, 114
Cory, William Johnson, 185
Ionica, 185
Cotton, G.E.L., 106, 122
Council of Europe, (1993), 7–8
Cowper, William, 29, 49–50
Tirocinium, 2, 49
Craig, A.R., 132, 139
crime, 50, 115, 116, 116n14, 149
criminal justice system, 117
Cunningham, Hugh, 160
curriculum, pre-Victorian, 30–32, 33–34
classical, 30, 34
feminizing of reform, 41–42
reform studies, 122–23
Cust, Lionel, 21
A History of Eton College (1899), 21
Custody of Children Act (1839), 98

Darwin, Clarence, 87, 87n21
The Descent of Man (1871), 170
Darwinism
anti-Darwin natural selection, 177, 193–95, 199
Social Darwinists, 145–46, 157–58, 179, 195, 195n200, 208
Davis, Cynthia Buffington, 20, 84
Day, S.P., 116–17
Day, Thomas, 15, 28, 29, 79, 116
death, 205, 210, 211, 233
debate, 30–31, 34–35, 42, 216–17
degeneration, 170, 173, 208, 215
democracy, 19, 94, 146, 166, 214
demonstrations, 2003 against Iraq War, 235–36
Department for Education and Science (UK), 8
Department of Education, 134
Dickens, Charles, 78
discipline; *see also* corporal punishment; *R* v. *Hopley*
and arguing, 128
by democratic schoolboy group, 132
earlier vs. modern boys, 144
evolutionary laws and, 160

and family focus, 114, 114n1
and Foucaldian model, 117–18, 119
medical control as, 51–52
and reasonable discipline, 114
school discipline, 114, 128–29
state controlled reform education and, 113–14, 123
and threat of damnation, 139–40
and violence, 144–45
Discipline and Punish, 118
Disraeli, Benjamin, 15, 18
Coningsby (1844), 18, 19, 59
diversity, argument against Social Darwinists, 192–93
domestic education, anti-domestic education, 49, 59
domestic life, 4, 44, 98–99
Dowling, Linda, 188
drama, 30–31, 40, 102, 122
Dying School Boy: By his Tutor, The (1863), 92–93

E.P., *Solomon's Precept: Or the Power of the Rod* (1861), 137–39
Eby, C.D., 196, 205
economics, 157–59, 173, 174–75, 195
and public school story genre, 5, 94
Edgeworth, Francis Beaufort, 38
Edgeworth, Maria, 21, 28, 38, 39–40, 41, 47, 57, 78, 79
The Barring Out, 39–40
Eton Montem (play), 39, 40–41, 122
Practical Education, 57, 78
Edgeworth, Richard Lovell, 15, 28
Edinburgh Review, 29, 33–34
education; *see also* combative learning
British positioning, 123, 175–76
class and, 2, 3, 166, 167, 196
classical education, 41
importance of, 48
instilling Christian character within reform, 27–29
laissez-faire system, 33, 75
liberal education movement, 7
progressive education of early twentieth century, 166
reform, compulsory education in mid-century, 114–15, 116–19

role, citizenship vs. academic, 7, 34
  Thomas Arnold on, 5–6
Education Act (1870), 114, 115
Education Act (1944), 7
Education Acts (1902), 158
Education Department, 114
educationalists, 160–61, 161n22, 166, 166n45 223
educators, 25, 83
effeminate adolescent boys, 69, 71, 71n66, 179–80, 192–93
effeminatus, 33
1834 New Poor Law, 54
1884 Reform Act, 7
elite (upper- and upper-middle-class) students, 2, 3, 5, 26, 177–78
Ellis, Havelock, 185, 186–87, 186n151, 188, 190
  Sexual Inversion, 180, 185
'English Boy of the Future', The' (1862), 145
enlightment, rational enlightment, 49
Essays on Duty and Discipline (1910), 158
Essays on a Liberal Education (1867), 83
Eton Candle, The ed. Brian Howard, 232
Eton Miscellany, 31
Eton school, 10, 22, 27, 32, 34n104, 40, 120, 122, 173, 185, 203, 209–10
  Clarendon Commission (1861–1864) enquiry, 105–106
  curriculum, 30, 122–23
  headmasters *see* Arnold, Thomas; Keate, John; Warre, Edmond
eugenics, 157–58, 158n3, 159, 195n200, 197
eugenics movement, 176, 179, 208n270
Evangelical reformers, 13, 27–28, 31, 37–38, 97, 106–107, 128
evolution, 110

Factory Acts, 98
fagging (Lancasterian or monitor system), 34, 51, 81, 130–31
fairy tales, 204–205
family, 17, 37–38, 43, 62; *see also* adolescents; father; fatherhood; girls; women
Family Herald, 128–29
family values, and reform, 37–38

Farrar, F.W., 11, 25, 34, 70, 83–84, 85, 93–94, 97,100, 102, 106, 107–108, 109, 128
  authorial voice, 109–10
  autobiographical sections of *Eric*, 97
  Ballantyne, contrast on, 90, 93, 107, 108
  biography, 97, 102, 106
  criticism of, 83, 84
  Hughes comparisons, 84, 85, 86, 88, 100, 107
  liberal education reform failure, 94–95, 104
  on paternalism, 97, 98, 110
  works
    Eric: Or Little by Little (1858), 3, 25, 83, 85–87, 88, 100, 116
    Essays on a Liberal Education (1867), 83, 85, 93–94, 176
    Julian Home: A Tale of College Life (1859), 83
    Present-Day Questions, 107
    Social and Present Day Questions (1891), 85
    St Winifred's: Or, The World of School (1862), 83, 84, 85, 100–102, 116
    The Young Man Master of Himself (1896), 85, 98–99
Farrar, Reginald, 97, 102, 106
father, 98, 200–201
father-son relationship, 196–97
fatherhood, 98, 118, 181–82, 184
  eugenics and homosexual panic, 181–82, 181n125, 196–97
fear, 139–40, 142–44
female, and corporal punishment, 124, 182
female development, 2, 163
feminists, agenda of school reform, 26, 30, 38–39
Fielding, Sarah, *The Governess: Or, the Little Female Academy* (1749), 4
fighting, 172; *see also* combative learning
film, *Dead Poets' Society* (Weir), 233
Finlay, Joseph, 169
Fitzgerald, Percy Hetherington, 11, 34–37, 67
  Schooldays at Saxonhurst, 23, 34, 35–36
Flagellant magazine, 32–33

flogging, 118, 119, 120, 123, 124, 128, 130, 132–33, 136
  anti-flogging writers, 133, 136
  pro-flogging, 134
Forster, William, 114
Foucauldian model, 117–18, 119
Foucault, Michel, *History of Sexuality*, 22, 186–87
Foyle College, 121
free choice, 47
free time, as positive, 34, 34n104, 37, 72, 80, 81–82, 102, 121–22
Freeman, Robert Massie, 170, 171–72
  Steady and Strong (1891), 170, 171–72, 174
French Revolution, influences of, 36, 39, 55, 65
Furnham, Adrian, 236

Gagnier, Regina, 117
Galton, Francis, 196
gay culture, eighteenth-century, 70–71
gay culture; *see also* homosexuality; Uranians
gender; *see also* girls; homosexuality; male identity; women
  deconstructing of gender norms, 182–86, 186n151
  feminization of boy characters in mid-nineteenth century, 38
  and recapitulation theory, 203
  women writers and crossgender writing, 38
genius, 18, 48, 163
Gentleman's Magazine, 40
Gibbon, Edward, 32
Gilligan, Carol, 129, 141
Gillis, John, 25
girls, 4, 41–42, 135, 141
girls' school stories, 4, 235
Gladstone, W.E., 1, 30, 32, 122–23
  'Ode to the Shade of Watt Tyler', 1
Gladstonian paternalism, 6–7
Glover, Richard, 33
God, 88–89, 91–92, 143–44
  and paternalism, 67, 97, 110
Golding, William, *Lord of the Flies*, 84, 233
Gollancz, Victor, 166, 216–17, 232

Political Education at a Public School (1918), 216–17
Goodlad, Lauren, 118, 119
Gosse, Philip, *The Aquarium* (1854), 88
gothic novel, 146
Gray, Thomas, 'Ode on a Distant Prospect of Eton College' (1747), 22
Griffin, Christine, 2, 9
Griffith, G., *The Life and Adventures of George Wilson* (1854), 149
Gunter, Barrie, 236

Hall, Donald, 107
Hall, Granville Stanley, 4, 53, 98, 157, 160, 161n22, 162–63, 188, 196
  Adolescence: Its Psychology and its Relations to Physiology, Anthropology, Sociology, Sex, Crime, Religion and Education (1904), 1, 157, 162–63
Hamilton, C.J., 213–14
Hanawalt, Barbara, 8, 25
Harrow, 10, 192
Hart, David, 236
Hayward, F.H., 166, 166n45, 213
  Day and Evening Schools (1910), 166
headmasters and teachers, 32–33, 26, 105–106, 142, 200, 214, 226
Heathorn, Stephen, 166
Hemyng, Bracebridge, 6, 11, 134–37, 147–49
  Butler Burke at Eton (1865), 134
  Butler Burke stories (1865–1870), 6, 134–37
  Eton School Days (1864), 134
  Jack Harkaway series, 134, 147
  Jack Harkaway's Schooldays (1871), 147–49
  London Labor and the London Poor (Mayhew and Hemyng), 134
heredity, 196–97
heroism, 16
heterosexual masculinity, 2
Higgins, Matthew, 105
Hilton, Boyd, 27
Hime, Maurice Charles, 121
History of a Schoolboy (1788) [Day], 15–17
Hobbesian view, 106–107, 134

home, and domestic values, 17, 41, 42–43, 101, 109
homosexual literature, 180, 181, 185–86, 190–92, 223
    Sturgis on, 185
homosexual panic, 181, 181–82n125
homosexuality
    anti-homosexuality law (1726), 71
    artificial homosexuality, 188
    class dynamic, 180–81
    and Darwinism, 179
    defending boy-friendships and sexuality, Waugh, 189n166, 223
    deflection of homosexual impulses, 95
    degeneration and, 208
    gay culture eighteenth-century, 70–71
    and homophobia, 70
    origin of, 184, 190
    in public school culture, 2, 6, 69, 71, 184
    stereotyping as deviant, 69, 70
    stigmatization, 70–71
honor, 140
Hood, Jack, 230–32
    The Heart of a Schoolboy (1919), 228
Hope, Arthur, 213
    The Higher Education of Boys in England (1909), 2, 213, 214
Hopley, Thomas, 125–27
    'Fact Bearing on the Death of Reginald Cancellor: With a Supplement and a Sequel', 126
Hughes, Thomas, 3, 11, 19, 21, 23–24, 25, 34, 55–56, 71, 72–73, 74, 81–82, 81n119, 150
    critics of, 56, 59, 60, 73
    and the fictional Arnold, 66, 67, 68, 76–77, 78
    identity, 61–62, 64, 65–66, 67, 68–69
    and paternalism, 60, 66–67, 98
    Richardson on, 61
    Stephens on, 37
    and Tom's evolution parallel to nation, 3, 4, 5, 55–56, 60–61, 62
    use of history and social issues, 60, 65, 66–67, 73, 149, 150
    works
        The Manliness of Christ (1879), 60, 73–74, 75

Tom Brown at Oxford (1861), 55–56, 59, 60–61, 74–75
Tom Brown series, 78, 155, 166, 166n45
Tom Brown's Schooldays (1857), 3, 11, 16–17, 19, 23, 34, 37, 78
Humanists, 47
Hurstpierpoint College, 10, 63
Huxley, T.H., 87

imagination, reading and overactive imagination, 57
immorality, 121, 229–30
imperialism, 170, 192, 202–203
independence, and practical and moral choices, 48
Indian Rebellion (1857), 75
Industrial Revolution, 17, 18, 19, 53–54
    and public school story genre, 5
innocence, 55, 96
intelligence, 144–45, 236
    criticism of, Mais, 215–16
Interdepartmental Committee on Physical Deterioration (1904), 176
intimacy communications, 191
Irish Nationalism, 23, 35

Jack Sheppard, 57
Jackson, Luke, *Freaks, Geeks and Asperger Syndrome: A User Guide to Adolescence*, 237
James, Henry, 'The Beast in the Jungle', Sedgwick on, 181
James, J.R., 214
Jermyn, Harry, *The Adolescence of Aubrey*, 2
Jesus Christ, 16, 107
Johnson, Claudia, 191
Johnson, W., 'Education of the Reasoning Faculties' (essay), 94, 94n49
Johnstone, C.D., 203
Johnstone, C.F., 21, 123, 191
juvenile delinquency, 50, 115–16, 149
Juvenile Depravity (1849), 115

Keate, John, 31
Keate school, 27
Keating, Peter, 98

Kidd, Kenneth, 163, 200, 203
Kilner, Dorothy, 21
Kincaid, James, 8, 54–55, 115
Kingsley, Charles, *Glaucus: Or, the Wonders of the Shore* (1855), 89
Kingsmill, Hugh, 83
Kipling, Rudyard, 11, 85, 121, 158, 198, 199, 201–205
  on adolescence and adulthood, 199, 201
  criticism of, 203, 205
  on Darwinian imperative, 199, 201
  and the feral boy, 203–204
  on school education, 201
  works
    Jungle Book stories, 201
    Kim, 202
    Stalky & Co. (1899), 4, 121, 161, 174, 190, 191, 198–203
    'The Janeites' (1924), 191
Kirchhoff, F., 182, 187
Kirkpatrick, R.J., 10, 84
  Encyclopaedia of boys School Stories, 12
Knoepflmacher, U.C., 200
Kohlberg, Lawrence, 129
Kosovsky Sedgwick, Eve, 180
Krafft-Ebing, W., 186

Lamb, Charles, 'Christ's Hospital Five and Thirty Years Ago' (1820), 50–51
Lancasterian system (monitor or fagging), 34, 51, 81, 130–31
Lancing College, 10
languages
  and Bakhtinian principles, 10, 24
  modern languages, 5
Leavis, F.R., 106
Leslie, Shane, 211–12
  The Oppidan (1922), 11, 209–12
Lesnik-Oberstein, Karín, 12, 106, 110
Lewis, George Cornewall, 124
liberalism, 6–7, 33–34, 45–46
libertarianism, 6, 33
Lister, Ian, 7
literature, mass-produced literature, 20–21; *see also* magazine publications; popular fiction; public school story genre

Locke, John, 45, 47, 79
  Arnold on, 45–46
  Some Thoughts Concerning Education, 126
Lockean tradition, 93, 128, 130
London School Board, 115
Lowe, Robert, 3
Lowell, J.R., *Stanzas on Freedom* (1843), 65
lower and working-class, 146, 196
lunacy, 51
Lunn, Arnold, 11, 217–19
  The Harrovians (1913), 11, 218–21, 224
Lyrical Ballads, 44

Macaulay, T.B., 33, 42
Machiavelli, 33
Macmillan, 134
magazine publications, 4–5, 20–21
Mais, S.P.B., 121, 166, 197, 214–16, 222, 232
  A Public School in War Time (1916), 215
male, 98
male citizen identity, 180–81
male citizenship, 30, 68, 75, 76–78, 107
male friendship, 180, 190, 191
male identity
  and imposed establishment categories, 71
  manliness as male and female identity, 68–69
  through literature, 78
  through rhetorical performance, 42
Malthus, Thomas, 74–75
Malthusian panic, 54, 54n224, 95
Mangan, J.A., 10, 36, 75, 122, 170
  Athleticism in the Victorian and Edwardian Public School, 170
  on Welldon, 192
Mansford, C.J., 113, 145
  Bully, Fag and Hero (1896), 145, 203
  In Playground and Schoolroom (1896), 145
Marlborough, 10, 34, 106, 122
Marshall, T.H., 6
Martin, M., 71n66
Martineau, Harriet, 21, 28, 38, 39, 42–43, 92
  The Crofton Boys (1841), 42–43
masculinity, 2, 38, 41, 43; *see also* muscular Christianity
Mason, Michael, 55

Matrimonial Causes Act (1857), 98
Matthews, John, 19
maturity, 226; *see also* adulthood
McCallum, Robyn, 10, 24
McInnes, Colin, *Absolute Beginners*, 233
Meagher, Thomas, 35
media, corporal punishment debate, 127
    and focus on homosexuality, 223,
        229–30, 230–31, 232
Melly, George, 11, 124, 130–32, 204
    School Experiences of a Fag (1854),
        11, 23, 130
mental health issues, 51, 108–109; *see also*
    R v. *Hopley*
middle class, 5, 29, 47
military training, 215–16
    Royal Military College, 223
Mill on the Floss, The (1860), 20, 98
molly culture, 70–71
monitor system (Lancaster or fagging), 34,
    51, 81, 130–31
moral abstract reasoning of boys, 141–42
moral behavior, 49, 55, 141–42, 167–68
moral development, 50, 54–55, 121, 129,
    130–32, 140–42
moral reasoning, corporal punishment,
    129–30, 132, 134
moral values, through public school stories,
    25, 150
More, Hannah, 27–28
Moretti, Franco, 99–100
mother, 49
Mudie's catalogue, 3
Muscular Christianity, 2, 12, 73–74, 122
Musgrave, Peter, 4, 23, 154
    From Brown to Bunter, 12
Muuss, Rolf, 46

National Association of Head Teachers, 236
National Curriculum, 7, 235
National Efficiency movement, 157–59,
    158n3, 208n, 212, 270
    public school story genre and, 173,
        174–75, 195
national identity, 6
national strikes, late nineteenth and early
    twentieth centuries, 155
natural history, 87–89

natural science literature, 88–89
nature
    and malignant spirits, 90, 91
    natural selection and educational
        control, 168, 170
    as savage and Edenic, 109, 179
    as teaching about God, 88–89
Neill, A.S., *Summerhill* (1921), 166
Neill, Alex, on Locke, 45
Nelson, Claudia, 9, 38, 92, 98, 145, 201
Nesbit, E., 80
    The Treasure Seekers, 200
New Lanark project (Woen), 28
Newbolt, Henry, 106, 232
    Vitae Lampada, 175
Newbolt Report, 155, 232–33
Newcastle Commission (1858–1861), 114
Newgate Chronicle, 57, 146
Newsagents' Publishing Company, 146
Nichols, John, 'The Boy Bishop. - Eton
    Montem. - Salt-bearers', 40–41
noblesse oblige, 183, 184
non-public schoolboy, 203–204
Northcliffe press, 216–17
Norton, Rictor, 70
Norwood, Cyril, 7
    *The Higher Education of Boys in
        England* (1909), 2, 213, 214
nouveaux riches, 75

obedience, 57, 140, 142–43, 143n174
Once a Week's, 145
Ong, Walter, 41
Orwell, George, 154
    Boys' Weeklies (1940), 154
Owen, Robert, 28

Paine, Thomas, 42
parenting, 37–38, 160, 195
Parent's Assistant, The, 39
Parker, Eric, 21, 122
pastorship, 119
Paterfamilias [Matthew Higgins], 105
paternalism, 6–7, 28, 97, 106–107, 118, 124
    Gladstonian paternalism, 6–7
Penny Bloods, 57
penny dreadfuls, 146–47, 149
personality, 31

Phillpott, Eden, 161, 162
  The Human Boy (1899), 161, 162
physical punishment, *see* corporal
  punishment; discipline
Pickering, Samuel, 48, 77–78
Pickwick and Nickleby, 20
Pilgrims Progress, The, 48
Place, Francis, 55
play, 22, 34, 37, 47, 72, 77–78, 79–80,
  103, 160
Playfellow, The, 42
political activism, industrialization and
  (1970s), 18
political conscientious, 7, 34–35,
  106–107, 236
political education, 30–31, 34–35, 217
political literature, 4, 154
political skills of adolescence, 40, 106–107,
  214–15
politics, 107
Politics for the People, 107
Pollock, Linda, 17
Poor Law debates, 28
popular fiction, 20–21, 57, 146
  comic novels, 235
postwar rejection by adolescence, 232
poverty, 107, 149, 150
  poor students, 29, 63, 114, 118–19
Prevention of Cruelty Act (1889), 115
Priestley, Joseph, 15, 28, 42, 213
  Essay on Education (1765), 44
prison reform, 50
progress, 58, 234–35
protection for adolescents, 57–58, 167–68
protest, *see* rebellion
psychology, 160–61, 166, 166n45
puberty, 8
Public Health Act (1848), 118
public persona, 31
public school history narratives, 21, 25
public school story genre
  adolescence response, 12–13
  audience for, 2, 3, 13, 23
  characters, 3, 10–11, 92, 154, 155–56, 209
  citizenship and, 2–3, 6–7, 15, 20, 78, 235
  criticism of, 17, 154
  defined, 2–3, 4–5, 9, 12, 15–16, 18–19,
    21–23, 47–48, 96, 209

exploitive use, 146, 150, 155, 222–24,
  227, 231
guidelines for successful story, 150
language of, 24, 191
late Victorian, 145–46
late-twentieth-century, 233
mid nineteenth, 38, 98
popularity of, 102
post WWI, 205, 209–10, 212–13,
  217–19, 227–28, 232–33
pre-Victorian era, 24–25, 26, 30, 57,
  235, 235n152
serious boy's school stories, 209
themes, 5–6, 7, 14, 24, 110
time period of, 11, 16–17
turn-of-twentieth century, 206–207,
  217–21, 222
vs. Penny Dreadfuls, 147
working class youth and, 108, 154,
  156, 232–33
public school system
  as all-male environment, 190
  Britishness of, 118–19, 121, 132
  civic education, Leslie, 212
  criticism of, 37–38, 50, 50n197, 98–99,
    193–95, 224
  defined, 10–11
  history, 10
  importance and goals, 17, 34, 65, 79,
    139–40, 205–206
  list of best, 10
  middle class view of, 29
  as miniature world, 79, 203,
    203–204, 228
  newer schools, 122, 184, 201
  pre-reform curriculum, 30–32
  structure of, 228
  student rebellions, 26–27
  student status, 30
public school system reform
  compulsory government program, 29,
    72, 114–15, 116–19
  curriculum, 41–42
  literary critics, 29–30
  physical environment, 120–21
  pre-Victorian issues for reform, 17–18,
    26, 26–28, 30, 33–34, 41–42, 145
Public Schools Act (1868), 118

publications, adolescent publications, 109, 150, 237, 237n160
   at school, 32–33, 217
pulp fiction, 146, 146n190
punishment, 123, 129; *see also* canning; corporal punishment; discipline; flogging

Quarterly Review of Education, 27
queer theorists, 180–81
Quigly, Isabel, 12, 151, 180, 205
   The Heirs of Tom Brown, 12

R v. *Hopley*, 113, 119, 124, 125–27
race, 168, 170; *see also* colonial subject
radicalism, 18
Ransome, Arthur, 80, 200
rational behavior, 49, 129–30, 167–68
rational choice, 48–49, 139–40
rational thinking, 44, 46–50, 133, 140, 146, 233
   2004 *The Primal Teen* (Strauch), 236–37
Raymond, Ernest, *Tell England* (1922), 197
reading, 57, 137
reading ability, 101–102
Reading School, 120
reasoning, 128–29
   adolescents and, 52–53, 135, 198–99
   moral decisions, boys vs. girls, 140–41
rebellion, 32–33
   and a boy's character, 40
   in pre-Victorian era, 25–26
   public school story genre, 39, 61–62, 65, 108, 136–37
rebels against society, 37
recapitulation theory, 53, 116, 203
Reed, Talbot Baines, 10–11, 150–52
   The Sixth Form at St Dominic's (1881), 3, 116, 150–52, 156
reform, educational reform. *see* public school system reform
religion, conversions, 211, 227; *see also under separate religions*
   fear of divine retribution, 143
Report of the Committee for Investigating the Causes of the Alarming Increase of Juvenile Delinquency in the Metropolis (1816), 50
reproduction, 54
Repton school, 216, 217
residential schooling, 51
Restoration, 106–107
revolutionary, 226
Rich, P.J., 38, 122
Richards, Frank, 11, 154
   Billy Bunter, 11
Richards, Jeffrey, 26, 61
   Happiest Days: The Public Schools in English Fiction, 12
Riehl, W.H., 25
rite of passage, 17
Robinson Crusoe, 42
role-play, 30, 34, 35, 79
Romanticism, 20, 22, 31, 42, 90
Romilly, Esmond, *Out of Bounds: The Education of Giles Romilly and Esmond Romilly*, 232n148
Rose, Jacqueline, 12, 155
Roslyn school, 93
Rossall school, 121, 197, 214
Rousseau, Jean-Jacques, 47, 77, 79
   Émile, 61, 77
Rousseauian principles, 61, 93
Rowling, J.K., *Harry Potter*, 233
Royal Commission on Children's Employment (1861), 114, 114n1
Royal Military College, 223
Rudduck, Jean, 236
Rugby school, 10, 11, 23, 37, 38–39, 76, 77, 124, 130–32; *see also* Arnold, Thomas

St Omers, *see* Stonyhurst College
St Paul's, 10
Saleeby, Caleb Williams, 195n200
Salinger, J.D., *The Catcher in the Rye*, 233
Salmon, Edward, 4, 147, 149, 150
   Juvenile Literature as It Is (1888), 149, 150
Salt, Henry, 133
   The Flogging Craze: A Statement Against Corporal Punishment (1916), 123
Sandhurst, 222

Saturday review, The, 3, 11, 83, 127, 145
savage, 3, 109, 109n146, 203–204
Schofield and Sims publishers, 3; *see also* National Curriculum
Scholastic Christianity, 46–47
school funding, Code of Grants (1862), 173–74
schoolboy, comparison to slaves, 15
  conception of nature, 85–86
  and Malthusian panic, 54
schoolboy savagery, 203–204
schoolboys' creed, 140
schools *see* boarding school; public school systems; state schools
science, 5, 208, 208n270
Scott, P.G., 78, 84, 97
Scottish education reform, 170
Searle, Geoffrey, 158, 175–76
Seccombe, Thomas, 223–24
Sedgwick,Eve, 181
self, 22–23
  inner self, 31
  sense of self, 18
self-determination, 64, 196–97
self-discipline, 55, 56
self-government, 214
self-reliance, 48
Serle, Geoffrey, 175
sex, as sin, 55
sexual abuse, 124
sexuality
  and behavior, 70, 148, 160, 167–68
  and Malthusian panic, 53–54
Shaftesbury, Lord, 28
Shakespeare, William, 78, 101
Sherborne school, 121, 214, 215
Shore, Heather, 50, 115, 116
Shrewsbury school, 10
Shrosbree, Colin, 34, 119
Shuttleworth, Sally, 183, 196
sin
  biological sin, 52–53, 55–57, 159, 168–69
  Christian sin, 54, 55, 56
Slaughter, John Willis, 165–66, 169
  The Adolescent (1911), 165
slavery, 65, 136
Smith, Adam, 74–75, 94
Smith, Sydney, 29

Smollett, Tobias, 29
Social Darwinists, 145–46, 157–58, 179, 195, 195n200, 208
social justice, 4–5, 6
social welfare, 63–64
socialism, 213
Societies for the Reformation of Manners, 71
society and adolescence, 2, 8
sociology, 1, 2
Sophocles, 227
Southey, Robert, 32, 125
Spacks, Patricia Meyer, 9, 163, 195–96
Spateman, Thomas, 1
  The Schoolboy's Mask (1742), 31, 48–49
Spectator, 11
Speenhamland System of poor relief, 63
Spencer, Herbert, 53, 133–34, 157, 159–60, 168
  Education: Intellectual, Moral and Physical (1861), 159
Spencerian education, 179–80
sports, 121–22, 170
Springhall, John, 17, 146, 147, 149
Stanley, A.P., 26, 28, 29–30, 44, 67, 69
state school system, 3, 114, 150–52, 158, 166, 176, 213, 228
statesmanship, 2, 5–6
Steedman, Carolyn, 22
Stephen, James Fitzjames, 21, 27–28, 73
Stonyhurst College, 10, 23, 34–35, 36
Strauch, Barbara, *The Primal Teen: What the New Discoveries About the Teenage Brain Can Tell Us About Our Kids* (2004), 236–37
strikes, 64–65
students
  comparison to colonized subjects, 203
  disabled/learning impaired. see *R* v. *Hopley* case
  ex-public schoolboys and conspiracy of silence on corporal punishment, 127
  poor students, 29, 63, 114, 118–19
Sturgis, H.O., 11, 87, 182–85
  critique of Tim (character), 187, 188
  Tim (pre 1890), 11, 179, 182
subjectivity, 24–25
suicides, 51
supernatural, 211, 233

Swinburne, A.C., 211, 212, 226
Symonds, J.A., 70, 185
   Sexual Inversion, 185

Tait's Edinburgh Magazine, review of *Tom Brown*, 73
Tanner, Lawrence, 30
Taunton Commission (1864–1867), 83, 114
technology careers, 5
teen novels, 12
Ten Hours Act of 1847, 28
Terasaki, Hiroaki, 125, 126–27
Thatcher government, 7
theater, 30–31, 40, 102, 122
Thomson, G.H., 187
Thornton, Henry, 27–28
Times Literary Supplement, The, 4, 11
Times, The, 127
Tom Brown (character) *see* Hughes, Thomas; Kilner, Dorothy
Tory, 6, 28, 137
Trimmer, Sarah, 21
twentieth century, writers of, 9

Unitarians, 28, 44
United States, 208n270
   American boys' periodicals of nineteenth century, 153–54
University College School, 10
Uppingham school, 122
Uranians, 94n49, 184, 185
Usborne, Richard, 59

Vachell, H.A., 175–79, 180–81, 190
   critique on male relationships in *The Hill*, 180–81, 192
   The Hill: A Romance of Friendship (1905), 11, 174, 175–79, 180, 185, 190
Valpy, Richard, 120
van Gennep, Arnold, 8
vernacular education, 111
vernacular scholarship, 42
vernacular teaching approach, 42, 45, 46
Vicinus, Martha, 197–98
violence
   adolescence in pre-Victorian era, 25–26

   as innate part of boyhood behavior, 45
   in school, 103, 137–39

Wallbank, M.V., 30
war, 145, 179, 211–12, 215–16, 227
Ward, E., *Boys and their rulers* (1853), 51
Warre, Edmond, 185, 209
Watson, Ian, 59, 60
Waugh, Alec, 11, 166, 189, 189n166, 213, 222–28
   Brideshead Revisted, 232
   criticism of, 222–23, 226, 229, 230
   Public School Life (1922), 189, 223
   The Loom of Youth (1917), 11, 209, 222, 224
Welldon, J.E., 158–59, 191, 192–94
   Gerald Eversley's Friendship (1895), 11, 179, 185, 190–91, 192
   Recollections and Reflections (1915), 123
Wells, H.G., 158, 212, 213
   The New Machiavelli, 5
Wellsian scientism, 212
Westminster, 10, 30–31, 32
Whately, Richard, 6, 28, 94
White, W.A., *The Court of Boyville* (1899), 164
Whiteley's 1909 catalogue, 3–4
Wilberforce, William, 27–28
Wilkinson, Rupert, 31
will, 47, 49
Wilson, James M., 97
Winchester school, 10, 26–27, 127
women
   fight against objectification, 197
   importance in boys' education, 42, 194–95, 230
   in public school story genre, 4, 41, 199
women writers, 20, 21, 38–39
women's suffrage, 213
women's textbooks, 4
Wood, Liz, 236
Woodard, Nathaniel, 10
Woodard schools, 10
Wordsworth, William, 22, 163
Wordsworthian principles, 85–86
work, 80, 81
working class, public school story genre and, 2, 3, 108, 152, 154–55

Working Men's College, 29
working-class education, 166
working-class family, 181, 190
working-class juvenile crime, 50, 149
working-class juveniles, 163, 164–65, 203–204
working-class radicals, 55
working-class student, 2, 3, 4, 114–15, 196, 203–204
World War I, and adolescence, 197, 212–13
Worsley, Henry, 115–16
Worth, G.R., 68
writers
    adolescent authors, 161, 162, 222, 228, 232, 237;. *see also* Browne, Martin; Hood, Jack; Phillpott, Eden
    autobiographies, 20, 22
    between 1890s and WWI, 160
    biographies, 21, 209
    goals as educationalists, 25
    male writers, and subject, 2, 5–6, 9, 12, 20, 21–22, 23, 24, 37
    pre-Victorian identity, 24–26
    reform, mid-nineteenth century onwards, Hughes, 108
    voice of, 23–24
    women writers, 20, 21, 38–39
    writing for youth, 38
    WWI era and shaken confidence, 209, 212, 227–28
writing, student vernacular creative writing, 103

YMCA, 74
Yonge, C.M., *What Books to Lend and What to Give*, 3
young people, 17, 115; *see also* adolescence
youth, 17